Taxation, Virtual Currency and Blockchain

Series on International Taxation

VOLUME 68

Series Editors

Prof. Ruth Mason, University of Virginia School of Law
Prof. Dr Ekkehart Reimer, University of Heidelberg

Introduction & Contents

The Series on International Taxation deals with a wide variety of topics in the global tax arena. The authors include many of the field's leading experts as well as talented newcomers. Their expert views and incisive commentary have proven highly useful to practitioners and academics alike.

Objective

The volumes published in this series are aimed at offering high-quality analytical information and practical solutions to international tax practitioners.

Readership

Practitioners, academics and policy makers in international tax law.

Frequency of Publication

2-3 new volumes published each year.

The titles published in this series are listed at the end of this volume.

Taxation, Virtual Currency and Blockchain

Aleksandra Bal

Wolters Kluwer

Published by:
Kluwer Law International B.V.
PO Box 316
2400 AH Alphen aan den Rijn
The Netherlands
E-mail: international-sales@wolterskluwer.com
Website: lrus.wolterskluwer.com

Sold and distributed in North, Central and South America by:
Wolters Kluwer Legal & Regulatory U.S.
7201 McKinney Circle
Frederick, MD 21704
United States of America
Email: customer.service@wolterskluwer.com

Sold and distributed in all other countries by:
Air Business Subscriptions
Rockwood House
Haywards Heath
West Sussex
RH16 3DH
United Kingdom
Email: international-customerservice@wolterskluwer.com

ISBN 978-94-035-0103-1

e-Book: ISBN 978-94-035-0104-8
web-PDF: ISBN 978-94-035-0105-5

Table of Contents

Preface

I began researching tax implications of virtual currencies in 2010, two years after the Bitcoin concept was announced. At that time, hardly anyone predicted that what was thought to be an electronic payment system based on cryptographic proof would become one of the greatest innovations of the 21st century with a profound impact extending well beyond the payment sector. Bitcoin began the virtual currency revolution and paved the way to the emergence of 1,600 virtual currency schemes that are currently in operation. However, in my view, Bitcoin's most important legacy is blockchain—the technological framework underlying the Bitcoin system. Nowadays, blockchain's potential as a standalone technology is widely recognized and this technology is being used by many companies to support and reshape their business processes and practices. Tax management and tax administration belong to the areas that could benefit from blockchain technology.

This book is a revised and updated version of my PhD thesis, which was finalized and defended at Leiden University in 2014. In contrast to my PhD thesis, which focused on tax implications of virtual currency used within online environments, the focus of this book is on blockchain and convertible decentralized virtual currency schemes (such as Bitcoin or Ethereum). This book covers developments until August 1, 2018.

As this book builds upon my doctoral thesis, I would like to convey my appreciation to all who gave their time and expertise in making my PhD research possible. First of all, I would like to express my sincere indebtedness to my supervisors, Professors Hank Vording and Koos Boer, for their guidance, advice and constructive observations. They helped me improve the quality of the thesis while allowing me sufficient flexibility to carry out my research project. My PhD research would not have been completed without the support of the International Bureau for Fiscal Documentation (IBFD) in Amsterdam. Finally, I would like to thank my family for their support and encouragement throughout the writing of both this book and my PhD thesis.

Part I Blockchain and Virtual Currency

CHAPTER 1

Introduction

§1.01 BACKGROUND

In 2018, Bitcoin[1]—the first decentralized virtual currency using blockchain technology—celebrated its 10th anniversary. When the Bitcoin concept was announced in 2008, hardly anyone would predict that what was thought to be an electronic payment system based on cryptographic proof would become one of the greatest innovations of the 21st century with a profound impact extending well beyond the payment sector. Virtual currency has experienced remarkable developments since its inception. The number of both its users and merchants willing to accept it as a valid form of payment has grown exponentially. The popularity of initial coin offerings (ICOs)[2] shows that virtual currency is no longer limited to serving as a payment alternative but is increasingly seen as a promising investment vehicle. Bitcoin paved the way to the development of 1,600 virtual currency schemes that are currently in operation[3] and triggered the emergence of an industry of virtual currency based businesses designed to facilitate transactions among virtual currency users.

Blockchain gained prominence as the technological framework in which Bitcoin operates. Although initially it was overshadowed by Bitcoin, its potential as a stand-alone technology was soon recognized in different industry sectors. Many companies started embracing blockchain technology to support and reshape their business processes and practices.

The growing mainstream use of virtual currency and blockchain is best illustrated by the numbers. In July 2018, the Bitcoin market capitalization was close to USD 128

1. Written without a capital letter, "bitcoin" or "ether" is used to describe virtual currency units. In its capitalized version, "Bitcoin" or "Ethereum" denote the concept of Bitcoin/Ethereum, or the entire network itself. *See* https://bitcoin.org/en/vocabulary#bitcoin.
2. Initial coin offerings (ICOs) are a new means of raising capital for the financing of commercial and development projects where new cryptocurrencies are sold for other cryptocurrencies or legal money. For a detailed description, *see* §3.02[D] Initial Coin Offerings (ICOs).
3. https://coinmarketcap.com/ (accessed July 22, 2018).

billion, with the currency price exceeding USD 7,400.[4] In 2017, the total cryptocurrency market capitalization exceeded USD 600 billon, which is nearly as much as the gross domestic product (GDP) of Argentina.[5] According to data collected by CoinDesk, ICOs raised more money in the first quarter of 2018 (USD 6 billion) than in the whole of 2017 (USD 5.5 billion).[6] An analysis of Google Trends data reveals a sharp increase in the popularity of the search terms "blockchain" and "Bitcoin," which reached its all-time high in December 2017.

Like any other innovation, virtual currency raises questions for which the existing tax systems may be unprepared. Although virtual currency shares similarities with both money and property, it has some unique characteristics and a different risk profile that the existing legislation may fail to account for. For a long time, virtual currency largely operated free of regulation or legal oversight. In view of its growing popularity, some countries have taken steps to clarify the tax landscape for virtual currency. Others have remained silent leaving the tax treatment of virtual currency under existing laws unsettled. Given the increasing use of blockchain and virtual currency, it is important to understand what these phenomena are, what technology they rely upon and how they function so that it can be ascertained whether virtual currency requires additional regulation or whether the law as it stands is adequate to administer its usage.

In 2013, the Organization for Economic Cooperation and Development (OECD) started examining tax challenges presented by the digital economy as part of its Base Erosion and Profit Sifting (BEPS) project.[7] In the March 2018 interim report discussing tax challenges arising from digitalization, virtual currency and blockchain have been listed among issues that require a more detailed and in-depth investigation. The OECD suggested examining "the risks of tax evasion posed by cryptocurrency and blockchain technology more generally, and the possible solutions, such as legislative measures which require digital asset exchange platforms or other third parties to report, and/or which allow tax administrations to request information on transactions regarding digital assets such as crypto-currency as well as targeted exchange of information."[8] In his recent report to the G20 finance ministers and central bank governors, the OECD Secretary-General observed that "technologies like blockchain give rise to both new, secure methods of record-keeping" and therefore "further work is required to ensure that governments can harness the opportunities these changes bring while ensuring the ongoing effectiveness of the tax system."[9]

---

4. https://coinmarketcap.com/ (accessed July 22, 2018).
5. World Bank, *GDP (current US$)*, https://data.worldbank.org/indicator/NY.GDP.MKTP.CD?year_high_desc=true (accessed July 22, 2018).
6. D. Floyd, *$6.3 Billion: 2018 ICO Funding has Passed 2017's Total* (April 19, 2018), www.coindesk.com/6-3-billion-2018-ico-funding-already-outpaced-2017/.
7. OECD, *Action Plan on Base Erosion and Profit Shifting* (OECD 2013). The fundamental idea behind the BEPS project was concerns about multinational enterprises being able to avoid tax by artificially separating income from activities that generate it. The BEPS Action Plan set out 15 Actions to counteract commonly employed BEPS strategies.
8. OECD, *Tax Challenges Arising from Digitalisation: 2018 Interim Report*, p. 208 (2018).
9. OECD, *OECD Secretary-General Report To The G20 Finance Ministers And Central Bank Governors*, p. 12 (March 2018).

§1.02 SCOPE OF THE BOOK

The emergence of virtual currencies has posed several tax questions. What is the status of virtual currency for tax purposes? Does it qualify as property, money or something else? Is it possible to treat all virtual currency types in a one-fits-all manner? When do disposals of virtual currency result in income and when in a capital gain? Is the mere possession of virtual currency subject to income tax? Does currency mining result in taxable income? When a person mining or selling virtual currency may be considered an entrepreneur for tax purposes? Under which circumstances does trade in virtual currency trigger a VAT registration obligation? Which transactions in virtual currency may benefit from a VAT exemption? What are the compliance obligations of persons mining and transacting in virtual currencies? What is the most optimal method of regulation for virtual currencies?

The purpose of this book is to provide an in-depth and comprehensive analysis of tax implications that result from activities involving virtual currency. These activities include exchanges of goods and services for virtual currency, exchanges of legal currency for virtual currency, exchanges of virtual currency for another virtual currency, currency mining, possession of virtual currency that appreciates in value and receipt of virtual currency (as gift or inheritance). The book seeks to ascertain whether virtual currency requires additional regulation or whether the law as it stands is adequate to administer its usage. The analysis of tax questions raised by virtual currency is restricted to two main types of taxes: individual income taxes levied on profits derived from activities involving virtual currencies and consumption taxes (value added tax and sales tax) levied on transactions in virtual currencies. The former are focused on the person earning the income, whereas the latter—on the transaction. They vary with respect to the point in time when an increase in the potential for private consumption is taxed: upon accrual or upon transformation into actual consumption. For both income and consumption taxes, the following three fundamental questions are considered:

- What is the optimal framework for taxing income from, and transactions in, virtual currencies?[10]
- To what extent do the existing tax rules in selected countries conform to the optimal framework?[11]
- How can the existing rules be improved to match (or to move closer to) the desired scenario?[12]

Exploring the application of tax laws to virtual currencies provides an opportunity to review some of the basic doctrines of substantive tax law (for example, the

10. The optimal framework is based on the generally accepted principles of taxation. For income taxation, *see* Chapter 4 Income Tax: General Considerations, for consumption taxation, *see* Chapter 7 Consumption Taxation: General Considerations.
11. For income taxation, *see* Chapter 5 Income Taxation: Selected Countries, for consumption taxation, *see* Chapter 8 Consumption Taxation: Selected Jurisdictions.
12. For income taxation, *see* Chapter 6 Income Taxation: Recommendations, for consumption taxation, *see* Chapter 9 Consumption Taxation: Recommendations.

concept of income and the destination principle) and to reexplore the connections of those legal doctrines to practicalities of modern tax administration. Modern technology provides opportunities for income generation in ways that were considered mere science fiction back in the days in which the tax concepts were developed. As trade in virtual currencies represents an extreme version of electronic commerce, the application of the existing rules to this phenomenon allows the evaluation of the flexibility of those rules and their potential to capture even more sophisticated (yet unknown) technological developments. The perspective of this book is both an interpretation *de lege lata* as well as a discussion of tax policy, an examination *de lege ferenda*.[13] This book is about traditional tax definitions which are embedded in the law and their ability (or inability) to encompass income generated by new types of economic activity in a manner that maintains both their theoretical justification and their practical implementation.

The book examines tax consequences of using convertible decentralized virtual currency schemes (such as Bitcoin or Ethereum) since such currency represents the vast majority of all virtual currency types. Tax implications of virtual currency used solely within an online environment (for example, World of Warcraft Gold) are outside the scope of this book.

Civil and financial law issues regarding virtual currency (for example, the status of virtual currency for the purposes of banking or securities regulations, the legal validity of smart contracts) are briefly mentioned only if it is relevant for the discussion of the main topic. Their detailed analysis is outside the scope of book. Those matters are left for examination by civil and financial law scholars.

§1.03 CONTENT OUTLINE

The book is divided in three main parts. Part I, which comprises the first three chapters, provides the background necessary to understand tax considerations discussed in Part II and Part III. Chapter 1 gives an introduction to the issues discussed in the book. It explains why virtual currency and blockchain are worth researching and how the book is organized. Chapter 2 focuses on blockchain and seeks to get the reader acquainted with technology that underlies the functioning of virtual currencies. Although blockchain gained prominence as the technological framework in which Bitcoin operates, blockchain technology can find applications in many other areas unrelated to virtual currencies. An important blockchain-based innovation is smart contracts—computer protocols intended to digitally facilitate the performance of contractual arrangements. Chapter 3 examines the concept and characteristics of virtual currencies. It makes a distinction between "virtual currency" and "cryptocurrency" and divided the latter category into "coins" and "tokens." Chapter 3 observes that although virtual currencies are a promising payment and investment innovation, their use bears a lot of risks. The materialization of these risks depends on the volume of virtual currency issued, its

13. "*De lege lata*" is a Latin expression meaning "the law as it stands." "*De lege ferenda*" means "future law" used in the sense of "what the law should be."

connection to the real economy, traded volume and user acceptance. Chapter 3 also explains the concept of initial coin offerings—a new means of raising capital where new cryptocurrencies are sold for other cryptocurrencies or legal money. Finally, Chapter 3 discusses the status of virtual currency and its classification as money, electronic money and securities.

Part Two (Chapters 4, 5 and 6) covers income tax aspects of virtual currencies. Chapter 4 provides a general introduction to the topic of income taxation. First, it describes two main types of income tax systems (global and schedular), the concept of income, income categories and income determination. Second, it introduces an evaluation model based on the general principles of taxation that will be used as a benchmark in the evaluation of the income tax treatment of virtual currency in four selected jurisdictions.

Chapter 5 examines whether income from transactions in virtual currency and virtual currency mining is subject to tax in four selected countries: the United States, the United Kingdom, Germany and the Netherlands. These countries were selected on the basis of their different approaches to income taxation (global versus schedular) and the different treatment of capital gains and accumulated wealth.

Chapter 6 builds upon the previous two chapters and seeks to make recommendations for the improvement of certain characteristics of the existing income tax systems that currently struggle with the imposition and enforcement of tax compliance obligations regarding transactions in virtual currency. It also proposes a methodology for creating an effective regulatory framework for the taxation of virtual currencies.

The third part of the book (Chapters 7, 8 and 9) is about consumption taxation. Chapter 7 provides a general introduction to the topic of consumption taxation. First, it describes various consumption tax systems and provides a brief history of consumption taxation (focusing on the digital economy and electronic commerce). Second, it describes the principles underlying an optimal consumption tax system that will be used as a benchmark in the evaluation of the consumption tax treatment of transactions involving virtual currencies in two selected jurisdiction—the European Union and the United States—which is undertaken in the next chapter of this book.

Chapter 8 describes the basic features of the EU value-added tax (VAT) and the US retail sales tax systems and applied them to transactions in virtual currencies. EU VAT is explained based on the EU VAT legislation, making references to the national rules if necessary. As regards the United States, since there is no federal sales tax, the features common to the majority of states are discussed. Although Chapter 8 focuses only on two jurisdictions, the issues identified in those jurisdictions may also be encountered in a wide range of other countries around the world which are trying to find the best way to tax virtual currency transactions.

Chapter 9 draws conclusions based on the analysis in Chapters 8 and 9. It examines to what extent the existing rules meet the characteristics of an optimal consumption system, identifies best practices for virtual currency transactions and makes recommendations for the improvement of the existing tax systems.

The final part of the book (Annex 1) provides an overview of tax regulations, administrative rulings and court decisions concerning virtual currency in various countries that were not examined in detail in the previous chapters of this book.

CHAPTER 2

Blockchain

§2.01 DEFINITION

Bitcoin was the first decentralized cryptocurrency to successfully implement the blockchain concept. Although blockchain gained prominence as the technological framework in which Bitcoin operates, blockchain technology can find applications in many other areas unrelated to virtual currency. Initially, Bitcoin overshadowed blockchain. However, things changed around 2014 when blockchain's potential as a stand-alone technology was recognized in different industry sectors. Many companies started embracing blockchain technology to support and reshape their business processes and practices.

Blockchain is entirely built with established and well-understood technologies (peer-to-peer network, cryptographic algorithm, distributed ledger[14] and decentralized consensus mechanism). Its genius is not the technology itself but the manner in which it combines earlier technologies. The four fundamental principles underlying blockchain technology are: (1) distributed database (no single party controls the system. Each party on a blockchain has access to the entire database and its complete history); (2) peer-to-peer transmission (communication occurs directly between peers); (3) irreversibility of records (once a transaction is entered into the database, the record cannot be altered); (4) pseudo-anonymity (each node or user has a unique address that identifies it. The identity of the parties is not disclosed during transactions).[15]

---

14. Blockchain is a type of distributed ledger technology (DLT). DLT is a set of technological solutions that enables a single, sequenced, standardized and cryptographically-secured record of activity to be safely distributed to, and acted upon by, a network of participants. This record can contain, for example, transactions, asset holdings or identity data. *See* Financial Conduct Authority, *Discussion Paper on Distributed Ledger Technology*, DP17/3 (April 2017).
15. M. Iansiti & Karim R. Lakhani, *The Truth About Blockchain*, Harvard Business Review (January 2017).

Blockchain is an open distributed ledger that records transactions between two parties efficiently and in a verifiable and permanent way.[16] In layman terms, blockchain can be seen as a large spreadsheet that sequentially records transactions among users operating within the network. A blockchain network consists of interconnected computers referred to as nodes. Each node can check and transmit transaction information using software designated for this purpose. Blockchain uses asymmetrical encryption methods that are referred to as "public" and "private" keys. Public keys are user addresses to which data is transmitted. Private keys work similarly to passwords and enable users to access their unit of accounts. Each node retains a copy of the whole blockchain which is automatically downloaded when connecting to the blockchain network and continuously updated. Every network node stores an up-to-date copy of the data. New transactions are grouped in a block and added to the blockchain every few minutes when the blockchain is automatically checked and brought to a consensus between all network participants.

Consensus mechanisms refer to the way in which blockchain participants reach an agreement about the validity of transactions. The traditional consensus mechanism is called proof-of-work (PoW). PoW is a system where the validity of transactions is verified in a process called mining. Miners solve a mathematical puzzle (known as proof-of-work problem) to verify transactions within each block. As the first miner who solves the problem is rewarded with new virtual coins, all network miners compete to be the first to find a solution. Since a problem cannot be solved in other ways than through brute force, solving it requires a huge number of attempts and a lot of computing power. The Bitcoin network consumes massive amounts of energy and is mostly fuelled by coal-fired power plants in China. This results in an extreme carbon footprint for each unique Bitcoin transaction. In a 2014 study, O'Dwyer and Malone showed that the electricity consumption of the Bitcoin network was likely to be approximately equivalent to the electricity consumption of a country like Ireland, i.e., an estimated 3 GW.[17] A potential solution to the huge energy costs generated by blockchain networks would be to opt for a different consensus mechanism.

Proof of Stake (PoS) is an alternative way of verifying and validating blockchain transactions. In contrast to PoW, where miners with a lot of computing power can be more successful in solving mathematical problems, the success in PoS-based systems depends on the participant's wealth (number of coins), also referred to as stake. The more coins one has, the more likely one is to validate the transaction. In PoS-based systems, the validators are rewarded with transactions fees as no new coins are generated. PoS is an energy-efficient and cheaper form of consensus. Validators do not have to use their computing power because the only factors that influence their

16. A good description of the functioning of blockchain technology can be found at: BaFin, *Blockchain technology*, www.bafin.de/EN/Aufsicht/FinTech/Blockchain/blockchain_node_en.html.
17. K. J. O'Dwyer & D. Malone, *Bitcoin Mining and its Energy Footprint* (June 2014).

chances are the total number of their coins and the complexity of the network. Also, PoS is more secure as it is less prone to 51% attacks[18] than a PoW-based system.[19]

There are public and private blockchains. Anyone can join a public blockchain and view the ledger content. Public blockchains can be further subdivided into permissioned and permissionless. A ledger is permissionless when anyone can read and write the ledger content. This means that everyone can view the content of the blockchain, validate transactions and contribute towards the blockchain's security and integrity. Permissioned public ledger means that only a preselected group of participants write the ledger content but anyone can read it. The advantages of public blockchains are a high level of security, low costs and avoidance of potential individual errors. The main disadvantages are limited scalability and the invariable transparency of all transactions, putting it at odds with privacy concerns.

In private (permissioned) blockchains, there is some form of central administration or at least a limited number of participants. Users need to be specifically invited to join the database. The two main criticism points of centralized blockchains are that there is a greater risk of manipulation and dependence on a central entity. However, private blockchains offer privacy and faster transaction processing.

§2.02 SMART CONTRACTS

[A] Background

Smart contracts are not a new phenomenon. The cryptographer Nick Szabo wrote an article about smart contracts as early as 1996.[20] In his article, he predicted that digital technology would change the way contracts are concluded and speculated that traditional contracts would not be used any more in the digital era. Szabo believed that smart contracts could be embedded into physical property ("smart property"). He

18. A 51% attack is a potential attack on a blockchain network by a group that controls the majority of the network mining power (in PoW-based systems) or the majority of the coins (in PoS-based systems). The group would be able to decide which transactions get approved and which not. PoS-based systems are less prone to 51% attacks for two reasons: (1) it would be difficult and expensive to accumulate 51% of all available coins in the market; and (2) a person with a 51% stake in the coin market would not have it in his best interest to attack a network in which he holds a majority share. If the value of the cryptocurrency fell, the value of his holdings would also fall. While the threat of 51% attacks has existed for years, the chances of it materializing appeared to diminish as more and more people joined cryptocurrency networks—which in theory makes it harder to obtain control of over half the network. However, in May 2018, the cryptocurrency Bitcoin Gold (a lesser known spin-off of the original Bitcoin) fell victim to a 51% attack. Unknown hackers compromised the Bitcoin Gold blockchain and stolen at least USD 18 million worth of Bitcoin Gold (BTG) from online exchanges platforms by using rented mining rigs to accumulate the majority of the Bitcoin Gold network's hashpower. The Bitcoin Gold example shows that 51% attacks are not just a theoretical concern but a real threat to any Bitcoin-like currency.
19. In addition to PoS and PoW, there are many other consensus mechanisms; for example, Proof-of-Importance, Delegated Proof-of-Stake, Delegated Byzantine Fault Tolerance (dBFT) and Proof-of-Burn.
20. N. Szabo, *Smart Contracts: Building Blocks for Digital Markets* (1996).

provided an example of a leased car whose embedded contract would automatically return control of the car to the lessor if the lessee failed to make payments on time.

Although Szabo's ideas were conceptually brilliant, they were much more advanced than the technology available at that time. Thus, they lay dormant for many years. The emergence of blockchain in 2008 led to the resurgence of the smart contract idea as blockchain provided both the foundational platform and the necessary ecosystem to implement the concept of smart contracts in practice.[21] With the currently available technology, what Szabo predicted over 20 years ago can soon become reality.

Smart contracts are said to revolutionize the way transactions are carried out, reduce transaction costs and even obviate the need for lawyers, notaries and other intermediaries. Allegedly, they can remedy many of the problems inherent in the operation of the legal system (such as ambiguity and subjectivity), secure contractual performance and ensure adherence to the law. The following sections confront these commonly made claims, examine the possibility of reducing contractual relationships into code and discuss the benefits and drawbacks of using smart contracts.

[B] What Is a Smart Contract?

There is no universally agreed definition of a smart contract. According to the simplest definition, smart contracts are agreements whose execution is automated. Szabo (1996) defined smart contracts as a set of promises, specified in digital form, including protocols within which the parties perform on these promises.[22] Savelyev (2016) provided the following definition: smart contract is a piece of software code, implemented on blockchain platform, which ensures self-enforcing and autonomous nature of its terms triggered by conditions defined in advance and applied to blockchain-titled assets.[23] According to Greenspan (2016), a smart contract is a piece of code which is stored on blockchain, triggered by blockchain transactions, and which reads and writes data in that blockchain database.[24] Brown (2015) defined a smart contract as "an event-driven programme, with state, which runs on a replicated shared ledger and which can take custody over assets on that ledger."[25] Based on the above definitions, the following features of smart contracts can be identified:

- *Digital form*. Traditional contracts may exist in many different forms. They can be concluded in writing or orally. Smart contracts may only exist in electronic form as the contractual terms are embedded in a computer code. They can relate to digital assets (for example, cryptocurrency) or to digital

21. Bitcoin blockchain itself is a form of a smart contract with the limited purpose of executing transactions that involve the exchange of virtual coins. Ethereum offers an enhanced ability to build more complex smart contracts using a specific language (Solidity).
22. Szabo, *supra* n. 20.
23. A. Savelyev, *Contract Law 2.0: Smart Contracts as the Beginning of the End of Classic Contract Law*, Working Paper Law WP BRP 71/LAW/2016.
24. G. Greenspan, *Beware of the Impossible Smart Contracts*, Blockchain news (April 12, 2016).
25. R. Brown, *A Simple Model for Smart Contracts* (February 10, 2015).

representations of physical assets (referred to as tokenized assets). Smart contracts require electronic digital signatures based on encryption technology.

- *Blockchain-based*. Blockchain technology is one of the core features of smart contracts as it allows automating the performance of contractual obligations by both parties. A smart contract can be programmed on both permissioned and permissionless blockchains. There are many blockchain-based platforms that can be used to create smart contracts. The most popular one is Ethereum, invented in 2013 by Vitalik Buterin.[26] Ethereum permits the transfers of any type of digital assets (in contrast to the Bitcoin system, which allowed the exchange of only one object—bitcoin units) and is today one of the fastest growing public blockchains and the second largest in terms of market capitalization.[27]
- *Conditional nature*. Computer code is generally based on conditional statements, such as "if X then Y." Similarly, in contact law, promises are made in exchange for other promises. The conditional structure is the fundamental element of smart contracts. It is said to reduce the level of ambiguity as the code does exactly what it is programmed to do.
- *Automated enforcement*. Once a smart contract is concluded, its execution should no longer be depended on the will of its parties or any approvals from their side. The computer verifies whether all conditions are met and executes the contract. There is no need for any human intermediary.
- *Event-driven*. Smart contracts offer event-driven functionality: they act upon information provided by external sources to modify other data. External data sources that send information to smart contracts are referred to as oracles.

[C] Are Smart Contracts Legally Enforceable Contracts?

Smart contracts have received a lot of attention from lawyers and legal scholars for the impact they may have on contract law and the role of lawyers. A question arises whether a smart contract can function as a stand-alone contract or whether it can only be used to supplement a traditional contract by automating its execution.

A contract is an agreement between two or more parties which is intended to give rise to a legally binding relationship or have some other legal effect. In other words, a contract establishes, amends or terminates legal relationships between parties. For the formation of a legally binding contract, the following elements are required: agreement between the parties (there has to be an offer and a corresponding acceptance), consideration and intention to create legal relations.

26. *See* §3.03[B] Ethereum.
27. As at June 6, 2018, the total Ethereum market capitalization exceeded USD 60 billion. *See* https://coinmarketcap.com/.

[1] Offer and Acceptance

An offer is an expression to another party or the public at large to be bound by the states terms. It is possible to find offer and acceptance in the process of smart contract formation. For example, in the case of a crowdfunding smart contract, the beneficiary posts the predefined terms of the contact (offer) and the person willing to contribute to the project accepts the offer by transferring certain assets to the pool. In the context of smart contracts, acceptance frequently occurs through the act of performance.

[2] Intention

A smart contact requires the will of the parties to take effect and be executed. A person must express its consent with the contractual terms and conditions and agree with the mode of contract execution although the person will have limited influence on the execution of the contract once it is entered into. The will of the party to enter into an agreement is manifested when the person transfer control over a digital asset or an online representation of a physical asset.

[3] Consideration

Consideration is often described as something given in exchange. It is not necessary that the contributions by both parties are of equal value. The focus is on reciprocity and not on equivalence of value. If a smart contract does not involve a reciprocal exchange, it cannot constitute a legally binding contract.

[4] Form

As contract law is inherently form free, there are no obstacles preventing parties from expressing their agreement in computer code. The fact that smart contracts exist only in electronic form and that the contractual terms are manifested in a computer code does not affect the contract's validity. In the European Union, Article 9 of the Electronic Commerce Directive (2000/31)[28] requires EU Member States to ensure that their legal systems allow contracts to be concluded by electronic means, and that the legal requirements applicable to the contractual process neither create obstacles for the use of electronic contracts nor result in such contracts being deprived of their legal effectiveness on account of their having been made by electronic means.

Numerous US states enacted, or are seeking to pass, legislation that seeks to clarify that contracts cannot be denied legal effect, validity or enforceability merely because the contract is processed or executed via a smart contract code. On May 29, 2017, Arizona Governor Doug Ducey signed Bill 2417, which recognized the legality of

28. *Directive 2000/31/EC of the European Parliament and of the Council of 8 June 2000 on certain legal aspects of information society services, in particular electronic commerce, in the Internal Market.*

blockchain's signatures and smart contracts.[29] Bill 2417 defines "smart contracts" as an "event driven program, with state, that runs on a distributed, decentralized, shared and replicated ledger that can take custody over and instruct transfer of assets on that ledger." It clarifies that records and signatures secured through blockchain technology are be considered electronic records and electronic signatures within the meaning of the Arizona Revised Statutes.[30] The bill also provides that a contract relating to a transaction may not be denied legal effect, validity or enforceability solely because that contract contains a "smart contract term." In New York, a similar bill that would update existing laws to include blockchain technology for electronic signatures and contracts is currently being considered.[31]

[5] Legal Validity

Finally, it needs to be observed that the mere existence of a smart contract does not establish the validity of the contractual relationship. The legal validity of a contract always concerns real-world events that cannot be seen or checked by blockchain. For example, a contract may be invalid because one of the parties lack legal capacity or acted under duress. Thus, blockchain may only validate a transaction in a technical sense but says nothing about the validity of the contract in the legal sense.

[6] Intermediary Conclusion

Based on the above-mentioned considerations, a smart contract may represent the entirety of an enforceable legal contact. However, it cannot be claimed that all smart contracts are legally binding. It needs to be established on a case-by-case basis whether the parties to a contract had the intention to enter into a contractual relationship and whether there was a reciprocal exchange. The general contract law of a particular jurisdiction will determine whether a smart contract gives rise to a legally binding contractual arrangement.

Smart contracts will remain subject to the same body of contract law as any other contract written in natural language. Even if it were possible to encode accurately the entirety of a complex natural-language contract, a smart contact cannot be relied on as the only record of rights and obligations between the parties. Legislation might impose additional contractual terms (for example, consumer protection law) that need to be adhered to. Thus, smart contracts cannot exist outside the legal system and need to rely on traditional legal instruments.

29. Arizona House Bill 2417.
30. The relevant passages of the statutes stipulate that records or signatures in electronic form cannot be denied legal effect and enforceability based on the fact they are in electronic form.
31. New York Assembly Bill 8780.

[D] Benefits and Drawbacks

[1] Eliminating Ambiguity?

Smart contracts allegedly provide numerous benefits in comparison with traditional contracts. First, they are said to increase contractual security. The terms of smart contracts are expressed in computer languages that have strictly defined semantics and syntax. The use of pre-defined programming languages and Boolean logic[32] reduces the risk of ambiguity and subjective interpretation. The computer code does not permit ambiguity: something either does or does not happen as a result of the code execution. In contrast, the interpretation of traditional contracts by humans may be affected by subconscious bias and subjective discretion. Thus, the reliance on strict syntax may result in increased clarity and certainty of the contractual terms.

However, it needs to be noted that the use of ambiguous language in contracts is not inherently bad. Contracts are frequently written is broad terms to ensure a certain degree of flexibility and to allow parties to adapt to changing circumstances without the need to renegotiate the agreement. In contrast, the use of precise language may make a contract rigid and inflexible. Terms may also be left vague on purpose because of the unwillingness to invest more resources in the negotiation process.

[2] Reducing Risk of Non-performance and Manipulation?

Smart contracts are said to ensure a higher degree of performance as once the contractual terms have been programmed into code, there is no longer a need to rely on the willingness of the parties to perform the contract. Subsequent changes of circumstances or intent by one of the parties are irrelevant. Smart contracts are said to reduce the risk of potential manipulation by a third party and of human error because the contract is managed automatically by blockchain. However, as it is shown below, smart contracts do not ensure a perfect execution of contractual obligations. Issues, such as non-performance and contract breach, may also occur in a smart contract context.

[3] Contract Modification

In traditional contracts, a need often arises for a variation of contractual terms. It is common to amend certain provisions to adapt to external circumstances, such as changes in commercial and regulatory landscape. It is also common to tolerate certain deviations from the agreed performance without formally amending the contract.[33] Smart contracts permit no such adjustments. Once a smart contract is programmed and put on the blockchain, it is set to run to its completion. This could result in a situation

32. Boolean logic is a form of algebra in which all values are reduced to either true of false.
33. Under contract law, deliberate non-performance is neither illegal nor prohibited as long as the party breaching the contract compensates the aggrieved party for his loss.

where a smart contract would continue to operate irrespective of any change in external circumstances, which could become commercially absurd or even illegal. The structure of smart contracts makes them rigid and deprives the parties of the ability to adapt to changing circumstances.

If the parties would like to retain the possibility to amend a smart contract subsequent to its conclusion, the possibility to allow contract modification would have to be programmed into the code. As the reasons for contract modification are rarely known at the outset and it is not possible to anticipate all potential events that could affect the contract operation during its lifetime, it would be necessary to include broad allowance into the code, which would lessen the level of certainty associated with the use of smart contracts. The benefits of self-enforcement would be lost if it was possible to amend the code to accommodate future events. However, a contract that would attempt to anticipate all possible events that may affect its operation would increase in volume and complexity. The longer the contract, the higher the risk of malfunction and the likelihood of errors.

[4] Contract Breach and Coding Errors

Like any other computer programme, smart contracts are vulnerable to bugs and coding errors. If an error is present, a smart contract will not function as it should. Therefore, it is necessary to stipulate what will happen if unforeseen circumstances beyond the control of any parties occur and allocate their risk of their occurrence by prior agreement.

Contrary to the popular belief, smart contracts can be breached by a party to it. A party can prevent the execution of a smart contract if circumstances have changed or he wishes to opt for a more profitable alternative. For example, a contract seeking to transfer some digital assets cannot be executed if the assets have been removed from, or have not been deposited in, a special account. It could also happen that the password to the account no longer works and the digital assets cannot be accessed during the contract execution. This means that all the legal remedies for breach of contract (for example, damages, penalties) are also relevant in the context of smart contracts. Also, there might be a need to seek enforcement by addressing the claims to a third party (a specialized government agency or judiciary).

Smart contracts deployed on public permissionless blockchains may give rise to problems in relation to legal enforceability as there is no central administering authority to decide a dispute between participants to a smart contract. There may be no obvious defendant against whom legal action could be brought (a blockchain network is not a legal entity) and it may not be clear what dispute resolution mechanism should apply. Finally, there might be difficulties in proving the existence or content of a smart contract in court proceedings where evidence exists only in electronic format on a distributed ledger.

Another issue is that smart contracts treat legal and illegal matters in the same way. Anything that can be implemented in a code can be the object of smart contracts. Although a contract may violate the fundamental principles of the legal order, it will be executed by programme code. Thus, smart contracts can be used for illegal purposes and magnify the scope of unlawful activities through automation.

For the reason explained above, it is recommended to couple the use of smart contracts with a traditional legal contract that will address various non-operational issues, such as breach, liability for coding error and the choice of jurisdiction. For example, the content of a smart contract could be duplicated in a separate natural-language contract—for every clause encoded into computer code, there would be a matching natural language version. Another possibility would be to apply the split contracting model where the entirety of the contractual terms would be split into two components: non-human performance would be encoded into computer code whereas general provisions would be written into a natural-language contract.

[5] Contract Drafting

The creation of smart contracts requires advanced programming skills. Such contracts are unlikely to be created by lawyers but by specialized programmers who will translate legal language into code. The parties to the contract and their lawyers will not be able to check whether the code correctly reflects the desired functionality. Potential errors may not become evident until the phase of implementation, i.e., when the contract is executed. As there is a huge gap of abstraction between legal and programming language, there is a risk of miscommunication and potential for discrepancies between what was agreed and what was implemented. Not all legal language is capable of a reduction into an algorithm and omitting a single word in legal documents may give rise to unintended legal consequences and prolonged disputes. Some contracts rely on abstract concepts, such as "reasonable steps" or "good faith," that do not lend themselves to encoding as they involve value judgments and are a question of degree. As words are ambiguous and capable of multiple interpretations, they may be incorrectly interpreted by those converting a particular obligation into code.

Many smart contracts will originate from natural-language contracts that are subsequently translated into code since programmers who create a smart contract cannot decide on its legal and commercial aspects. As legal language includes lengthy sentences, subordinate clauses and references to abstract concepts, translating a legal agreement into code will be a tedious labor-intensive process. Although smart contract are believed to reduce transaction costs, it cannot be concluded that they are cheaper to use than traditional contracts. As smart contracts can be developed by people with advanced programming skills, the costs associated with the "drafting" of a smart contract will be relatively high.

To remedy the above-mentioned problems of translating legal language into executable code, lawyers should draft agreements with encoding in mind. They should write contractual terms in a way that enables their subsequent translation into code by using logical, clear and unambiguous language that the programmers can understand.

[6] Links to the Real World

Smart contracts cannot function without input from external sources (oracles). They need to communicate with the real world to establish whether a certain event took place. To ensure a smooth smart contract execution, it is necessary to find a reliable oracle that obtains data from a trustworthy information provider. To mitigate the risk of an oracle's non-functioning, it may be wise to create a network of oracles that obtain information from multiple independent data sources.

§2.03 BLOCKCHAIN AND TAXATION: USE CASES

Many blockchain-based initiatives are currently taking place in various sectors. This section presents some (potential) use cases of blockchain that can be relevant in the context of taxation.[34]

[A] Recordkeeping

Blockchain could be useful in the field of organizational management, especially, in all areas where central databases or registers are used. It has the potential to change the way we regulate and maintain administrative control. Many business processes necessitate intensive cross-checking of different data sources from various business units. Blockchain technology could simplify the processes and help reduce inconsistencies. The advantage of blockchain is that the ledger is replicated in a large number of identical databases, each hosted and maintained by an interested party. When changes are entered in one copy, all other copies are simultaneously updated. There is no need for a third-party verification or manual reconciliation of records. In this way, blockchain technology could be used by group companies to manage intra-group transactions and make transaction information available to all entities.

In some countries, blockchain technology is already used by publicly traded companies to keep record of stock ownership. Knowing who owns which shares is a fundamental corporate governance requirement. Publicly traded corporations need a reliable stock ledger to ensure accurate ownership, voting and dividend payments. On August 1, 2017, the amendments to the Delaware General Corporation Law, which allows corporations to maintain shareholder lists and other corporate records using blockchain technology, became effective.[35] As Delaware is widely regarded as the corporate capital of the United States, legal and commercial developments in Delaware have the potential to affect the entire United States economy. The corporate law amendments were part of the Delaware Blockchain Initiative, a new project seeking to clarify the state's law and welcome the blockchain industry into the state.

34. Some of these use cases were originally discussed in: A.M. Bal, *Blockchain, Initial Coin Offerings and Other Developments in the Virtual Currency Market*, 20 Derivs. & Fin. Instrums. 2 (2018).
35. J. Roberts, *Companies Can Put Shareholders on a Blockchain Starting Today* (August 1, 2017), http://fortune.com/2017/08/01/blockchain-shareholders-law/.

[B] Government Services

It is widely believed that blockchain may revolutionize the public sector as it has the potential to bring security, efficiency and speed to a wide range of government services and processes. In the past years, agencies in more than a dozen countries have been experimenting with blockchain-based applications for both internal and external use.

Dubai plans to become the world's first blockchain-powered government and is investing in technology as a way to diversify away from relying too heavily on oil revenues. The Dubai Blockchain Strategy that establishes a roadmap for the introduction of blockchain technology is built on three pillars: government efficiency, industry creation and international leadership. The first pillar (government efficiency) will result in all government entities using blockchain technology by 2020. The move to blockchain is expected to improve the delivery of basic government services, saving over 25 million productivity hours per year.[36] By 2020, the emirate wants all visa applications, bill payments and license renewals, which account for over 100 million documents each year, to be transacted digitally using blockchain. An important technical milestone was achieved in 2017 when the Dubai Land Department (DLD), the government agency tasked with overseeing land purchases, became the world's first government entity to adopt blockchain technology.[37] DLD has created a blockchain-powered database that records all real estate contracts and connect homeowners and tenants to property-related billers, such as electrical, water and telecommunications utilities. In addition to adopting blockchain in real estate, Dubai also launched its own blockchain-based cryptocurrency, called, emCash, that people can use to pay for government and non-government services. The currency is said to have many advantages, including faster processing, improved delivery time, less complexity and cost, that will improve ease of doing business in Dubai.

The Swedish Land Registry Authority (*Lantmäteriet*) examined the use of blockchain for recording property transactions. *Lantmäteriet* used a private blockchain to investigate how buyers, sellers, banks and authorities can track a transaction digitally, instead of using paper records. According to some estimates, the switch to blockchain could save the Swedish taxpayer over EUR 100 million a year by eliminating paperwork, reducing fraud, and speeding up transactions.[38]

In Estonia, a country that is often named as a leader in tech literacy and e-services, the government seeks to implement blockchain-based solutions for voting. It has announced that Estonia's e-Residency platform would be facilitating a blockchain-based e-voting service to allow shareholders of companies listed on

36. M. Kassem, *Smart Dubai close to rolling out 20 blockchain-based services* (January 14, 2018), www.thenational.ae/business/smart-dubai-close-to-rolling-out-20-blockchain-based-services-1.695280.
37. Gulf News, *Dubai has world's first government entity to conduct transactions through Blockchain network* (October 7, 2017), http://gulfnews.com/business/property/dubai-has-world-s-first-government-entity-to-conduct-transactions-through-blockchain-network-1.2101819.
38. J. Wong, *Sweden's blockchain-powered land registry is inching towards reality* (April 3, 2017) https://qz.com/947064/sweden-is-turning-a-blockchain-powered-land-registry-into-a-reality/.

Nasdaq's Tallinn Stock Exchange to vote in shareholder meetings.[39] The country's e-Residency platform is an electronic identity system used by both Estonian residents and those with business interests in the country to access government services through e-Residency digital authentication.

In the public sector, blockchain may provide significant benefits where many stakeholders use the same information or the same information needs to be provided to many public sector agencies. Blockchain offers the ability to aggregate and verify data from multiple sources and present a shared view of the same record. It has the potential to reduce discrepancies, operational costs and the risks of data loss. A promising use case for blockchain would be the management of beneficial ownership registers. The availability and international exchange of beneficial ownership information is part of the ongoing initiatives to enhance transparency over corporate vehicles, trusts and similar legal arrangements undertaken by the Financial Action Task Force (FATF)[40] and OECD Global Forum on Transparency and Exchange of Information for Tax Purposes.[41] Currently, countries face many challenges when implementing measures designed to collect beneficial ownership information. The most common issues are insufficient accuracy and accessibility of company ownership information, insufficient customer due diligence measures and obstacles to information sharing in the form of data protection and privacy laws. In order to comply with anti-money laundering legislation, financial institutions and other obliged entities must conduct customer due diligence processes to verify beneficial ownership. These procedures are quite inefficient as customers are frequently required to provide identical information to various institutions. To eliminate these inefficiencies, a number of countries have proposed the

39. Nasdaq, *Nasdaq's Blockchain Technology to Transform the Republic of Estonia's e-Residency Shareholder Participation* (February 12, 2016), http://ir.nasdaq.com/releasedetail.cfm?releaseid=954654.
40. Formed in 1989 by the G7 countries, the Financial Action Task Force on Money Laundering (FATF) is an intergovernmental body whose purpose is to develop and promote an international response to combat money laundering. As of March 2018, its membership consists of 37 countries and territories. In April 1990, the FATF issued a report containing a set of Forty Recommendations, which were intended to provide a comprehensive plan of action needed to fight against money laundering. The FATF Recommendations are recognized as the international standard for combating of money laundering and the financing of terrorism, and form the basis for a co-ordinated response to these threats to the integrity of the financial system The FATF Recommendations were revised in 1996, 2003 and most recently in 2012 to ensure that they remain up to date and relevant. Currently, there are 49 recommendations. Countries seen as not sufficiently compliant with these recommendations may be subject to financial sanctions.
41. *See*, for example, FATF, *Concealment of Beneficial Ownership* (July 2018); FATF, *FATF Report to the G20: Beneficial Ownership* (September 2016). At the EU level, the issue of beneficial ownership was addressed in the 4th and 5th Anti-Money Laundering Directives (AMLD). *See Directive (EU) 2018/843 of the European Parliament and of the Council of 30 May 2018 amending Directive (EU) 2015/849 on the prevention of the use of the financial system for the purposes of money laundering or terrorist financing, and amending Directives 2009/138/EC and 2013/36/EU* (AMLD 5) and *Directive (EU) 2015/849 of the European Parliament and of the Council of 20 May 2015 on the prevention of the use of the financial system for the purposes of money laundering or terrorist financing, amending Regulation (EU) No 648/2012 of the European Parliament and of the Council, and repealing Directive 2005/60/EC of the European Parliament and of the Council and Commission Directive 2006/70/EC* (AMLD 4).

establishment of centralized registers containing basic beneficial ownership information. The information would be stored in a single repository and shared among financial institutions, tax administrations and companies. Blockchain could be used to provide a platform for such centralized registers. Its immutability, transparency and real-time updates make it ideally suited for storing and sharing beneficial ownership information among many participants.

[C] Supply Chain Management

Over the last years, trade has been growing exponentially and this trend is certain to continue. To meet the needs of customers who expect online-ordered items to be delivered next day, the speed with which goods are moving along the supply chains has increased. Growing trade volumes (especially the increasing number of imported low value consignments) imply a higher workload for the customs administration.

One of the main tasks of customs administration is to ensure security of cross-border supply chains. Customs authorities should prevent dangerous and counterfeit goods from entering a country's territory and, in doing so, they should interfere as little as possible with the flow of commerce. Examples of traditional measures to address the issue of supply chain security are: the submission of pre-arrival information for all goods imported into the European Union, the concept of trusted entities (e.g. Authorized Economic Operator,[42] C-TPAT[43]), and the US Container Security Initiative.[44]

Another area of customs administration where security issues are paramount is the trade in dual-use goods that pose a risk of being diverted from legal trade for illegal misuse. The European Union and many other jurisdictions control the export, transit and brokerage of dual-use items by requiring traders dealing with these items to obtain authorizations and to keep records of how these goods are used across the supply chain. Dual-use export controls affect a wide-range of industries (for example, energy,

42. The EU Authorized Economic Operator (AEO) program took effect on January 1, 2008. AEOs may benefit from simplifications provided for by the customs rules (AEOC) and/or facilitation with regard to customs controls related to security and safety (AEOS). *See* European Commission, *Authorized Economic Operator,* https://ec.europa.eu/taxation_customs/general-information-customs/customs-security/authorised-economic-operator-aeo/authorised-economic-operator-aeo_en#what_is.
43. The US Customs –Trade Partnership Against Terrorism (C-TPAT) is a voluntary government-business initiative to strengthen US border security. An entity that wishes to join the C-TPAT programme must address a broad range of security topics and present security profiles that list action plans to align security throughout the supply chain. *See* Customs and Border Protection (CBP), *CTPAT: Customs Trade Partnership against Terrorism,* www.cbp.gov/border-security/ports-entry/cargo-security/ctpat.
44. The Container Security Initiative (CSI) is a program under which high-risk maritime cargo containers are checked before they are loaded aboard vessels bound for the United States. CSI is operational at around 60 ports in North America, Europe, Asia, Africa, the Middle East, and Latin and Central America. It allows pre-screening over 80% of all maritime containerized cargo imported into the United States. *See* CBP, *CSI: Container Security Initiative,* www.cbp.gov/border-security/ports-entry/cargo-security/csi/csi-brief.

aerospace, telecommunications and information security, life sciences, chemical, and electronics).

In the area of customs administration, blockchain technology would permit tracing the origin and flow of (high-value) goods to their final destination by means of tokenized assets (which are digital representations of real assets). When a high-value product is manufactured, a corresponding digital token would be created by a trusted entity that would authenticate the origin of the product. A digital "certificate of origin" would be more difficult to forge or falsify than one issued in a paper form. Any movements of the product across the supply chain and changes of ownership would be recorded in the blockchain. By recording all data in one register that would be shared among various stakeholders, efficient control over the movement of goods would be possible. One central register would eliminate inefficiencies related to storing and processing the same information by different bodies, duplication of processes and manual data entry. By being able to trace the origins and pathways of goods they procure, distributors and retailers would be sure that there are no illegal labor or environmental practices involved at any stage of the supply chain. The main difficulty of using blockchain for customs purposes is that the participation of a large group of stakeholders (traders, brokers, ports, customs authorities) would be necessary to make the system fully operational.

Some companies are using blockchain as a way to simplify their supply chains and strengthen oversight over the movement of goods. The diamond sector has been one of the first to embrace the blockchain technology, which permitted diamond suppliers and intermediaries to replace a paper certification process with a digital ledger. Determined to stop the spread of fake and "blood" diamonds, a London-based company Everledger has been using blockchain to track the provenance of diamonds. It has placed more than 1.6 million diamonds on a blockchain by recording digitally each diamond's myriad attributes and a certificate number (that is also inscribed on the stone). In this way, Everledger helps intermediaries and consumers ensure that a stone is authentic and has been obtained through reputable means.[45]

In January 2018, the world's largest container shipping firm Maersk and IBM announced the intention to establish a joint venture to provide more efficient and secure methods for conducting global trade using blockchain technology.[46] Two main objectives that this project seeks to achieve are paperless trade and supply chain transparency. The project aims at providing end-to-end supply chain visibility that enables all parties involved in global shipping transactions to securely and seamlessly record shipment events in real time and at digitalizing and automating paperwork filings for the import and export of goods by enabling end users to securely submit, stamp and approve documents across national and organizational boundaries.[47] A

45. J. Roberts, *The Diamond Industry Is Obsessed With the Blockchain* (September 12, 2018) http://fortune.com/2017/09/12/diamond-blockchain-everledger/.
46. M. White, *Digitizing Global Trade with Maersk and IBM* (January 16, 2018), www.ibm.com/blogs/blockchain/2018/01/digitizing-global-trade-maersk-ibm/.
47. According to Maersk, a shipment of refrigerated goods from East Africa to Europe can go through nearly 30 people and organizations and involve more than 200 different communications. Documentation and bureaucracy can be as much as a fifth of the total cost of moving a container.

blockchain-based platform should link ports, customs authorities, logistics companies and traders, helping them manage and track millions of shipping containers. The success of the proposed platform depends on acceptance of all participants.

[D] Tax Compliance

As smart contracts may have a variety of applications in the payment sector especially where the need to make a payment is dependent on the occurrence of certain events, they could be used in the area of tax compliance and remittance. Payroll and withholding tax compliance seems to be an ideal use case for blockchain and smart contracts. Smart contracts would automatically determine the correct tax withholdings and transfer payments to the tax administration with the residual net amount deposited in the employee's or recipient's bank account.

To successfully implement a blockchain-based withholding tax system, the payment service provider would need to secure the cooperation of various banks and all government agencies involved. The large number of participants that would need to be included in the system requires an extreme level of coordination, which is compounded many times when international transactions are considered.

The payment service provider would need to make sure that data used in his withholding tax calculations is complete and up-to-date. He would need to find reliable external data feeds (oracles) that would provide the necessary tax information. Without oracles, smart contracts cannot do much more than moving digital tokens around. The use of oracles is also necessary to connect smart contracts to the traditional payments systems that make the transfers of real money to the bank accounts of the parties involved in a transaction.

[E] Value Chain Analysis

In 2013, the OECD initiated the Base Erosion and Profit Shifting (BEPS) project with the aim to improve the international tax framework.[48] One of the objectives of the BEPS project was to ensure that profits are taxed where economic activities generating the profits are performed and where value is created.[49] BEPS Actions 8-10 specifically call for "aligning transfer pricing outcomes with value creation."[50]

See J. Gronholt-Pedersen, *Maersk, IBM to launch blockchain-based platform for global trade* (January 16, 2018), www.reuters.com/article/us-maersk-blockchain-ibm/maersk-ibm-to-launch-blockchain-based-platform-for-global-trade-idUSKBN1F51DE.

48. *See supra* n. 7.
49. On the concept of value creation, *see* J. Hey, *"Taxation Where Value is Created" and the OECD/G20 Base Erosion and Profit Shifting Initiative*, 72 Bull. Intl. Taxn. 4/5 (2018); R.J.S. Tavares & J.P. Owens, *Human Capital in Value Creation and Post-BEPS Tax Policy: An Outlook*, 69 Bull. Intl. Taxn. 10 (2015).
50. OECD, *Actions 8-10: Aligning Transfer Pricing Outcomes with Value Creation* (OECD 2015).

As the fundamental principle underlying blockchain technology is transparency, blockchain could be used to support the global efforts to identify value-generating activities and impose taxes accordingly. For example, if related-party transactions were included in the blockchain, each group company (and tax authorities) would be able to see the complete history of transactions. Having a good picture of transaction-level data could lead to a better understanding of the value creation process across the supply chain. This distributed ledger could be part of transfer pricing documentation, supplementing the information presented in the master file, local file and country-by-country report. Each stakeholder would have an up-to-date copy of the whole ledger, eliminating the risk of loss of records and the need for manual data reconciliation.

The use of blockchain for value chain analysis may have its limitations. Although blockchain can capture transaction-level data, not all value drivers can be traced back and allocated to particular transactions. For example, although brand awareness and the availability of customer data are often tremendously important profit drivers, there may be no stage in the value chain (and thus in the blockchain recording this value chain) where they are directly measurable. In other words, blockchain could be useful to trace the movement of goods across the supply chain; however, it may have its limitations when it comes to certain value-adding intangibles.

[F] VAT Fraud Detection

Another interesting area of application for blockchain and smart contracts is VAT compliance and VAT fraud prevention. The EU VAT system is vulnerable to cross-border frauds. These are known as missing trader intra-Community (MTIC) and missing trader extra-Community (MTEC) frauds. Fraudsters take advantage of weaknesses in the structural design of the VAT system and in the administration of the tax in the following way: a supplier sells goods to another country and this transaction is zero-rated (meaning that the supplier does not charge VAT but is allowed to deduct VAT that was charged to him). The recipient that is supposed to account for VAT on the acquisition of the goods fails to do so although he re-sells the goods to another party and collects the VAT. The tax authorities currently do not have any means for real-time detection of cross-border fraud. They rely on auditing VAT returns (filed one or more months after the transaction has taken place) and intra-Community exchanges of transaction data.[51] The total amount of VAT lost in the European Union in 2015 was estimated at EUR 151 billion. This represented a loss of 12% of the total expected VAT revenue.[52]

51. Traders supplying goods or services to another Member State are required to file recapitulative statements. The information from recapitulative statements is compiled in national databases that can be accessed by the tax authorities of other EU countries. In this way, the tax authorities can check whether all intra-Community supplies of goods and cross-border provision of services have been duly taxed. The main flaws of this approach are that it is request-based, provides aggregate data (not invoice-level granular data) and data exchange is delayed a few months after a suspect transaction has taken place.
52. European Commission, *VAT Gap*, https://ec.europa.eu/taxation_customs/business/tax-cooperation-control/vat-gap_en.

Several authors have proposed the implementation of a VAT blockchain that would function as a private permissioned distributed ledger and record all VAT-relevant transactions.[53] To join the VAT blockchain, a taxpayer would need a valid VAT identification number. All VAT-relevant transactions would be registered on a distributed ledger and verified by tax administrations nodes, i.e., government-owned computer facilities that would match transactions entered by various parties and perform artificial intelligence-facilitated risk analysis to identify potential fraudsters, replicating a real-time government audit. If a transaction was not validated by the tax administration nodes, a valid VAT invoice could not be issued. The seller would not be entitled to collect VAT from the buyer and the buyer would not be allowed to deduct VAT paid. The VAT blockchain would use smart contracts that, upon entering the transaction data by the trader, would determine the applicable VAT rates and calculate the VAT to be paid. The proposed system could not use PoW as a consensus mechanism since, in PoW-based systems, transaction verification depends on the network power that one controls. Consequently, if tax authorities did not have more than 50% of the network power, they would not be able to control the blockchain.

A well-functioning VAT blockchain would allow real-time VAT remittance and refund, and would facilitate detection of fraudulent activity. Another benefit of the proposed system is that VAT returns would be prepared by the government through an automated assessment system rather than by taxpayers through the more burdensome self-assessment system. This would mean that the government would prepare the return for taxpayer review as opposed to the taxpayer preparing the return for tax authority review. The proposed system would also eliminate the need for recapitulative statements, which are currently obligatory for all EU entrepreneurs involved in intra-Community supplies.

Just as in the case of the potential use of blockchain for tax compliance purposes,[54] the two main challenges to the creation of a VAT blockchain are (1) a huge coordination effort that would need to be undertaken to develop a system that would connect tax administrations of various countries and an extremely large number of suppliers and service providers and (2) finding reliable oracles that would deliver the required VAT information and connect the VAT blockchain to the traditional payment systems.

Ainsworth (2016) went one step further and proposed the concept of VATCoin—a government-mandated cryptocurrency used for VAT compliance purposes.[55] Under his proposal, VATCoins would be "minted" by the tax authorities and sold to businesses that would use them in their commercial transactions. VATCoins would act as the only means for the payment of VAT: it would not be possible to pay

53. R.T. Ainsworth & M. Alwohaibi, *The first real-time blockchain VAT: GCC solves MTIC fraud*, Tax Notes International (May 22, 2017); R.T. Ainsworth & A.B. Shact, *Blockchain technology might solve VAT fraud*, Tax Notes International (September 26, 2016). T. Loy, *Umsatzsteuerbetrug im innergemeinschaftlichen Erwerb: Konzept eines Blockchain-basierten Lösungsansatzes*, 22 Deutsches Steuerrecht (2018).

54. *See* §2.03[D] Tax Cmpliance.

55. R.T. Ainsworth et al., *VATCoin: Can a Crypto Tax Currency Prevent VAT Fraud?* 84 Tax Notes International 703 (November 14, 2016).

tax in legal currency and only governments would be allowed to convert VATCoins into legal currency. Thus, if VATCoins were stolen, they would immediately become worthless. The proposed system would eliminate missing trader fraud, which always involves a trader who holds VAT on the government's behalf and disappears without filing a return and remitting the tax. VATCoin would prevent this fraud by taking VAT out of the hands of the traders.

§2.04 WHEN DOES IT MAKE SENSE TO USE BLOCKCHAIN FOR TAX PURPOSES?

Although blockchain is frequently seen as a solution to all problems of data management and data storage, the same characteristics that make it a very appealing technology (transparency, disintermediation and immutability) may hamper its widespread adoption in the tax sector. Before embarking on blockchain projects, one should consider what added value a blockchain solution will provide and whether there are any alternative solutions (for example, a traditional database)[56] that could achieve the same outcome in a more efficient way.[57] The following sections explain in which circumstances a blockchain-based solution may be beneficial. Diagram 1 lists the most important questions that one should ask while considering the use of blockchain technology.

56. A database is a collection of information that is organized in a way to be easily accessed, managed and updated. A database is stored as a file or a set of files. The information in these files may be broken down into records, each of which consists of one or more fields. Fields are the basic units of data storage, and each field typically contains information pertaining to one aspect or attribute of the entity described by the database. Records are also organized into tables that include information about relationships between its various fields. *See* www.britannica.com/technology/database.
57. Some of the ideas in this section were originally discussed in A.M. Bal, *Does the Tax Sector Need Blockchain?* (April 4, 2018) White Paper IBFD.

Figure 2.1 List of Questions to Determine Whether Blockchain Is the right Technology to Use

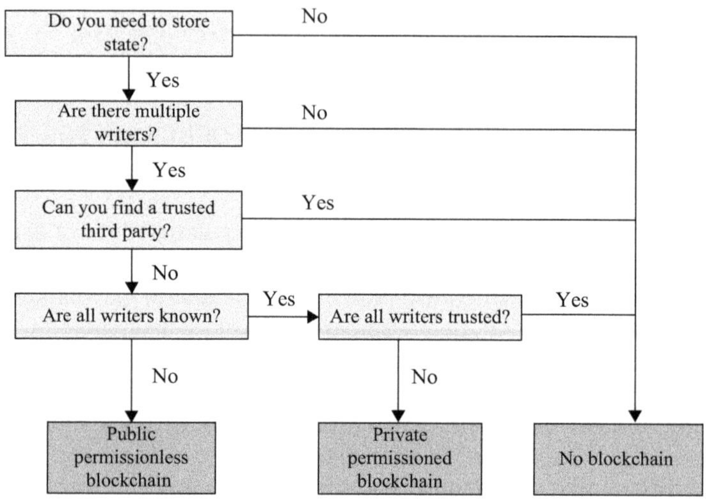

Source: K. Wüst & A. Gervais, Do you need a Blockchain? (2017), https://eprint.iacr.org/2017/375.pdf.

[A] Transparency

Blockchain is all about transparency and making data visible to anyone who can access the network. Every blockchain participant can see every transaction on the distributed ledger although he cannot determine the identities of the parties carrying out the transactions. In contrast, tax-related information is confidential and companies are generally not willing to disclose the details of their tax affairs to the public. Therefore, a blockchain-based solution where everyone has access to the same information does not seem suitable for tax purposes. Given data protection and confidentiality concerns, a private blockchain or a traditional database where a central administrator (for example, the tax administration) determines the rights of all participants and may prevent some of them from viewing some of the contents seems to be a better option.

Blockchain's transparency is a double-edged sword. Many blockchain networks make their source code fully transparent, allowing anybody to verify their functionality and hoping to gain the trust of potential users. However, the more transparent a blockchain network is, the better the opportunity to search for errors and vulnerabilities in the computer code. As the DAO example discussed in §2.04[E] 'New Versus Traditional Technology' shows, transparency makes bugs easy to find and exploit for illicit purposes.

[B] Disintermediation

Traditional databases are managed centrally by a trusted entity which ensures that all operations are executed according to the agreed set of rules and which protects the database against malicious modifications. In contrast, a blockchain-based database does not need a central administrator that would verify the transactions. All nodes in the network work together to ensure the integrity of information. Newly added nodes can verify the database contents from scratch and do not need to trust other participants.

Blockchain removed the need for trusted intermediaries by enabling several parties to interact directly with one another. The question that one must inevitably ask is whether there is an urgent need for disintermediation in the tax sector. Is there anything wrong with a central party who manages a database with tax information and verifies the correctness of entries? In the tax sector, in a domestic context, a trusted intermediary can be identified—it is the tax administration or another government entity.

The lack of a central entity may have a negative impact on the performance of blockchain networks. In terms of performance, blockchain-based databases will always be slower than traditional databases. Whereas in traditional databases transactions are processed once, in blockchain networks they must be processed independently by each node, meaning that a lot more work is done for the same result. Blockchain is based on duplication of processes as all nodes in the network (at least in public blockchains) do exactly the same things: they verify the same transactions according to the same rules and they store the entire database history, which requires downloading large chunks of data. Moreover, blockchains use consensus mechanisms, such as proof-of-work, that may involve a lot of back and forth communication among the nodes.

[C] Immutability

Immutability is said to be one of the hallmarks of blockchain technology. Whereas in traditional databases information can be deleted or changed relatively easily, once a blockchain transaction has been validated, the commonly held view is that it can never be reversed or modified. This is not entirely correct. Immutability is not guaranteed in private blockchains which depend on the behavior and reliability of their validators. Similarly, in public blockchains, if enough participants decide to act against the rules, there is nothing to stop them. There is always at least a theoretical possibility of a so-called 51% attack, meaning that a group controlling the majority of the network mining power could take control over the whole network. This may seem extremely unlikely; however, if one realizes that the top mining pools currently control more than 50% of all computing power of the Bitcoin network,[58] the threat of a 51% attack becomes more real. To conclude, no blockchain is perfectly immutable.

58. https://blockchain.info/pools.

As explained above, although it is not entirely impossible, it is extremely difficult to modify a once validated blockchain transaction. Based on this fact, it can be assumed that blockchain creates permanent and unalterable records. The only practical way to reverse a previous entry is to add a new entry that will be visible to all participants. The benefit of irreversibility of transactions is that it protects information from unauthorized modifications. However, in the tax (and legal) domain, there is often a need to make corrections with retroactive effect. This is currently nearly impossible in public blockchain networks.

[D] Data Correctness

Although blockchain applications uses pre-programmed algorithms and computational logic, it cannot be assumed that they will always produce legally correct records. Just like any software application, blockchain faces the inherent problem of the interface between the digital and physical world: someone must program the distributed ledger and make sure that proper entries are made. As input needs to be provided by people, what enters the blockchain can be subject to manipulation. For example, two related parties may agree to include fictitious transactions or fictitious prices in the ledger. If these entries are validated by the network, blockchain is technically correct but not legally correct. There are many ways in which validators who digitally sign the blocks they create in a private blockchain can manipulate the database contents. If enough validators collude maliciously, they can prevent a particular transaction for being confirmed.

To perform many activities, smart contracts need real-world data, i.e., information from outside their network. Otherwise, all they can do is to move digital assets around the blockchain. External sources of information (oracles) are a necessary step forward in the practical utilization of smart contracts. For more complex tasks, smart contracts will need multiple data feeds with various types of information. Therefore, finding reliable oracles is a necessary precondition for a well-functioning smart contract. If oracles deliver incorrect data, smart contracts will not perform as anticipated. In other words, a decentralized system of smart contracts will need a reliable centralized oracle to carry out its functions.

[E] New Versus Traditional Technology

Traditional databases, such as Oracle or SQL, have the advantage of efficiency and simplicity as they have been subject to extensive testing and debugging prior to their release. Their performance is constantly improved by the continuous series of software updates. In contrast, blockchain technology is still in its infancy. Although blockchain applications are generally released after security audits and thorough testing, they may be vulnerable to bugs.

In June 2016, the Ethereum software suffered a devastating attack when a loophole in a smart contact called the Decentralized Autonomous Organization (DAO) was exploited to drain almost USD 50 million. The DAO was a network of smart contracts established as a new type of decentralized crowdfunding vehicle where participants could invest cryptocurrency and collectively vote on projects looking for funding. DAO participants were given the possibility to withdraw their funds any time, thereby keeping the risk of their investment low. The DAO quickly collected ether worth around USD 150 million but was hacked by unknown attackers. Some hackers exploited loopholes in the withdrawal mechanism to obtain over 12 million units of ether, valued at over USD 50 million at that time.[59] Through a contentious emergency procedure (knows as "hard fork"),[60] the core developers of Ethereum were able to rewrite the history of their blockchain and restore all funds to investors. The hard fork led to a split of the Ethereum blockchain into mainstream Ethereum and Ethereum Classic, whose supporters continue to maintain that the hackers rightfully exploited a bug in the smart contract and that the diverted funds should not have been returned to the investors.

Traditional databases and software packages have been used for tax purposes for decades. The majority of companies is already using automated payroll records and tax management systems. These software packages have the benefit of flexibility (incorrect data entry can be easily amended) and efficiency (speedy transaction processing), and they are integrated with the company's ERP systems and relatively easy for their users to operate. Being a revolutionary idea that breaks away from the conventional computer systems, blockchain-based innovations can be hard to comprehend for people who use and invest in them. Only experts are capable of examining the underlying program code in order to assess whether the code does not contain programming errors and is not vulnerable to manipulation.

Finally, implementing a new technology is always a labor-intensive and costly undertaking. New technology frequently needs to interact and share data with one or more legacy systems and this may make it difficult to integrate it in the existing processes. Blockchain-based applications require people with specialist technical knowledge to develop, test and evaluate. Tax officials and tax managers are frequently missing advanced IT skills, such as coding, programming, cryptography. They would need to rely on specialized IT staff to verify the accuracy and reliability of blockchain applications. An important question that has not received much attention yet is how to audit blockchain. For many traditional auditors (even IT auditors), this would be an entirely new field.

§2.05 CONCLUSIONS

Blockchain is often referred to as the cure-all panacea for all world's problems. To its enthusiasts, it has the potential to make a similar impact as the Internet has had. The

---

59. D. Siegel, *Understanding the DAO attack* (June 25, 2016), www.coindesk.com/understanding-dao-hack-journalists/.
60. A fork occurs when a single cryptocurrency/blockchain splits in two due to the code changes. Forks can be soft and hard. A hard fork is meant to create two blockchains, whereas a soft fork is meant to result in one. After a hard fork, the previous version and the new one are completely separated, there is no communication or transaction option between the two. Usually, the new version inherits all the historic transactions.

author is of the opinion that as blockchain technology matures, more people will adopt this new mode of collaboration. Blockchain will be slowly moving into the mainstream, with more and more organizations exploring how it can be implemented for their businesses. However, as with any innovation, it is difficult to predict to what extent it will change the current ways of working. In the author's opinion, there are serious limitations to the widespread adoption of the blockchain technology in the tax sector.

Before embarking on a blockchain project, one should ask the question whether blockchain technology will genuinely add value in the particular situation. In many cases, a project can be well managed by means of a traditional database. The use of traditional databases is preferable where a trusted entity to manage the information can be found and where warranting confidentiality is an important issue. In contrast, blockchain is a good solution for repositories of information where every user should be able to validate and view all information. In other words, blockchain has a strong use case where disintermediation and transparency are more important than performance and confidentiality.

The hallmarks of the blockchain technology (transparency, disintermediation and immutability) are typical of public blockchains. Private blockchains do not guarantee these features. The paradox is that companies and institutions that praise the features of public blockchains tend to shy away from these characteristics when they implement their own blockchain-based applications. They would like to implement something over which they have more control and which does not require exposing all transactions publicly. Thus, they wish to benefit from the characteristics of a public blockchain but frequently end up having nothing more than a shared database.

Smart contracts are one of the most important blockchain-based innovations. A smart contract is a contract represented in code and executed by computers. The idea of smart contracts appeared in mid-1990s but remained abstract until the invention of Bitcoin and blockchain. Given the enormous interest in blockchain technology, the number of smart contracts will increase in the future and they will become more and more relevant for the execution of contractual obligations.

Smart contracts offer benefits in terms of clarity, predictability and ease of enforcement. It is widely believed that the use of programming languages with strictly defined syntax and automated execution reduce room for ambiguity and provide a greater level of certainty. However, the use of smart contracts raises a lot of technical challenges related to contract coding, reliance on oracles and the risk of programming errors.

As smart contracts face the same issues as natural-language contracts (validity, breach, non-performance) and are subject to the risk of malfunctioning, it would be wise to supplement the use of smart contracts with a written natural language-contract that would resolve liability issues in case the smart contract does not perform as it should. Another possibility is to opt for the split contracting model where non-human performance in represented in computer code, and general contractual obligations are contained in a traditional written contract.

CHAPTER 3

Concept of Virtual Currency

§3.01 BACKGROUND

Money is a social institution which has exhibited a great capacity to evolve and adapt to the character of the era. In early times, people used commodities as means of payment. Later on, those commodities were gradually replaced by coins and paper money. For a long time, private monies were commonplace—no government even thought to claim a formal monopoly over the issue and use of money within its political territory. The notion of absolute monetary sovereignty began to emerge in the 19th century with the formal consolidation of the powers of the nation state in Europe and later elsewhere in the world. Monetary instruments were standardized and the legal tender status was reserved to the national currency. The era of territorial money reached its zenith in the middle of the 20th century with the invention of exchange and capital controls. However, this trend has clearly reversed in the recent years. Financial and monetary systems have become increasingly integrated, capital controls tend to disappear, and we see greater competition among currencies.

Money has undergone another evolution due to the development of electronic payment systems. These systems have taken the concept of money beyond its physical and notational forms to intangible data that exists only online. Valuable physical coins and nicely printed banknotes have started playing a marginal role: money is no longer a physical object but a large system consisting of computer networks. The emergence of virtual currencies can be seen as a logical next step in the process of dematerialization of money.

Virtual currencies first became popular as a medium of exchange within virtual communities, i.e., places within cyberspace where individuals interact and follow mutual interests or goals. Virtual socializing began in chat rooms and community websites, and later on expanded into more sophisticated environments: virtual worlds.[61] For virtual world participants, the acquisition of virtual items for virtual money was an essential activity to increase their social or power status within the online environment.

In 2008, a person (or persons) operating under the pseudonym Satoshi Nakamoto created Bitcoin—a virtual currency traded online via a peer-to-peer network, allowing its users to interact with one another anonymously and without a third-party intervention.[62] Nakamoto's decentralized currency was a response to the financial crisis, governments' reactions to it and to the role of banks and other payment intermediaries in mediating financial transactions.[63] The first bitcoins were transacted in January 2009 and by June 2011 there were 6.5 million Bitcoins in circulation among an estimated 10,000 users.[64] In July 2018, bitcoins were traded at around USD 6200 and their number exceeded 17 million.[65] The number of virtual currency schemes grew tremendously: from one in 2009 to 1,640 in 2018.[66]

It is important to note that the idea of a stateless decentralized currency emerged long before Bitcoin entered the marketplace. In 1976, the Nobel laureate Friedrich Hayek proposed a system of denationalized money shaped exclusively by market forces.[67] In his opinion, macroeconomic performance would be improved if state control of money could be wholly erased, leaving currencies to be created solely by private financial institutions. Hayek argued that traditional government-backed currencies are prone to a number of weaknesses, such as susceptibility to inflation and political corruption. Private currencies are more stable than traditional currencies because they do not share these weaknesses.

61. Virtual worlds are persistent computer-generated environments in which participants interact with each other using avatars. Although there is much diversity among virtual worlds and each one is unique, two main categories can be distinguished: structured (game-like) worlds and unstructured environments. Game-like worlds (e.g., World of Warcraft) resemble traditional computer games—they have defined objectives and a significant amount of operator-developed content. Unstructured worlds (e.g., Second Life) lack pre-set challenges and utilize more user-generated content. For a detailed analysis of tax consequences of transactions in virtual worlds, *see* A.M. Bal, *Taxation of Virtual Currency*, PhD Thesis (Leiden University 2014).
62. S. Nakamoto, *Bitcoin: A Peer-to-Peer Electronic Cash System* (2008), http://bitcoin.org/bitcoin.pdf.
63. The idea to use virtual currency as an alternative to the existing financial systems is not a novelty. In 1983, David Chaum described the concept of secure digital cash which could be spent in a manner that is untraceable by banks or any other party (D. Chaum, *Blind signatures for untraceable payments* (1983), www.hit.bme.hu/~buttyan/courses/BMEVIHIM219/2009/Chaum.BlindSigForPayment.1982.PDF). He developed DigiCash—a digital currency that ultimately failed due to poor management and missed deals (I. Grigg, *How DigiCash Blew Everything* (February 10, 1999), http://cryptome.org/jya/digicrash.htm). In 1998, Wei Dai wrote an article seeking to create a medium of exchange that avoided government involvement and the need for intermediaries in electronic transactions (Wei Dai, *B-Money* (1998), http://weidai.com/bmoney.txt).
64. F. Reid & M. Harrigan, *An Analysis of Anonimity in the Bitcoin System* (2012).
65. https://coinmarketcap.com/ (accessed on July 14, 2018).
66. https://coinmarketcap.com/ (accessed on July 17, 2018).
67. F.A. Hayek, *Denationalization of Money: The Argument Refined*, 3rd ed. (IEA 1990).

§3.02 DEFINITIONS

For tax and other regulatory purposes, it is necessary to develop a definition of virtual currency and a classification of different virtual currency schemes. A common set of terms describing how virtual currency operates is a crucial first step to enable governments and legislators to develop a regulatory framework governing virtual currency transactions.

The use of correct terminology is very important: governments and legislators that intend to regulate virtual currency must have a good understanding of what they will regulate. Otherwise, there is a risk that the proposed legislation will be under- or overinclusive: certain types of virtual currencies that were supposed to be included may be unintentionally left out or the other way round. For example, a regulation that is drafted in very broad terms may capture virtual currency that is exclusively used within an online game although the intention of the regulator was to regulate decentralized cryptocurrencies, such as bitcoin or ether.

[A] What Is Virtual Currency?

There are many definitions of the term "virtual currency." Although they vary in detail, some common elements can be identified. There seem to be a general agreement that virtual currency is a digital representation of value that does not have a legal tender status in any jurisdiction. Another common feature is that the criterion of convertibility is used to divide virtual currency schemes into different categories. As neither domestic tax legislation nor administrative guidelines provide a comprehensive definition of virtual currency,[68] this section examines the definitions of virtual currency suggested by the European Central Bank, FATF[69] and the EU 5th Anti-Money Laundering Directive.[70]

68. The only piece of legislation providing a detailed definition of virtual currency is the Australian GST Act (A New Tax System (Goods and Services Tax) Act 1999). It defines virtual currency as a digital unit of value that has all of the following characteristics: (1) fully interchangeable with another unit of the same digital currency for the purpose of its use as payment, (2) can be provided as payment for any types of purchases, (3) generally available to the public free of any substantial restrictions, (4) not denominated in any country's currency, (5) the value is not derived from or dependent on anything else, and does not give an entitlement or privileges to receive something else. The legislation specifies that the following is not covered by the virtual currency definition: (1) loyalty points provided by retailers that can only be redeemed for products and services specified by that loyalty scheme, (2) "currency" used in online multi-player games that cannot be used outside the game under which the "currency" is made available; and (3) "digital currency" with value based on something else or that gives an entitlement or privileges to something else (e.g. ICO tokens).
69. *See supra* n. 40.
70. *Directive (EU) 2018/843 of the European Parliament and of the Council of 30 May 2018 amending Directive (EU) 2015/849 on the prevention of the use of the financial system for the purposes of money laundering or terrorist financing, and amending Directives 2009/138/EC and 2013/36/EU.*

[1] European Central Bank

The European Central Bank (ECB) defines virtual currency as a digital representation of value, not issued by a central bank, credit institution or e-money institution, which, in some circumstances, can be used as an alternative to money.[71] The ECB divides virtual currency schemes into three categories based on their interactions with real money and the real economy:[72]

The first category is closed virtual currency schemes. These schemes have almost no link to the real economy and are sometimes called "in-game only" schemes. Users usually pay a subscription fee and earn virtual money based on their online performance. This type of virtual currency can only be spent by purchasing virtual goods and services offered within the virtual community and, at least in theory, it cannot be traded outside the virtual community. An example of closed virtual currency schemes is World of Warcraft (WoW) Gold—a medium of exchange used in the well-known online role-playing game designed by Blizzard Entertainment. Buying and selling WoW Gold in the real world is strictly forbidden under the terms and conditions established by Blizzard Entertainment.

The second category includes virtual currency schemes with unidirectional flow. This type of virtual currency can be purchased directly using real currency at a specific exchange rate, but it cannot be exchanged back to the original currency. The conversion conditions are established by the scheme administrator. An example of virtual currency with unidirectional flow is Facebook Credits (which allow users to buy virtual goods in any application on the Facebook platform) and Nintendo points (which can be redeemed in Nintendo's shops and in their games but cannot be converted back to legal money).

The third category includes virtual currency schemes with bidirectional flow. This type of virtual currency is similar to any other convertible currency with regard to its interoperability with the real world. It allows for the purchase of both virtual and real goods and services. Examples of virtual currency schemes with bidirectional flow are Linden Dollar[73] and Bitcoin.

71. European Central Bank (ECB), *Virtual Currency Schemes—A further analysis* (February 2015). Previously, the ECB defined virtual currency as a type of unregulated digital money, which is issued and usually controlled by its developers, and used and accepted among the members of a particular virtual community (European Central Bank, *Virtual Currency Schemes*, p. 13 (October 2012)). The ECB amended this definition for the following reasons: (1) the word "money" was deleted since virtual currencies did not have the nature of a highly liquid asset and had not reached the level of acceptance commonly associated with money; (2) the word "unregulated" was deleted as in some jurisdictions legislation addressed some aspects of virtual currency; (3) to avoid misunderstandings as regards any theoretical limits on the acceptance of virtual currency, "used and accepted among the members of a specific community" was also deleted (ECB, *Virtual Currency Schemes—A further analysis*, p. 25).
72. ECB, *Virtual Currency Schemes*, *supra* n. 71, at p. 13.
73. Linden Dollars is the virtual currency issued in Second Life, a virtual world where users create "avatars," i.e., digital characters that can be customized. Second Life has its own economy where users can buy and sell goods and services from and to each other. In order to do so, they need Linden Dollars, which can be purchased with US dollars and other currencies according to the exchange rates established in the currency trading market. Users can sell their spare Linden Dollars in return for US dollars.

[2] Financial Action Task Force

A similar definition of virtual currency has been proposed by the Financial Action Task Force (FATF).[74] According to FATF, virtual currency is a digital representation of value that can be digitally traced and functions as (1) a medium of exchange; and/or (2) a unit of account; and/or (3) a store of value, but does not have a legal tender status in any jurisdiction. FATF proposes dividing virtual currency into two basic types: convertible and non-convertible.

Non-convertible (or closed) virtual currency is intended to be specific to a particular virtual domain or world, such as a Massively Multiplayer Online Role-Playing Game (MMORPG), and under the rules governing its use, cannot be exchanged for legal currency. All non-convertible virtual currencies are centralized: by definition, they are issued by a central authority that establishes rules making them non-convertible. A non-convertible characterization is not necessarily static. Even if, under the terms set by the administrator, a currency is officially transferrable only within a specific virtual environment, it is possible that an unofficial secondary black market may arise and provide an opportunity to exchange the "non-convertible" virtual currency legal currency or another virtual currency. The development of a robust secondary black market in a particular "non-convertible" virtual currency may, as a practical matter, effectively transform it into a convertible virtual currency.

Convertible (or open) virtual currency (for example, Bitcoin or Linden Dollar) has an equivalent value in legal currency and can be exchanged back-and-forth for legal currency. The notion of "convertible currency" does not in any way imply an *ex officio* convertibility but rather a *de facto* convertibility (i.e., because a market exists). A virtual currency is "convertible" only as long as some private participants make offers and others accept them since the "convertibility" is not guaranteed at all by law. Convertible virtual currencies may be either of two sub-types: centralized or decentralized.

Centralized virtual currencies have a single administrating authority that controls the system. An administrator issues the currency, establishes the rules for its use, maintains a central payment ledger and has the authority to redeem the currency (withdraw it from circulation). The exchange rate for a convertible virtual currency may be either floating (determined by market supply and demand for the virtual currency) or pegged (fixed by the administrator at a set value measured in legal currency or another real-world store of value, such as gold or a basket of currencies). Decentralized virtual currencies (also known as cryptocurrencies) are distributed, open-source, math-based, peer-to-peer virtual currencies that have no central administrating authority, and no central monitoring or oversight. Given their importance, cryptocurrencies are discussed in more detail in §3.02[B] 'What Is Cryptocurrency?'.

74. FATF, *Virtual Currencies: Key Definitions and Potential AML/CFT Risks* (July 2014).

[3] EU 5th Anti-Money Laundering Directive

The EU 5th Anti-Money Laundering Directive (AMLD5) has introduced the following definition of virtual currency:

> a digital representation of value that is not issued or guaranteed by a central bank or a public authority, is not necessarily attached to a legally established currency, and does not possess a legal status of currency or money, but is accepted by natural or legal persons, as a means of exchange, and which can be transferred, stored and traded electronically.

The directive clarifies that local currencies (also known as complementary currencies) that are used in very limited networks, such as a city or a region, and in-games currencies that can be used exclusively within the specific game environment should not be considered virtual currencies. It also makes it clear that virtual currencies should not be confused with the term "electronic money"[75] or with the concept of "funds."[76]

The definition of virtual currency provided in AMLD5 is very broad. The preamble to AMLD5 clarifies that the objective of the directive is to cover all potential uses of virtual currency, which in addition to being a means of payment can be used "for other different purposes and find broader applications such as means of exchange, investment purposes, store-of-value products or uses in online casinos."

[B] What Is Cryptocurrency?

Although the terms "virtual currency" and "cryptocurrency" are frequently used interchangeably, they do not mean the same thing. "Cryptocurrency" is a subcategory of virtual currency and refers to decentralized convertible virtual currency that is protected by cryptography. It relies on public and private keys to transfer value from one person to another.[77]

Cryptocurrencies can be divided into two categories: (1) alternative cryptocurrency coins (also called altcoins, cryptocoins, currency tokens or simply "coins") and (2) tokens. Although the terms "coins" and tokens" are often used interchangeably, there are significant differences among those two categories. Coins (for instance, Bitcoin) are a cryptocurrency type that operates independently of any other platform. In other words, a coin has its own blockchain-powered platform. The purpose of a coin

75. Article 2(2) *Directive 2009/110/EC of the European Parliament and of the Council of 16 September 2009 on the Taking Up, Pursuit and Prudential Supervision of the Business of Electronic Money Institutions Amending Directives 2005/60/EC And 2006/48/EC and Repealing Directive 2000/46/EC.*
76. Article 4(25) *Directive (EU) 2015/2366 of the European Parliament and of the Council of 25 November 2015 on payment services in the internal market, amending Directives 2002/65/EC, 2009/110/EC and 2013/36/EU and Regulation (EU) No 1093/2010, and repealing Directive 2007/64/EC.*
77. The classification of cryptocurrency was originally discussed in: A.M. Bal, *Blockchain, Initial Coin Offerings and Other Developments in the Virtual Currency Market*, 20 Derivs. & Fin. Instrums. 2 (2018).

is to act like money. In contrast, a token is a unit value that operates on an existing blockchain. It is a cryptocurrency which requires another platform, such as Ethereum, to exist and operate. Tokens are issued by means of ICOs[78] and can be equipped with multiple functionalities: (1) utility tokens can be exchanged for services or goods once such services or goods are ready to be marketed; (2) equity tokens are similar to equity shares in a company: they permit the investors to earn "dividends" (rewards based on the successful performance of the company) and sometimes carry the right to vote on major company proposals; and (3) debt tokens are the equivalent of short-term loans and embody the right to variable or fixed interest during a specified time period.[79] All three types of tokens have in common that they serve as a means of financing: offerors issue digital tokens to collect funds to finance their future projects. A recent empirical study (surveying 253 ICOs) found that 26% of tokens offered profit rights, 68% of the survey tokens contained a utility component (they offered access to platform services) and 20% included a currency component.[80]

From the above analysis, it is clear that cryptocurrency is not a uniform category. Coins and tokens are different in terms of their technical properties and purpose. Even among tokens, several categories can be distinguished. Therefore, virtual currency transactions cannot be treated in a one-fits-all manner and a case-by-case approach is necessary.

[C] Virtual Currency Ecosystem

This section defines participants in a typical virtual currency system. The "ecosystem" of virtual currency includes some new categories of actors which were not present in the traditional payment environments.

In centralized virtual currency schemes, the administrator (issuer) of virtual currency plays a crucial role. An administrator is a person or entity engaged as a business in issuing (putting into circulation) virtual currency, establishing the rules for its use, and maintaining a central payment ledger. The administrator has also the authority to redeem the virtual currency (withdraw it from circulation).[81]

In decentralized virtual currency schemes, there is no single entity managing the whole system. New units of virtual currency can be created automatically as a result of activities performed by "miners," who receive these units as a reward. Miners are persons, sometimes working as a group, who voluntarily make computer processing power available in order to validate a set of transactions made with a decentralized

78. *See* §3.02[D] Initial Coin Offerings (ICOs).
79. Strategic Coin, *Utility, Equity, and Debt Tokens: an Overview for Institutional Investors*, http://strategiccoin.com/utility-equity-debt-tokens-overview-institutional-investors/. Another way of classifying tokens is to divide them into two categories: (1) security tokens that represent equity or debt of a start-up company and (2) utility tokens that represent the right to use of a product or service, *see* TokenMarket, *What is Token?* https://tokenmarket.net/what-is/what-is-token/.
80. S. Adhami et al., *Why Do Businesses Go Crypto? An Empirical Analysis of Initial Coin Offerings* (October 3, 2017).
81. FATF, *Virtual Currencies: Key Definitions and Potential AML/CFT Risks, supra* n. 74.

virtual currency system and to add this to the payment ledger. As a reward for their work, miners normally receive a specific number of currency units. Miners can also require a transaction fee from those who initiate a transaction. The name "miner" is supposed to be an analogy to people spending time and energy on extracting a valuable mineral from the earth.[82]

Virtual currency exchangers and trading platforms function as gateways or entry and exit points to and from a virtual currency system. An exchanger is a person or entity engaged as a business in the exchange of virtual currency for legal currency or other types of virtual currency for a fee (commission).[83] Exchangers, most of whom are non-financial companies, can be either issuer-affiliated or a third party. They generally accept a wide range of payment options, including cash, credit transfers and payments with other virtual currencies. Moreover, some exchangers also provide trade statistics, act as wallet providers and offer (immediate) conversion services for merchants who accept virtual currencies as an alternative payment method.

Trading platforms function as marketplaces, bringing together buyers and sellers of virtual currencies by providing them with a platform on which they can offer and bid among themselves. In contrast to exchanges, trading platforms do not engage in the buying and selling themselves.[84]

A wallet provider is an entity that provides a virtual currency wallet (i.e., a software application for holding, storing and transferring virtual currency). A wallet holds a user's private keys, which allow the user to spend virtual currency allocated to his virtual currency address in the blockchain.[85] There are basically two types of wallets, which differ as regards their immediate usability versus their safety from cyber crime: online wallets and offline wallets. In the context of wallets, it is important to note that users do not hold any virtual currency units in their wallets. The wallets actually hold keys which give access to a certain account balance that is stored in the blockchain.

[D] Initial Coin Offerings (ICOs)

Initial coin offerings (ICOs) are a new means of raising capital for the financing of commercial and development projects where new cryptocurrencies (tokens) are sold for other cryptocurrencies or legal money.[86] ICOs are similar to crowdfunding and are sometimes referred to as crowdsales.

In order to conduct an ICO, it is not necessary either to have a particular legal form or to carry out any business activities in general. Even individuals who do not run

82. ECB, *Virtual Currency Schemes—A further analysis*, *supra* n. 71, at p. 7.
83. FATF, *Virtual Currencies: Key Definitions and Potential AML/CFT Risks*, *supra* n. 74.
84. ECB, *Virtual Currency Schemes—A further analysis*, *supra* n. 71, at p. 8.
85. FATF, *Virtual Currencies: Key Definitions and Potential AML/CFT Risks*, *supra* n. 74.
86. An overview of ICOs and returns they generate can be found at https://icostats.com/. Information about upcoming ICOs can be obtained from www.icoalert.com/ and https://tokenmarket.net/ico-calendar. Initial coin offerings were originally discussed in A.M. Bal, *VAT Treatment of Initial Coin Offerings*, 29 Intl. VAT Monitor 3 (2018).

a business operation may offer tokens as long as they are technically capable to do so. Most frequently, the offeror is a blockchain technology start-up company looking for capital to finance future projects. A typical ICO is structured as follows: the offeror first describes its project intentions and the functioning of the offered tokens in a white paper (occasionally it also publishes other terms and conditions). Second, the generated tokens are sold to interested investors in an unregulated public bidding process, either by publishing the public address to which the funds have to be transferred or via crypto-brokers. If the money raised does not meet the minimum funds required by the offeror, the money is returned to the investors and the ICO is deemed to be unsuccessful. If the funds requirements are met within the specified timeframe, the money raised is used to finance the project.

Once the tokens are issued, they can be resold to others in a secondary market on exchange platforms or directly between individuals. The purchased tokens are accessed through specialized wallets that manage the private and public keys needed for token transactions. The wallet does not contain the tokens which remain to be recorded in the blockchain. The owner of the wallet controls the tokens on the network by signing transactions with the keys stored in the wallet.

ICO investors are motivated to buy newly-issued tokens in the hope that the project becomes successful and the value of the tokens they have purchased will increase. An example of a successful ICO project that was profitable to early investors is Ethereum.[87] In 2014, the Ethereum project was announced and its ICO raised USD 18 million in bitcoins (USD 0.40 per ether). The project went live in 2015 and in 2016 the ether value went up as high as USD 14.

The term "ICO" stems from that of "initial public offering" (IPO). Despite the similar acronyms, there are substantial differences between IPOs and ICOs, both from a technical and legal standpoint. In contrast to the prospectus of a share issue, the content of the ICO white paper is neither prescribed by law nor checked for completeness by a supervisory authority. Because stock corporation law does not apply to ICOs, the tokens are not required to carry any membership rights, information rights, control rights or voting rights. The offeror is completely free to decide which rights or entitlements they grant to the investor with the tokens. The costs associated with the issuance of tokens are extremely low in comparison to those of issuing shares.

As ICOs generally remain unregulated, investors are exposed to several risks and high legal uncertainty. Several regulatory authorities, including US Securities and Exchange Commission (SEC)[88] and European Securities and Markets Authority (ESMA),[89] warned about the risks of both investing in and organizing ICOs. In September 2017, China announced that it was banning all ICOs. The People's Bank of China issued a sharp statement labelling token sales "illegal and disruptive to economic

87. *See* §3.03[B] Ethereum.
88. SEC, *Investor Bulletin: Initial Coin Offerings* (July 25, 2017).
89. ESMA, *ESMA highlights ICO risks for investors and firms* (November 13, 2017).

and financial stability."[90] An overview of risks that an investor may face is shown in Table 3.1.

The investor bears the risk of the offeror's providing incorrect information. The offeror alone determines the content of the white paper, meaning that the documentation may be insufficient, incomprehensible or misleading. Moreover, offerors can change the white paper at any time, both before and during the ICO. Should a dispute arise, claims against token offerors domiciled abroad can only be asserted with substantial effort and difficulty, if at all. Another risk is that ICO projects are usually in their very early stages and their assumptions may have not been tested from a business perspective. The projects are generally complex so that extensive technical knowledge is necessary in order to be able to assess them properly. Only experts are capable of examining the underlying program code in order to assess whether the functionality described in the white paper is accurate and whether the code does not contain programming errors and is vulnerable to manipulation. The investor may lose the amounts invested without compensation. He bears the risk of not being able to sell the tokens at all or only being able to sell them at a price below the purchase amount. As tokens often experience significant price fluctuations, the amount for which they will be traded on secondary market platforms may not meet the investor's expectations. The investor bears the sole responsibility for the safekeeping of the private digital key which is required for any access to his tokens. The loss or theft of this private key is equivalent to losing all of the tokens associated with it. The risk of investors losing the sums invested is further increased by the possibility of authorities taking measures against the offeror in case they conclude that the ICO violated the existing legal regulations.

Table 3.1 Overview of Risks Associated with ICOs

Risk of loss	ICOs are a highly risky and speculative form of investment. A total loss of the sum invested is possible.
Lack of regulation	Many ICOs are conducted in an unregulated environment.
Lack of protection	There are often no relevant consumer protection provisions, no investor protection instruments specific to the capital market and no protection of personal data.
Insufficient information	Investors may receive objectively insufficient, incomprehensible or misleading information in the form of white papers.
Complexity	Extensive technical, knowledge is necessary to be able to assess an ICO project comprehensively.
Projects in early phases	Projects to be financed using ICOs are still in their very early, in most cases experimental, stages. Therefore, their performance and business models have never been tested.

90. W. Zhao, *China's ICO Ban: A Full Translation of Regulator Remarks* (September 5, 2017), www.coindesk.com/chinas-ico-ban-a-full-translation-of-regulator-remarks/.

Volatility	Substantial price fluctuations are possible. There is often no secondary market. Tokens might also turn out to be completely illiquid.
Risk of fraud	The structures of ICOs can entail a significant potential for abuse and fraud. The program code might also contain errors that can be exploited by third parties.

Source: BaFin, www.bafin.de/SharedDocs/Veroeffentlichungen/EN/Fachartikel/2017/fa_bj_1711_ICO_en.html.

Commercial offerors of token sales and operators of brokerage platforms may also face substantial risks. They may not be aware that their activity may be subject to investment and banking regulations. For example, in Germany, as cryptocurrency constitutes financial instruments within the meaning of the German Banking Act (*Kreditwesengesetz*, KWG), anyone who sells or purchases tokens on a commercial basis or operates secondary market platforms on which tokens are traded is generally required to obtain authorization from Federal Financial Supervisory Authority (*Bundesanstalt für Finanzdienstleistungsaufsicht*, BaFin) in advance. Based on the specific formulation of the contract for each ICO, BaFin decides on a case-by-case basis whether the offeror is required to obtain authorization pursuant to the KWG, Investment Code (*Kapitalanlagegesetzbuch*, KAGB), Payment Services Supervision Act (*Zahlungsdiensteaufsichtsgesetz*, ZAG) or Insurance Supervision Act (*Versicherungsaufsichtsgesetz*, VAG) and whether he must fulfil prospectus requirements. If BaFin receives information indicating dealings which might be prohibited, it investigates them and, where necessary, intervenes by administrative means. Independently of this, trading without the required authorization is punishable by law and the law enforcement authorities are responsible for the prosecution of such criminal offenses.[91]

§3.03 POPULAR VIRTUAL CURRENCY SCHEMES

[A] Bitcoin

Bitcoin has been the first and so far the most popular convertible decentralized virtual currency. It was invented in 2008, when a person (or persons) using the pseudonym Satoshi Nakamoto published a design paper that described the features of the virtual currency and its operation.[92] The first transfer of bitcoins took place on January 12, 2009 and in October 2009 the first Bitcoin-USD exchange rate (USD 1 = 1,309.03 BTC) was established, using an equation that included the cost of electricity to run a computer that generated bitcoins. In March 2010, the first real-world transaction using bitcoins took place when a Florida programmer paid 10,000 bitcoins for a pizza on the Bitcoin Forum. At the time, the exchange rate put the purchase price for the pizza at

91. BaFin, *Initial coin offerings: High risks for consumers* (November 15, 2017).
92. Nakamoto, *supra* n. 62.

around USD 25. Bitcoin's market capitalization exceeded 1 million USD in November 2011.[93]

Bitcoins are composed of unique strings of numbers and letters that constitute units of the currency and have value only because individual users are willing to pay for them. The upper limit of bitcoins cannot exceed 21 million. Bitcoins are divisible to eight decimal places.

There are three main ways to obtain bitcoins. First, users can exchange legal currency for bitcoins. To accommodate growing demand, several Internet platforms offer exchanges between Bitcoin and traditional currencies.[94] The price of Bitcoins floats against the price of other currencies and is dependent on the supply and demand. Second, users can obtain bitcoins in exchange for (virtual or real) goods or services. Third, users can mine Bitcoins by volunteering their computer processing power to solve complicated computer algorithms.

As the technical aspects of the Bitcoin system are complex and not easy to understand without a sound technical background, a comprehensive explanation of the technical mechanism of Bitcoin lies outside the scope of this book.[95] The following paragraphs contain a very simplified description of the Bitcoin system operation. A person wishing to make payments in bitcoins needs to download the Bitcoin client software from the Internet. Once the software runs, it connects the user to the decentralized network of all Bitcoin users. The software generates a pair of unique mathematically linked keys (public and private key). To transfer a bitcoin, the Bitcoin software performs a mathematical operation combining the recipient's public key and the transferor's private key. Bitcoins are not transferred in the sense of putting one unit somewhere else, but a defined amount is subtracted from one account balance and added to another account balance within the blockchain. To initiate a payment in bitcoins, the sender sends a transfer instruction, signed with his private key and identifiable with the public key, to the whole network. At certain intervals, all transactions during the preceding period are bundled together into a block. Within each block, there is a cryptographic puzzle which, when solved, validates the chain as a whole. Solving the puzzle is a computationally demanding process and requires large amounts of computing power. The miner that decodes a block receives the ability to create a fixed quantity of new bitcoins as a reward. The validated block of transactions is added to the blockchain, which functions as a database of all approved transactions (which can be thought of as a giant shared accounting ledger). This public ledger records which bitcoins have been spent or accepted, but it does not record any information on the parties' identity. Bitcoin has solved the double spending problem without resorting to a third-party intermediary: the database of transactions across the peer-to-peer network keeps a record of all transfers, so that the same bitcoin cannot be spent twice.

---

93. http://historyofbitcoin.org/.
94. The most popular exchange platforms are Bitstamp (www.bitstamp.net), Bitfinex (www.bitfinex.com), Coinbase (www.coinbase.com), Gemini (https://gemini.com/) and Kraken (www.kraken.com). Until its collapse in February 2014, Mt. Gox enjoyed the status of a monopolist as it dominated an estimated 80%-90% of the Bitcoin-Dollar trading volume.
95. For detailed explanations, *see* Nakamoto, *supra* n. 62.

The value of bitcoin shows great volatility. Over a five-day period beginning on July 12, 2010, the exchange value of bitcoin increased ten times from USD 0.008 to USD 0.080. In October 2011, one bitcoin was worth approximately USD 2. In April 2013, the bitcoin price was USD 135. Next, it grew steadily to reach USD 800 in January 2014 and dropped to USD 300 in January 2015. In December 2017, the value of bitcoin reached its all-time high of USD 19,500. In July 2018, bitcoin was worth USD 6,600.[96]

As the network of Bitcoin users grew, it took more and more time to process bitcoin transactions. Bitcoin's transaction speed became very slow at around 7 transactions per second. As a comparison, Visa performed around 24,000 transactions per second. Thus, it became clear that there were too many transactions to handle and some reform was required in order to allow Bitcoin to scale further. To increase the speed of transaction processing, in August 2017, Bitcoin was split into Bitcoin and Bitcoin Cash[97] using a process called "hard fork."[98] Following the hard fork, Bitcoin Cash became a new separate currency and everyone who had bitcoins before the hard fork received the same amount in Bitcoin Cash wallet. Bitcoin Cash implemented an increased block size of 8MB to accelerate the verification process (initially, Bitcoin's block size limit was 1MB). This increased limit made it possible to process around two million transactions per day. Bitcoin and Bitcoin Cash are now completely separate and operate independently of each other.[99]

[B] Ethereum

Ethereum was proposed in late 2013 by Vitalik Buterin, a cryptocurrency researcher and programmer, who argued that Bitcoin needed a scripting language to support the development of decentralized applications. The development of the Ethereum platform was funded by an online public crowdsale, where the participants were buying the Ethereum value token (ether) with bitcoins. The platform went live on July 30, 2015.

Ethereum is an open-source blockchain platform that enables developers to build and deploy decentralized applications (Dapps). Bitcoin is an example of a Dapp that is used for value transfers without any intermediary. In other words, although both Bitcoin and Ethereum run on blockchain, Bitcoin uses blockchain only for one purpose (to facilitate online peer-to-peer payments), whereas Ethereum allows developers to create applications for any purpose they want. Both Ethereum and Bitcoin benefit from the blockchain properties, such as security (resistance to fraud and data manipulation by third parties), lack of a central point of failure and pseudo-anonymity.

The idea behind Ethereum is simple: online applications should not be controlled by one central entity. Currently, thousands of people are using document storage services, such as Google Docs or Evernote, that are managed by a single service

96. https://coinmarketcap.com/ (accessed on July 14, 2018).
97. The use of the word "cash" was not accidental—the creators intended the new virtual currency to become a new form of cash.
98. *See supra* n. 60.
99. Cointelegraph, *Difference Between Bitcoin and Bitcoin Cash*, https://cointelegraph.com/bitcoin-cash-for-beginners/btc-bch-differences#neutral-opinion.

provider. If the service provider decides to discontinue the service, all user data will be lost. The aim of Ethereum is to eliminate a single point of control over online applications.

Although both Bitcoin and Ethereum are powered by the principle of distributed ledgers and run on blockchain technology, they differ in their technical characteristics and purpose. The Ethereum platform is built with a Turing-complete language, whereas Bitcoin operates in a scripting stack based language. Other differences include block time: Ethereum transactions are confirmed in seconds, whereas Bitcoin transactions in minutes. Bitcoin was designed to act as a means of payment, whereas the primary purpose of Ether is not to establish itself as a payment alternative but to facilitate the functioning of Ethereum to enable developers to build and run distributed applications. Ethereum is currently the most popular platform to build smart contracts.[100]

As the Ethereum network uses a lot of computer power, it has its own "currency" that is used to pay for the use of computational resources needed to run an application. The "currency" of the Ethereum blockchain is called ether. It is listed under the code ETH and traded on cryptocurrency exchanges.

In 2016 a DAO, a set of smart contracts developed on the Ethereum platform, raised a record USD 150 million in a crowdsale to fund its projects.[101] The DAO was exploited when USD 50 million in ether were stolen by anonymous hackers. To reappropriate the affected funds, Ethereum performed a contentious "hard fork" and was split into two separate blockchains—the new separate version became Ethereum (ETH), and the original continued as Ethereum Classic (ETC).

§3.04 BENEFITS OF USING VIRTUAL CURRENCIES

Decentralized virtual currencies can provide an efficient infrastructure for the transfer of value by lowering transaction costs and eliminating the need for intermediaries to oversee the value transfer process and verify whether the transaction is valid.

The costs related to the usage and acceptance of virtual currencies are generally low. Transaction fees are either absent or low as the payer can choose whether to offer a fee to incentivise miners to process his transaction more quickly. In any case, fees are fixed, regardless of the transaction size. To receive virtual currency, the recipient just needs to open a virtual currency account and wallet. Even if he chooses to use the services of a payment service provider, the costs are much lower than those related to the use of traditional payment instruments, such as credit cards. The costs advantages of virtual currencies are most notable in the context of cross-border transactions. Remitting money abroad can currently involve fees of around 8% of the total payment amount.[102] When using virtual currency, as opposed to a currency that needs to be converted, there is no foreign exchange cost. Therefore, it is very cost-efficient to use

100. *See* §2.02 Smart Contracts.
101. *See* §2.04[E] New Versus Traditional Technology.
102. HM Treasury, *Digital currencies: response to the call for information*, p. 6 (March 2015).

virtual currency for cross-border payments. Due to its low transaction costs, virtual currency could also be efficiently used in the micropayment sector.

In addition to potential benefits for the payers and recipients, virtual currency could present some advantages for the payment system at a general level. The fact that in decentralized virtual currency schemes the processing costs are distributed over multiple subjects allows the network to reach reasonable computing power without requiring any major single investment, and it grants the network a strong scalability, as long as enough miners are willing to participate.[103]

Another potential field of application for virtual currency could be value transfers within a particular online community. Internet companies could decide to issue a centralized virtual currency to facilitate payments on their platforms or to integrate the existing types of currencies into their online environments.

The use of virtual currencies can speed up transaction processing. The existing inter-bank payment systems can take several hours or days to move money between accounts. Traditional payment services are only available during banking hours, whereas virtual currency transactions are processed 24 hours a day. Some virtual currency schemes provide for a relatively short time for the verification and settlement of payment transactions. Furthermore, the speed of verification and settlement are not linked to the geographical location of the sender and receiver.

Virtual currencies offer benefits in terms of privacy as the payer does not need to disclose any personal information to the recipient or payment intermediary. This could be beneficial for businesses that currently incur costs and bear risks associated with securing sensitive customer payment data.[104]

Having a decentralized distributed network of miners verifying transactions mitigates the risk of a single entity being able to manipulate transactions and a single point of failure that could bring the system down. Virtual currency keeps middlemen away not only from profiting from transaction fees but also from "invading" transaction privacy. Payment intermediaries can be extremely powerful and effectively shut down an organization by refusing to transfer funds to it. When accounts of those accepting donations for *WikiLeaks* were frozen by PayPal and other payment systems, Bitcoin soon became *WikiLeaks*' preferred donation mechanism.[105]

To sum up, virtual currencies are a promising innovation in payment technology as they have the potential to create cheaper and faster payment systems. They provide advantages in terms of lower fees, global reach, anonymity of the payer and speed of settlement. These benefits make virtual currencies an interesting value transfer option for payments within virtual communities and for cross-border payments.

103. European Central Bank, *Virtual Currency Schemes—A further analysis*, *supra* n. 71, at p. 19.
104. HM Treasury, *supra* n. 102, at p. 6.
105. B. Maurer, T.C. Nelms & L. Schwarz, *"When Perhaps the Real Problem Is Money Itself": The Practical Materiality of Bitcoin*, 23 Social Semiotics 2 (2013).

§3.05 RISKS OF USING VIRTUAL CURRENCIES

Despite the potential advantages of decentralized currencies, their widespread adoption faces a number of obstacles. The main one is uncertainty surrounding their operation and growth. People can easily download virtual currency wallets and start using virtual units although they do not fully understand how the system works and which risks they take. The lack of an underlying legal framework, unclear legal status and the possibility of a government crackdown pose additional problems. As digital currencies lack regulation or public oversight, they are subject to credit, liquidity and consumer protection risks. Virtual currency transactions are irreversible and the system has no built-in anti-fraud capabilities, whereas traditional financial services companies have invested millions of USD in protecting customers against fraud. Blockchain technology is clearly an area where technology has outpaced the law. Due to lack of regulatory oversight across the digital currency sector, scams and market manipulation are commonplace. Investors may lose their virtual coins and tokens either due to either regulatory enforcement action or insufficient investor protection legislation.

Just like any other computer and network system, virtual currencies are subject to operational risks. These risks range from technical failures to hacking, both of which can occur both at individual level (loss or theft of private cryptographic keys or user credentials)[106] and on a wider scale (disruption to, or hacking of, the technical infrastructure of the key actors). The media reported on several thefts of bitcoins, leading to losses to users. In June 2011, Mt. Gox was hacked: 25,000 coins worth somewhere between USD 375,000 and USD 500,000 were stolen. The hacker tried to sell them at once, causing the Bitcoin price to drop from USD 17.50 to USD 0.01. Mt. Gox responded by freezing trading and rolling back all accounts and trades to a pre-hack state.[107] In February 2014, Mt. Gox closed its website and filed for bankruptcy protection in Japan after 850,000 Bitcoins (approximately USD 450 million) belonging to customers and the company were stolen due to hacking into its computer system.[108] In the case of decentralized virtual currency schemes, there is no central body that can solve issues, such as the loss of cryptographic keys or arrange for the reimbursement of the lost currency units. It is not even clear who should provide information to users in the case of technical problems.

---

106. Keeping bitcoins on one's computer can be as dangerous as keeping large sums of cash in one's physical wallet. Malware, system failures or human errors may cause an accidental loss of the wallet file which stores the private keys needed to spend the coins. If this happens, the person cannot use his bitcoins anymore and the coins turn into zombies. (Zombie coins are coins whose private key has been forgotten or destroyed. Such coins cannot be used any more, resulting in shrinkage of the money base. *See* S. Barber, X. Boyen, E. Shi & E. Uzun, *Bitter to Better—How to Make Bitcoin a Better Currency*, in *Financial Cryptography and Data Security*, pp. 399-414 (Springer 2012).
107. J. Mick, *Inside the Mega-Hack of Bitcoin: the Full Story* (June 19, 2011), www.dailytech.com/Inside + the + MegaHack + of + Bitcoin + the + Full + Story/article21942.htm.
108. BBC News, *Mt. Gox bitcoin exchange files for bankruptcy* (February 28, 2014), www.bbc.com/news/technology-25233230.

One of the most serious drawbacks of virtual currency schemes is their potentially high volatility. Such volatility is a major concern for users because they will at some point either have to cash back their virtual currency holdings into legal currency or use them to buy goods, the price of which is usually quoted in legal currencies and therefore unstable in the case of payments in virtual currency. In the case of some virtual currency schemes, the change in exchange rates over 24 hours can easily exceed 10%, and can be over 100%.[109]

Another technological limitation of some virtual currency schemes is the long time that is necessary for transactions to settle. Due to their encrypted and distributed nature, Bitcoin transactions can take longer to process than those settled via traditional payment systems, such as cash or debit cards. This makes Bitcoin relatively impractical as a payment solution.

A remarkable property of virtual currency is that they provide no support for identity management and authentication of parties who act as payers, payees and miners. All parties preserve their anonymity in transactions. Although all transactions are published on the distributed ledger, the blockchain only identifies users by their virtual currency "addresses" which play the role of pseudonyms. As it is hardly possible to link the pseudonyms with the real persons or organizations behind it, fraudsters could take advantage of this, for instance, by misleading users about the real beneficiary of the payments. In addition, the impossibility of reversing transactions increases the risk of such frauds.[110] Due to the pseudo-anonymity, Bitcoin attracted those hoping to buy illegal goods and services online. It became associated with the website Silk Road, a "digital black market" accessible only through the anonymized browsing service.[111]

Virtual currencies face the problem of network externalities. The benefits of using virtual currency depend on the number of other people using it. Continuity of virtual currency schemes is not guaranteed. As virtual currency is not pegged to any legal currency and its exchange rate is determined solely by supply and demand in the market, the whole system could collapse if people try to get rid of their currency units and are not able to do so because of its illiquidity. Users face the risk that an abrupt stop in activities of key actors will leave them with valueless units. The activities of key actors may be discontinued not only as a result of bankruptcy but also for any other reason (for example, lack of profitability). Acceptance of virtual currency by retailers is based on their free decision and can cease at any moment, again leaving users with valueless units. As virtual currency schemes are susceptible to irrational bubbles, a loss of confidence may collapse demand relative to supply.

Some scholars claim that decentralized currencies possess the traditional characteristics of tax havens: earnings are not subject to taxation and taxpayers' anonymity is maintained. It is possible that tax evaders who use bank accounts in tax-haven

109. European Central Bank, *Virtual Currency Schemes—A further analysis*, *supra* n. 71, at p. 16.
110. *Id.*, at p. 22.
111. FATF, *Virtual Currencies: Key Definitions and Potential AML/CFT Risks*, *supra* n. 74, at p. 11.

jurisdictions opt out of traditional tax havens in favor of cryptocurrencies.[112] Traditional anti-tax-evasion mechanisms cannot successfully address Bitcoin-based tax evasion since Bitcoin's operation is not dependent on the existence of a sovereign jurisdiction that could provide information. Given the growing popularity of decentralized currencies, tax evasion associated with them may become more common in the future.[113]

§3.06 QUALIFICATION AS MONEY

No virtual currency has so far been declared the official currency of a state. This means that virtual currencies do not have a legal tender status and can be used only as "contractual money" when there is an agreement between the buyer and the seller in order to accept a given virtual currency as a means of payment. No creditor is obliged to accept payment with virtual currency to discharge a debtor of its debt.

Although it is clear that virtual currencies do not have a legal tender status in any jurisdiction, one of the most frequently asked questions is whether virtual currency constitutes money. To answer this questions, one must first have an idea of what constitutes money.

Monetary theory has not provided a universal definition of money yet; nor has it explained how money should be created—the concept of money has become quite important without having been properly defined. What may count as money for one observer need not qualify as money for another one. However, regardless of the form, money is traditionally associated with three different functions.[114] First, money is a medium of exchange (barter catalyst) used as an intermediary in trade to avoid the inconveniences of a barter system. Second, money provides a unit of account. It acts as a standard numerical unit for the measurement of value of goods and services to make different offerings on the market more comparable. However, to serve as an efficient unit of account, a currency must be more than decimal and readily divisible. It must provide a measure of relative worth that users can understand on a nearly intuitive level. Otherwise, users must expend time and effort to determine what the currency and its associated unit of account really mean. Moreover, a currency can serve as an effective unit of account only if users accept its legitimacy. Third, currency serves as a store of value of current earnings for future spending. Non-circulating money can circulate in the future and that potential for future circulation represents wealth or value that an individual participant can take advantage of.

How do virtual currencies perform the three main monetary functions? Virtual currencies may act as a medium of exchange, either among members of a particular virtual community (for example, Linden Dollar) or globally (for example, Bitcoin).

---

112. O. Marian, *Are Cryptocurrencies Super Tax Havens*? 112 Michigan Law Review First Impressions 38 (2013).
113. *Id.*, at p. 43.
114. ECB, *Virtual Currency Schemes, supra* n. 71, at p. 10; K.L. Macintosh, *How to Encourage Global Electronic Commerce: The Case for Private Currencies on the Internet*, p. 756, 11 Harvard Journal of Law and Technology 733 (1998).

However, given the limited number of venues accepting them, virtual currency is still a weak barter catalyst. It has a very low level of acceptance among the general public compared to other alternative payment solutions. Evans (2014) compared the number of daily Bitcoin transactions with the number of transactions on mPesa, a mobile payment solution which was launched in Kenya in 2007. mPesa followed the classic path for a successful new payment method and is now used by one-third of the Kenyan population, whereas the number of transactions with Bitcoin grew at first but then levelled out.[115] When considering virtual currencies as a means of exchange, their price volatility should be taken into account: the change in exchange rates over 24 hours can easily exceed 10%, and can be over 100%.[116]

To serve as an efficient unit of account, a currency must meet three criteria: it must act as a numerical measurement unit, have legitimacy among its users and provide an almost intuitive measure of relative worth. Virtual currencies can be used to measure the value of goods and services on the market: they are numerical and divisible. However, Bitcoin requires retailers to quote the prices of common retail goods and services out to four or five decimal places with leading zeros. This practice is contrary to consumer marketing strategies as such price quotations are likely to confuse both sellers and buyers. Decentralized currencies derive their legitimacy among their users from the trust that the users place in the computer code (cryptographic algorithm). Users do not need to rely on a government, a bank or a payment intermediary which may follow their own interests. As regards the third element (measure of relative worth), it is questionable whether virtual currencies can be considered intrinsically and intuitively valuable. To determine how much virtual currencies are worth, users usually translate their value into value expressed in a familiar unit of account. By looking at the string of data, hardly anyone can identify its value. It is impossible to determine the value of particular goods in Bitcoin without knowing the Bitcoin exchange rate at a particular time.

When assessing a currency as a store of value, the key question is whether the currency is viewed as reliable and stable enough to operate effectively. Traditional currencies are often accepted as stores of value because they are backed by governments and this gives them a sense of legitimacy and stability in the eyes of the users. But government backing is a double-edged sword: maintaining a stable currency is not the only economic goal of governments and central banks. They can freely print large amounts of money to cover deficits or for other purposes, for example, to redistribute income and wealth between creditors and debtors or as a means to reduce unemployment. In contrast, decentralized currencies are resistant to inflation and answer to market forces, rather than policies of governments and various interests they represent. As they have no central authority, no one can decide to increase the money supply. Thus, the independence of decentralized currencies from direct political influence makes them a more stable store of value than traditional currencies. However, the high volatility renders virtual currency useless as a store of value even for short-time

115. D.S. Evans, *Bitcoin Payments: Igniting Or Not?* (February 17, 2014) www.globaleconomicsgroup.com/financial-regulation/bitcoin-payments-igniting-or-not/.
116. European Central Bank, *Virtual Currency Schemes—A Further Analysis*, *supra* n. 71, at p. 16.

purposes, let alone for the purpose of being a longer-term savings instrument. Storing wealth in any medium that is easily susceptible to collapse or price fluctuations is unwise.

Finally, Bitcoin faces a long-term structural economic problem related to the absolute limit of 21 million units that can ever be issued. If Bitcoin became extremely successful and replaced legal currencies, it would exert a deflationary force on the economy since the money supply would not increase in line with the economic growth. This would require workers to accept pay cuts every year and such a situation would surely meet fierce resistance in society.

To sum up, decentralized currencies have the potential to perform each of the monetary functions. However, at present, due to their limited use, lack of intrinsic value and enormous volatility, virtual currencies cannot serve as a unit of account, medium of exchange and store of value. Therefore, they cannot be considered money in the economic sense[117] but resemble a speculative investment.

§3.07 QUALIFICATION AS ELECTRONIC MONEY

This section compares the concepts of virtual currency and electronic money. As there is no universally accepted definition of electronic money, it is necessary to look at various attempts to define this term and to identify some common characteristics of electronic money.

According to the White Paper published by the US Treasury in 1996,[118] "electronic money" involves tokens of value expressed in digital form, in the same sense that a casino chip is a token of value expressed in a physical form. Electronic money may take a wide variety of forms, including credit cards, smart cards and online payment systems, such as PayPal. In general, electronic money exhibits the following characteristics: it is issued by an identifiable institution, permits its users to move funds electronically, relies upon advanced technology and requires "loading" from funds held within the financial system. The White Paper differentiates between accounted and unaccounted systems. In the former, the e-money issuer maintains a complete or partial audit trail of transitions and can identify the person to whom electronic money is issued as well as people and businesses receiving electronic money as it flows through the economy. In the latter, electronic money may operate much like paper currency, moving through the economy anonymously.

The ECB defines "electronic money" as "an electronic store of monetary value on a technical device that may be widely used for making payments to undertakings other than the issuer without necessarily involving bank accounts in the transaction, but

117. Sometimes the concept of "near-money" is used to refer to a system that satisfies so many characteristics of money that is a candidate for becoming money. Money is always a near-money. *See* J.A. Bergstra & K. de Leeuw, *Bitcoin and Beyond: Exclusively Informational Money* (2013).

118. US Treasury, *Selected Tax Policy Implications of Global Electronic Commerce* (November 22, 1996).

acting as a prepaid bearer instrument."[119] It distinguishes electronic money from access products (such as debit cards where payments are settled by means of transfers between bank accounts) and single-purpose electronic payment instruments (i.e., payments made for goods and services where the issuer is expected to deliver at a later stage, for example a pre-paid telephone card). Further, the ECB divides electronic money products into hardware-based and software-based products, depending upon the storage device. In the case of hardware-based products, purchasing power resides in a device containing hardware-based security features (for example, a chip). In contrast, software-based products employ specialized software on a personal computer, allowing electronic value to be transferred via telecommunications networks.

In the European Union, electronic money is also defined in Article 2 of the Electronic Money Directive (2009/110) as monetary value as represented by a claim on the issuer, which is issued on receipt of funds for the purpose of making payment transactions and which is accepted by persons other than the issuer.[120] Article 11 of the Electronic Money Directive (2009/110) adds that "Member States shall ensure that, upon request by the electronic money holder, electronic money issuers redeem, at any moment and at par value, the monetary value of the electronic money held."

Although there is no generally accepted definition of electronic money, some general observations can be made. All the definitions rely the concept of an identifiable issuer and a link to the traditional monetary system. In contrast, in virtual currency schemes, the link between the electronic money and the traditional money is not preserved. Virtual currency is not expressed in the same unit of account (for example, USD, EUR), but in a different one (for example, ether or bitcoins). Neither do virtual currency schemes require "loading" since virtual "coins" can also be mined by the users themselves. The link between virtual currency and currency with a legal tender status is not regulated by law, which might be problematic or costly when redeeming funds (if this is permitted). Finally, in decentralized currency schemes is it not possible to identify the issuer. Thus, virtual currencies cannot be regarded as electronic money.

§3.08 QUALIFICATION AS SECURITY

There is no uniform definition of a security and the meaning of this term varies per country. In the United States, section 2(a) of the Securities Act of 1933[121] lists a number of instruments considered to be securities. These include not only stocks and bonds but also the catch-all term of "investment contracts." Section 5 of the Securities Act of 1933 requires all securities offered for sale be registered with the Securities and Exchange Commission (SEC) unless an exemption applies.

119. European Central Bank, *Issues Arising from the Emergence of Electronic Money*, ECB Monthly Bulletin (November 2000).
120. *Directive 2009/110/EC of the European Parliament and of the Council of 16 September 2009 on the Taking Up, Pursuit and Prudential Supervision of the Business of Electronic Money Institutions Amending Directives 2005/60/EC And 2006/48/EC and Repealing Directive 2000/46/EC.*
121. The Securities Act of 1933 was codified at 15 USC § 77a et seq.

The US Supreme Court gave a definition of an investment contract in *the Howey* judgment.[122] According to this decision, an investment contract consists of four elements (the "*Howey* test"): (1) investment of money into (2) common enterprise with (3) the reasonable expectation of profits derived (4) from the entrepreneurial or managerial efforts of others. In its investigative report of July 2017, the SEC applied the *Howey* test to the DAO tokens[123] and concluded that they were securities.[124] The SEC noted that it was immaterial that the consideration for the DAO tokens was given in ether and not in USD. Since ethers were a valuable contribution to the issuer, buyers did "invest money" into a "common enterprise" (the DAO vehicle). Pursuant to the promotional materials, investors had a reasonable profit expectation, whereby "profits" included "dividends and other periodic payments" and "the increased value of the investment." These profits were expected not only from the interplay of market forces but from substantial efforts of DAO promoters. Thus, the SEC concluded that all the criteria of the *Howey* test were fulfilled. The SEC came to the same conclusion in securities fraud investigations against the initiators of the REcoin Group Foundation and Diamond Reserve Club[125] and in its order against the Mnuchee Inc.[126] The SEC opinions show how easily a token sale could fall into the investment contract category. However, because the *Howey* test is fact-dependant, the outcome of the *Howey* test for any given token sale can be different.

The SEC opinion on the security status of virtual currency was confirmed by the United States District Court in Sherman, Texas, in the case *Securities and Exchange Commission v. Trendon T. Shavers and Bitcoin Savings and Trust.*[127] The District Court held that Bitcoin is a currency or form of money and investments into Bitcoin Savings and Trust met the definition of a security.

In the European Union, the prospectus legislation[128] applies three formal criteria to define a security: transferability, negotiability and standardization. Transferability means that the units can be assigned to another person. The mere contractual restriction of the transfer of units does not deprive them of their status of transferability. Negotiability concerns the ease with which ownership can be transferred. Standardization requires units be defined by common characteristics so that it is sufficient

---

122. *SEC v. W.J. Howey Co.*, 328 US 293 (1946).
123. *See* §2.04[E] New Versus Traditional Technology.
124. SEC, *Report of Investigation Pursuant to Section 21(a) of the Securities Exchange Act of 1934: The DAO* (July 25, 2017). The SEC report did not mention whether tokens with a different design than that of the DAO (utility tokens, coins) were also securities.
125. SEC, *SEC Exposes Two Initial Coin Offerings Purportedly Backed by Real Estate and Diamonds* (September 29, 2017).
126. SEC, *Company Halts ICO After SEC Raises Registration Concerns* (December 11, 2017).
127. *Securities and Exchange Commission v. Trendon T. Shavers and Bitcoin Savings and Trust*, Case No. 4:13-CV-416. For more details on the case, *see* §5.01[B] Virtual Currency Regulations in the United States.
128. *Regulation (EU) 2017/1129 of the European Parliament and of the Council of 14 June 2017 on the prospectus to be published when securities are offered to the public or admitted to trading on a regulated market, and repealing Directive 2003/71/EC.*

to refer to the type and number of units to trade them.[129] The Markets in Financial Instruments Directive (2014/65)[130] combines these three criteria with a non-exhaustive list of examples that constitute securities. This list includes three broad categories: shares, bonds and other securities. To constitute securities, an instrument must be comparable to these typical securities.

Tokens are generally transferable as they can be sold on secondary markets. However, if due to technical limitations the transfer of token ownership to third parties is impossible, tokens lack transferability and the security status. The fact that tokens are actively traded on cryptocurrency platforms is a clear indication that they are negotiable on capital markets. As all tokens issued by a single issuer in one round of financing share the same characteristics, they are deemed to be standardized. Based on their structure and functionality, equity and debt tokens can be comparable to shares or bonds. Therefore, debt and equity tokens may be considered securities in the European Union, whereas coins and utility tokens are exempted from EU securities regulation.

§3.09 CONCLUSIONS

Money has been affected by the technological developments and the widespread use of the Internet: the result is the emergence of virtual currencies. Originally, such currencies were limited to virtual worlds and used as a medium of exchange between avatars. Nowadays, they exist independently of any virtual environments, competing with legal currencies. The culmination in the process of monetary decentralization was the creation of Bitcoin—a decentralized, peer-to-peer currency not controlled by any institution. The emergence of virtual money can be considered as a natural development: the monetary history traces a path from more to less tangible: from barter via precious metals, coins, paper money, checks and credit cards to purely digital value (strings of numbers and letters flashing across a computer screen).

Virtual currency can be defined as a digital representation of value without legal tender status. Depending on its links with the real world, virtual currency can be either convertible or non-convertible. Convertible virtual currency can be divided into centralized and decentralized based on the way the currency system is administered. Convertible decentralized virtual currency is commonly referred to as cryptocurrency. Cryptocurrency can be further subdivided in coins and tokens. The former intend to act like money, whereas the latter resemble a means of investment.

Virtual currency schemes present advantages in the areas of usage possibilities, speed and costs of value transfer. Although they are a promising payment alternative and financial investment innovation, their use bears a lot of risks. The materialization

129. For a detailed discussion of whether tokens may constitute securities, *see* P. Hacker & C. Thomale, *Crypto-Securities Regulation: ICOs, Token Sales and Cryptocurrencies under EU Financial Law*, SSRN Electronic Journal (January 2017).

130. *Directive 2014/65/EU of the European Parliament and of the Council of 15 May 2014 on markets in financial instruments and amending Directive 2002/92/EC and Directive 2011/61/EU.*

of these risks depends on the volume of virtual currency issued, its connection to the real economy, traded volume and user acceptance.

ICOs are a new means of raising capital for the financing of commercial and development projects where new cryptocurrencies (tokens) are sold for other cryptocurrencies or legal money. Although the term ICO stems from that of initial public offering (IPO), those two ways of financing are fundamentally different, both from a technical and legal standpoint. As any new form of doing business involving novel technology, ICOs face great regulatory uncertainty and carry a lot of risks for both offerors and investors.

At present, virtual currency cannot be considered money in the economic sense due to its limited use, lack of intrinsic value and enormous volatility. Neither does it constitute electronic money as it is not linked to the traditional monetary system and frequently the currency issuer cannot be identified. In the United States, virtual currency seems to fall within the scope of federal securities regulation. In the European Union, debt and equity tokens are considered securities, whereas coins and utility tokens are exempted from EU securities regulation.

PART II Income Taxation

CHAPTER 4

Income Tax: General Considerations

Chapter 4 provides a general introduction to the topic of income taxation. First, it describes two main types of income tax systems (global and schedular), the concept of income, income categories and income determination. Second, it introduces an evaluation model based on the general principles of taxation that will be used as a benchmark in the evaluation of the income tax treatment of virtual currency in four selected jurisdictions—the United States, the United Kingdom, Germany and the Netherlands—which will be undertaken in the next chapter. Finally, Chapter 4 lists the most important income tax questions raised by the emergence of virtual currencies that the next chapter seeks to answer.

§4.01 SYSTEMS OF INCOME TAXATION

[A] Global and Schedular Systems

The income tax in its modern form originated in the United Kingdom at the end of the 18th century and was adopted by most industrialized countries about hundred years later. In the development of the tax internationally, the influence of three countries—Germany, the United Sates and the United Kingdom—has been predominant. The tax systems of other countries can trace their origins back to these three.[131]

From a structural viewpoint, two basic types of income tax systems can be distinguished: schedular and global.[132] A schedular system distinguishes income categories (salaries, dividends, business profits) and determines gross income and deductible expenses for each one of them. Different tax rates and procedures for tax reporting, assessment and collection apply to each category. In other words, a pure

131. V. Thuronyi et al., *Comparative Tax Law*, p. 209-210 (Wolters Kluer 2016).

132. L. Burns & R. Krever, *Individual Income Tax*, pp. 1-3 in: *Tax law design and drafting* (V. Thuronyi ed. IMF 1998); S. Plasschaert, *The Definition of Gross Taxable Income in Schedular or Global Income Taxes*, 31 Bull. Intl. Fisc. Doc. 12, p. 535 (1977).

schedular system consists of a coordinated set of separate taxes on various types of income. In a global system, all receipts and expenses are considered together in the calculation of net income. The purpose of this approach is to distribute interpersonal tax burdens, vertically and horizontally, according to the ability-to-pay principle. In practice, most existing income tax systems lie on the spectrum between global and schedular (mixed systems). Many countries have become partially schedularized by the use of withholding taxes on particular income types or distinguish between income categories, but aggregate them and tax at a common rate. Another common technique is to define income according to various categories but then to establish a residual category encompassing income items that do not belong to any of the specific categories. How comprehensive the residual category is depends on the underlying concept of income. If the underlying concept is broad, the residual category includes any accession to wealth that is not enumerated in the other categories. If the concept of income is narrow, the residual category will include only clearly defined items. Thus, the same words "other income" can mean different things in the tax laws of different countries.[133]

The global system is considered to be superior to the schedular one because the separation of income into many categories makes it difficult to impose progressive taxation and to provide for personal tax relief.[134] Under a schedular system, a progressive marginal rate structure is applied to selected categories of income, leading to inequalities between taxpayers who earn income from different sources. Similarly, personal tax relief must be either applied wholly against one category of income, such as employment income, in which case the relief may not be fully effective, or divided among various categories of income, which increases complexity. The schedular system is also more difficult to administer: administrative resources are wasted on classification issues arising at the borders between the various schedules. For border-line cases, one must closely investigate how tax law and judicial interpretation shape the tax treatment of a particular item. Any differences in the final tax burdens imposed on income in different categories may be exploited by taxpayers engaging in tax planning and restructuring to ensure that their income fits within the most advantageous category. Moreover, the schedular system involves a risk that if an item is not included into any income category, it is not included in the income at all. This risk has been overcome in some countries by including an open-ended residual income category.[135]

On the basis of the historical record, schedular systems appear to be typical for countries at less advanced levels of development. The existence of these systems also owes to cultural factors. As a Latin phenomenon, they are common is Southern Europe and developing countries in which the tax system was profoundly shaped by French and Spanish influences. As from 19th century, many countries moved from a schedular

133. Thuronyi et al., *Comparative Tax Law, supra* n. 131, at p. 212.
134. Burns & Krever, *Individual Income Tax, supra* n. 132, at pp. 2–3.
135. *Id.*

to a mixed or global system.[136] This transition resulted from the widespread recognition of the ability-to-pay principle and the drawbacks of the schedular system mentioned in the previous paragraph. Currently, a pure schedular system exists almost nowhere.[137]

The tax systems of the four jurisdictions examined in the next chapter of this book include the characteristics of both global and schedular systems.

In the United States, the income tax system has been of a global nature from its inception in 1913. Under the Internal Revenue Code (IRC), receipts from whatever source derived are subject to tax. The limits of the income concept are determined on a case-by-case basis by courts and administrators.

The United Kingdom is the first country where the modern income tax system was introduced (1799-1783). The British system evolved from an originally schedular model to a more global one which views all types of income aggregately for the purposes of applying the tax rates. Although the law lists items of income that are subject to tax, there is a residual category comprising income not mentioned in other categories. In 1965, a fully-fledged capital gains tax (CGT) was introduced. Although legally distinct, this tax can, in terms of substance, be viewed as integrated with the income tax system.[138]

The German income tax system is of a mixed nature. Tax is levied on items belonging to particular income categories, which are subsequently combined for the purpose of imposing a progressive tax rate and providing a personal tax relief. A logical structure and the global-type paradigm has been a prominent feature of the German system since its introduction in Prussia in 1891.

The Netherlands has a mixed system with a distinct preponderance of the schedular layer. The total taxable income is the sum of net incomes assessed separately in three boxes. Each box has its own rules for the income determination. The distinctive feature of the Dutch system is the fact that the wealth tax has been partially incorporated in the income tax system (although officially it has been abolished).

[B] Concept of Income

The first step to determine a tax liability is to ascertain gross taxable income. The proper definition of gross income was for a long time the subject matter of considerable debate and gave rise to many competing theories. The two main income theories are the source theory and the wealth accrual model (also called the Schanz-Haig-Simons concept).

The source theory (*Quellentheorie*) was developed by Bernhard Fuisting and implemented as early as in the Prussian Income Tax Act of 1891.[139] According to this

136. Plasschaert, *The Definition of Gross Taxable Income in Schedular or Global Income Taxes*, *supra* n. 132, at p. 543.
137. S. Plasschaert, *First Principles about Schedular and Global Frames of Income Taxation*, 30 Bull. Intl. Fisc. Doc. 3, p. 109 (1976).
138. S. Plasschaert, *The Definition of Gross Taxable Income in Schedular or Global Income Taxes*, *supra* n. 132, at p. 544.
139. W. Blümich, B. Heuermann, P. Brandis et al., *Einkommensteuergesetz. Loseblatt-Kommentar*, sec. 2 (26) (C.H. Beck Verlag 2009).

concept, a receipt constitutes income if it is periodic and comes from a permanent source.[140] Franz Guth described income as "any increase in economic ability, which flows with a certain regularity from a given source. The recipient may enjoy income, consume it, or destroy it without impairing his 'stock' ... ." For Thomas Malthus, income was "portion of stock of wealth which the possessor may annually consume without injury to his permanent resources." While the expression "source" is by no means perfectly clear, it is usually linked to the traditional categories in the functional distribution theory, i.e., land, capital, labor and entrepreneurship. The source theory derives from the "harvest tradition" in agricultural societies, where land produces its fruit at regular intervals. In this concept, capital gains,[141] increases in asset value, windfalls, awards and gifts should not be subject to income tax.

During the late 19th century, a wealth accrual concept of income was first developed. Georg von Schanz wrote the first definitive exposition of income in terms of wealth accrual in Germany in 1896. In his view:

> the concept of income is related to the economic ability of persons. When we wish to determine an individual's income, we must ask what economic power has accrued to a given person over a given period of time. In other words, we wish to know what means came within the disposing power of a given person, who, during the period in question, neither impaired his capital nor incurred personal debts.[142]

Twenty-five years later, in the United States, Robert Haig wrote the second major dissertation on this topic.[143] Haig interpreted income as "the money value of the net accretion to one's economic power between two points of time." The elements that enhance one's economic power included: cash, any goods or services obtained in kind (also those obtained by way of gift), any unrealized increases in the value of assets held during the period and the value of benefits obtained from non-market events. According to Haig's interpretation, an increase in an individual's economic power over a period is an increase in his capacity to command more resources. Therefore, when wealth accrual is adopted as the tax base, taxation is imposed on a person's capacity to do something in the future. Tax is not imposed on the exercise of that ability. Haig stressed that a benefit must be susceptible of valuation in terms of money to constitute income.

Henry Simons developed a similar concept of income, also based on increases in a person's economic power derived in monetary or non-monetary form.[144] However, he took a step further by combining wealth accrual and consumption. Haig's definition

---

140. A description of the preservation of source doctrine can be found in P.H. Wueller, *Concepts of Taxable Income—The German Contribution*, 53 Political Science Quarterly 1 (1938).
141. Capital gains are thought to result from a disposition of the source itself and therefore are not in the nature of income. *See* Thuronyi et al., *Comparative Tax Law, supra* n. 131, at p. 214.
142. G. von Schanz, *Der Einkommensbegriff und die Einkommensgesetze*, Finanz-Archiv (1896) translated in Wueller, *supra* n. 140.
143. R. Haig, *The Concept of Income—Economic and Legal Aspects*, in: R. Haig (ed.), *The Federal Income Tax*, p. 2 (Columbia University Press 1921).
144. H. Simons, *Personal Income Taxation—The Definition of Income as a Problem of Fiscal Policy* (University of Chicago Press 1983).

did not deal explicitly with consumption as consumption arose after the economic power had been obtained: it was sufficient to determine when the power was accrued without examining how it was subsequently applied. Simons measured income at a later stage and broke down Haig's accrual of economic power into two ways it could be applied: consumption expenditure and savings. Under Simons's model, one had to wait to see how Haig's *a priori* economic power was actually applied by an individual before his income could be identified. He defined income as the market value of rights exercised in consumption and an increase in the value of a person's store of property rights. Whether a benefit had a market value greater than zero depended on whether the underlying rights were transferable. If not, it had no market value.

The approach described in this section has become the foundation measure of income in the 20th century economics. It is commonly known as the Haig-Simons concept of income. In recognition of Schanz's initial contribution, it is termed here as the Schanz-Haig-Simons model.

[C] Income Categories

In both schedular and global systems, three main income categories can be distinguished: employment income, business income, and investment income. Under a schedular system, it is common for a different tax regime to be imposed on each of these types. Under a global system, special rules, particularly tax accounting rules, may apply to business income.[145] However, not all amounts derived by a taxpayer fit neatly into one of the categories specified above. There are some areas in which the problem of defining gross income has proven more stubborn (for example, windfall gains, benefits in kind and capital gains). This section outlines some income categories which, due to their potential relevance for virtual currencies, deserve closer attention. These are business income, windfall gains, benefits in kind, investment income and capital gains.

[1] Business Income

The starting point in determining whether an item of income is business income is to determine whether the underlying activity is properly characterized as a business. In the absence of a definition in the income tax law, the term "business" has its ordinary meaning. In broad terms, a business is a commercial or industrial activity of an independent nature undertaken for profit.[146] The definitions of business income in common law jurisdictions generally include income from professional activities.[147] In

145. L. Burns & R. Krever, *Taxation of Income from Business and Investment*, p. 2 in *Tax law design and drafting* (V. Thuronyi ed. IMF 1998).
146. *Id.*
147. Sec. 995-1 Australian Income Tax Assessment Act ("business includes any profession, trade, employment, vocation or calling, but does not include occupation as an employee"); sec. 248 Canadian Income tax Act ("business" includes a profession, calling, trade, manufacture or undertaking of any kind whatever").

contrast, some civil law countries make a distinction between income from commercial trading activities, on the one hand, and income from professions and vocations, on the other.[148] There are no persuasive tax policy reasons for this distinction, which developed out of historical, non-tax rationale. From a tax administration perspective, it is much simpler to have a single set of rules dealing with all business and professional activities.[149]

Although business activity generally requires a profit motive, a clear distinction between consumption-oriented and profit-seeking activities is difficult. Such distinction depends on the intent of the taxpayer as activities standing alone cannot be classified as consumption or profit-seeking. As making assumptions about the intent requires a case-by-case analysis of a taxpayer's state of mind, it is usually necessary that the profit motive is supported by objective evidence, for example, certain amounts of revenue or profit regularity.

[2] Windfall Gains

Windfalls constitute unexpected accretions to wealth. They are generally understood to be a transfer of property from one party to another for no (or inadequate) consideration given by the recipient.[150] The Schanz-Haig-Simons concept of income recognizes that gifts and windfall gains enhance the economic power of an individual and should be recognized as income.

In most jurisdictions with schedular definitions of income, windfalls simply fall outside the categories included in gross income. Although there are no persuasive tax policy grounds for excluding them from the income tax base, political considerations and administrative difficulties in assessing these gains most often explain why they are not taken into account.[151]

A type of windfall payment is a prize or an award. Generally, tax systems distinguish between prizes and awards that are won by the taxpayer in a purely personal capacity, which are usually not taxable, and prizes and awards given in recognition of a taxpayer's business or employment activities, which are usually taxable.[152] Windfalls may also result from gambling or betting activities. However, if those activities are the primary income source for taxpayers and are carried out in a manner resembling business activity, they generate taxable business income.

[3] Benefits in Kind

A benefit in kind is a benefit derived in a form other than cash. The most obvious category of benefit in kind arises in barter transactions. Under the Schanz-Haig-Simons

148. Secs. 15 (*Gewerbebetrieb*) and 18 (*Selbstandige Arbeit*) German Income Tax Act (*Einkommensteuergesetz*).
149. Burns & Krever, *Taxation of Income from Business and Investment*, *supra* n. 145, at p. 30.
150. Burns & Krever, *Individual Income Tax*, *supra* n. 132, at p. 31.
151. *Id.*
152. *Id.*

concept, the value of goods exchanged in barter is income, provided that it results in consumption or in a net increase in wealth. One often thinks of barter transactions in the context of primitive societies which have not developed a medium of exchange. However, fringe benefits (for example, free medical treatment, free use of recreational facilities or free meals) given by employers to employees in return for labor services provided by the latter to the former are also a form of barter transactions. Their tax treatment varies from jurisdiction to jurisdiction.

In transactions where the consideration does not involve monetary amounts but benefits in kind, the determination of value becomes a pivotal issue. Market value is the basic valuation standard in many countries. In some of them, an unambiguous definition of the market value is provided in the tax legislation. For example, in Germany, market value (*gemeiner Wert*) is defined as the price which would be obtained on disposal of an asset in the ordinary course of business, whereby all circumstances (except personal and extraordinary ones) are to be taken into account.[153] Under US tax law, the fair market value is the price at which an asset would change hands between a willing buyer and a willing seller, neither being under any compulsion to buy or sell and both having reasonable knowledge of the relevant facts.[154]

All the definitions have some common characteristics: they define market value as the amount for which an asset could be exchanged between knowledgeable individuals in an arm's-length transition. Market value is based on a hypothetical ordinary transaction and hypothetical knowledgeable and willing participants and assumes informational symmetry and profit maximization. Under perfect competition, there would be only one market price in a long-term equilibrium. However, as most markets are characterized by informational asymmetry, uncertainty and imperfect competition, an asset can have more than one market value.

[4] Investment Income

Investment income includes interest, dividend, royalties and rents. The characterization of an amount as investment income is important in both schedular and global income tax systems. Under a schedular system, characterization determines which tax regime applies to the income. Under a global system, there are frequently specific rules for the taxation of investment income.

Interest is the compensation earned by a creditor for the use of his money during the period of the loan. Fundamental to the ordinary notion of interest is that there is a debt obligation. As modern commercial law contracts make it possible to convert interest on debt into a variety of other forms, the definition of interest often includes a general formula to more effectively cope with the flexibility available to taxpayers in the way they structure their financial transactions. For example, interest can be defined

153. Section 9 German Valuation Act (*Bewertungsgesetz*).
154. Treas. Reg. 1.170A-1(c)(2).

to include "any other amount that is functionally equivalent to interest."[155] The Commentary to the OECD Model (2017) defines interest as "income from debt-claims of every kind, whether or not secured by mortgage and whether or not carrying a right to participate in profits."[156]

The term "dividends" generally means a sum of money paid regularly by a company to its shareholders out of the company's profits or reserves. The Commentary to the OECD Model (2017) includes in the dividend concept all distributions when repayment depends largely on the performance of the company's business as it assimilates to shares all securities that carry a right to participate in the company's profits without being debt-claims.[157]

Many countries impose final withholding taxes on investment income paid to private individuals. The main reason for this is administrative simplicity: as for the majority of the population, the only sources of income will be wages, interest and dividends, taxing these amounts through withholding means that most individual will not have to file returns. Another important issue in the taxation of investment income is the allowance of deductions, the most important of which tends to be interest expense.[158]

[5] Capital Gains

A capital gain is gain on disposal of certain fixed assets. What may constitute a fixed asset and, therefore, give rise to a capital gain varies from country to country and is often strongly fact-dependent. In some countries, capital gains are subject to a separate tax or no tax, while in others they may be subject to different tax treatment under the general income tax legislation. Gains may be classified as long-term or short-term according to the length of time the assets are held. They are generally taxed by reference to the difference between disposal proceeds and acquisition cost.[159] Capital assets also include intangibles that are controlled by the taxpayer through legal rights. Expenditures related to patents, copyright and trademark are capitalized and amortized over their useful life.

Equity considerations provide a strong case for taxing capital gains as comprehensively as it appears feasible. Otherwise, receipts which provide a taxpayer with spending power are left untaxed. Moreover, capital gains tend to be heavily concentrated among high-income individuals. Leaving them untaxed undermines the vertical distribution of the tax burden. However, a comprehensive taxation of capital gains would require each taxpayer to keep a balance sheet showing his properties. As obliging individuals to maintain accounting records is utterly unenforceable and politically unacceptable, the taxation of capital gains tends to be restricted to a few

155. Burns & Krever, *Taxation of Income from Business and Investment, supra* n. 145, at p. 18.
156. OECD, *Commentaries on the Articles of the OECD Model Tax Convention, Commentary on Article 11 Concerning the Taxation of Interest*, para. 18 (November 21, 2017).
157. OECD, *Commentaries on the Articles of the OECD Model Tax Convention, Commentary on Article 10 Concerning the Taxation of Interest*, para. 24-25 (November 21, 2017).
158. Thuronyi et al., *Comparative Tax Law, supra* n. 131, at p. 229.
159. Capital gain, IBFD Glossary, IBFD Tax Research Platform, available at: www.ibfd.org.

selected assets, among which real estate and securities are by far the most prominent.[160]

[D] Income Determination

Income tax is imposed on persons who have earned taxable income for the relevant tax period. Therefore, four central concepts underpinning the income tax system can be distinguished. First, the person liable to tax must be identified (income is allocated to a person who earns it by personal services or by virtue of owning property).

Second, the taxable income of that person must be calculated separately for each tax period, which means that it is necessary to provide accounting rules for the allocation of income and expenses to particular tax periods. Income is usually determined on a cash or accrual basis. The accrual method seeks to allocate both income and deductions to the tax year in which the taxpayer's economic activity produces them. The records should reflect expenses definitely incurred and income definitely earned without regard to whether payment has been made or whether payment is due. This method is more resistant to manipulation as it is irrelevant whether taxpayers arrange for payment in a later tax period. The cash method takes account of income when it is received and of expenses when they are paid. Taxpayers are allowed to use this method because of its simplicity.

Third, the tax base must be defined. All income tax systems, whether global or schedular, seek to impose taxation on a net amount (gross income minus deductions) because this amount properly reflects a person's increase in his economic capacity for the tax period. The gross income is the total amount of taxable receipts derived by a person during the tax period. In many global systems, the definition of gross income provides little guidance to the income concept, often including the term that it purports to define. For example, in the United States, gross income is defined as "all income from whatever source derived."[161] Therefore, even under a global system, the inclusion of amounts in gross income is often specified by reference to particular categories (for example, employment, business, investment). The gross income of a person does not include amounts that are exempt from tax. An amount (welfare payment, scholarship) or an entity (charitable, or education institution) may be exempt for social compassion reasons. Exemptions may also result from international conventions, for example, to prevent double taxation. Finally, an amount may not be included in the tax base for administrative or political reasons (for example, windfall gains). The total amount of deductions consists of expenses incurred by the person in deriving amounts subject to tax plus any other amounts allowed as a deduction.[162] A deduction of business and investment losses is part of the logic of taxing net income. To earn income, one must incur the risk, and sometimes also the actuality, of loss which is just a cost of doing business. To tax gains but not allow an offset of losses would bias the income tax

160. Plasschaert, *The Definition of Gross Taxable Income in Schedular or Global Income Taxes*, *supra* n. 132, at p. 540.
161. Section 61 IRC.
162. Burns & Krever, *Individual Income Tax*, *supra* n. 132, at p. 8.

against risk. If income tax is to remain neutral as to the risk and investment decisions, it must allow a deduction for losses in profit-seeking activities.

The fourth basic element is the method of calculation of the amount of tax payable. In most cases, this involves applying the relevant tax rates to the taxable income of the taxpayer and then subtracting any tax offsets that may be available.[163]

§4.02 EVALUATION MODEL

This section introduces an evaluation model that will be used as a benchmark in the evaluation of the income tax treatment of virtual currency in four selected jurisdictions—the United States, the United Kingdom, Germany and the Netherlands—which will be undertaken in the next chapters.

The evaluation model is based on the generally accepted principles of taxation that most of the existing tax systems tend to follow. Principles are the normative basis for the creation of legal rules and function as the essential criteria of evaluation for lawmaking. They are a way of classifying policy considerations that go into making decisions about tax law. The Court of Justice of the European Union (CJEU) and many national courts frequently refer to the general principles of law as a support for the interpretations they give. According to Ronald Dworkin, a principle is a "standard that is to be observed not because it will advance or secure an economic, political or social situation deemed desirable, but because it is a requirement of justice or fairness or some other dimension of morality."[164] Every society is organized around the existence of identifiable general principles issued for the guidance of conduct. These principles play a central role in the legal system and form the basis for all laws and regulations. However, it should be noted that, although principles may provide supporting arguments, they do not offer a certain and technically correct solution to a legal problem. Making decisions about taxation involves a trade-off among the relevant criteria and, therefore, political or value judgments.

Although there are considerable variations in the income tax rules from country to country, the underlying taxation principles are common to all jurisdictions. The main four axioms upon which a tax system ought to be based were set out by Adam Smith in *The Wealth of Nations*.[165] They are: equity, certainty, convenience and efficiency. Although these canons were developed in 1776, they still influence tax policy today.[166] As virtual currency is part of the digital economy, the general principles of taxation laid down by the OECD in the Ottawa Report (1998) are also used as a benchmark. Those principles are: neutrality, efficiency, certainty, simplicity, effectiveness, fairness and flexibility.[167]

---

163. *Id.*, at p. 7.
164. R. Dworkin, *Taking Rights Seriously*, Ch. 2 (Harvard University Press 1978).
165. A. Smith, *An Inquiry into the Nature and Causes of the Wealth of Nations*, Book V, Chapter II (1776).
166. G.K. Morse & D. Williams, *Principles of Tax Law*, p. 5, *6th* ed. (Sweet & Maxwell 2008).
167. OECD, *A Borderless World: Realizing the Potential of Global Electronic Commerce* (1998).

The following sections look at each of the principles in more detail. They discuss (1) equity (fairness), (2) certainty and flexibility, (3) administrative feasibility (which combines efficiency, effectiveness, simplicity and convenience) and (4) neutrality.

[A] Equity

Widespread consensus exists that the fundamental principle of individual income tax is the equity principle, which requires the establishment of a fair relationship between the resources available to the taxpayer and the amount of tax paid by him. It dates back to Adam Smith's canon of equality of taxation:

the subjects of every state ought to contribute towards the support of the government as nearly as possible in proportion to their respective abilities; that is in proportion to the revenue, which they respectively enjoy under the protection of the state.[168]

There are two dimensions to the notion of fairness: vertical and horizontal. Horizontal equity means equal treatment of individuals considered to be in equal positions, which should result in people with similar tax capacity facing similar tax liabilities. Arbitrary deviations from equal treatment create dissatisfaction among taxpayers who are subject to discrimination and result in pressures for the enactment of additional special benefits which legislators find it difficult to resist. Horizontal equity can be achieved by widening the tax base to ensure that all gains and benefits are included in it and by equating the tax treatment of income from different sources. It is breached if a tax system exempts certain categories of income to achieve other social or economic aims. The difficult thing about horizontal equity is to determine which factors are taken into account (and which factors are excluded) in ascertaining the relative positions (or tax bases) of individuals. Deciding which characteristics are caught and which are omitted depends on policymakers' ideas of fairness and on what society considers equitable.[169]

Vertical equity means that people in different circumstances should pay an appropriately different amount of tax since it is fair for a heavier tax burden to fall on people who are better able to bear it. It presupposes progressive income tax rates (or at least higher nominal taxes for high-income earners than for individuals with low income) and permits discrimination between taxpayers in order to facilitate redistribution between the rich and the poor.[170] Vertical equity is closely related to the ability-to-pay principle.

The main question that arises in the context of equity is when taxpayers can be considered to be in a similar position. Under the Schanz-Haig-Simons concept, the value of an individual's consumption and changes in the net value of his assets need to be compared to decide whether taxpayers are similarly situated. Neither the form (cash or benefits in kind) nor the source of income is relevant. Income is also deemed to exist if assets appreciate in value. If a taxpayer has no money inflow but only unrealized

168. Smith, *supra* n. 165, at Ch. 2.
169. R.A. Musgrave, *In Defense of an Income Concept*, 81 Harvard Law Rev. 45, (1967).
170. J. Kirkbridge & A.A. Olowofoyeku, *Revenue Law, Principles and Practice*, p. 11 (Tudor Business Publishing 1992).

increases in non-cash assets (for example, plots of unrented vacant land), he obtains a greater share of economic resources. If these assets are converted to cash at that increased value, greater consumption rights fall upon the owner. Thus, under the Schanz-Haig-Simons concept, unrealized gains should be subject to taxation, whereas the application of the realization doctrine would constitute an unfair deviation from the income concept.

Many scholars agree with the proposition of the Schanz-Haig-Simons concept that realization is an unnecessary and undesirable concept of income tax law.[171] In their view, income should be deemed to occur when an economic benefit is derived, which is the time when an asset increases in value and not when realization occurs. The ability to defer tax on asset appreciation confers a benefit on the taxpayer due to the time value of money. Consequently, taxpayers with income in the form of appreciated assets bear a lower tax burden than taxpayers with an identical amount of income from other sources. The deferral creates an incentive to invest in property generating returns in the form of capital appreciation, thereby distorting investment decisions and affecting economic efficiency. The realization requirement is also said to violate vertical equity since the benefits of the deferral accrue mainly to wealthy taxpayers who tend to own greater amounts of capital. A market-to-market system, in which every taxpayer would have to report as income an annual increase in the value of his assets, would eliminate the above-mentioned problems.

In the context of virtual currency, it needs to be considered whether the possession of virtual currency that appreciates in value should have tax consequences. Following the Schanz-Haig-Simons income concept, unrealized increases in the value of virtual currency should be subject to taxation. Accumulated virtual currency can be converted to cash and if this happens, greater consumption rights fall upon the owner. However, in the author's view, it makes a substantive difference for taxpayers whether their gain is realized or not and whether an increase in wealth is accompanied by a receipt of liquid assets.[172] Taxpayers having cash can easily settle their tax liability, whereas taxpayers without liquid resources have to monetize their assets or borrow the necessary funds and such transactions are far from costless, either psychologically or financially. Taxpayers selling their assets incur transaction costs. The imposition of tax on unrealized appreciation may dissuade taxpayers from investing in assets which cannot be easily converted into cash. This fear could prevent economic resources from being directed to their most efficient uses.[173] Forcing taxpayers to mortgage their assets is also problematic. Property that is not easily marketed is not easily borrowed against. When the property is speculative, leveraging the investment increases the level of risk

171. J. Kwall, *When Should Asset Appreciation Be Taxed?: The Case for a Disposition Standard of Realization*, 86 Indiana Law Journal 77 (2011); D. Elkins, *The Myth of Realization: Market-to-Market Taxation of Publicly-Traded Securities*, 10 Florida Tax Review 5 (2010); V. Thuronyi, *The Concept of Income*, 46 Tax Law Review, p. 58 (1990).
172. S. Pareja, *Taxation without Liquidation: Rethinking "Ability to Pay,"* Wisconsin Law Review 841 (2008). Pareja observes that although the common view is that the ability to pay does not consider liquidity, liquidity is a significant issue in the tax context. He suggests dividing assets transferred by gift or bequest into two classes—liquid assets and illiquid assets. With respect to the latter, the recipient should be able to avoid immediate income inclusion.
173. Elkins, *supra* n. 171, at p. 381.

of holding the asset. Taxpayers may not be willing to incur additional risk and they may be reluctant to invest in speculative assets knowing that the tax system may force them to increase the level of risk in the future.[174]

Excluding unrealized increases in the value of assets from taxation could also be deduced from Adam Smith's canon of convenience:[175]

> every tax ought to be levied at the time, or in the manner, in which it is most likely to be convenient for the contributor to pay it. A tax upon the rent of land or of houses, payable at the same term at which such rents are usually paid, is levied at the time when it is most likely to be convenient for the contributor to pay; or, when he is most likely to have wherewithal to pay. Taxes upon such consumable goods as are articles of luxury are all finally paid by the consumer, and generally in a manner that is very convenient for him. He pays them by little and little, as he has occasion to buy the goods. As he is at liberty, too, either to buy, or not to buy, as he pleases, it must be his own fault if he ever suffers any considerable inconveniency from such taxes.

The most convenient moment to settle a tax liability seems to be to the author the time when the taxpayer has liquid resources that allow him to meet his tax liability.

In the author's view, the decision whether taxpayers are similarly situated has to take into account the form and source of their income. Since taxes cannot be paid in the form of any non-monetary assets, differentiating between realized and unrealized gains appropriately reflects the limitations inherent in the tax system. Taxpayers who dispose of virtual currency for legal currency are not faced with problems similar to those that taxpayers having virtual currency that appreciates in value are confronted with (lack of liquidity), so those two groups of taxpayers cannot be regarded to be in a comparable situation. Thus, the principle of horizontal equity permits a different treatment of taxpayers with realized and unrealized gains in virtual currency.

[B] Certainty and Flexibility

One of the most important norms in the legal systems of nearly all countries is the Rule of Law. The Rule of Law is a multi-faceted ideal but its core element is legal certainty and predictability. Citizens—it is said—need predictability in the conduct of their lives and business. If people know in advance how the law will operate, they can act in a way that allows them to avoid a detrimental impact of the law on their affairs. The state should operate in an orderly predictable way, giving its citizens advance notice by publicizing the general norms on which its actions will be based, and it should stick to these norms and not arbitrarily depart from them even if it seems politically advantageous to do so.[176]

174. *Id.*, at p. 379.
175. Smith, *supra* n. 165, at Ch. 2.
176. J. Waldron, *The Concept and the Rule of Law*, Public Law and Legal Theory Research Paper Series, Working Paper No. 08-50 (November 2008).

The principle of legal certainty has also its source in the Latin expression "*nullum tributum sine lege*," which, in the context of taxation, expresses the requirement that in the assessment and enforcement of taxes, governments must act on the basis of enacted laws rather than rulings related to individual cases. In many countries, the principle of certainty is backed up by the constitution. Taxpayers must be able to predict the consequences of their actions. A retroactive application of law is not acceptable, and a legal provision may not have effect until it is published and becomes known to the taxpayers. In the case of non-compliance with the principle of certainty, legal remedies must be provided in order to protect the person concerned.[177]

Adam Smith stated that:[178]

> the tax which each individual is bound to pay ought to be certain, and not arbitrary. The time of payment, the manner of payment, the quantity to be paid, ought all to be clear and plain to the contributor, and to every other person
>
> ...
>
> not near so great an evil as a very small degree of uncertainty.

Certainty requires a tax system be clear, so that a taxpayer can understand and anticipate the tax consequences of his actions.[179] The predictability of law protects those who are subject to the law from arbitrary state interference with their lives. Legal certainty enables people to plan their future. The OECD and the European Union have emphasized the need for legal certainty through clear, transparent and predictable tax obligations.[180] Thus, income tax liability cannot depend on a variety of imprecise legislative terminology subject to various interpretations. Any subjectivity inherent in the tax legislation must be reduced to a minimum.

In the context of virtual currency, the principle of certainty requires that taxpayers are well-informed about, and can predict, the tax consequences of their dealings in virtual currencies. This, in turn, requires (1) enacting legislation or administrative guidelines about the tax implications of virtual currency transactions, and (2) communicating these rules to taxpayers in a clear and unambiguous manner.

While legal certainty is an important principle of taxation, it seems unlikely that tax legislation could provide legal certainty with regard to all taxpayers' activities. Therefore, in its Ottawa Report on the taxation of electronic commerce, the OECD emphasized the principle of flexibility which requires taxation systems to be flexible and dynamic to ensure that they keep pace with technological and commercial developments. In other words, tax rules should exhibit a certain degree of adaptability to the changing circumstances. The principle of legal certainty must be balanced against the ability of a tax system to respond to changes in economic circumstances.[181]

177. B. Westberg, *Cross-border Taxation of E-commerce*, p. 65 (IBFD 2002).
178. Smith, *supra* n. 165, at Ch. 2.
179. OECD, *A Borderless World*, *supra* n. 167, at p. 4.
180. *Id.*; European Commission, *Communication on Electronic Commerce and Indirect Taxation*, COM(1998)374 final (June 17, 1998).
181. OECD, *A Borderless World*, *supra* n. 167, at p. 4.

When lawmaker and tax administrations enact laws and guidelines, they must choose between using rules and standards to achieve the desired objective.[182] This choice requires a trade-off between certainty and flexibility. A rule is precise and ex ante in nature. It indicates to the taxpayer whether his actions will violate or comply with the law. Rules are costly to design because lawmakers must, at the outset, identify and analyze all potential scenarios to which a rule may apply. A standard is imprecise and leaves the specification of what conduct is permissible to the adjudicator. The exact content of law comes after an individual acts as adjudicators determine whether the individual's specific behavior violates or complies with the standard. Thus, standards generate uncertainty because taxpayers do not know up front whether their behavior will be deemed by the adjudicator to comply with the standard.

In the context of virtual currency, rules may be prone to error and imprecise as they must be defined ahead of time. New types of virtual currency or new potential applications of virtual currency may appear that may not fit well within the existing rule-based legislation. Thus, rules may be poorly calibrated to the developments as they actually occur. In the author's opinion, the legislators should not put a lot of effort into prescribing precise rules to regulate virtual currency transactions. Designing rules for a quickly-evolving phenomenon can be wasteful as the anticipated scenarios may never arise or may materialize in a different from that renders a rule inapplicable. Instead, legislators should enact broad standards and let the tax administration convert those standards into more precise regulations.[183]

[C] Administrative Feasibility

Because public law is enforced by the government and potentially applicable to everyone, administrative ease should be a centrally important value. A legal rule is administrable to the extent that it can be applied easily and without excessive controversy by the governmental agency charged with its enforcement.[184] The tax system should exhibit the characteristics of effectiveness, efficiency, convenience and simplicity.

A legal solution can be considered to be effective when it is adequate to produce the intended result and as efficient when it performs or functions in the best possible manner with the least waste of time and effort. In other words, being effective is about doing the right things, whereas being efficient is about doing things in the right manner. Tax rules should produce the right amount of tax revenue at the right time. The potential for tax evasion and avoidance should be minimized, while keeping counter-acting measures proportionate to the risks involved.[185] The costs that a tax system imposes on both taxpayers (in complying with the laws) and governments (in

182. L. Kaplow, *Rules Versus Standards: An Economic Analysis*, 42 Duke Law Journal 557 (1992); J.O. McGinnis & S. Wasick, *Law's Algorithm*, 66 Florida Law Review 991 (2014), A. Casey & A. Niblett, *The Death of Rules and Standards*, Coase-Sandor Working Paper Series in Law and Economics No. 738 (2015).
183. *See also* §6.03 Developing a New Regulatory Framework.
184. A.G. Abreu & R.K. Greenstein, *Defining Income*, 11 Fla. Tax Rev. 295, p. 332 (2011).
185. OECD, *A Borderless World*, *supra* n. 167, at p. 4.

collecting taxes) should be kept at a minimum. Adam Smith considered administrative costs to be a major threat to tax efficiency:[186]

> tax levying may require a great number of officers, whose salaries may eat up the greater part of the produce of the tax, and whose perquisites may impose another additional tax upon the people ... By subjecting the people to the frequent visits and the odious examination of the tax-gatherers, it may expose them to much unnecessary trouble, vexation, and oppression.

He concluded that taxes are frequently much more burdensome to the people than they are beneficial to the government.

Taxing income from virtual currency transactions will prove effective if it helps reach the main goal of taxation which is to raise revenue. There is no point in taxing a source of income if costs of tax collection exceed the collected revenue or if large amounts of tax remain uncollected despite effects to the contrary. While that consideration is often labeled administrative convenience, it is pure common sense.

Furthermore, whether the revenue-raising goal of taxation can be achieved depends on taxpayers' behavior and enforcement possibilities. Tax compliance is a multi-causal phenomenon and cannot be guaranteed only by a deterrence strategy. Although some taxpayers are deterred from underreporting of income by the threat of penalties, the enforcement of tax laws may also have a negative effect on tax compliance: punishment simply suggests that others do not cooperate and this undermines any cooperation norm.[187] The tax determination process ultimately rests on taxpayers disclosing their financial affairs and paying what they owe without overt government compulsion. It is each citizen's self-enforcement of the legal duty that keeps the tax system running smoothly. The tax system is based on "voluntary compliance." This term does not mean that taxpayers have any choice in the matter of paying taxes. Rather, it describes the motivation of some taxpayers to fulfil their duties at their own volition.[188]

A core problem for enforcement of tax laws is asymmetric information. The taxpayer knows the facts regarding the relevant transaction but tax authorities have to obtain this information either from the taxpayer himself or from a third party.[189] It is well known that tax compliance can be improved by involving third parties in the procedure of tax assessment.[190] The fact that tax authorities can obtain information from a third party and the taxpayer knows about it fosters taxpayer honesty. Information reporting is efficient if it is imposed on parties who are fewer in number and who

---

186. Smith, *supra* n. 165, at Ch. 2.
187. E. Posner, *Law and Social Norms: The Case of Tax Compliance*, 86 Virginia Law Review 1781, p. 1786 (2000); D. Kahan, *Signaling or Reciprocating? A Response to Erich Posner's Law and Social Norms*, 36 Richmond Law Review 367, p. 369 (2002).
188. R. Seer, *Voluntary Compliance*, 67 Bull. Intl. Taxn. 11 (2013); L. Lederman, *Reducing Information Gaps to Reduce the Tax Gap: When Is Information Reporting Warranted?* 78 Fordham Law Review 1733, p. 1737 (2010).
189. Lederman, *supra* n. 188, at p. 1735.
190. *Id.*, at p. 1737; L. Lederman, *Statutory Speed Bumps: The Roles Third Parties Play in Tax Compliance*, 60 Stanford Law Review 695 (2007); E. Cheng, *Structural Laws and the Puzzle of Regulating Behaviour*, 100 Northwestern University Law Review 655, p. 675-676 (2006).

have appropriate infrastructure (for example, a bookkeeping system). In an ideal scenario, the information provided by third parties can be matched with the amounts on the taxpayer's return. In the context of virtual currency, the exchange platforms can play a major role in closing the information gap. Exchange platforms operate at the intersection of the virtual and real commercial channels and serve as a gateway to the traditional financial system. Thus, they could assist government agencies in monitoring compliance among virtual currency users.

The principle of simplicity requires the tax rules be clear and simple to understand so that taxpayers can anticipate the tax consequences in advance of a transaction, including knowing when, where and how the tax is to be accounted.[191] Thus, it is closely related to the principle of certainty. Convenience, as defined by Adam Smith, implies that taxes should be levied at the time, or in the manner, in which it is most convenient for the taxpayers to them. As both convenience and simplicity were discussed in the previous sections, the statements made there also apply in the context of administrative feasibility.

[D] Neutrality

The principle of neutrality has many meanings. The first one relates to capital export neutrality (CEN) and capital import neutrality (CIN).[192] The second one is concerned with the influence on taxpayers' behavior. A neutral tax system does not interfere with other economic, environmental or social policy objectives, which should be pursued by non-tax measures. The design of a tax system should only be influenced by tax considerations and do not result in an adaptation of the taxpayer's behavior. Taxpayers' decisions should be motivated by economic rather than tax considerations.[193] However, in practice, neutrality is difficult to achieve, and governments often want to interfere with people's choices deliberately to ensure that certain behavior is encouraged or discouraged.

The concept of neutrality implies that the obligation to pay taxes should not force people to undertake any actions to obtain resources necessary to satisfy it.[194] Since the function of the state is to protect liberty and property, the government should not use the tax system to reduce the scope of permissible individual choices and to change the pattern of individuals' preferences.[195] It also means that legislators should not introduce extensive monitoring and reporting requirements, since those may eventually harm certain activities. As the US Supreme Court once noted, "the power to tax

191. OECD, *A Borderless World*, *supra* n. 167, at p. 4.
192. CEN means that there is no tax incentive to locate an investment within or outside a certain country. To achieve CEN, the principle of taxation in the state of residence should be applied. The investment is taxed in the residence state independent of the country where it is made. CIN refers to the tax neutrality between domestic and foreign investments in a certain country. To achieve CIN, the principle of taxation in the source state should be applied. Foreign as well as domestic investments are taxed in the source state. *See* Westberg, *supra* n. 177, at sec. 4.3.1.
193. OECD, *A Borderless World*, *supra* n. 167, at p. 4.
194. This issue is discussed in more detail in §4.02[A] Equity.
195. R.A. Epstein, *Taxation in a Lockean World*, 4 Social Philosophy and Policy 1, p. 55 (1986).

involves the power to destroy."[196] The principle of neutrality should prevent the tax system from exercising that power.

§4.03 QUESTIONS RAISED BY VIRTUAL CURRENCIES

The emergence of virtual currencies has posed several income tax questions. As income taxes may generally be levied on both realized and unrealized income and gains, the following events involving virtual currency may have tax implications:

- exchanges of goods and services for virtual currency;
- exchanges of legal currency for virtual currency;
- exchanges of virtual currency for another virtual currency;
- currency mining;
- possession of virtual currency that appreciates in value;
- receipt of virtual currency (as gift or inheritance).

For each of the following events, a number of questions must be answered in order to determine its treatment for income tax purposes. First of all, there must be a clear understanding of what is the status of virtual currency for income tax purposes. Does it qualify as property, currency or something else? For the schedular tax systems, it needs to be determined which income category is applicable. Furthermore, when do disposals of virtual currency result in income and when in a capital gain? Is the mere possession of virtual currency subject to income tax? Does currency mining result in taxable income? When transactions in virtual currency give rise to business income? If dealings in virtual currencies result in taxable income, taxpayers must be aware of their compliance obligation and the tax authorities must have effective methods to monitor and enforce compliance. Chapter 5 seeks to answer these questions by examining the relevant parts of the income tax systems of the United States, United Kingdom, Germany and the Netherlands.

---

196. *McCulloch v. Maryland*, 17 US 316, 431 (1819).

CHAPTER 5

Income Taxation: Selected Countries

§5.01 THE UNITED STATES

[A] Basic Features of the Tax System

[1] Introductory Remarks

The United States first adopted individual income tax in 1864 to finance the Civil War (1861-1865). This tax, which was repealed in 1872, affected only 1% of potential taxpayers due to generous exemptions. The next Income Tax Act was enacted in 1913 after the adoption of the 16th Amendment to the Constitution.[197] This Amendment gave Congress broad powers to implement income tax. It made clear that Congress may use taxes to discourage any activities without considering how the revenue will be affected. Moreover, Congress may favor some groups with tax preferences without favoring all groups as long as the distinction is not based on a suspect classification.[198] In *Regan v. Taxation with Representation of Washington* (1983), the Supreme Court confirmed that Congress had "broad latitude in creating classifications and distinctions in tax statutes."[199]

Individual income tax is levied on citizens, residents and non-residents. Taxpayers belonging to the first two groups are taxed on their worldwide income, whereas those falling within the latter category, only on their US source income. A person is considered a resident if he holds a green card under the US immigration laws or has a substantial presence in the United States over a three-year period. The substantial presence test is met if the person is present in the United States for at least 31 days during the current calendar year and for at least 183 days during the current and prior

197. J.R. Repetti, *The United States*, sec. 1 in: *Comparative Taxation: A Structural Analysis* (H.J. Ault & B.J. Arnold eds., Kluwer Law International 2010).
198. *Id.*, at sec. 2.
199. *Regan v. Taxation with Representation of Washington*, 461 US 540 (1983).

two years, determined by counting each day of presence in the current year as one day, each day of presence in the first prior year as one-third of a day and each day in the second prior year as one-sixth of a day.[200] US citizens residing anywhere in the world are liable for US income tax, irrespective of the income type and source. Persons who renounce their US citizenship may be subject to income tax on the net unrealized gain on their worldwide property as if the property had been sold for fair market value on the day before expatriation.[201]

Within the United States, taxes based on income are imposed at the federal, state and sometimes at local levels. Although the tax system within each jurisdiction may define taxable income separately, many states refer to the federal concepts for determining the taxable income. This chapter exclusively deals with the federal income tax law.

Although the US income tax system is of global nature, it has tended towards a schedular income concept in the recent years. Several categories of expenses are limited in their deductibility to similar categories of income. For example, investment expenses are deductible only from investment income.[202]

[2] Gross Income

The starting point for determining which earnings are taxable for federal income tax purposes is the concept of gross income. The Internal Revenue Code (IRC) does not classify income by specific categories or sources. Instead, section 61 of the IRC states that "except as otherwise provided in this subtitle, gross income means all income from whatever source derived." This provision emphasizes that taxpayers have gross income when they receive anything of economic value, whether in the form of cash, property, services or other benefits in kind. Prizes, awards and lottery winnings are also included.[203] The gross income definition applies regardless of whether the underlying activity is legal or illegal. In the case *James vs. United States* (1961), the Supreme Court said that "when a taxpayer acquires earnings, lawfully or unlawfully, without the consensual recognition, express or implied, of an obligation to repay and without restriction as to their disposition, he has received income that he must report, even though it may still be claimed that he is not entitled to retain the money, and even though he may still be adjudged liable to restore its equivalent."[204]

Section 61(a) of the IRC lists 15 examples of items included in the gross income. These are: (1) compensation for services, including fees, commissions, fringe benefits, and similar items; (2) gross income derived from business;[205] (3) gains derived from

200. Section 7701(b) IRC.
201. Section 877A IRC.
202. Repetti, *supra* n. 197, at sec. 5.1.
203. Section 74 IRC.
204. *James v. United States*, 366 US 213 (1961).
205. In the case of business activity (manufacturing, merchandising or mining business), gross income amounts to gross profit and not to gross receipts. It is determined by deducting costs of goods sold from gross receipts (Treas. Reg. 1-61-3).

dealings in property; (4) interest;[206] (5) rents; (6) royalties; (7) dividends;[207] (8)alimony and separate maintenance payments; (9) annuities; (10) income from life insurance and endowment contracts; (11) pensions; (12) income from discharge of indebtedness; (13) distributive share of partnership gross income; (14) income in respect of a decedent; and (15) income from an interest in an estate or trust. This list is not exhaustive. Therefore, unless the IRC specifies that something is excluded from the gross income definition, the assumption is that it is enclosed.

Exceptions to what is included in gross income can be found under sections 101-140 of the IRC. With respect to individuals, the most significant exclusions encompass: minor fringe benefits,[208] compensation received for injuries or sickness,[209] gain from sale of principal residence,[210] gifts and inheritance of property.[211] The characterization of a payment as either a gift or income must be made on a case-by-case basis.[212] Gifts made by an employer to an employee usually qualify as a (non-taxable) fringe benefits or employee achievement awards.[213] Any income derived from the gift, including profit upon its sale, is taxable.[214]

[3] Capital Gains

Gains from the disposition of capital assets also form part of gross income. A capital asset is defined as property other than property held primarily for sale to customers in the ordinary course of business,[215] depreciable or real property used in the trade or business, copyright produced by the taxpayer or given to him by the creator, or derivative financial instruments held by a dealer.[216] The Supreme Court ruled that the definition of a capital asset must be broadly interpreted, and only assets coming within one of the statutory categories of non-capital assets are excluded.[217]

To compute the tax liability correctly, it is necessary to distinguish between short- and long-term gains (the latter are subject to a preferential tax rate of up to 20 %,

206. Interest from corporate bonds, government bonds, convertible bonds, profit-sharing bonds, bank deposits, mortgage loans, and ordinary loans, is included in gross income for federal income tax purposes, regardless of whether received from domestic or foreign sources. An exception applies to interest on certain bonds issued by the US states or their political subdivisions, which are generally exempt from federal income tax.
207. Dividends, whether paid in cash or in kind, and whether from domestic or foreign sources, are included in gross income for federal income tax purposes. Dividends in kind are valued at the fair market value of the property distributed on the date of the distribution.
208. Section 132 IRC.
209. Section 104 IRC.
210. Section 121 IRC.
211. Section 102 IRC.
212. CCH, *US Master Tax Guide 2013*, sec. 702 (CCH 2013).
213. Sections 74.c and 132.a IRC.
214. Section 102.b IRC.
215. When the taxpayer holds an asset for dual purposes—to rent or to sell, whichever becomes more profitable—he generally gets capital treatment since he did not hold it primarily for sale to customers (K. McNulty & D.L. Lathrope, *Federal Income Taxation of Individuals*, sec. 98, 8th ed. (West 2002)).
216. Section 1221 IRC.
217. *Arkansas Best Corporation v. Commissioner*, 485 US 212 (1988).

whereas the former are taxed just like other ordinary income). The following conditions must be met for the preferential treatment to apply: the objects sold are considered property, the sale does not occur within one year from their purchase, the objects are not primarily held for sale to customers and they do not constitute copyright produced by the taxpayer or given to him by the creator.

An unrealized gain (an increase in the market value of an asset) is not subject to tax.[218] Correspondingly, a decrease in the value of property is not taken into account, unless the property is sold, abandoned or destroyed. Capital losses may be deducted in a tax year to the extent of capital gains for that year, with a USD 3000 limit on any excess.[219] The excess may be carried forward indefinitely.[220]

[4] Adjusted Gross Income

In order to arrive at taxable income, adjusted gross income must be determined first. It is computed by subtracting allowable deductions from gross income. Unlike gross income, which is broadly defined in section 61 of the IRC and expansively interpreted by the courts, deductions are cast in narrow statutory language, which, in turn, is construed strictly against the taxpayer. Those deductions mainly include ordinary and necessary trade and business expenses.[221] An activity qualifies as a trade or business if it is regular, continuous and has a profit motive.[222] In determining whether there is a profit motive, the following must be taken into consideration: the manner in which the taxpayer carries on the activity, the expertise of the taxpayer, the time and effort expended by the taxpayer in carrying on the activity, the taxpayer's history of income or losses with respect to the activity, his financial status and any elements of personal pleasure or recreation.[223] Expenses are ordinary if they generally accepted in the particular business sector (taxpayer need not often make them) and necessary if they are helpful and appropriate to the conduct of the trade and business.[224]

Taxpayers frequently try to deduct expenses/losses claiming that they are incurred in the production of income; however, the activity turns out to be not profitable. To prevent this abuse, the IRC allows deductions for activities not engaged in for profit (hobby losses) only to the extent of income produced by that activity. An activity is presumed not to be a hobby if profits result in any three of five consecutive tax years unless the IRS proves otherwise.[225] In general, a taxpayer may deduct losses related to trade or business activity which have not been compensated by insurance or

218. The Supreme Court held in *Cottage Savings Association v. Commissioner*, 499 US 554, 559 (1991) that: "Under an appreciation-based system of taxation, taxpayers and the Commissioner would have to undertake the 'cumbersome, abrasive, and unpredictable administrative task' of valuing assets on an annual basis to determine whether the assets had appreciated or depreciated in value."
219. Section 1211.b IRC.
220. Section 1212.b IRC.
221. Section 62 IRC.
222. *Commissioner v. Groetzinger*, 480 US 23 (1987).
223. Treas. Reg. 1.183-2.
224. *US Master Tax Guide 2013*, *supra* n. 212, at sec. 901.
225. Section 183 IRC.

otherwise.[226] To be deductible, a loss must be evidenced by closed and completed transactions and fixed by identifiable events. No deduction can be made if there is a reasonable prospect of loss recovery.[227] No deduction is allowed for payments which are illegal under the federal or state law (but only if such state law is generally enforced) if such a transfer subjects the payer to a criminal penalty or the loss of license or privilege to engage in a trade or business.[228]

After computing adjusted gross income, personal exemptions, and standard or itemized deductions are subtracted to arrive at taxable income.[229] Taxable income is the amount to which the tax rate[230] is applied to determine the amount of the tax due. The standard deduction is a general tax-exempt amount. It cannot be claimed if a person chooses to itemize his deductions. Itemized deductions are any deductions permitted under the IRC which are not used to arrive at adjusted gross income. They include: medical expenses,[231] gambling losses (to the extent of gambling income),[232] expenses incurred in producing income as well as managing and holding of income producing assets.[233] The reason for the itemized deductions is that not every profit-seeking activity may be characterized as "trade or business" which gives rise to the deductions of necessary and ordinary business expenses laid down in section 162 of the IRC (for example, handling one's own investments in the stock market is not considered business activity).[234]

[5] Accounting and Reporting

The federal income tax is based on an annual system of reporting. The year for which a taxpayer's income is reported may be either a calendar year (one that ends on the last day of December) or a fiscal year (one that ends on the last day of any other month than December). In order to ascertain what income is to be included and what deductions are to be taken, the taxpayer must use an accounting method on the basis of which he regularly computes his income.[235] Generally speaking, the taxpayer may adopt any method as long as it clearly reflects income and is applied consistently. The two basic methods are cash and accrual accounting. It is important to note that those methods are not related to financial accounting methods.

226. Section 165.a IRC.
227. *US Master Tax Guide 2013*, *supra* n. 212, at sec. 1104.
228. Section 162.c IRC.
229. Section 63 o IRC.
230. Taxpayers fall into one of seven brackets, depending on their taxable income: 10%, 15%, 25%, 28%, 33%, 35% or 39.6%.
231. Section 213 IRC.
232. Section 165.d IRC.
233. Section 212 IRC.
234. McNulty & Lathrope, *supra* n. 215, at sec. 37. Sec. 212 of the IRC applies in situations where a taxpayer has incurred significant expenses to produce income, but fails to meet sec. 162's trade or business requirements. The standard for deductions under sec. 212 is the same as under sec. 162. If a taxpayer lacks profit motive, sec. 183 may be applied.
235. Section 446 IRC.

The cash method requires an individual to report income when it is received and make deductions when they are actually paid.[236] Since income need not be received in the form of cash to be taxable, the cash method entails the reporting of a cash equivalent, for example the fair market value of property (doctrine of cash equivalence).[237] Income is also charged to tax if it has been constructively received, which occurs when income is made available for an individual, so that he may draw upon it at any time. However, income is not constructively received if the taxpayer's control of its receipt is subject to substantial limitations or restrictions.[238] The accrual method requires an individual to report income when the right to receive it is fixed, the amount in question can be reasonably determined and no substantial uncertainty about collection exists.[239] On the deduction side, a parallel statement can be made.

An individual not engaged in business must report income on the cash basis. Accrual method is prescribed when, for example, the IRC requires an individual to maintain an inventory to clearly reflect his income.[240] Change from one accounting method to another requires an IRS approval and recognition of any income escaping taxation under the change.[241]

[B] Virtual Currency Regulations in the United States

[1] Taxation

In its 2013 Annual Report to Congress, the United States Taxpayer Advocate considered need to issue guidance addressing the tax treatment of virtual currencies to be one of the most serious problems facing the IRS.[242] This report noted that the use of virtual currencies is growing and that it is the government's responsibility to inform the public about the rules they are required to follow. The National Taxpayer Advocate recommended that the IRS answer, *inter alia*, the following questions: when receiving or using virtual currency will trigger gains or losses, whether these gains will be taxed as ordinary income or as capital gains and what information reporting, withholding and recordkeeping requirements apply to virtual currency transactions.

In May 2013, the Government Accountability Office (GAO) published a report exploring potential tax compliance risks associated with virtual currencies.[243] The GAO recommends that IRS find relatively low-cost ways to provide information to taxpayers

236. Section 451 IRC.
237. McNulty & Lathrope, *supra* n. 215, at sec. 70.
238. Treas. Reg. 1.451-2.
239. Treas. Reg. 1.451-1.
240. Treas. Reg. 1.446-1(c)(2)(i) and 1.471-1.
241. Section 446.e and 481 IRC.
242. National Taxpayer Advocate, *2013 Annual Report to Congress*, p. 249.
243. GAO, *Report to the Committee on Finance, U.S. Senate. Virtual Economies and Currencies. Additional IRS Guidance Could Reduce Tax Compliance Risks* (May 2013).

on various matters regarding virtual currencies. In commenting on a draft of this report, the IRS agreed to implement this recommendation.[244]

On March 25, 2014, the IRS issued a notice *Virtual Currency Guidance* to describe how the existing general tax principles apply to transactions using convertible virtual currency.[245] This notice provides answers to 16 frequently asked questions (FAQ) on virtual currencies. The IRS defines virtual currency as a digital representation of value that functions as a medium of exchange, a unit of account, and/or a store of value, but does not have legal tender status in any jurisdiction. Virtual currency that has an equivalent value in legal currency, or that acts as a substitute for legal currency, is referred to as "convertible" virtual currency. The notice states that virtual currency is treated as property (and not as a currency) for US federal tax purposes. The same general tax principles that apply to property transactions apply to transactions using virtual currencies. A taxpayer who mines or receives virtual currency as payment for goods or services must include the fair market value of the virtual currency in computing his gross income. The fair market value of virtual currency paid as wages is subject to federal income tax withholding, Federal Insurance Contributions Act tax, and Federal Unemployment Tax Act tax and must be reported on Form W-2, Wage and Tax Statement. Payments using a virtual currency made to independent contractors are taxable, and the self-employment tax rules apply. Generally, payers must issue a Form 1099-MISC, Miscellaneous Income, to the IRS and to the payee. The character of gain or loss from the sale or exchange of a virtual currency depends on whether the virtual currency is a capital asset in the hands of the taxpayer. A payment made using a virtual currency is subject to information reporting to the same extent as any other payment made in property. A person who settles payments made in virtual currency on behalf of merchants that accept virtual currency from their customers may be subject to the reporting requirements for third party settlement organizations.

On November 8, 2016, the US Treasury Inspector General for Tax Administration (TIGTA)[246] publicly released a report *As the Use of Virtual Currencies in Taxable Transactions Becomes More Common, Additional Actions Are Needed to Ensure Taxpayer Compliance*,[247] which discusses additional actions that the IRS should take to address income produced through virtual currencies. The report states that, although the IRS issued Notice 2014-21 with guidance on virtual currency transactions, there has been little evidence of coordination between the responsible functions to identify and

244. Letter from Steven T. Miller, Deputy Comm'r for Servs. and Enforcement, IRS, to James R. White, US GAO (May 3, 2013), reprinted in the GAO report, *supra* n. 243.

245. IRS, *Virtual Currency Guidance*, Notice 2014-21 (March 25, 2014). Notice 2014-21 also directs taxpayers to Publication 15, (Circular E), *Employer's Tax Guide*; Publication 334, *Tax Guide for Small Businesses*; Publication 515, *Withholding of Tax on Non-resident Aliens and Foreign Entities*; Publication 525, *Taxable and Non-taxable Income*; Publication 535, *Business Expenses*; Publication 544, *Sales and Other Dispositions of Assets*; Publication 551, *Basis of Assets*; and Publication 1281, *Backup Withholding for Missing and Incorrect Name/TINs*, for additional guidance on virtual currencies.

246. The TIGTA was established in January 1999 in accordance with the Internal Revenue Service Restructuring and Reform Act of 1998 to provide independent oversight of IRS activities.

247. TIGTA, *As the Use of Virtual Currencies in Taxable Transactions Becomes More Common, Additional Actions Are Needed to Ensure Taxpayer Compliance*, 2016-30-083 (September 21, 2016).

address, on a programme level, potential taxpayer non-compliance issues for transactions involving virtual currencies. The report also states that, although employers and businesses are required to report taxable virtual currency transactions, the current third-party methods of reporting taxable transactions to the IRS do not separately identify transactions related to virtual currencies. The report made the following recommendations to the IRS:

- developing a coordinated virtual currency strategy that includes outcome goals, a description of how the agency intends to achieve those goals and an action plan with a timeline for implementation;
- providing updated guidance to reflect the necessary documentation requirements and tax treatments needed for the various uses of virtual currencies; and
- revising third-party information reporting documents to identify the amounts of virtual currencies used in taxable transactions.

In November 2016, a federal court in the Northern District of California permitted the IRS to serve a John Doe summons on Coinbase (a company operating a virtual currency wallet and exchange business headquartered in San Francisco), which seeks information about US taxpayers who conducted transactions in convertible virtual currency via the Coinbase's website. The IRS uses John Doe summonses to obtain information about possible violations of tax laws by individuals whose identities are unknown. The summons initially served by the IRS on Coinbase sought "information regarding United States persons who at any time during the period January 1, 2013 through December 31, 2015 conducted transactions in a convertible virtual currency." In the face of opposition by Coinbase and due to an apparent acknowledgement that most Coinbase users conduct numerous low-value transactions, the IRS later narrowed its initial request and filed a "Notice of Narrowed Summons Request for Enforcement." The "Narrowed Summons" sought information regarding accounts "with at least the equivalent of USD 20,000 in any one transaction type ... in any one year during the 2013-2015 period." The "Narrowed Summons" excluded a user "(a) who only bought and held bitcoin during the 2013-15 period; or (b) for which Coinbase filed Forms 1099-K during the 2013-15 period." The Court granted the petition and ordered disclosure of certain documents related to virtual currency transactions.

[2] Anti-money Laundering

Decentralized and untraceable virtual currencies are said to be a channel for money laundering, illicit financing and tax evasion. There are concerns that virtual currency is used by terrorists to shift money across borders and by those who wish to conduct illegal activities online anonymously. Given these obvious attractions of virtual currency to criminals and terrorists, the US Financial Crimes Enforcement Network (FinCEN),[248] which is the US regulatory agency in charge of preventing money

248. FinCEN is one of the US Treasury's primary agencies to oversee and implement policies to prevent and detect money laundering. This is accomplished in two ways. First, FinCEN uses

laundering and terrorist financing, started investigating virtual currency in order to prevent criminals from benefiting from the innovative payment systems.

In March 2013, FinCEN published guidance entitled *Application of FinCEN's Regulations to Persons Administering, Exchanging, or Using Virtual Currencies*,[249] which addressed the applicability of the Bank Secrecy Act (BSA)[250] to persons creating, obtaining, distributing, exchanging, accepting, or transmitting virtual currency. The guidance provides information to help taxpayers determine whether their activities with virtual currencies classify them as a money service business (MBS), which are types of non-bank financial institutions that are regulated by the BSA. The FinCEN guidance states that a user who obtains virtual currency and uses it to purchase real or virtual goods or services is not an MSB. Importantly, the FinCEN guidance states that an administrator[251] or exchanger[252] that (1) accepts and transmits a virtual currency or (2) buys or sells virtual currency for any reason is a money transmitter (an MSB) under FinCEN's regulations and is subject to the BSA monitoring and reporting requirements unless a limitation to or exemption from the definition applies.

In January 2014, the FinCEN issued clarifying rulings on virtual currency miners and investors.[253] The first ruling states that to the extent a user creates or "mines" a virtual currency solely for a user's own purposes, the user is not a money transmitter under the BSA. The second ruling states that a company purchasing and selling virtual currency as an investment exclusively for the company's benefit is not a money transmitter.

FinCEN began to take action against companies that fail to comply with their registration and reporting obligations. In May 2015, FinCEN assessed a USD 700,000 penalty against Ripple Labs, a company headquartered in San Francisco that provides virtual currency exchange services, for violating the Bank Secrecy Act by not registering with FinCEN and by failing to implement an adequate anti-money laundering programme designed to protect its products from use by money launderers or terrorist

---

counter-money laundering laws (such as the Bank Secrecy Act) to require reporting and record keeping by banks and other financial institutions. Second, FinCEN provides intelligence and analytical support to law enforcement. *See* http://www.fincen.gov/about_fincen/wwd/faqs.html.

249. FinCEN, *Application of FinCEN's Regulations to Persons Administering, Exchanging, or Using Virtual Currencies* (March 18, 2013), http://fincen.gov/statutes_regs/guidance/pdf/FIN-2013-G001.pdf.

250. The Bank Secrecy Act (BSA) creates a number of reporting obligations upon financial institutions and money services businesses (MSB). MSB include check cashers, issuers and redeemers of travelers' checks and money orders, and money transmitters. MSB are subject to the BSA reporting requirements, including Currency Transaction Reports and Suspicious Activity Reports. The IRS has BSA enforcement responsibilities for financial institutions not regulated by a federal bank agency or another federal regulator.

251. An administrator is a person who is engaged as a business in using (putting into circulation) a virtual currency and who has the authority to redeem (to withdraw from circulation) such virtual currency.

252. An exchanger is a person engaged as a business in the exchange of virtual currency for real currency, funds, or other virtual currency.

253. FinCEN, *FinCEN Publishes Two Rulings on Virtual Currency Miners and Investors* (January 30, 2014).

financiers.[254] Following the assessed penalty, Ripple Labs agreed to take steps to ensure compliance with the anti-money laundering rules (for example, by monitoring all future transactions and reporting any suspicious ones, and having regular independent compliance reviews).

On July 25, 2016, a Florida judge for the Eleventh Judicial Circuit ruled that Bitcoin does not qualify as money.[255] In the case *Florida v. Espinoza,* the judge dismissed the state's money laundering claims against Michell Espinoza, who had been charged with illegally transmitting and laundering USD 1,500 worth of bitcoins. He sold them to undercover detectives who told him they wanted to use the money to but stolen credit card numbers. The Court found that virtual currency is not separately included as a category in the definition of a monetary instrument under the Florida law and thus cannot be the object of money laundering.[256] The Court observed that the Florida legislature may choose to adopt laws regulating virtual currency, but in the meantime "attempting to fit the sale of Bitcoin into a statutory scheme regulating money services business is like fitting a square peg in a round hole."

[3] Securities Regulation

On September 18, 2014, the United States District Court in Sherman, Texas, decided the first case involving virtual currency (*Securities and Exchange Commission v. Trendon T. Shavers and Bitcoin Savings and Trust*).[257] Shavers established and operated Bitcoin Savings and Trust (BTCST) and made a number of solicitations aimed at enticing lenders to invest in Bitcoin-related investment opportunities. The District Court found that Shavers knowingly and intentionally operated BTCST as a sham and a Ponzi scheme, and repeatedly made materially false and misleading representations to BTCST investors and potential investors concerning the use of their bitcoins, how he

254. FinCEN, *FinCEN Fines Ripple Labs Inc. in First Civil Enforcement Action against a Virtual CurrencyExchanger* (May 5, 2015).

255. *Florida v. Espinoza*, Fla. Cir. Ct., F14-2923, 7/25/16. The judge set forth detailed reasons for her conclusion that Bitcoin could not be considered "money" for purposes of the Florida statutes: "Bitcoin may have some attributes in common with what we commonly refer to as money, but differ in many important aspects. While Bitcoin can be exchanged for items of value, they are not a commonly used means of exchange. They are accepted by some but not by all merchants or service providers. The value of Bitcoin fluctuates wildly and has been estimated to be eighteen times greater than the U.S. dollar. Their high volatility is explained by scholars as due to their insufficient liquidity, the uncertainty of future value and the lack of a stabilization mechanism. With such volatility they have a limited ability to act as a store of value, another important attribute of money. Bitcoin is a decentralized system. It does not have any central authority, such as a central reserve, and Bitcoins are not backed by anything. They are certainly not tangible wealth and cannot be hidden under a mattress like cash and gold bars. This Court is not an expert in economics, however, it is very clear, even to someone with limited knowledge in the area, that Bitcoin has a long way to go before it is the equivalent of money."

256. Florida law defines a "monetary instrument" as "coin or currency of the United States or any other country, travelers' checks, personal checks, bank checks, money orders, investment securities in bearer form or otherwise in such form that title thereto passes upon delivery." *See* Fla. Stat. sec. 896.101(2)(e).

257. *Securities and Exchange Commission v. Trendon T. Shavers and Bitcoin Savings and Trust*, Case No. 4:13-CV-416.

would generate the promised returns, and the safety of their investments. One of the questions before the Court was whether BTCST investments qualify as securities.[258] Shavers argued that the BTCST investments are not securities because Bitcoin is not money, and is not part of anything regulated by the United States. The SEC argued that the BTCST investments are both investment contracts and notes, and, thus, are securities. In a memorandum opinion issued on August 6, 2013, the District Court ruled that Bitcoin is a currency or form of money and investors wishing to invest in BTCST provided an investment of money. Thus, the BTCST investments met the definition of a security.

On July 25, 2017, the SEC issued an investigative report cautioning market participants that sales of digital assets are subject to the requirements of the federal securities laws.[259] The SEC's report stems from an inquiry that the agency launched into whether the DAO[260] and associated entities and individuals violated federal securities laws with unregistered offers and sales of DAO tokens in exchange for ether. The SEC found that DAO tokens were securities and therefore subject to the federal securities laws. The SEC came to the same conclusion in securities fraud investigations against the initiators of the REcoin Group Foundation and Diamond Reserve Club[261] and in its order against the Mnuchee Inc.[262] The SEC statements imply that issuers of distributed ledger or blockchain technology-based securities must register offers and sales of such securities unless a valid exemption applies.

On July 27, 2017, the US SEC issued an Investor Bulletin to make investors aware of potential risks of participating in ICOs.[263] In view of the SEC, virtual tokens may qualify as securities. If they are securities, the offer and sale of these tokens in an ICO are subject to the federal securities laws that require professionals and their firms who offer, transact in, or advise on securities to be licensed or registered. The SEC pointed out that although investors in an ICO may have rights under the federal securities laws, their ability to recover the amounts invested in the event of fraud or theft may be significantly limited as third-party wallet providers, exchange platforms and other parties involved in virtual currency transactions may be located overseas or be operating unlawfully. The SEC may be unable to obtain information from persons or entities located overseas. Also, as traditional financial institutions are not involved with ICOs or virtual currency transactions, it is difficult to follow the flow of money. Finally, as there is no central authority that collects virtual currency user information,

258. The term "security" is defined in sec. 77b of the US Code as "any note, stock, treasury stock, security future, security-based swap, bond ... [or] investment contract ... ." An investment contract is any contract, transaction, or scheme involving (1) an investment of money, (2) in a common enterprise, (3) with the expectation that profits will be derived (4) from the efforts of the promoter or a third party. *See SEC v. W.J. Howey & Co.*, 328 US 293, 298-99 (1946). *See* also §3.08 Qualification as Security.
259. SEC, *U.S. Securities Laws May Apply to Offers, Sales, and Trading of Interests in Virtual Organizations* (July 25, 2017).
260. *See* §2.04[E] New Versus Traditional Technology.
261. SEC, *SEC Exposes Two Initial Coin Offerings Purportedly Backed by Real Estate and Diamonds* (September 29, 2017).
262. SEC, *Company Halts ICO After SEC Raises Registration Concerns* (December 11, 2017).
263. SEC, *Investor Bulletin: Initial Coin Offerings* (July 27, 2017).

the SEC must rely on multiple other sources for this type of information. Following the publication of the Investor Bulletin addressing the risks of ICOs, the SEC issued several others investor alerts, bulletins and statements on ICOs and cryptocurrency-related investments, including with respect to the marketing of certain offerings and investments by celebrities and others.[264]

[C] Taxation of Income from Virtual Currency Transactions

[1] Income Definition

The statement "all income is taxable" seems to be clear and easy to apply in practice. However, its key problem is that the term "income" has never been defined in the tax law. The IRS claims that income is whatever it says it is. The 16th Amendment to the Constitution gave the federal government the power to tax every single receipt that it deems to be income.[265] According to the IRS, anything of value may constitute taxable income if it regards it as such.

The Schanz-Haig-Simons concept is widely accepted as the basis for the taxable income definition.[266] It holds that an individual's income consists of his consumption plus accumulation during the taxable period. The Schanz-Haig-Simons concept is an economic one. It is very broad and goes far beyond what tax law requires, including, for example, unrealized capital gains and imputed income in the income definition. Despite its wide acceptance, it remains ambiguous, since the terms "consumption" and "accumulation" are open-ended. Taking it as a sole basis for defining taxable income would ignore the practical requirement that income must be something that can be reliably measured, reported, and paid.

The judicial interpretations helped clarify the term income. In *Eisner v. Macomber* (1920), the Supreme Court had to decide whether a pro-rata stock dividend was income.[267] In holding that it was not, the Supreme Court defined income as "the gain derived from capital, labor or from both combined, provided it be understood to include profit gained through a sale or conversion of capital assets." By requiring the gain be "derived" or "served" from the property, the Supreme Court gave birth to the realization requirement, which remains part of the definition of income today. The narrow *Macomber* definition did not cover many things one thinks of as income (embezzled funds, found money, prizes and awards).

More than three decades after it decided *Macomber*, the Supreme Court had to rule in *Commissioner v. Glenshaw Glass Co.* (1955) whether punitive damages were

264. SEC, *Statement on Potentially Unlawful Promotion of Initial Coin Offerings and Other Investments by Celebrities and Others* (November 1, 2017); *Investor Alert: Public Companies Making ICO-Related Claims* (August 28, 2017); *Statement on Cryptocurrencies and Initial Coin Offerings* (December 11, 2017).
265. The 16th Amendment states: "Congress shall have power to lay and collect taxes on incomes, from whatever source derived, without apportionment among the several States, and without regard to any census or enumeration."
266. Thuronyi, *The Concept of Income*, *supra* n. 171, p. 46.
267. *Eisner v. Macomber*, 252 US 189 (1920).

income.[268] Unlike compensatory damages, punitive damages bear no relationship to the labor or capital of the plaintiff but are paid solely to punish the defendant. Hence, they are a windfall for the plaintiff. As windfalls do not proceed from the recipient's labor or capital or both combined, the punitive damages received by Glenshaw Glass could not be income under the *Macomber* definition. The lower courts had consistently held so. To treat punitive damages as income, the Supreme Court needed to redefine the term.[269] Thus, in *Glenshaw Glass*, the Supreme Court laid down what has become the modern understanding of taxable income. It declared that income taxes could be levied on "accessions to wealth, clearly realized, and over which the taxpayers have complete dominion." If these requirements are met, any increase in wealth falls within the taxable income definition, unless Congress makes a specific exemption. The *Glenshaw Glass* definition, which is the Schanz-Haig-Simons concept limited by realization, is neither too broad, as the Schanz-Haig-Simons concept alone would be, nor too narrow, as the *Macomber* definition was. By retaining realization while moving to embrace the Haig-Simons-Schanz model, the Supreme Court seemed to develop the right income definition.[270]

The reminder of this section looks at the three components of the gross income definition (accession to wealth, realization and complete dominion) in more detail.

[a] Accession to Wealth

An accession to wealth means that taxpayers gain access to valuable resources. They are able to use more resources than before. It is irrelevant whether their accession is legal or not (illegal income is also taxable).

The receipt of virtual currency increases the spending power of an individual. Although virtual currencies are nothing more than a computer code existing in the computer network, they can be exchanged for a number of (real or virtual) goods or services. The fact that the user's ability to convert virtual currency to usable wealth (i.e., legal currency) may be contingent on factors beyond his control (e.g. sudden price decrease, theft) is not important. Wealth does not mean money or things convertible into money. Permission to use is what makes an item valuable, not just permission to sell it. The Supreme Court once held that use is almost as big a stick in the bundle of property rights as is alienability.[271] Thus, the receipt of virtual currency represents an accession to wealth.

[b] Realization

Although the requirement of realization is firmly embedded in US tax law, no general definition of realization has achieved widespread acceptance yet. The realization requirement has evolved in an unprincipled manner and remains ambiguous to this

268. *Commissioner v. Glenshaw Glass Co.*, 348 US 426 (1955).
269. Abreu & Greenstein, *supra* n. 184, at p. 301.
270. Abreu & Greenstein, *supra* n. 184, at p. 305.
271. *United States v. Craft*, 535 US 274, 283 (2002).

day.[272] Although it acquired constitutional status after the first Supreme Court decisions in income tax matters, it is widely accepted today that realization is not a constitutional requirement but a rule of administrative convenience and that Congress is authorized to tax unrealized gains if it chooses to do so.

In one of its first decisions regarding the 16th Amendment to the Constitution, *Eisner v. Macomber* (1920) (which authorized Congress to impose tax on "income from whatever source derived"), the Supreme Court held that "income" means only realized income.[273] The Supreme Court was called upon to decide whether a stock dividend declared and issued by a corporation to its shareholders constituted the shareholders' income. In ruling that it did not, the Court stated that realization required not only a mere transfer of property but also the receipt of a contemporaneous benefit by the transferor. After the *Macomber* decision, realization appeared to be a constitutional requirement.

Twenty years later, in *Helvering v. Bruun* (1940), the Supreme Court held that a landlord whose tenant built a building upon the leased land and then abandoned the lease had income in the amount of the value of the new building.[274] The landlord's legal relationship to the building changed upon the tenant's abandonment of the lease because, as a result of the abandonment, the landlord acquired rights which it did not have before (for example, the right to take possession of, or re-lease, the building). The *Bruun* decision marked a retreat from the *Macomber* standard of realization. It suggested that any definite event (for example, the forfeiture of a leasehold) could constitute realization.

Eight months after the *Bruun* decision, in *Helvering v. Horst* (1940), the Supreme Court explicitly acknowledged that the realization requirement was found on administrative convenience.[275] The Court reiterated this view in *Cottage Savings v. Commissioner* (1991).[276] In that case, the Supreme Court found that a taxpayer who exchanged a pool of mortgages with a fair market value of USD 4.5 million for another pool with the identical fair market value had a realization event, despite the equivalence of the market values, because the underlying mortgages in each pool were different. In the Court's view, the difference in the identity of the properties and obligors in the underlying mortgages sufficed to create realization. The Supreme Court stated that a realization event occurs when there is a sale or exchange of property that is materially different in kind. To determine whether properties are materially different in kind, the Supreme Court rejected the idea of comparing the economic substance of the properties involved and, instead, evaluated whether the properties being exchanged had legally distinct entitlements.

272. D.N. Shaviro, *An Efficiency Analysis of Realization and Recognition Rules Under The Federal Income Tax*, 48 Tax Law Review 1 (1992). According to *Black's Legal Dictionary*, realization is "an event or transaction, such as the sale or exchange of property, that substantially changes a taxpayer's economic position so that income tax may be imposed or a tax allowance granted."
273. *Eisner v. Macomber*, 252 US 189 (1920).
274. *Helvering v. Bruun*, 309 US 461 (1940).
275. *Helvering v. Host* 311 US 112 (1940).
276. *Cottage Savings Assoc. v. Commissioner*, 499 US 554 (1991).

Although the receipt of money in exchange for property is the most common form of realization, this requirement does not mean that property must be sold for cash. The exchange of any services or items for other services or items may constitute realization. If person A gives person B an item in exchange for USD 100, person A has gross income irrespective of whether the item given away was his property.

As virtual currency is considered property, exchanges of virtual currency into legal currency, other virtual currency or goods and services should be taxable events because a disposition of property may constitute a realization for federal income tax purposes.[277] Once an exchange transaction is complete, the participant has a different set of rights and can dispose of more virtual resources. Thus, all exchanges of virtual currency constitute realization events. So does the receipt of virtual currency without consideration (either through mining or as a gift). The received virtual currency changes a taxpayer's economic position. As a result of the mining process or a donation, he acquires a right to use virtual currency he did not have before.

[c] Complete Dominion

The Supreme Court shed more light on the term "complete dominion" in the case *CIR v. Indianapolis P & L* (1990).[278] Indianapolis Power and Light Co. (IPL) required certain customers to make deposits with it to assure prompt payment of future electric bills. Although the deposits were at all times subject to the company's unfettered use and control, IPL did not treat them as income at the time of receipt, but carried them on its books as current liabilities. The question arose whether the purpose of those payments was to serve as a security or as advance payments for electricity. The Supreme Court held that although IPL derived some economic benefit from the deposits, it did not have the complete dominion over them at the time they were made. IPL had an obligation to repay the deposits upon termination of service and, thus, its right to retain them was contingent upon events outside its control. The customer controlled the ultimate disposition of a deposit. The circumstance that IPL enjoyed unrestricted use of the money was not decisive. The Supreme Court stated that:

> In determining whether a taxpayer enjoys "complete dominion" over a given sum, the crucial point is not whether his use of the funds is unconstrained during some interim period. The key is whether the taxpayer has some guarantee that he will be allowed to keep the money.

IPL's receipt of these deposits was accompanied by no such guarantee. If some other person can decide how, when, or whether the taxpayer can take actual possession of the funds, those funds are not realized income to the taxpayer. Another negative example is a loan. The borrower is unrestricted in his use of the loan funds received; however, he also has a current obligation to repay the funds, and, therefore, he realizes no taxable income from the loan.

277. Section 1001 of the IRC mentions "realization" in connection with the sale or other disposition of property.
278. *CIR v. Indianapolis P & L*, 493 US 203 (1990).

In general, taxpayers have complete dominion over any decentralized universal currency they receive as they can access and use coins accumulated in their wallets as they deem fit. However, the question of complete dominion could be problematic in centralized virtual currency systems where the supply of virtual currency is controlled by a central entity. In centralized virtual currency schemes, the contractual terms and conditions need to be investigated to determine the set of rights that taxpayers have in their currency. If the issuer of the virtual currency retains the right to terminate the users' virtual currency accounts or remove the virtual coins from circulation, the users will not have a complete dominion over their accumulate coins.

[2] Income Determination

Notice 2014-21 clarified that, for federal tax purposes, virtual currency is treated as property. Virtual currency is not treated as currency that could generate foreign currency gain or loss for US federal tax purposes. Therefore, the general tax principles applicable to property transactions apply to transactions using virtual currency.

[a] Earning Virtual Currency

The receipt of virtual currency will result in gross income. A taxpayer who receives virtual currency must, in computing gross income, include the fair market value of the virtual currency, measured in USD, as of the date that the virtual currency was received. When a taxpayer successfully mines virtual currency, the fair market value of the virtual currency as of the date of receipt is includible in gross income. Taxpayers are required to pay tax on any income they receive, irrespective of whether they spend it or not. Even if they leave the currency in their wallets, the currency is still considered taxable income upon receipt. When taxpayers spend their virtual currency, another taxable event occurs.

Notice 2014-21 states that taxpayers are required to determine the fair market value of virtual currency in USD as of the date of payment or receipt. If a virtual currency is listed on an exchange platform and the exchange rate is established by market supply and demand, the fair market value of the virtual currency is determined by converting the virtual currency into USD at that exchange rate, in a reasonable manner that is consistently applied. However, as virtual currency exhibits enormous price volatility, its price may change from minute to minute. It is not clear whether taxpayers should use the average price of a particular day, the price as of the moment of receipt or the day's high or the day's low. Taxpayers may be tempted to use a higher price when purchasing virtual currency and a lower when selling it.

[b] Gains or Losses

When a taxpayer exchanges virtual currency for property or legal currency, he may have a gain or loss on the transaction. Gain or loss is calculated by subtracting cost basis from proceeds. If the fair market value of property received in exchange for virtual currency exceeds the taxpayer's cost basis of the virtual currency, the taxpayer has taxable gain. The taxpayer has a loss if the fair market value of the property received is less than the cost basis of the virtual currency.

When virtual currency is sold for legal currency, the transaction is treated as the sale of intangible property that may result in a taxable gain or loss. For example, Anna sells one unit of virtual currency to Mike for USD 1000. If Anna's basis in one unit of virtual currency was USD 300, Anna has realized a USD 700 gain on account of the sale. Mike has no gain or loss on the transaction. However, if he later sells the virtual currency to Jane for USD 1500, he will have a gain of USD 500. It is important to stress that every conversion of virtual currency into legal currency produces a taxable gain or loss. This could have significant financial implications for sellers who accept payments in virtual currency as they would have to record two transactions: (1) sale of property for virtual currency and (2) disposal of virtual currency for legal currency, and the value of virtual currency may fluctuate during the time period between these two events.

When virtual currency is exchanged for goods and services, the transaction should be treated as barter. For example, Mike sells two books to Anna and he receives from her one unit of virtual currency. The fair market value of the currency unit is USD 600 and Anna's basis is USD 200. The fair market value of the books is also USD 600 and Mike's basis is USD 100. In this case, both Anna and Mike have a taxable gain. Anna has realized USD 400 and Mike USD 500 on the transaction. Thus, every time a person uses virtual currency to purchase goods or services, he realizes a gain or loss on the disposition of the virtual currency. This makes virtual currency rather impractical for daily transactions because of the accounting and recordkeeping burden.

For exchanges of virtual currency into another type of virtual currency that took place before December 31, 2017, section 1031 of the IRC could be relevant. This provision allowed a taxpayer to sell a property, to reinvest the proceeds in a new like-kind property and to defer all capital gains taxation. For transactions concluded prior to December 31, 2017, to qualify as a like-kind exchange, both properties that were exchanged had to be held for use in a trade or business or for investment and be of the same nature, character or class. Quality or grade did not matter.[279] Certain types of property were specifically excluded from section 1031 treatment.[280] Notice 2014-21 did not address whether virtual currency could be the subject of a 1031 exchange. However, as virtual currency qualified as property for federal income tax purposes, it could be assumed that exchanges of virtual currency for other virtual currency could benefit from the like-kind provision. For like-kind exchanges concluded after December 31, 2017, the Tax Cuts and Jobs Act of 2017 amended section 1031 to make it clear that the only permissible property is a business or investment real estate.[281] Thus,

279. IRS, *Like-Kind Exchanges Under IRC Code Section 1031*.

280. Sec. 1031 did not apply to exchanges of inventory or stock in trade, stocks, bonds, or notes, other securities or debt, partnership interests and certificates of trust.

281. Sec. 1031 (a)(1) states: "No gain or loss shall be recognized on the exchange of real property held for productive use in a trade or business or for investment, if such real property is exchanged solely for real property of like-kind which is to be held either for productive use in a trade or business or for investment."

exchanges of virtual currency into another type of virtual currency are now treated as barter transactions that cannot benefit from the 1031 treatment.

[c] Capital Gains versus Ordinary Income

The character of gain or loss generally depends on whether virtual currency qualifies as a capital asset in the hands of the taxpayer. A taxpayer generally realizes capital gain or loss on the sale or exchange of virtual currency that is considered a capital asset (i.e., property other than property primarily held for sale to customers). For example, stocks, bonds, and other investment property are generally capital assets. In contrast, a taxpayer generally realizes ordinary gain or loss on the sale or exchange of virtual currency that is not a capital asset in the hands of that taxpayer. Inventory and other property held mainly for sale to customers in a trade or business are examples of property that is not a capital asset.

Gains and losses that arise from investing in virtual currency (treated as capital assets) must be reported as short-term or long-term gains or losses. If virtual currency is held for one year or more, the seller may benefit from the favorable rate for long-term capital gains. Short-term gains are taxed at the ordinary rates. Capital losses can be used to offset capital gains and the excess amount can be deducted from ordinary income, with a maximum of USD 3000 per year.

[d] Recordkeeping

Because virtual currency is treated as property, taxpayers must keep careful account of basis to calculate the taxable gain or loss. However, Notice 2014-21 does not indicate what type of accounting method should be used. Two most commonly used valuation methods are last-in, first-out (LIFO) and first-in, first-out (FIFO). The impact of both methods on the taxable gain is shown Table 2. This example assumes that a taxpayer intends to sell five units of virtual currency at the current price (5000). Under the FIFO method, the taxable gain will be 4000, whereas the LIFO method will result in a taxable gain of 2000.

Table 5.1 Taxable Gain under the FIFO and LIFO Valuation Methods

Date of Receipt	*Amount*	*Cost Basis*	*Sales Price (Now)*	*Gain*
July 2014	5	1000	5000	4000 (FIFO)
December 2014	5	2000	5000	3000
July 2015	5	3000	5000	2000 (LIFO)

[e] Trade or Business

If a taxpayer's virtual currency transactions constitute a trade or business, and are not undertaken by the taxpayer as an employee, the net earnings resulting from those activities (generally, gross income derived from carrying on a trade or business less allowable deductions) constitute self-employment income and are subject to the tax rules for the self-employed.

An activity qualifies as a trade or business if it is regular, continuous and has a profit motive.[282] In determining whether there is a profit motive, the following must be taken into consideration: the manner in which the taxpayer carries on the activity, the expertise of the taxpayer, the time and effort expended by the taxpayer in carrying on the activity, the taxpayer's history of income or losses with respect to the activity, his financial status and any elements of personal pleasure or recreation.[283]

Self-employed taxpayers file a Schedule C (Form 1040) and bear the responsibility for paying their own social security, Medicare and income taxes. They can deduct ordinary and necessary business expensed from their income.

[3] Income Reporting

A payment made using virtual currency is subject to information reporting to the same extent as any other payment made in property. For example, a person who in the course of a trade or business makes a payment of fixed and determinable income using virtual currency with a value of USD 600 or more to a US non-exempt recipient in a taxable year is required to report the payment to the IRS and to the payee on Form 1099-MISC. If interest is paid in virtual currency, the taxpayer needs to issue the payee a 1099-INT.

Payments made by means of virtual currency are subject to backup withholding to the same extent as other payments made in property.[284] A taxpayer making reportable payments using virtual currency must solicit a taxpayer identification number (TIN) from the payee. The payor must backup withhold from the payment if a TIN is not obtained prior to payment or if the payor receives notification from the IRS that backup withholding is required. For example, if a taxpayer is going to pay someone virtual currency worth USD 600 or more in a calendar year in the course of his trade or business and the payee has refused to give him his TIN, the taxpayer is required to withhold 28% (24% for tax years 2018-2025) of the amount to be paid and send it to the IRS.

There are IRS information reporting requirements for a person who settles payments made in virtual currency on behalf of merchants that accept virtual currency from their customers. A third party that contracts with a substantial number of unrelated merchants to settle payments between the merchants and their customers is a third party settlement organization (TPSO). A TPSO is required to report payments

282. *Commissioner v. Groetzinger*, 480 US 23 (1987).
283. Treas. Reg. 1.183-2.
284. IRS, *Topic Number 307—Backup Withholding*.

made to a merchant on a Form 1099-K, Payment Card and Third Party Network Transactions, if, for the calendar year, both (1) the number of transactions settled for the merchant exceeds 200, and (2) the gross amount of payments made to the merchant exceeds USD 20,000. When determining whether the transactions are reportable, the value of the virtual currency is the fair market value of the virtual currency in US dollars on the date of payment.

[4] Foreign Account Tax Compliance Act (FATCA)

No US tax law has ever had a more global reach than FATCA (the Foreign Account Tax Compliance Act). FATCA's aim is to prevent tax evasion by US citizens with foreign bank accounts by imposing compliance obligations on financial institutions. Not only banks, but also many entities outside the traditional financial services sector are affected by FATCA's operation.

US citizens who own certain foreign financial accounts with a total value of at least USD 50,000 at the end of the tax year are subject to FATCA reporting obligations (Form 8938 must be submitted to the IRS). The penalty for failure to file is generally USD 10,000 and may increase to up to USD 60,000 for continuing failures to file.

FATCA requires that a foreign financial institution report financial accounts held by US citizens; otherwise withholding taxes will apply. In a FATCA context, the definitions of both "financial account" and "foreign financial institution" are very broad. A foreign financial institution includes entities that accept deposits in the ordinary course of a banking or similar business; hold financial assets for the account of others; or engage in the business of trading securities or commodities. The term "financial account" includes any depository or custodial account.

No guidance on the treatment of virtual currency under FATCA has been provided so far. The IRS guidelines on the tax treatment of virtual currencies do not address the FATCA issue. However, due to the broad definitions of both foreign financial institution and financial account, there is a strong possibility that foreign virtual currency exchanges and payment services may be considered foreign financial institutions subject to FATCA reporting obligations. Many of these businesses operate in a similar way to banks, in that they offer a customer the possibility to transfer the customer's virtual currency to an account and record the customer's balance on their books.

The FATCA reporting requirement is separate from the reporting requirement for purposes of foreign bank account reporting (FBAR).[285] Under FBAR, US persons with over USD 10,000 in foreign financial assets must report a financial interest in, or signature authority over, a foreign financial account to the FinCEN. The FBAR reporting obligation may exist even if there is no associated taxable income. The filing is treated quite seriously by the financial authorities, with no filing deadline extensions

285. For a comparison of both reporting requirements, *see* IRS, *Comparison of Form 8938 and FBAR Requirements*.

and penalties for failure to report ranging from USD 10,000 to USD 100,000 per violation.

There is still no clear statement as to whether virtual currency accounts are subject to the FBAR reporting. However, under the FinCEN guidance of 2013,[286] virtual currency exchange businesses should be regarded as financial institutions for FBAR purposes. Also, the 2014 decision of the US District Court for the Northern District of California in *United States v. Hom* (2014) could have significant implications for Bitcoin accounts.[287] The Court ruled that online poker sites operated as financial institutions and the gaming accounts represented foreign financial accounts subject to FBAR reporting. Based on that decision, a US individual storing bitcoins with any of the exchange businesses could be subject to the FBAR reporting requirements if the value of his bitcoin holdings exceeded USD 10,000 at any time during the year.

[D] Conclusions

Section 5.1. examined whether income from transactions in virtual currency may be subject to federal income tax in the United States and described the income tax consequences for participants in virtual currency transactions. At the outset, the section observed that the United States applies a global income definition, taxing "all income from whatever source derived." In other words, all receipts, irrespective of whether they exist in monetary or non-monetary, tangible or intangible form, are subject to tax unless a specific exemption applies. Based on this definition, all receipts of virtual currency (both through mining and exchange transactions) are considered taxable income. The fair market value of the currency as of the day of receipt should be recorded for federal tax purposes.

According to the IRC, virtual currency should be treated as property for federal income tax purposes, meaning that every time a person spends virtual currency, no matter how small the amount, there is a taxable transaction. The IRS has not provided any *de minimis* threshold below which disposals of virtual currency would be disregarded. This creates a serious problem for taxpayers that want to use virtual currency in their everyday transactions as they have to keep track of the cost basis of all coins they own. It is not clear which valuation method (FIFO or LIFO) should be used. Disposals of virtual currency may result in a capital gain or loss if virtual currency is considered capital asset in the hands of the taxpayer. Long-term capital gains may benefit from a preferential tax rate. Transactions in virtual currency (mining and disposals) may qualify as a trade or business if they are regular, continuous and have a profit motive. If this is the case, the taxpayer has to follow the rules for the self-employed. A payment made using virtual currency is subject to information reporting to the same extent as any other payment made in property and may trigger the obligation to file Forms 1099-K, 1099-MISC, 1099-INT and W2.

286. FinCEN, *Application of FinCEN's Regulations to Persons Administering, Exchanging, or Using Virtual Currencies*, *supra* n. 249.
287. *United States v. Hom*, Case 3:13-cv-03721-WHA.

The SEC considers virtual currency to be securities subject to the federal securities law. The IRS has not commented on the qualification of virtual currency as securities so far. It is unclear whether it may also apply for tax purposes.

§5.02 THE UNITED KINGDOM

[A] Basic Features of the Income Tax System

In the United Kingdom, income tax was introduced in 1798 and has remained in force ever since, except for a gap between 1816 and 1842. It was completely overhauled in 1803 by the introduction of the schedular system backed up by an extensive system of withholding at source. The Finance Act of 1803 established a set of Schedules for different income categories. Each Schedule was subject to different rules. Income that did not fall within any schedule was not subject to tax.[288]

As time passed, the UK tax law became lengthy and complex. Referring to a particular provision of income tax law, Lord Reid held in the House of Lords that it "is so obscure that no meaning can be given to it. I would rather do that then seek by twisting and contorting the words to give to the subsection an improbable meaning. Parliament is so accustomed to obscure drafting in finance Bills that no one may have noticed the defects in this subsection."[289] Following the criticism that tax law became complex and incomprehensible, the Tax Law Rewrite Project was established and commissioned with the task of rewriting tax legislation into a more logical and user-friendly format. As a result of the Tax Law Rewrite Project, the UK income tax legislation is now included in three principal statutes:

- Income Tax (Earnings and Pensions) Act 2003 (ITEPA 2003), which covers income from employments pensions, social security benefits, and replaces the former Schedule E;
- Income Tax (Trading and Other Income) Act 2005 (ITTOIA 2005), which covers income from trade, professions, vocations, property, savings and investment, and replaces the six cases of former Schedule D, A and F;
- Income Tax Act 2007 (ITA 2007), which covers basic provisions about the charge to income tax, tax rates and personal relief.

Income tax has been of schedular nature since its introduction in 1798. There is no statutory definition of income, beyond the statement that income is taxable if it falls within one of the income categories.[290] Section 3 of the ITA 2007 lists the following income sources: employment, pension, social security, trading, property, savings and investment, and a miscellaneous category. Each category has its own rules to compute taxable income. Losses can only be offset within the categories.[291] If there is no source,

288. J. Tiley, *The United Kingdom*, sec. 1 in: *Comparative Income Taxation: A Structural Analysis* (H.J. Ault & B.J. Arnold eds. Kluwer Law International 2010).
289. *Fleming v. Associated Newspapers Ltd* (1972) 48 TC 382.
290. J. Tiley et al., *Tiley and Collison's UK Tax Guide* 2012-2012, sec. 9.3 (LexisNexis 2012).
291. *Id.*, at sec. 9.6.

there is no taxable income. Profits from illegal activities or legally unenforceable contracts are also allocated to the sources and subject to tax.[292]

Total income consists of the taxpayer's income from all sources, calculated according to the provisions under which it arises and after deducting expenses appropriate to a particular category. To arrive at taxable income, allowable payments (pension payments, loss relief, gifts to charities) and personal reliefs (age-related allowance, tax reduction for married couples) are deducted.[293] Income tax is a self-assessed tax. Individuals are taxed at rates ranging from 0% to 45%.[294] Taxpayers must calculate their tax due no later than January 31 following the end of their tax year. The year of assessment runs from April 6 to April 5 in the next year. Trading and professional income is assessed on the basis of the accounting year ending in the year of assessment. For certain types of income (for example, dividends), tax is deducted at source.

UK residents are taxed on their worldwide income. There is no statutory definition of residence. In determining it, reliance is placed on the Her Majesty's Revenue and Customs (HMRC) guidance contained in *HRMC 6 Residence, Domicile and the Remittance Basis*.[295] The UK tax law distinguishes between residence, ordinary residence and domicile. Domicile[296] is mainly important for inheritance tax purposes, whereas capital gains and income tax are founded on residence. To be resident, an individual must be present in the United Kingdom during some part of the year of assessment. An individual who is present in the United Kingdom for 183 days or more in a tax year is always considered resident for that year. If an individual spends less than six months in the United Kingdom, he may still be regarded as resident depending upon whether his visits are frequent and substantial.[297] Ordinary residence implies continuity or habitual residence. It is referred to a man's abode in a particular place or country which he has adopted voluntarily and as a part of the regular order of his life for the time being. It is possible to be resident but not ordinarily resident in a country and vice versa. For example, if an individual is abroad for a full tax year, he may be ordinarily resident in the United Kingdom without being resident.[298]

Revenue receipts must be distinguished from capital receipts which attract CGT. What is income and what capital has to be determined in the light of all the circumstances and the weight to be given to a particular circumstance depends on common sense rather than any legal principle. The two main tests used in distinguishing income and capital are: whether receipts relate to assets that form part of the permanent business structure or whether they relate to circulating or fixed capital.

292. *Id.*, at sec. 14.9.
293. N. Lee et al., *Revenue Law: Principles and Practice*, sec. 7.4 and 7.21, 28th ed. (Bloomsbury 2010).
294. For tax year 2018/2019, no income tax is levied on amounts up to GBP 11,850. The highest tax rate of 45% applies to income exceeding GBP 150,000.
295. HMRC, *Residence, domicile and the remittance basis* (October 3, 2013).
296. Domicile is where the individual has a settled intention to reside permanently. Everybody must have a domicile and a person can only be domiciled in one place at a time. *See* CCH, *British Master Guide*, sec. 227 (CCH 2012).
297. *Id.*, at sec. 224.
298. *Id.*, at sec. 226.

Circulating capital is acquired to be used or sold, whereas fixed capital is retained in the business with the object of making profits.[299] Capital expenditure is not deductible in computing profits, even though incurred wholly and exclusively for business purposes. The difficulty of determining whether payments are income or capital receipts was expressed in *IRC v. British Salmson Aero Engines Ltd* (1938): "in many cases it is almost true to say that the spin of the coin would decide the matter almost as satisfactorily as an attempt to find reasons."[300]

[B] Basic Features of the Capital Gains Tax System

An individual who is either resident or ordinarily resident in the United Kingdom is subject to CGT on his worldwide capital gains. The statutory provisions relating to CGT are laid down in the Taxation of Chargeable Gains Act (TCGA) 1992. The distinction between income and capital still remains central to the UK tax system, despite a certain amount of convergence. According to section 39 of the TCGA 1992, an income tax characterization takes priority over one for CGT purposes.

When income tax was first introduced, various forms of capital were already subject to other taxes. Trust law made a sharp distinction between income and capital receipts. As income tax was seen as temporary, there was little room for extending it to capital gains.[301] CGT was eventually introduced in 1965 on the grounds of equity rather than for yield because taxpayers started exploiting opportunities to convert income into capital to escape taxation. Originally, CGT was charged at a significantly lower rate than income tax. This encouraged the proliferation of sophisticated devices, whereby an income profit was turned into a capital gain. The scope of this type of arrangements was reduced by the alignment of the tax rates and the extensive anti-avoidance legislation.[302]

CGT is levied on gains from the disposal of assets. Some assets are exempt; for example, a private car, personal possessions (tangible and moveable assets) that are individually worth GBP 6,000 or less and "wasting assets" (i.e., assets with a lifespan of up to 50 years that often lose their value over time).[303] The chargeable gain is found by taking the disposal consideration and deducting from that figure the allowable expenditure. If the latter exceeds the former, the taxpayer has made a loss for CGT purposes.[304] For basic rate taxpayers (i.e., those subject to the 20% income tax rate), the CGT rate depends on the size of the gain, the taxable income and whether the gain is from residential property or other assets. Higher or additional rate taxpayers (i.e., those subject to the 40% or 45% income tax rates) pay 28% on gains from residential property and 20% on gains from other chargeable assets. Capital losses may be only set off against capital gains of the same or subsequent years. There is an annual tax-free

299. *British Master Guide, supra* n. 296, at sec. 630.
300. *IRC v. British Salmson Aero Engines Ltd* (1938) 2 KB 482.
301. Tiley, *The United Kingdom, supra* n. 288, at sec. 1.
302. *British Master Guide, supra* n. 296, at sec. 202.
303. HMRC, *Capital Gains Tax on personal possessions.*
304. Lee, *supra* n. 293, at sec. 19.21.

allowance (known as the Annual Exempt Amount), which for the tax year 2018-19 is GBP 11,700 for an individual.[305]

[C] Virtual Currency Regulations in the United Kingdom

HMRC set out its position on the tax treatment of income received from activities involving bitcoins and other similar cryptocurrencies in Brief 09/14 of March 3, 2014.[306] The Brief states that such income is subject to the general rules of income tax and GCT. The question whether any profit on bitcoin transactions is chargeable must be answered on the basis of the individual facts of each case, taking into account the relevant legislation and case law. For VAT purposes, the HMRC is of the opinion that mining is outside the VAT scope, exchanges of bitcoins into traditional currencies are exempt and supplies of goods and services for bitcons are subject to VAT under the general rules. The HMRC observed that, given the evolutionary nature of cryptocurrencies, the position outlined in Brief 09/14 is provisional.

The UK Financial Conduct Authority (FCA), which is the main financial regulatory body in the United Kingdom, has published numerous information statements and warnings about the risks associated with the use of virtual currency. In its opinion on the ICOs,[307] the FCA clarified that it can only be decided case by case whether an ICO falls within the FCA's regulatory boundaries or not. Many ICOs will fall outside the regulated space. However, depending on how they are structured, some ICOs may involve regulated investments and firms involved in an ICO may be conducting regulated activities. Also, some tokens may constitute transferable securities and therefore may fall within the prospectus regime.

In November 2017, the FCA issued warnings about risks involved with contracts for differences (CFDs).[308] CDFs are cash-settled derivative contracts in which the parties to the contract seek to secure a profit or avoid a loss by agreeing to exchange the difference in price between the value of the CFD contract at its outset and at its termination. In other words, CFDs are complex financial instruments which allow speculating on the price of an asset (for example, bitcoin or ether). The FCA considered cryptocurrency CFDs to be extremely high-risk investments and listed some of the main investor risks related to price volatility, price transparency and high charges.

In April 2018, the FCA issued a statement on cryptocurrency derivatives, such as cryptocurrency futures (a derivative contract in which each party agrees to exchange cryptocurrency at a future date and at a price agreed by both parties), CFDs and cryptocurrency options (a contract which grants the beneficiary the right to acquire or dispose of cryptocurrencies).[309] In the FCA view, cryptocurrency derivatives may qualify as financial instruments under the Markets in Financial Instruments Directive

---

305. HMRC, *Capital Gains Tax*.
306. HMRC, *Brief 09/14: Tax Treatment of Activities Involving Bitcoin and Other Similar Cryptocurrencies* (March 3, 2014). Previously, UK tax authorities classified bitcoin as a taxable voucher.
307. FCA, *Initial Coin Offerings* (September 12, 2017).
308. FCA, *Consumer warning about the risks of investing in cryptocurrency* CFDs (November 14, 2017).
309. FCA, *Cryptocurrency derivatives* (April 6, 2018).

(2004/39),[310] meaning that firms conducting regulated activities in cryptocurrency derivatives must comply with all applicable rules provided in the FCA's and EU regulations.

The FCA intends to develop a coherent strategy for dealing with the issues and risks that cryptocurrencies raise. In March 2018, it announced that it was working with the Bank of England and the UK Treasury on a discussion paper for cryptocurrencies that will be published later in 2018. The three organizations will also create a cryptocurrency task force to look into how to both regulate and support crypto technologies.[311]

[D] Taxation of Income from Virtual Currency Transactions

Having provided a brief description of the UK tax system, it will now be examined whether and to what extent virtual currency transactions may have income tax or CGT consequences. The following events involving virtual currency may have tax implications:

- exchanges of goods and services for virtual currency;
- exchanges of legal currency for virtual currency;
- exchanges of virtual currency for another virtual currency;
- currency mining;
- possession of virtual currency that appreciates in value;
- receipt of virtual currency (as a gift).

Income from those activities is subject to tax only if it falls within one of the source categories (for example, trading, miscellaneous) or constitutes a capital gain. This is examined in the following sections.

[1] Trading Income

Trading income is dealt with under Part 2 of the ITTIOIA 2005. The term "trade" is incompletely defined in the legislation, which states that this concept includes "every trade, manufacture, adventure or concern in the nature of a trade."[312] Without precise legislative guidance, it must be studied on a case-by-case basis whether a transaction under consideration measures up to the usual characteristics of trade.[313] Those characteristics were developed by case law and were divided by the Royal Commission

310. *Directive 2004/39/EC of the European Parliament and of the Council of 21 April 2004 on markets in financial instruments amending Council Directives 85/611/EEC and 93/6/EEC and Directive 2000/12/EC of the European Parliament and of the Council and repealing Council Directive 93/22/EEC.*
311. M.J. Zuckerman, *UK Financial Regulator To Release Crypto Review This Year With BoE And Treasury* (April 9, 2018), https://cointelegraph.com/news/uk-financial-regulator-to-release-crypto-review-this-year-with-boe-and-treasury.
312. Section 832(1) Income and Corporation Taxes Act 1988.
313. *British Master Guide, supra* n. 296, at sec. 555.

of 1955 into six badges: subject-matter, period of ownership, frequency of transactions, supplementary work, circumstances responsible for sale and motive.[314]

The first badge (subject-matter) states that some forms of property, such as commodities or manufactured articles, are normally the subject of trading and only very exceptionally the subject of investment. When a person buys an item for investment, he intends to keep it for a reasonable time, i.e., long enough to develop a feeling that he will enjoy the possession or use of the item purchased.[315] Property that neither yields income nor gives personal enjoyment to its owner is more likely acquired with the object of a deal.[316] A gain made from the sale of assets held for investment may give rise to a charge under the CGT rules.

The second badge (period of ownership) assumes that if property is meant to be dealt in, it is sold within a short time after acquisition. A quick sale is more consistent with a trading activity rather than an investment that is likely to be long-term.[317]

The third batch (frequency of transactions) presumes that if realizations of the same sort of property occur in succession over a period of years, the taxpayer has been engaged in trade.[318] Nonetheless, an isolated transaction may be an adventure in the nature of the trade depending on the facts of an individual case.[319] Some cases illustrate this principle. In the first one, a money lender bought one million of toilet paper rolls while being on business trip abroad. He sold the paper to a single purchaser on his return to the United Kingdom and made a profit of GBP 10,000. The court held that the taxpayer was engaged in an adventure in the nature of a trade and that he made the purchase of such a vast quantity obviously for no other purpose than that of reselling it at a profit.[320] Trade was also assumed in another case where a woodcutter who had never previously traded in whisky bought three lots of it and sold them two years later at a profit.[321] Thus, the nature and size of the transaction are more important than its frequency in determining whether a particular activity may constitute trade.

Later transactions may color earlier ones and trigger a trading income tax liability on them.[322] This statement is well illustrated by the case in which a taxpayer started a driving school and sold it at a profit. Subsequently, he set up and sold some 30 driving schools. The court held that the sales that followed the first one had tainted it. The first transaction could also be considered a trading transaction, even though initially there might not have been any intention to sell the first driving school. The subsequent sales made the court believe that there must have been.[323]

314. Royal Commission on the Taxation of Profits and Income, Final Report Cmd 9474 (1955), Comments on what is a trade.
315. *British Master Guide*, *supra* n. 296, at sec. 558; Tiley, *UK Tax Guide*, *supra* n. 290, at sec. 14.10.
316. *British Master Guide*, *supra* n. 296, at, at. 562; Lee, *supra* n. 293, at sec. 10.23.
317. *British Master Guide*, *supra* n. 296, at sec. 564; Lee, *supra* n. 293, at sec. 10.24.
318. *British Master Guide*, *supra* n. 296, at 566.
319. *T. Beynon & Co Ltd v. Ogg* (1918) 7 TC 125.
320. *Rutledge v. IRC* (1929) 14 TC 490.
321. *IRC v. Fraser* (1942) 24 TC 498.
322. Lee, *supra* n. 293, at sec. 10.25.
323. *Pickford v. Quirke (HMIT)* (1927) 13 TC 251.

The fourth badge (supplementary work) states that if property is worked up in any way during the ownership to bring it into a more marketable condition or if any special efforts are made to attract purchasers, there is evidence of trading.[324]

Under the fifth badge (circumstances responsible for the sale), the knowledge that a purchase will increase in value is insufficient evidence to find that a transaction is in the nature of trade. Many people buy things to keep and enjoy but at the same time they know that these objects will increase in value and may be sold at a profit. If the resale appears to be the only reason for the purchase, it can be concluded that the taxpayer is trading.[325] The fact that an asset is sold in response to a sudden opportunity negates the idea that any plan of dealing prompted the original purchase.[326] A forced sale to raise cash for an emergency raises a presumption that the transaction is not a trade.[327]

If there is clear evidence upon which it can be decided whether the taxpayer is trading, the taxpayer's motive (the sixth badge) is irrelevant. However, if the evidence is ambiguous, the motive can be considered. A desire to make a profit is not sufficient evidence to support a finding of trading since it is uppermost in the minds of all who buy for investment. The question of motive is important where the taxpayer buys for investment and quickly thereafter changes his mind and decides to sell or the other way round. Providing that there is clear evidence that the asset was bought for investment, a quick resale will not make the transaction an adventure in the nature of trade. If a taxpayer who bought an item with the intention of reselling it at a profit decides to retain it, he will not be trading when he decides to sell it later on.[328]

A scheme which inevitably involves a loss may not be a trading transaction.[329] However, operations of the same kind and carried out in the same way as those which characterize ordinary trading are not excluded from trading operations because they make a loss or there is no intention to make profits.[330] HMRC advises taxpayers to be consistent in their approach to transactions that may be trading transactions, irrespective of whether they lead to a profit or a loss.[331]

With regard to hobby activities, the HMRC acknowledges that "in some cases the person's hobby can lead them to make substantial supplies and may grow to become a business activity. Many successful businesses grow out of a hobby or private interest."[332] The distinction between a hobby and a trade, profession or vocation is a question of fact and degree.[333] It seems that the main criterion to distinguish between hobby and trade is the manner in which the activity is organized and its profitability in

324. *British Master Guide, supra* n. 296, at sec. 568; Lee, *supra* n. 293, at sec. 10.26.
325. *British Master Guide, supra* n. 296, at sec. 564.
326. *Id.*, at sec. 570.
327. Lee, *supra* n. 293, at sec. 10.27; Tiley, *UK Tax Guide, supra* n. 290, at sec. 14.24.
328. *British Master Guide, supra* n. 296, at sec. 571.
329. *FA and AB Ltd v. Lupton* (1971) 3 All ER 948, 47 TC 580.
330. *JP Harrison (Watford) Ltd v. Griffiths* (1960) 40 TC 281.
331. HMRC, *Meaning of trade: general: hobbies and artificial trades.*
332. HMRC, *VAT Business and Non-Business activities: hobbies.*
333. HMRC, *Athletes: Trade or hobby.*

general. If profits are an isolated event in the overall picture of continuing losses, trade cannot be assumed.[334]

In order to establish whether transactions in virtual currencies may give rise to trading income, it is necessary to have regard to the entire context in which they are made. As there are no precise legal rules on income characterization, case law is the only frame of reference for distinguishing among various income categories. One of the main reasons for purchasing virtual currencies is to benefit from their increase in value as taxpayers want to make a profit by reselling them. If objective circumstances imply that the taxpayer acts as a trader (i.e., sells and buys currency in large quantities), trading income will be deemed to exist. A one-off deal (for example, the sale of a large quantity of virtual currency) may be considered an adventure in the nature of trade. Trading income is likely to be assumed if the time between the acquisition and sale is relatively short. A taxpayer who made some occasional sales of virtual currency before commencing a more intensive trading activity runs the risk that all his previous transactions will be considered trade.

It is questionable whether virtual currency mining can give rise to trading income. At the first sight, it may appear that virtual currency miners perform a service: they solve complicated cryptographic algorithms to verify transactions and prevent double spending. Those calculations require computer hardware, large amount of electricity and a lot of processing power. In exchange for their services, miners may receive new units of virtual currency. However, not every miner is rewarded with new currency units. As more and more miners compete for a limited supply of blocks (ledgers of past transactions) to verify, not everyone receives a reward for his mining efforts. In order to have a realistic chance to mine new currency units, one must invest in specialized equipment. If mining activity is carried out on a large scale (including the use of proper mining software and hardware), the received units of virtual currency could be seen as trading income. However, if a person intends to mine virtual currency with an ordinary computer, mining should be seen as a gamble given the extremely low likelihood of success. Gambling winnings are not subject to income tax and the related expenses are not deductible.

If transactions in virtual currency give rise to trading income, it is necessary to outline how to compute the taxable profit. Profits are defined as the surplus by which the receipts from trade or business exceed the expenditure.[335] Trading profits are usually computed on the earning basis, i.e., on sums earned in the period of account as opposed to sums received (the cash basis).[336] Accounts prepared for commercial purposes according to generally accepted accountancy practice[337] rarely show the

334. HMRC, *Trade: general: hobbies and artificial trades* states that "taxpayer who wants tax relief for losses, which are not, in truth, trading losses may point to a profit in a particular year to support the trading assertion. This factor would normally carry little weight if that profit were an isolated event in an overall picture of continuing losses."
335. *Russell v. Aberdeen Town and County Bank* (1888) 2 TC 321 at 327.
336. *British Master Guide, supra* n. 296, at 590.
337. Generally accepted accounting practice has no legal definition in the United Kingdom. It encompasses the principles set out in the accounting standards and other statements issued by the Accounting Standards Board (ASB) but goes beyond that to include the requirements of

taxable trading profits, although over the years the accounting and tax profits have become more aligned. Small businesses with turnover lower then GBP 150,000 are allowed to use the cash basis.[338]

The right to deduct expenses in computing taxable income does not rest on any express statutory provision but rather on the absence of any express prohibition. It is interfered from the fact that it is the profit and not the receipts that are taxed.[339] The right to deduct is limited by a number of rules: expenses must be incurred "wholly and exclusively" for the purpose of trade (principle of remoteness and duality), they must be income and not capital,[340] and a deduction must not be prohibited by a statute.[341] The word "wholly" refers to the quantum of the money expended, whereas the word "exclusively," to the motive accompanying it.[342]

Expenditure for personal purposes is not deductible. The duality rule prevents the deduction of expenditure for mixed purposes. There have been numerous cases where this principle was strictly applied. The leading case on that matter is the decision of the House of Lords in *Mallalieu v. Drummond* (1983), in which a lady barrister sought to deduct the cost of clothes bought to wear in court since such clothes were required by court etiquette.[343] The undisputed evidence was that the taxpayer's expenditure was motivated solely by thoughts of court etiquette. However, the House of Lords disallowed the deductibility as, in addition to the business purpose, there were the purposes of warmth and decency. In *Prince v. Mapp* (1969), a guitarist in a pop group could not deduct the cost of an operation on his little finger because he played the guitar partly for business and partly for pleasure.[344] The dual-purpose cases show that if the taxpayer incurs the expenditure for two purposes, one business and the other personal, none of expenditure is deductible.

However, an exception is made if it is possible to split a payment into a portion which is incurred for business purposes and a portion which is not.[345] Section 34(2) of the ITTOIA 2005 provides that if an expense is incurred for more than one purpose, a deduction can be made for any identifiable part which is incurred wholly and exclusively for the purposes of trade. This approach was followed in *Copeman v Flood* (1941) where a 17-year old daughter of the managing director of a company was also appointed as director. The tax authorities claimed that the entire salary expense was not wholly and exclusively incurred for business purposes.[346] In order to judge whether an item of expenditure is deductible in computing profits, it is necessary to look at the

company law, industry-specific requirements, regulatory factors and pronouncements by HMRC (Lee, *supra* n. 293, at sec. 10.64).

338. HMRC, *Cash basis*.
339. Tiley, *UK Tax Guide, supra* n. 290, at sec. 14.99.
340. To classify expenditure as income or capital, similar tests to those for deciding whether a receipt is income or capital apply. A payment is capital if it is made to bring into existence an asset for the enduring advantage of the trade (Lee, *supra* n. 293, at sec. 10.131).
341. *Id.*, at sec. 10.130.
342. Tiley, *UK Tax Guide, supra* n. 290, at sec. 14.100.
343. *Mallalieu v. Drummond* [1983] STC 665, [1983] 2 AC 861, HL.
344. *Prince v. Mapp* [1969] 46 TC 169.
345. Tiley, *UK Tax Guide, supra* n. 290, at sec. 10.137.
346. *Copeman v. Flood* [1940] 24 TC 53.

nature of the activity of the taxpayer in incurring that expenditure. Sums spent for earning profits will be deductible even if no profit is expected that year. Losses which are incidental to the carrying out of the business are deductible.[347]

Taxpayers who mine and sell virtual currency will need to determine a reasonable key to allocate part of their expenses, such as electricity and Internet costs, to trading activities in order to claim deductions. The dual-purpose cases show that courts tend to interpret deductions very narrowly. The costs of the necessary computer equipment are not deductible as trading expenses but may qualify for capital allowances.[348]

Traders who accept virtual currency as consideration for goods and services perform barter transactions. According to IAS 18 (which provides guidance on accounting for revenue from the sale of goods and provision of services), in barter transactions, the fair market value of goods and services received (if it is reliably measurable) should be recorded as revenue.[349] If this fair market value cannot be measured, the value of the goods and services given up (determined by reference to non-barter transactions) should be used (SIC 31).

[2] Miscellaneous Income

Section 687 of ITTOIA 2005 includes a residual category to catch receipts not covered by any other provisions. However, the HMRC has made clear that although the miscellaneous income provisions are "sweep up" sections, this does not mean that these provisions tax all profits that fall outside the other charging provisions of the Tax Acts. Excluded are, for example, voluntary receipts (gifts), gambling winnings from wagers and bets, and capital accretions on isolated transactions in assets.[350]

The courts have named three requirements for profits to qualify as miscellaneous income: they must possess a quality of recurrence, be of income nature and not be gratuitous.[351] There is no rule that profits must recur each year to be taxable. Case law does not provide guidance on how frequently a particular activity must be pursued. A profit on the sale of a single item that is not a trading venture will be a capital accretion and not miscellaneous income.[352] Profits from a series of sales may amount to a trade.[353] A large number of transactions (50 transactions a year over an eight year period) were found assessable under the miscellaneous income provisions.[354] However, the HMRC observes that such a case might also be viewed as giving rise to trading income.[355]

347. *Id.*, at sec. 14.109.
348. HMRC, *Claim capital allowances.*
349. Under IAS 18, fair value is the price that would be received to sell an asset or paid to transfer a liability in an orderly transaction between market participants at the measurement date.
350. HMRC, *Miscellaneous income: scope of the provisions: overview.*
351. Tiley, *UK Tax Guide*, *supra* n. 290, at sec. 18.4.
352. HMRC, *Miscellaneous income: scope of the provisions: isolated sales of assets.*
353. HMRC, *Miscellaneous income: scope of the provisions: series of sales of assets.*
354. *Cooper v. Stubbs [1925] 10 TC 29.*
355. HMRC, *Miscellaneous income: scope of the provisions: series of sales of assets.*

To be of income nature, a receipt must have a source and be distinct from that source. Hence, a gift or the receipt of gambling winnings is not subject to tax.[356] When profits are derived from the provision of services or exploitation of a capital asset, such profits are treated as having income quality. Those derived from the disposal of a capital asset are of capital nature.[357]

According to case law, the following activities may give rise to miscellaneous income: sale of cotton futures, letting racehorses for share of prize money, sale of rights in life story to newspaper and the receipt of commissions.[358]

Income from occasional transactions in virtual currency, which do not qualify as trade (for example, they are rarely carried out), may constitute miscellaneous income provided that virtual currency is not a capital asset in the hands of the taxpayer.[359] It is difficult to draw the line between trade and other income-generating activity as there are no precise guidelines on that matter. It is not clear what intensity, frequency and turnover an activity must have to become trade.

Miscellaneous income can be computed on either a cash or an accrual basis. Miscellaneous losses cannot be set off against income under another heading of the same year. They can be carried forward into next taxable periods.[360]

[3] Capital Gains

CGT is levied on a gain a taxpayer makes when he disposes of an asset. Under section 21(1) of the TCGA, all forms of property should be considered assets and, in particular, incorporeal property, any currency other than sterling[361] and any form of property created by the person disposing of it. The word "property" is not expressly defined in the legislation. It is generally believed that it should encompass anything which is capable of being owned.[362] The following were recognized as assets: a lease,[363] goodwill,[364] loans,[365] royalty rights,[366] the right to an action for damages[367] and rights under a service contract.[368] These examples show that "asset" is a very broad term; rights that do not seem to constitute property in its ordinary sense may nevertheless constitute assets for capital gains purposes. A right may qualify even if it is incapable of valuation or assignment.[369] In *Marren v. Ingles* (1980), the right to receive an

356. Tiley, *UK Tax Guide, supra* n. 290, at sec. 18.4. More recently, in *Anise v. Hammond* [2003] STC (SCD) 258, gambling profits were held not to be taxable income because they had been received by chance.
357. *Id.*, at sec. 13.3.
358. Tiley, *UK Tax Guide, supra* n. 290, at sec. 18.6.
359. *Id.*, at 13.6.
360. Tiley, *UK Tax Guide, supra* n. 290, at sec. 18.13.
361. Currency in sterling is not an asset. It is a means by which the gain on other assets is measured.
362. P.G. Whiteman et al., *Whiteman on Capital Gains Tax*, sec. 6-04 (Sweet & Maxwell 2008).
363. *Bayley v. Rogers* (1980) TC 420.
364. *Kirby v. Thorn EMI* [1987] STC 621.
365. *W.T. Ramsay Ltd. v. IRC* (1981) 54 TC 101.
366. *Rank Xerox v. Lane* (1979) 53 TC 185.
367. *Zim Properties v. Procter* (1984) 58 TC 371.
368. *O'Brien v. Benson's Hoisery* (1979) 53 TC.
369. Whiteman, *supra* n. 362, at sec. 6-37 and 6-38.

unquantifiable sum in the future was considered to be an asset.[370] Each asset is treated as a distinct item, so that tax only arises on the disposal of that asset and is computed in the light of the expenditure on that asset. An exception is made for shares and securities of a company of the same class and held by one person.[371]

There is no general definition of the word "disposal" either. It is believed that "disposal" encompasses the transfer of beneficial ownership (whether legal or equitable), or some parts of it, from one person to another.[372] Section 22 of the TCGA provides that there is a disposal of assets even where a capital sum (i.e., money or money's worth) is derived, notwithstanding the fact that no asset is acquired by the person paying the capital sum. As an example, it mentions capital sums received as consideration for use or exploitation of assets. A disposal under the contract is treated as made even though the contract itself is unenforceable.[373]

Virtual currency constitutes assets (property) for CGT purposes as it is capable of being owned and transferred. Any contractual restrictions imposed on the use of virtual currency do not affect its characterization as property. Even if the status of virtual currency as capital asset was doubtful, a capital sum may be received upon its sale, creating a "disposition of assets."

For virtual currency whose value is subject to fluctuations, section 24(2) of the TCGA may also be relevant in the case of significant price drops. According to this provision, if an asset becomes of negligible value, the taxpayer is deemed to have disposed of and immediately acquired the asset at its market value (nil), enabling him to claim loss relief. Should the value of the asset subsequently increase, the result will be that on a later disposal, the base value will be nil so that all the consideration received will be treated as gain. According to the HRMC, negligible value should be less than 5% of the original value.[374]

The chargeable gain is calculated by deducting allowable expenditure, which is defined as expenditure incurred wholly and exclusively in the acquisition, disposal of the asset and any enhancements of its value. Deductions must be computed with regard to the disposal of a particular asset and not a group of assets.

[E] Conclusions

UK income tax law is schedular in nature. It imposes income tax on several categories of receipts. Transactions in virtual currency may result in trading income or miscellaneous income, or they may give rise to capital gains that are taxed by means of a separate CGT. Under UK law, it does not matter whether income is generated in a monetary or non-monetary, tangible or intangible form. Non-monetary receipts are subject tax based on to the rules on benefits in kind (their fair market value is recorded as revenue).

370. *Marren v. Ingles* (1980) 54 TC 76.
371. Section 104(1) of the TCGA 1992.
372. Whiteman, *supra* n. 362, at sec. 7-04.
373. *Thompson v. Salah* [2000] STC 113.
374. Tiley, *UK Tax Guide, supra* n. 290, sec. 27.22.

Whether income from virtual currency disposals and virtual currency mining may constitute trading income must be established a case-by-case basis using the six criteria developed by the case law (the six badges of trade). Repetitive and frequent transactions may imply trade. If the requirements of trade are not met (for example, in the case of occasional sales of virtual currency), taxpayers' profits may be covered by the miscellaneous income provision provided that virtual currency is not considered capital assets in the hands of the taxpayer.

A CGT is imposed on disposals of capital assets. The terms "asset" and "disposal" have been extended by the legislation to cover transactions that would not fall within their common-sense meaning: tax liability arises if a capital sum is received, even if the person paying the sum does not acquire any asset. A profit on the sale of virtual currency held for investment purposes constitutes a capital gain (provided that the sale is not a trading venture based on its characteristics and size).

However, as there are no numerical indicators, it is difficult to draw an unambiguous distinction among various income sources and decide which category receipts from virtual trade will be allocated to. Any attempts to do so by the taxpayer will result in uncertainty because a particular transaction may be found by the tax authorities and courts to fall within a different category. An incorrect characterization of the income source results in the wrong computation of the tax liability, which may lead to the imposition of penalties and interest.

HMRC have not provided any guidance on the tax treatment of virtual currency, except for the statement that the general rules apply and a case-by-case analysis is necessary.

§5.03 GERMANY

[A] Basic Features of the Income Tax System

The German concept of income has undergone many changes since its introduction. The Prussian Income Tax Act of 1981 followed the source theory (*Quellentheorie*), under which a receipt constitutes income if it is periodic and comes from a permanent source. Under the influence of Georg von Schanz, the Income Tax Act of 1920 contained an accrual income concept. The current system follows a mixed approach: tax is levied on inputs from several categories which follow either the source or the accrual income theory.[375]

Income of individuals is taxable in Germany either because of a nexus between the country and the individual earning the income (residence taxation) or because of a nexus between the country and the activity which generates the income (source taxation). Individuals whose domicile or habitual place of abode is in Germany are considered residents and are subject to tax on their worldwide income. According to section 8 of the General Tax Code (*Abgabenordnung*, AO), an individual's domicile is

375. W. Schön, *Germany*, sec. 6.1.1 in *Comparative Income Taxation: A Structural Analysis* (H.J. Ault & B.J. Arnold eds., Kluwer Law International 2010).

the place where he occupies a home in circumstances which indicate that he will retain and use it (only actual facts are relevant and not the intention of the taxpayer). An individual's habitual place of abode is the place where he is present in circumstances which indicate that his stay is not just temporary. Such a place is deemed to exist if an individual has been continuously present in Germany for a period of more than six months.[376]

Income tax liability of individuals is increased by a solidarity surcharge (*Solidaritätszuschlag*), which was introduced in 1995 to raise money for the financial reconstruction of the federal states in the eastern part of Germany following the German reunification.[377] Solidarity surcharge amounts to 5.5% of the payable income tax. Individuals carrying on a trade or business (excluding agricultural and professional sector) are also subject to business tax (*Gewerbesteuer*).[378] Business tax is an important source of revenue for municipalities. Its rate varies from one municipality to another.[379] Foreign businesses are only subject to trade tax if they have a permanent establishment in Germany.

Unlike the US tax system, the German tax law does not contain an all-encompassing provision that would tax income from whatever source derived. The German income definition is of schedular nature. Tax is only levied on seven income categories (*sieben Einkünftsarten*) that are listed in section 2(1) of the Individual Income Tax Act (*Einkommensteuergesetz*, EStG).[380] These are:

1) income from agriculture and forestry (section 13 of the EStG),
2) business income (section 15 of the EStG),[381]
3) income from independent personal services (section 18 of the EStG),
4) income from employment (section 19 of the EStG),
5) capital investment income (section 20 of the EStG),[382]

376. Section 9 AO.
377. D. Grashoff & F. Kleinmanns, *Aktuelles Steuerrecht 2012*, sec. 2.1 (229) (Verlag C.H. Beck 2012).
378. The taxable income for the business tax is generally determined in the same manner as for income tax purposes, subject to certain adjustments. These adjustments refer to certain expenses which may be deducted for income tax purposes but not for business tax purposes and vice versa. A personal exemption of EUR 24,500 is granted to individuals. The effective rate of business tax depends on a federal rate (Steuermesszahl) and a municipal coefficient (Hebesatz). The amount of the business tax is determined by applying the basic federal rate to the taxable business income, which results in a basic tax amount. The coefficient is then applied to this basic tax amount to determine the actual tax burden. The coefficient is fixed by the municipalities and may vary according to their financial needs from 200% to 490%.
379. *Id.*, at sec. 2.3 (331).
380. The term "*Einkünfte*" means net income (receipts minus expenses).
381. Business income is called in Germany "*Einkünfte aus Gewerbebetrieb.*" The term "*Gewerbebetrieb*" has a different meaning in the German Commercial Law Act (*Handelsgesetzbuch*, HGB). It is also not equivalent to the term "entrepreneur" (*Unternehmer*) or "enterprise" (*Unternehmen*) used in the German VAT Act (C. Herrmann, G. Heuer, A. Raupach et al., *Einkommensteuergesetz. Kommentar*, sec. 15 (1003) (Otto Schmidt Verlag 2008)).
382. With respect to dividends, a distinction is made between private shareholdings and shareholdings held as business assets. Dividends derived by resident individual shareholders from private investments are subject to a final flat withholding tax, irrespective of the degree of participation, the holding period or the activity of the company. Expenses economically

6) rental income (section 21 of the EStG), and
7) miscellaneous income (sections 22, 23 of the EStG).

The last category is not an open-ended group encompassing sources that are not referred to in the previous provisions,[383] but includes a conclusive list of income items, which contains, among others, annuities and private short-term capital gains. If a taxpayer's income does not fall into any of the above-mentioned categories, it is not subject to income tax. Among financial benefits that are not covered by the list are gifts, bequests and lottery winnings.[384] Prizes are subject to tax only when they arise in connection with one of the income categories (for example, an architect creates a prize-winning item within his professional activity). If they are granted for personal achievements or a successful participation in an event (for example, tournament for amateur sportsmen, quiz show), they are not taxable.[385] Activities performed by a taxpayer that fall within more than one income category should be considered separately. However, if they are economically connected with one another, they should not be artificially split but treated according to their dominant element.[386]

The income categories are not of equal rank. There is a priority order among them. Income items are first allocated to the main income categories (*Haupteinkünftsarten*): agriculture, business, self-employment and employment. Within this group, business income is subordinated to income from agriculture and independent personal services: it is deemed to exist only if an activity does not meet the requirements of sections 13 and 18 of the EStG. If none of the four categories mentioned above is appropriate, income items may be assigned to the remaining three groups (*Nebeneinkünftsarten*).[387]

For the computation of taxable income, two different methods exist (*Dualismus der Einkünfteermittlung*). Section 2 (2) of the EStG divides the seven income categories into two types: profit categories (*Gewinneinkünfte*, categories 1 to 3) and surplus categories (*Überschusseinkünfte*, categories 4 to 7), and prescribes a different method for the determination of net income for either of them.[388] The main difference between these categories concerns capital gains and losses from the disposition of assets.

---

connected to the dividends are not deductible. An allowance of EUR 801 (*Sparer-Pauschbetrag*) is granted. Business income of individual shareholders is taxed under a partial-income system (*Teileinkünfteverfahren*): only 60% of dividends derived by resident individual shareholders are taxed, irrespective of the degree of participation, the holding period or the activity of the company. Correspondingly, only 60% of the expenses related to the dividends are deductible. *See* secs. 3 Nr. 40, 32d and 43(5) EStG.

Interest is also subject to the final flat withholding tax. If the interest income is attributable to the operation of a business, it is taxed as business income.

383. G. Niemeier et al., *Einkommensteuer*, p. 51 (Erich Fleischer Verlag 2009).
384. K. Tipke & J. Lang, *Steuerrecht*, sec. 8 (124), 21st ed. (Otto Schmidt Verlag 2013); H. Endriss et al., *Steuerkompendium, Band 1: Ertragsteuern*, p. 40 (NWB, 2007).
385. Herrmann et al., *supra* n. 381, at sec. 2 (80).
386. *Id.*, at sec. 2 (92); P. Kirchhof et al., *Einkommensteuergesetz. Kommentar*, sec. 2 (50) (Otto Schmidt Verlag 2011).
387. Niemeier, *supra* n. 383, at p. 50; Blümich, *supra* n. 139, at sec. 2 (52).
388. Blümich et al., *supra* n. 139, at sec. 2 (41).

Taxable income for profit categories is the profit accounted for on an accrual basis by way of comparing the tax balance sheet results for the current year with those for the preceding year (net worth comparison method, *Betriebsvermögensvergleich*).[389] Economic events are recognized regardless of when cash transactions occur. The profit calculation is based on generally accepted accounting standards (*Grundsätze ordnungsmäßiger Buchführung*), which are in turn based on commercial law (*Handelsgesetzbuch*, HGB). In the first place, the accounts have to be complete and faithful.[390] Profits that are not yet certain are not taken into account (the prudence principle), whereas losses are recognized when they are expected.[391] An increase in the value of business assets is not included in profits (the realization principle).[392] In Germany, there is a strong connection between tax and commercial accounting (*Maßgeblichkeit*). An interpretation by the Federal Tax Court holds that whenever there is an accounting choice, the taxpayer must use, for tax purposes, the option that results in a higher taxable income.[393] However, currently, there is a growing pressure on the legislature to delink the relationship between financial and tax accounting.[394]

The cash method (*Einnahmen-/Überschussrechnung*) may be used for profit categories by taxpayers who are neither under a legal obligation to keep the accounts nor keep them voluntarily.[395] The obligation to maintain accounting records could arise from tax or commercial law provisions.[396] Under the General Tax Code, entrepreneurs are required to keep the accounts if their profit and turnover exceed certain thresholds (EUR 60,000 and EUR 600,000 respectively). Neither tax nor commercial law imposes a bookkeeping obligation on independent service providers.

Net income from surplus categories is determined on a cash basis per calendar year by deducting income-related expenses from gross income. Gross income may take the form of cash or benefits in kind (*geldwerte Vorteile*). The value of the benefits in kind is determined as the price that the taxpayer would have to pay to purchase the same goods at the same place and at the same time.[397] Under the cash method, income and expenses are reported in the year that they are actually paid or received (*Zu- and Abflussprinzip*). *Überschusseinkünfte* follow the source theory as they capture revenue

389. Section 4 (1) and (5) EStG.
390. Section 239 HGB and sec. 146 AO.
391. Section 252 HGB.
392. Section 252 HGB.
393. Federal Financial Court (*Bundesfinanzhof*, BFH), February 3, 1969, GrS 2/68, BStBl. II S. 251; BFH, October 21, 1993, IV R 87/92, BFHE 172, 462, BStBl II 1994, 176.
394. Schön, *supra* n. 375, at sec. 10.1.
395. Section 4 (3) EStG.
396. Section 1 and 238 et seq. HGB and sec. 140 and 141 AO. According to the Commercial Code, people carrying on commercial business activity (*Handelsgewerbe*) are required to keep the accounts and prepare annual financial statements. Commercial business activities are any business activities, except those that do not require a commercial business operation. Whether such an operation is necessary depends on many quantitative and qualitative factors (range of business relations, use of external financing, number of employees, fixed assets, turnover, branches, size of business activity). *See* A. Baumach et al., *Handelsgesetzbuch*, sec. 1 (23) (C.H. Beck Verlag 2010).
397. Section 8 (2) EStG.

derived from certain sources but not the sources themselves (sales of assets used to earn income are not taxable).[398]

Under both methods, expenses incurred in producing taxable income are generally deductible. The condition is that they must be directly related to gross income.[399] Restrictions apply, in particular with respect to expenses of personal character (for example, gifts and the use of company cars for travelling from home to work). The costs of living are not deductible. This also applies to personal expenses that are also likely to support an individual's career.[400] An exception is made for expenses that can be allocated either to business or private use based on an objective and verifiable method.[401]

Losses may be fully set off against income arising in the same tax year (subject to certain restrictions). In general, losses up to EUR 1 million may be carried back to the preceding year, whereas the rest may be carried forward.[402] It is important to note that losses cannot be offset if they are generated by a hobby (*Liebhaberei*) as profits from a hobby remain non-taxable. German law does not know a provision similar to section 183 of the US IRC.[403] A hobby activity exists if an individual has no intention to make a profit.

The net results of all categories are aggregated.[404] The sum of net income is reduced by certain allowances (for example, for children, elderly taxpayers) as well as special and extraordinary hardship costs (*Sonderausgaben und aussergewöhnliche Belastungen*).[405] The general income tax rate is progressive and depends on the amount of income, whereby a tax-free threshold for the minimum standard of living (*Grundfreibetrag*) exists.[406] Income tax is assessed annually. The assessment period is the calendar year. However, taxpayers earning business income may choose a year which is different from the calendar year. Individual income tax is imposed at progressive rates ranging between 0% and 45%.

Germany does not have a CGT. Capital gains derived from the sale of business assets are treated as ordinary business income, whereas those from the selling of non-business assets generally remain tax free. There are however two exceptions.

398. Kirchhof, *supra* n. 386, at sec. 2 (28).
399. Endriss, *supra* n. 384, at p. 54.
400. Section 12 EStG.
401. R 12.1 of the Individual Income Tax Guidelines (*Einkommensteuerrichtlinien*). Administrative guidelines (*Richtlinien*) are non-statutory rules issued by the tax administration. Although they are only binding for lower-level tax administration, they are often used by taxpayers as guidance. A taxpayer who wishes to deviate from the guidelines must generally do so through court proceedings.
402. Section 10d EStG.
403. Section 183 of the IRC allows the deduction of hobby losses up to the amount of hobby profits.
404. An exception is private capital investment income (category five), which is taxed separately by way of a final flat withholding tax.
405. Special expenses are those incurred in connection with an individual's private lifestyle (e.g., education costs, life and health insurance contributions), which are acknowledged as deductible by tax law. By virtue of equity reasons, the legislator allows individuals to deduct unusual and inevitable expenses for personal purposes (e.g., high expenses for medical care, funerals, damages caused by violence) if they exceed expenses borne by a comparable group of taxpayers with a comparable income. *See* sec. 10 and 33 EStG.
406. The tax-free threshold for a single person was EUR 9,000 in 2018.

Gains derived from private transactions are taxable if their total amount exceeds EUR 600 during the tax year and they arise from the disposal of immovable property within ten years of the date of acquisition or other assets within one year of the acquisition date.[407]

[B] Virtual Currency Regulations in Germany

[1] Financial Supervision

In July 2013, the German Federal Financial Supervisory Authority (*Bundesanstalt für Finanzdienstleistungsaufsicht*, BaFin) issued a statement explaining the status of bitcoin for the purposes of the German Banking Act (*Kreditwesengesetz*, KWG).[408] The BaFin recognized bitcoin as a "unit of account," comparable to foreign exchange accounting units. Although bitcoin does not have legal tender status, it was considered similar to private or regional money.

Sometime later, BaFin issued an extensive opinion on the treatment of virtual currency for financial supervision purposes.[409] According to the BaFin opinion, virtual currencies are considered financial instruments. This legal classification applies to all currency schemes, irrespective of the software and encryption technologies they use. Virtual currencies that are not issued and managed by a central entity cannot be considered electronic money as they do not represent any claims on the issuer. The situation is different for digital means of payment which are backed by central entities. Such companies usually carry out e-money business pursuant to the German Payment Services Supervision Act (*Zahlungsdiensteaufsichtsgesetz*, ZAG). The use of virtual currency as means of payment and mining activities do not require authorization. However, a commercial handling of virtual currencies may trigger the authorization requirement under the German Banking Act.[410] Failure to obtain authorization generally constitutes a criminal offense.

On March 29, 2018, BaFin published an advisory letter in which it states its position on the regulatory classification of tokens for the purposes of securities

407. Section 23 EStG.
408. BaFin, *Hinweise zu Finanzinstrumenten nach § 1 Abs. 11 Satz 1 Nummern 1 bis 7 KWG (Aktien, Vermögensanlagen, Schuldtitel, sonstige Rechte, Anteile an Investmentvermögen, Geldmarktinstrumente, Devisen und Rechnungseinheiten)* (July 2013).
409. BaFin, *Virtual Currency*.
410. The German Banking Act implements the Basel Accords into German law. It is binding for banks (*Kreditinstitute*) and other institutes providing financial services (*Finanzdienstleistungsinstitute*). It regulates the provision of those banking and financial services for which a licence is required and constitutes the legal basis for the prudential supervision of credit and financial services institutions by the German Federal Financial Supervisory Authority and the German Federal Bank (*Deutsche Bundesbank*). The provisions of the Act cover not only licensing requirements but also the protection of liquidity and savings deposits as well as caps on bank employees' variable remuneration. The Banking Act contains numerous reporting obligations to be met by supervised institutions and requires banks to have a proper business organization.

supervision.[411] The key message of the advisory letter is that BaFin assesses on a case-by-case basis whether a token constitutes a financial instrument within the meaning of the German Securities Trading Act (*Wertpapierhandelsgesetz*, WpHG) or the Markets in Financial Instruments Directive (2004/39),[412] a security within the meaning of the German Securities Prospectus Act (*Wertpapierprospektgesetz*, WpPG), or a capital investment within the meaning of the German Capital Investment Act (*Vermögensanlagengesetz*, VermAnlG). Because of the large number of different token structures on the market, a general statement regarding their legal nature would be too sweeping. A supervisory classification is not possible without assessing all individual circumstances and features. The decisive factor is the rights that are associated with the respective token. A typological designation is not a determining factor, although a categorization—for example as an "investment token," "utility token" or "payment token"—may give an initial indication of the token type.

[2] Taxation

In June 2013, Frank Schäffler (a member of the German parliament) asked the Ministry of Finance about the income tax treatment of bitcoin transactions and bitcoin mining. The Ministry replied that bitcoin transactions may result in business income (section 15 of the EStG) and miscellaneous income (section 22(3) and 23 of the EStG).[413] In August 2013, the Ministry of Finance replied to two other questions raised by Frank Schäffler. In response to the first question, the Ministry of Finance admitted that it was not clear which valuation method (for example, FIFO, LIFO) should be applied to determine the taxable gain where bitcoins with different cost bases were held in the same wallet.[414] In its second letter, the Ministry considered bitcoins to be private money and stated that bitcoin transactions could not benefit from the VAT exemption.[415]

On January 5, 2018, the Ministry of Finance clarified some questions regarding the treatment of cryptocurrencies for tax and financial regulatory purposes in response to questions posed by some other members of the German parliament.[416] The Ministry confirmed that BaFin considers bitcoins to be financial instruments within the meaning of the German Banking Act. This classification means that exchange platforms are subject to BaFin supervision and regulations. In the Ministry's opinion, occasional mining activity may give rise to other income (*Einkünfte aus sonstigen Leistungen*) within the meaning of section 22(3) of the Individual Income Tax Act. Such income is tax-free up to the amount of EUR 256. Exchanges of virtual currency into another type

411. BaFin, *Initial Coin Offerings: Advisory letter on the classification of tokens as financial instruments* (March 29, 2018).
412. *Directive 2004/39/EC of the European Parliament and of the Council of 21 April 2004 on markets in financial instruments amending Council Directives 85/611/EEC and 93/6/EEC and Directive 2000/12/EC of the European Parliament and of the Council and repealing Council Directive 93/22/EEC.*
413. BMF, *Letter to Frank Schäffler* (June 20, 2013).
414. BMF, *Letter to Frank Schäffler* (August 7, 2013).
415. BMF, *Letter to Frank Schäffler* (August 7, 2013).
416. Deutsche Bundestag—19. Wahlperiode, Drucksache 19/370, question 24 and 25.

of virtual currency or legal currency within one year from its purchase may result in the application of section 23(1) of the Individual Income Tax Act (short-term capital gains). If the mining of or trading in virtual currency has a commercial character, it will generate business income. Regarding the VAT treatment of virtual currency transactions, the Ministry of Finance referred to the CJEU decision in *Hedqvist* (Case C-264/14).[417] According to the CJEU, the use of bitcoins as means of payment for goods and services is not taxable. Exchanges of bitcoins into legal currency are VAT exempt. As the CJEU decision did not mention mining activities in its decision, the Ministry of Finance concluded that the treatment of such activities for EU VAT purposes had not been clarified yet.

On February 27, 2018, the Ministry of Finance issued a circular in which it clarified the VAT treatment of virtual currency transactions.[418] In the circular, the Ministry confirmed the application of principles developed by the CJEU in the *Hedqvist* judgment to transactions involving bitcoins and similar virtual currency.[419] Accordingly, exchanges of virtual currency into legal currency are treated as exempt currency transactions. The transfer of bitcoins as payment for goods are services is treated in the same way as the transfer of legal currency (i.e., it is outside the VAT scope). If supplies of goods and services are remunerated by means of bitcoins, the taxable amount is the value of bitcoins in EUR determined by using the last exchange rate of the day when the transaction occurred. This rate has to be recorded by the supplier. Bitcoin mining is outside the VAT scope as it does not involve a reciprocal relationship. The provision of virtual currency wallets is an electronically supplied service, whereas the operation of exchange platforms constitutes the provision of IT infrastructure and services that cannot benefit from a VAT exemption. However, if the platform operator purchases and sells virtual currency in his own name, he may benefit from a VAT exemption.

[C] Taxation of Income from Virtual Currency Transactions

Having provided a brief description of the German tax system, it can be examined whether and to what extent virtual currency transactions may have income tax consequences. The following events involving virtual currency may have tax implications:

- exchanges of goods and services for virtual currency;
- exchanges of legal currency for virtual currency;
- exchanges of virtual currency for another virtual currency;
- currency mining;
- possession of virtual currency that appreciates in value;
- receipt of virtual currency (as a gift).

417. *See* §8.01[B][3] *Hedqvist* (Case C-264/14).
418. BMF, *Umsatzsteuerliche Behandlung von Bitcoin und anderen sog. virtuellen Währungen*, III C 3—S 7160-b/13/10001, 2018/0163969 (February 27, 2018).
419. *See* §8.01[B][3] *Hedqvist* (Case C-264/14).

Income from those activities is subject to tax only if it falls within one of the source categories (for example, business or miscellaneous income). This is examined in the following sections.

[1] Business Income

Section 15(2) of the EStG defines business activity as an independent repetitive activity that is undertaken with a profit motive and involves business relations with third parties. The activity may not qualify as agriculture, forestry, asset management or independent personal services.[420] The distinction between these groups is important as only business income is subject to business tax. Business activity may take many different forms: trade, production, supply of services—there are no restrictions on its type.[421] It does not require any capital investment. It is sufficient if the taxpayer's own work is the only input.[422]

Business income must be earned through transactions with other market participants (*Beteilgung am allgemeinen Wirtschaftsverkehr*).[423] The activity must be offered at the market against consideration which does not have to be a fixed price but may be performance-related.[424] It is sufficient if goods/services are offered to selected groups and not to the general public.[425] The market participation requirement is not met in the case of gifts, lottery winnings, income derived from self-performed services and utilization of self-owned property.[426] Thus, the receipt of virtual currency as a gift will not have any income tax consequences. As regards winnings, the Federal Tax Court (*Bundesfinanzhof*) distinguishes between games of chance (wagering, lottery, roulette) and those whose outcome depends on the skills of the player (Skat, Backgammon, and Poker).[427] The former do not result in taxable income due to the lack of a market exchange. A lottery fee is paid in return for the lottery participation and not for the drawn prize since the chance of winning depends on circumstances beyond the player's (and the organizer's) control. Consequently, a lottery win is given without any consideration. However, if a game result depends on the player's skills, the player can more or less influence it. He does not take a huge risk since players with better skills are likely to be more successful in the long run. There is a market exchange: the player pays his initial stake in return for other players promising him to give him their contributions in case he wins. The consideration he receives depends on the game outcome.[428]

All income derived from virtual currency exchange transactions is generated through market participation. Virtual currency is exchanged for legal currency, other

---

420. BFH, July 3, 1995, GrS 1/93, BStBl II 95, 617; Tipke & Lang, *supra* n. 384, at sec. 8 (414).
421. Niemeier, *supra* n. 383, at p. 630.
422. Blümich, *supra* n. 139, at sec. 15 (15-16).
423. Tipke & Lang, *supra* n. 384, at sec. 8 (413).
424. BFH, November 11, 1993, XI R 48/91.
425. Kirchhof, *supra* n. 386, at sec. 15 (30).
426. Tipke & Lang, *supra* n. 384, at sec. 8 (124); Kirchhof, *supra* n. 386, at sec. 2 (47).
427. BFH, November 11, 1993, XI R 48/91.
428. A. Schmidt-Liebig, *Einkommensteuerbarkeit und Einkunftsqualifikation von Spiel-und ähnlichen Gewinnen*, Steuer und Wirtschaft 2, p. 162 (1995).

type of virtual currency or goods and services offered by other market participants. It does not matter that (at least) one part of the transaction is in a non-monetary form. In barter transactions, the market value (*gemeiner Wert*) is generally used as valuation standard.[429]

It is questionable whether virtual currency mining involves market participation. It may seem that virtual currency miners perform a service: they solve complicated cryptographic algorithms to verify transactions and to prevent double spending. Those calculations require computer hardware, large amounts of electricity and a lot of processing power. In exchange for their services, miners may receive new units of virtual currency. However, not every miner is rewarded with new units. As more and more miners compete for a limited supply of blocks to verify, not everyone receives a reward for his mining efforts. In order to have a realistic chance to mine new currency units, one must invest in specialized equipment. If mining activity is carried out on a large scale (including the use of proper mining software and hardware), the miner has some (although limited) influence on the mining outcome. However, if a person intends to mine virtual currency with an ordinary computer, the mining activity resembles a game of chance given the extremely low likelihood of success. Winnings resulting from a game of chance are not subject to income tax as there is no market participation and the associated costs are not deductible.

The profit intention (*Einkünfteerzielungsabsicht*) is a desire to earn a favorable financial return on an activity.[430] It does not have to be the main reason for engaging into a transaction.[431] It may initially not be present, later appear and subsequently disappear.[432] As an inner component, the profit intention has to be determined on the basis of external circumstances.[433] A mere declaration of the intention to make profits is not sufficient.[434] The actual profit realization is not necessary; it merely implies that an activity is performed with a profit motive.[435] If losses are generated for a longer period, the taxpayer must take measures to improve his economic performance.[436] It is also necessary to estimate whether there are sound economic reasons to expect profits in the future (*positive Ergebnisprognose*). A mere chance to realize them is not sufficient.[437] The prediction can be based on business plans, cash-flow statements or other accounting documents. No minimum amount of profits is required; however, the amount should be economically relevant (unfortunately, the case law does not state what is "economically relevant").[438] Activities that are not undertaken for the purpose of making profits are regarded as a non-taxable hobby. To sum up, the following

429. For definition, *see* sec. 9 of the Valuation Act.
430. Niemeier, *supra* n. 383, at p. 52.
431. BFH, January 20, 2004, IV B 203/03, BStBl II 04, 355; Tipke & Lang, *supra* n. 384, at sec. 8 (414); Endriss, *supra* n. 384, at p. 69.
432. Blümich, *supra* n. 139, at sec. 15 (50).
433. L. Schmidt et al., *Einkommensteuergesetz. Kommentar*, sec. 2 (22) (C.H. Beck 2012); Blümich, *supra* n. 139, at sec. 15 (45); Niemeier, *supra* n. 383, at p. 51.
434. BFH, November 15, 1984, IV R 139/81, BStBl 1985 II, 205.
435. Endriss, *supra* n. 384, at p. 70.
436. L. Schmidt et al., *supra* n. 433, at sec. 2 (22).
437. BFH, March 2, 1994, VII R 59/92, BStBl II 96, 219.
438. BFH, June 26, 1985, IV R 149/83, BStBl II 85, 549.

circumstances imply that an activity is not undertaken with a profit motive: business misconduct (no measures taken despite heavy losses), no sound profit prediction, part-time activity, the use of income generated from other activities to cover losses and hobby character of an activity.[439] Profit intention has to be determined on a case-by case basis taking into consideration the principles outlined above. There are no general monetary thresholds above which a profit intention would be assumed.

Mining and selling virtual currency may be regarded as a pastime. There are people who want to experiment with innovative payment technologies while pursuing other careers for their income-earning purposes. They are unable to predict whether and how much income they will generate from their activities in virtual currency. For some taxpayers who occasionally buy and sell virtual currency, the trade may be motivated by curiosity and not by monetary reasons. Thus, in some cases, the profit intention is likely to be denied. A strong indication of the profit intention is the volume of sales activity. A person that trades in virtual currency on a large scale and generates a significant amount of revenue is likely to have a profit motive.

The burden of proof regarding the profit intention rests on the tax authorities. If they want to tax profits derived from transactions in virtual currency, they must come forward with evidence that the activities ceased to be a mere hobby and became an income-generating activity.[440] However, if a taxpayer wants to deduct losses from his transactions in virtual currency, he must prove that he is engaged in business activity.

Other requirements of business activity are independence and repetitive character. An activity is independent if the taxpayer acts in his own name and on his own account.[441] He must bear business risk and develop business initiative. Repetitive character (*Nachhaltigkeit*) requires an activity be performed regularly or at least with an intention to repeat it.[442] It is not sufficient that a taxpayer purchases inputs needed for the activity on a regular basis. He must have the intention to make the activity a permanent income source. The activity need not be performed continuously. It may be performed occasionally or temporary. However, the taxpayer must have the intention to repeat it when an appropriate opportunity appears.[443]

There are two methods of net business income determination: cash method (*Einnahmen-Überschussrechnung*) and accrual method (*Betriebsvermögensvergleich*). Transactions in virtual currency may trigger the obligation of keeping the accounts and applying the accrual method if they result in turnover being higher than EUR 600,000 and profit exceeding EUR 60,000. Below those thresholds, the cash method can be used to determine the net amount of income from transactions in virtual currency. Under this method, revenues are recorded during the period they are received and expenses in the period, in which they are actually paid (*Zu- and Abflussprinzip*).

---

439. N. Braun, *Objektivierung der Gewinnerzielungsabsicht bei der Liebhaberei*, 55 Betriebsberater 6, p. 283 (2000).
440. Schmidt et al., *supra* n. 433, at sec. 15 (35).
441. Niemeier, *supra* n. 383, at p. 631; Tipke & Lang, *supra* n. 384, at sec. 8 (413).
442. Niemeier, *supra* n. 383, at p. 632; Tipke & Lang, *supra* n. 384, at sec. 8 (413); Schmidt et al., *supra* n. 433, at sec. 15 (17).
443. Hermann et al., *supra* n. 381, at sec. 15 (1040).

Business-related expenses can be deducted from the gross income. A division of expenses between expenses caused by business and private motives must be made on a case-by-case basis by weighing all the individual circumstances. If a clear allocation to a private or business sphere is not possible, no deduction is allowed.[444] Business income is taxed at progressive rates ranging between 0% and 45% and is also subject to business tax.

[2] Miscellaneous Income

Miscellaneous income comprises various categories. One of them are gains derived from disposal of assets if the time period between the purchase and sale of the asset does not exceed one year and the total profits from such transactions exceed EUR 600.[445] Disposals may be both barter and sales transactions.[446] The term "asset" (*Wirtschaftsgut*) is very broad. It includes all benefits (both tangible and intangible) which are capable of valuation and can be used for a longer period.[447] Objects of everyday life that are not likely to increase in value are excluded from the scope of this provision.[448]

Virtual currencies are capable of valuation on the basis of the daily exchange rates. As almost every type of virtual currency has value, those objects can be regarded as assets for the purposes of section 23 of the EStG. They cannot fall within the excluded category of objects of everyday life given their significant volatility and price fluctuations. An exclusion cannot be applied to objects that are likely to increase in value.

The gain is determined as the difference between the purchase and sales price of the asset. In the case of self-generated virtual currency, the purchase price may include the software, hardware and Internet costs as expenses necessary to obtain the currency unit.[449] If a person has virtual currency from different sources (i.e., currency both

444. BFH, September 21, 2009, GrS 1/06, BStBl II 10, 672.
445. Section 22 No. 2 and 23(1) No. 2 EStG.
446. Schmidt et al., *supra* n. 433, at sec. 23 (50) and (71).
447. Blümich, *supra* n. 139, at sec. 23 (62-63); H 4.2. (1) of the Individual Income Tax Guidelines.
448. Section 23(1) No. 2 EStG.
449. P. Eckert, *Steuerliche Betrachtung elektronisher Zahlungsmittel am Beispiel sog. Bitcoin-Geschäfte*, Der Betrieb 38, sec. IV.1 (2013). The sale of self-made assets is not subject to income tax under sec. 23 of the EStG. To fall within the scope of this provision, an asset must be purchased. The term "purchase" is to be interpreted broadly and does not require a reciprocal or any other legal relationship. An asset received through a barter transaction is also deemed to be purchased. However, assets that were received free of charge are excluded from the scope of the provision (Blümich, *supra* n. 139, at sec. 23 (91-97). In the author's view, the receipt of virtual currency through mining could be seen as a currency purchase within the meaning of sec. 23 of the EStG as the miner incurs costs to obtain the currency. However, a different view was expressed by the Finance Ministry of Hamburg (*Finanzministerium/ Finanzbehörde der Freien und Hansestadt Hamburg*) and the Regional Tax Office North Rhine-Westphalia (*Oberfinanzdirektion Nordrhein-Westfalen*) in their opinions on the income tax treatment of virtual currency. *See* Finance Ministry of Hamburg, *Ertragsteuerliche Behandlung des Handels mit Bitcoins auf der privaten Vermögenssphäre*, S 2256—2017/003-52 (December 11, 2017) and Regional Tax Office North Rhine-Westphalia, *Ertragsteuerliche Behandlung von virtuellen Währungen (Kryptowährungen)* (April 20, 2018).

purchased at different exchange rates and self-generated), he may use the first-in first-out (FIFO) method, under which the oldest items are recorded as sold first, but this do not necessarily mean that they are actually sold first.[450]

To sum up, miscellaneous income includes private short-term capital gains from disposals of virtual currency within a year from its purchase if the total profit from disposal of private assets has exceeded the threshold of EUR 600 in a calendar year. If sales of virtual currency are seen as business activity resulting in business income, the miscellaneous income provision cannot be applied.

Another type of miscellaneous income that could be relevant for virtual currency transactions is other income as defined in section 22(3) of the EStG. According to this provision, income not covered by any other income category may be considered miscellaneous income if it exceeds EUR 256 per year. Occasional mining activity that does not meet the requirements of commercial business activity and does not resemble a game of chance could fall into this category. Occasional sales transactions are likely to be covered by section 23 of the EStG (short-term private capital gains) that takes priority.

[D] Conclusion

German income tax law is schedular in nature. It imposes income tax on seven categories of receipts. Receipts that do not fall within any of the categories are not subject to income tax. Under German law, it does not matter whether income is generated in a monetary or non-monetary form. The latter is subject to tax based on the rules for benefits in kind. Transactions in virtual currency may result in business income or miscellaneous income. Income from both sources is aggregated and taxed at the progressive rates ranging from 0% to 45%.

Business activity requires an independent repetitive activity that involves market participation and a profit motive. Trading in or mining virtual currency on a large scale that requires a commercial business operation may give rise to business income (section 15 of the EStG). If a taxpayer's mining or trading activity constitutes business income, the income resulting therefrom is also subject to business tax. If a taxpayer attempts to mine virtual currency without using proper equipment, the mining activity resembles a game of chance given the extremely low likelihood of success. Winnings from a game of change are not taxable and the associated costs are not deductible.

If a taxpayer's activity does not qualify as business, transactions in virtual currency may result in miscellaneous income. Miscellaneous income includes short-term private capital gains (section 23 of the EStG) which are taxable if the time period between the purchase and sale of the asset does not exceed one year and the total gain from disposals of private assets has exceeded EUR 600 in a calendar year. If a

450. Schmidt et al., *supra* n. 433, at sec. 23 (22); Finance Ministry of Hamburg, *supra* n. 449; Regional Tax Office North Rhine-Westphalia, *supra* n. 449.

taxpayer's receipts from transaction in virtual currency or virtual currency mining cannot be considered short-term capital gains or business income, they may be considered another type of miscellaneous income (other income as defined in section 22(3) of the EStG) provided that they exceed EUR 256 per year.

The German Ministry of Finance has provided some guidance on the tax treatment of virtual currency transactions. In response to questions posed by some members of the German parliament, the Ministry clarified that transactions in virtual currency (including currency mining) may result in business or miscellaneous income. The Ministry also issued a circular on the application of VAT to virtual currency transactions in which it confirmed the principles developed by the CJEU in the *Hedqvist* judgment.

§5.04 THE NETHERLANDS

[A] Basic Features of the Income Tax System

Dutch individual income tax (*inkomstenbelasting*) is levied on the basis of the Individual Income Tax Act of 2001 (*Wet inkomstenbelasting*, IB). The income tax was radically reformed in 2001; the reform brought about a schedular system with different rates for each income category and the abolition of the net wealth tax. Until 2001, all income was added together and the tax was levied on the total using one rate structure.[451]

Income tax is levied on the worldwide income of individuals resident in the Netherlands. There is no clear definition of residence in the Dutch tax law. Under section 4 of the General Tax Act of 1959 (*Algemene wet inzake rijksbelastingen*, AWR), residence is to be determined "according to the circumstances," such as the availability of a permanent home, the place where the spouse and under-aged children live and the place of personal and economic relations (for example, the place of employment).[452] In general, an individual is deemed to reside in a country if he is physically present there. A resident of the Netherlands who leaves the country without becoming a resident of another state and returns within one year is deemed to have remained resident for this entire period.[453]

Under the schedular tax system effective as from January 1, 2001, taxable income is divided into three categories known as "boxes." A different method of income calculation and a different tax rate apply to each box.[454] Income that does not fall within any of the boxes is not taxable. Among financial benefits that are not covered by the list are gifts, bequests and lottery winnings. The three categories (boxes) are:

451. P. Siekman & N. Luijsterburg, *Personal Income Taxation in the Netherlands*, 60 Bull. Intl. Taxn. 8, p. 316 (2006).
452. R. Offermanns, *The Netherlands*, sec. 1.1 in: *Global Individual Tax Handbook* (IBFD 2017).
453. Section 2. IB.
454. L.G.M. Stevens, *Elementair belastingrecht voor economen en bedrijfsjuristen—Theorieboek*, sec. 4.1, 28th ed., (Kluwer 2012).

- Box 1: income from labor and owner-occupied dwelling (*belastbaar inkomen uit werk en woning*), which includes income from the following sources: present and past employment, business activities, other activities, periodical payments and owner-occupied dwellings;[455]
- Box 2: capital gains and other income from a substantial shareholding in a company (*belastbaar inkomen uit aanmerkelijk belang*);[456]
- Box 3: income from savings and investments / net wealth income (*belastbaar inkomen uit sparen en beleggen*).[457]

Within Box 1, a special provision applies to owner-occupied property. Such property is taxed at a notional rental value assessed according to the statutory tables. This applies only to the main residence; second homes and other property fall under Box 3. The net results of the various income sources of Box 1 are aggregated and then personal deductions (*persoonsgbonden aftrek*)[458] and progressive rates are applied. Box 1 income is subject to tax rates ranging from 8.9% to 52%.

Income from substantial shareholdings that falls within Box 2 is taxed at the flat rate of 25%. A substantial shareholding exists if the taxpayer owns alone or together with his spouse, directly or indirectly, at least 5% of the issued share capital in a company with a capital divided into shares.

Income from Box 3 includes all types of income from capital other than income derived from a dwelling, dividends and capital gains from substantial shareholding (which are taxed in Box 1 and 2). Before January 1, 2017, Box 3 assets were deemed to produce an annual notional yield of 4%. This notional yield was taxed at a flat rate of 30%, resulting in an effective tax of 1.2% on the annual average value of the net assets. With effect from January 1, 2017, Box 3 taxation is based on a weighted notional yield on net assets. The weighted notional yield is assigned to fictional "savings" and fictional "investment" portions of the assets which are subsequently taxed at the flat rate of 30%. For 2018, the weighted notional yield and the effective tax rate are presented in Table 5.2.[459]

455. Section 3.1-3.157 IB.
456. Section 4.1-4.53 IB.
457. Section 5.1-5.23 IB.
458. Personal deduction (sec. 6.1 of the IB) consist of expenses that reduce a person's ability to pay (e.g., educational expenses, medical expenses). It is first subtracted from income from Box 1. Any reminder can be deducted from the income from Box 3. If there is still a portion left, it can be deducted from income from Box 2 (Stevens, *supra* n. 454, at sec. 4.3.a.).
459. Section 5.2. IB.

Table 5.2 Box 3 Taxation in the Netherlands

Net value of Assets (EUR)			*Weighted Notional Savings Yield (0.36%)*	*Weighted Notional Investment Yield (5.38%)*	*Total Notional Yield (%)*	*Effective Tax Rate (%)*
0	–	70,800	67	33	2.017	0.605
70,800	–	978,000	21	79	4.326	1.2978
Over		978,000	0	100	5.38	1.614

The assets and debts are valued at the market value that they have on January 1. A personal tax exemption applies to income from Box 3. The exempt standard amount for 2018 is EUR 30,000.[460] A number of assets are specifically exempt from Box 3 taxation. The exemption includes, for example, short-term periodical income received in installments during a period of less than a year on an asset owned by the taxpayer and amounts up to EUR 527 in cash.[461]

With respect to portfolio dividends (i.e., dividends from a taxpayer's shareholding that is less than 5%) that fall within Box 3, income tax is not levied on the amount of dividends received. Gross dividend income (including the withholding tax) does not form part of the taxpayer's taxable income from savings and investments, but the shares are classified as Box 3 assets. Similarly, interest received is not subject to income tax as such. Instead, the instruments on which the interest income arises are classified as Box 3 assets and taxed accordingly.

There is an order of priority where the sources of income overlap: an item of income is considered to belong to the category of income first mentioned in the Income Tax Act 2001. The order of priority applies not only among the boxes but also within a particular box.[462] Thus, if income qualifies both as income from business (Box 1) and from a substantial shareholding (Box 2), it is deemed business income. If income qualifies as both income from business and income from employment, it is deemed business income. Furthermore, net assets (whether or not exempt) which generate taxable income in Box 1 or 2 are not included when determining the deemed yield for the purposes of Box 3.[463]

Income from all boxes is determined separately and not aggregated; a negative result of one box cannot be set off against a positive result of another. Only income from Box 1 and 2 may result in a loss.[464] The income tax due is calculated on the sum of income from all three boxes (*verzamelinkomen*).[465] A tax credit is granted against

460. Section 5.5. IB.
461. Section 5.10d and 5.12 IB.
462. Section 2.14 IB.
463. Section 2.14 IB.
464. Offermanns, *supra* n. 452, at sec. 1.8.
465. Section 2.18 of the IB; R.E.C.M. Niessen et al., *De Wet inkomstenbelasting 2001 met hoofdzaken loonbelasting,* sec. 3.0.4 (Sdu 2012); P. Kavelaars et al., *Inkomstenbelasting: inclusief hoofdzaken loonbelasting en premieheffing,* sec. 2.5, 8th ed. (Kluwer 2012).

the total amount of tax due. It is comprised of a general rebate (*algemene heffingskorting*) and supplementary ones (for example, for single parents, the handicapped and the elderly).[466]

Capital gains are not taxed in the hands of private individuals with the exception of capital gains from a substantial shareholding in a company (Box 2). Gains derived in the course of business are taxed as a part of ordinary business income.[467] Before the Income Tax Act 2001 came into force, the absence of capital gains taxation and the relatively high tax rates applicable to ordinary income constituted a strong incentive for taxpayers to try to convert ordinary income into a tax-free capital gain or into a substantial interest gain (that was taxed at 20%). The new statute eliminated such avoidance tactics by the introduction of deemed taxation of capital income and by subjecting both income and capital gains to the same 25% rate in substantial interest cases.[468]

Taxable income is computed on a cash basis (*kasstelsel*), except for business income and income from other activities which is usually determined on an accrual basis (*vorderingenstelsel*). Under the former, revenue and expenses are recognized when they are received or paid, whereas under the latter, economic events are recognized irrespective of when the cash transaction occurs.[469] Income is received when it has been put at the disposal of the taxpayer or when it can be claimed and collected without any further difficulty. Income in kind is taken into account at the market value. If the benefit cannot be exchanged for cash or it is unusual to do so, the value is estimated or based on the amount saved by the taxpayer (for example, in the case of free living).[470]

The taxable period is the calendar year. For an entrepreneur, a deviating book year may be applied.[471] The latter applies as long as the taxpayer keeps accounts on a regular basis and the nature of business justifies a deviating financial year.

[B] Virtual Currency Regulations in the Netherlands

The Dutch Finance Ministry (*Ministerie van Financiën*) presented its first opinion on Bitcoin in a letter of April 10, 2013.[472] According to this letter, Bitcoin cannot be regarded as traditional money since it lacks central supervision and stability. Neither can it be treated as electronic money or financial product. The letter also mentions that taxpayers engaged in Bitcoin trading and mining are subject to the general tax rules.

466. Niessen, *supra* n. 465, at sec. 3.0.3; Stevens, *supra* n. 454, at sec. 4.4.a.
467. A.J. van Soest et al., *Belastingen: inkomstenbelasting, vennootschapsbelasting, besluit voorkoming dubbele belasting 2001*, p. 54, 23rd ed. (Kluwer 2007).
468. K. van Raad, *The Netherlands*, sec. 5.1 in: H.J. Ault & B.J. Arnold, *Comparative Taxation: A Structural Analysis* (Kluwer Law International 2010).
469. Niessen, *supra* n. 465, at sec. 2.0.7; Stevens, *supra* n. 454, at sec. 4.3.e.
470. Section 144 IB.
471. Section 3.66 IB.
472. Finance Ministry (*Ministerie van Financiën*), *Antwoord van de Minister van Financiën op vragen van het lid Nijboer (PvdA) aan de minister van Financiën over de opkomst van de Bitcoin als digitale betaaleenheid (ingezonden 10 april 2013)*.

On May 28, 2018, the Finance Ministry answered some fundamental tax questions about virtual currency in a letter to the upper house of parliament.[473] The letter observes that the tax treatment of activities depends on whether they form a "source of income." If this is the case, the activities will be subject to Box 1 taxation. It needs to be determined on a case-by-case basis whether virtual currency mining may constitute a source of income. If the result of mining activity is not influenced by the labor performed, mining will be a speculative non-taxable transaction. However, if the outcome of the mining process can be attributable to labor performed, a source of income will be deemed to exist. If Box 1 taxation is not applicable, virtual currency will be treated as Box 3 asset and taxed accordingly. The letter also observes that wages paid in virtual currency are considered benefits in kind and, for wage tax purposes, virtual currency must be converted into EUR at the moment the wage is enjoyed. If a business receives a payment for the provision of goods and services in virtual currency, it must convert it into EUR for the purposes of profit determination. Virtual currency may be considered current assets or inventory and valued at the lower of cost and market value for balance sheet purposes.

The Dutch tax authorities (*Belastingdienst*) indicate on their website that bitcoins and other virtual means of payment are Box 3 assets and their value as at January 1 should be taken into account in calculating Box 3 income.[474]

The Netherlands Authority for the Financial Markets (*Autoriteit Financiële Markten*, AFM), which is the financial services regulatory authority for the Netherlands (a SEC-comparable institution), published several documents on the subject of virtual currency.[475] In November 2017, AFM issued several warnings about investing in virtual currency and ICOs.[476]

[C] Taxation of Income from Virtual Currency Transactions

Having provided a brief description of the Dutch tax system, it can be examined whether and to what extent virtual currency transactions may have income tax consequences. The following events involving virtual currency may have tax implications:

- exchanges of goods and services for virtual currency;
- exchanges of legal currency for virtual currency;
- exchanges of virtual currency for another virtual currency;
- currency mining;
- possession of virtual currency that appreciates in value;
- receipt of virtual currency (as a gift).

473. Finance Ministry, *Beantwording vragen vaste CIE Financiën fiscale aspected cryptovaluta* (May 28, 2018).
474. Belastingdienst, *Overige Bezittingen*.
475. AFM, *Virtuele valuta's*; and *Wat is blockchaintechnologie?*
476. AFM, *Reële risico's bij cryptocurrencies* (November 13, 2017); and *AFM waarschuwt voor grote risico's bij Initial Coin Offerings* (November 13, 2017).

Income from these activities is subject to tax only if it falls within one of the boxes. The following sections first examine whether income from virtual currency activities could be considered Box 1 income. They discuss the general characteristics of income items in Box 1 (the income concept) and two income sources (business income and miscellaneous income). Subsequently, Box 3 taxation (income from savings and investment) is discussed.

[1] Income Concept

Dutch tax law does not contain a definition of the term "income." The notion of income was influenced by several income theories, the most important of which was the source theory (*Bronnentheorie*).[477] Under this concept, a benefit may be regarded as income if it comes from a permanent source (*bron*).[478] The disposition of the source itself is not taxable.[479] A "source of income" exists in situations where the taxpayer engages in an economic activity with the intention to derive a benefit therefrom and where such benefit can be reasonably expected to materialize. Thus, the following three requirements must be met:

- participation in economic life (*deelname aan het economische verkeer*);
- intention to obtain income (*voordeel beogen*) (subjective criterion);
- a reasonable income expectation (*voordeel verwachten*) (objective criterion).[480]

The first criterion (participation in economic life) implies that an individual has to offer goods or services on the market for consideration. He has to make it visible to others that he is willing to exchange these goods and services.[481] There must be a reciprocal relationship between the parties engaged in the transaction.[482] Illegal activities are also a form of participation in the economic life. Under the principle of fiscal neutrality, it is irrelevant for income tax purposes whether income is generated in a lawful or unlawful manner.[483] According to some decisions of the Dutch Supreme Court (*Hoge Raad*), the first criterion is decisive for establishing whether a source of income exists as neither subjective intention nor expectations (the second and third criterion) influence the ability to pay. A benefit obtained from participation in economic life should be subject to tax, irrespectively of whether it was intended or not.[484] The second and third criteria are relevant in cases where no profit has been generated yet, transactions may have speculative nature or may be performed in a

477. Van Raad, *supra* n. 468, at sec. 5.1.
478. The *Bronnentheorie* is reflected in the structure of Box 1, which names five sources of income.
479. Kavelaars, *supra* n. 465, at sec. 0.12b; Niessen, *supra* n. 465, at sec. 2.0.7.
480. Niessen, *supra* n. 465, at sec. 2.0.7; Stevens, *supra* n. 454, at sec. 4.3.b; HR, October 23, 1923, B. 3307; HR, January 25, 1933, B. 5365; HR, November 26, 1930, B. 4857.
481. Kavelaars, *supra* n. 465, at sec. 0.12b.
482. J.E.A.M. van Dijk, *Vermogensbeheer*, WFR 1976/5258.
483. HR, June 20, 1951, B. 9055; HR, June 24, 1992, 27327, BNB 1993/18; HR, June 24, 1992, 28156, BNB 1993/19.
484. HR, October 3, 1990, BNB 1990/329; HR, April 14, 1993, 28847, BNB 1993/203.

private capacity. The function of the profit-related criteria is to prevent deductions of expenses in situations that are not likely to produce any income.[485]

All income derived from virtual currency disposals is generated through market participation. Virtual currency is offered for sale (for legal currency or other type of virtual currency) to anyone who is potentially interested in purchasing it. However, it is questionable whether there is market participation in the case of currency mining. Miners do not engage in reciprocal transactions with other market participants. They use their resources (software and hardware) to verify blocks of transactions and may be remunerated for their efforts with new units of virtual currency. They cannot be sure that their efforts will be remunerated although the more powerful equipment they use, the greater the chance that they receive new units of virtual currency. Thus, market participation may not always be present in the case of virtual currency mining.

The second and third criteria (profit intention and reasonable profit expectation) are related to each other. Although subjective in nature, the profit intention must be deduced from the objective facts and not from the statements by the taxpayer.[486] The profit expectation is reasonable when it is supported by factual circumstances and the profit occurrence is viable from the point of view of a rational person.[487] The judicial interpretation of these requirements is very broad. For example, the Supreme Court (*Hoge Raad*) ruled that the collector of mammoth bones who created a complete mammoth skeleton and sold it to a museum may be considered as having a reasonable profit expectation. Income may arise if the taxpayer does not expect any profits, but the objective facts imply that such profits can be realized.[488]

Profit expectations and motives are of vital relevance in cases concerning activities mainly regarded as hobbies. In general, incidental benefits from a hobby or amateur sport are not taxable and the related expenses are not deductible.[489] A comparison of costs and benefits is frequently used to distinguish commercial activities from non-taxable pastimes. A hobby is deemed to exist if the expenses are likely to exceed the revenue in the long run.[490]

Thus, to determine whether virtual currency mining is an income-generating activity or a non-taxable hobby, it is necessary to consider the amount of revenue and losses (together with the prospect of their recovery), the time devoted to the activity and the investment made. In the case of a miner whose expenses continuously exceed the revenue obtained, no reasonable profit expectation can be assumed.[491]

485. HR, April 14, 1993, 28847, BNB 1993/203; R.E.C.M. Niessen, *Algemene en bijzondere bronkenmerken*, Weekblad voor Fiscaal Recht 3, p. 4 (1997).
486. HR, February 22, 1978, BNB 1978/194.
487. Kavelaars, *supra* n. 465, at sec. 3.4.2a; Stevens, *supra* n. 454, at sec. 4.3.c.
488. HR, February 27, 2009, V-N 2009/18.27.
489. Hof Arnhem, June 27, 1983, no. 645/1982, BNB 1985/9.
490. H. Mobach, *Cursus belastingrecht: Inkomstenbelasting*, sec. 3.4.3.B.b5.I (Deventer Gouda Quint 2011). *See also* Hof's-Gravenhage, November 21, 1996, no. 95/1035, FED 1997/117. The case concerned an accountant who also played in an amateur music band. As amounts earned from incidental performances did not exceed the costs, the court concluded that the activity was outside the scope of income tax law.
491. However, the miner must have an opportunity to provide evidence of objective facts that imply that profits may be realized.

No profit expectations can be assumed in the case of speculative dealings where the outcome of the transaction depends exclusively on circumstances beyond the taxpayer's control.[492] This does not apply if speculative transactions are carried out as a part of business activities of an entrepreneur.[493] The Supreme Court applied this reasoning in the case concerning pyramid schemes.[494] It ruled that participants of such schemes could not have had any reasonable profit expectations due to the speculative character of their dealings. This did not apply to the organizers who were held to derive business income. In the author's view, virtual currency mining cannot be regarded as a purely speculative transaction as it does not depend exclusively on factors beyond the miner's control. Miners can increase their changes of receiving new unit of virtual currency by employing more powerful equipment. Thus, it needs to be determined on a case-by-case basis whether virtual currency mining may be considered a source of income.

[2] Business Income

Section 3.2 of the IB stipulates that "taxable business profits are the total amount of profits which the taxpayer as an entrepreneur derives from one or more enterprises less the entrepreneur deduction." The IB defines the term "entrepreneur" (*ondernemer*) as the person for whose account a business is carried on and who is directly liable for the obligations entered into with respect to the business.[495] The IB does not provide a definition of the term "business" (*onderneming*), but the jurisprudence of the Supreme Court indicates that a business is an organization of capital and labor with certain degree of permanence, which participates in the market with the intention of making a profit.[496] Points of particular interest are: the way the activities are organized, their extent, the period in which the activities are performed, the amount of the profits, the presentation towards clients and suppliers, the risks borne and the level of investment made by an individual.[497] A series of unrelated transactions cannot be classified as durable even if all of them generate profits.[498] The Supreme Court decided that a freelance journalist working for various principals cannot be considered as maintaining a durable organization of labor and capital.[499]

The required degree of permanence does not mean that transactions have to be performed on a continuous basis. For example, permanence is assumed if transactions are repeated seven times over a three-and-a-half-year period.[500] There are no precise statutory limits on how much time must be spend on business activity per week;

492. HR, January 18, 1967, BNB 1967/71.
493. Stevens, *supra* n. 454, at sec. 4.3.c.
494. HR, February 1, 2002, no. 35848, 36238 and 36668, BNB 2002/127-129. A pyramid scheme is a business model that involves promising participants payments for enrolling other people into the scheme.
495. Section 3.4 IB.
496. HR, January 11, 1989, BNB 1989/63.
497. Belastingdiesnt, *Wanneer bent u ondernemer voor de inkomstenbelasting?*
498. H. Mobach, *Cursus belastingrecht, Inkomstenbelasting, supra* n. 490, at sec. 3.2.2.B.b.
499. HR, September 6, 1995, no. 30237, BNB 1995/298.
500. Hof Arnhem, March 29, 2004, NTFR 2004/649.

however, according to Niessen (2012), it can be deduced from the case law that at least ten hours a week and two-third of the minimum salary should be generated from business activities.[501] The case law of the Supreme Court on the permanence of business activities is not always consistent. In the case involving a candidate notary who took care of a notary office for a period of one year after the death of the notary, the Supreme Court ruled that no business was carried out because of the short period of the activities (despite the fact that the notary practice was carried out for the account and risk of the candidate notary).[502]

An individual who carries on an independent profession also qualifies as a person for whose account a business is carried on.[503] The rules for taxation of professional income are the same as for taxation of business income. A definition of the term "profession" is not included in Dutch statutory tax law. According to the case law, one of the main characteristics of a profession is that considerable time is spent carrying out the activities; the use of one's skills, personal qualities and labor are decisive while capital input is not required.[504]

The most important requirement for entrepreneurship, which distinguishes it from employment, is independence. This criterion is met if an individual carries out activities in his own name and assumes any responsibility and risk.[505] The main difference between wealth management (Box 3) and business is that in the case of the latter, the taxpayer must perform work to make his property profitable. There must be a causal connection between the profit and this work.[506]

Transactions in virtual currency and currency mining may give rise to business income if the taxpayer maintains a durable organization of labor and capital. The Dutch tax law sets high requirements to assume the presence of an enterprise since it offers various incentives for entrepreneurs.[507] Only those for whom virtual currency activities have become a regular source of income could fall under the scope of the entrepreneurship rules. In evaluation the entrepreneur status, the following factors are considered: the amount of investment (both in terms of time and money), the risk borne and the revenue obtained.

Business profits have to be calculated in accordance with the principles of sound business practice (*goed koopmansgebruik*), including a consistent policy, independent of its possible fiscal consequences. The taxpayer can use any calculation method which is in accordance with the business practice, unless it contravenes a tax regulation.[508] In calculating the annual profit, the principle of prudence has to be taken into account.

501. Niessen, *supra* n. 465, at sec. 5.2.
502. HR, December 5, 1990, BNB 1991/38.
503. Section 3.5 of IB.
504. HR, November 20, 1968, BNB 1969/13.
505. Niessen, *supra* n. 465, at sec. 5.2.
506. H. Mobach, *Cursus belastingrecht: Inkomstenbelasting, supra* n. 490, at sec. 3.2.2.B.d.d1.
507. These are: self-employed allowance (*zelfstandigenaftrek*), research and development deduction (*aftrek voor speur- en ontwikkelingswerk*), start-up allowance (*startersaftrek*) and cooperation deduction (*meewerkaftrek*). Under sec. 3.6 of the IB, many of those deductions are not allowed if entrepreneurs do not work for a sufficient number of hours (*urencriterium*). *See* Belastingdienst, *Urencriterium*.
508. HR, May 8, 1957, BNB 1957/208.

This principle implies that profits which have not been realized yet should be excluded whereas losses may be included at the moment they are expected but not realized.[509] In the Netherlands, the rules on tax and commercial accounting diverge substantially to reflect different aims of these two sets of provisions. Commercial accounting rules are to provide information necessary to judge the financial policy and operations of a business undertaking, while tax accounting rules aim to determine the basis for tax payable to the government.[510]

The total profit is usually calculated according to the wealth comparison method (*vermogensvergelijking*), under which the balance sheet value at the end of a taxable period must be reduced by its value at the beginning of the period and adjusted for any contributions (*stortingen*) and withdrawals (*onttrekkingen*).[511] For balance sheet purposes, virtual currency may be treated as current assets and inventory and be valued at the lower of cost and market value. The cash method is only allowed for small businesses which cannot be reasonably expected to have a bookkeeping system[512] and for freelancers with activities on a limited scale.[513] It is more commonly applied by taxpayers having income from other activities, which is calculated in the same way as business profit.[514]

All expenses incurred in the course of business are deductible, irrespective of whether they were necessary in the view of the tax authorities. In other words, the tax authorities may not interfere in business policy: they are not allowed to make a judgment as to whether the expenses were reasonable.[515] Expenses incurred in respect of the acquisition of the income source itself are not deductible.[516] Other limitations on expenses deductibility are contained in sections 3.14-3.17 of the IB.[517]

[3] Income from Other Activities

Under section 3.90 of the IB, income derived from other activities (*belastbaar resultaat uit overige werkzaamheden*) is subject to tax. The aim of this provision is to capture all benefits derived from one's labor exercised outside the framework of an employment contract or business enterprise.[518]

As the term "*werkzaamheid*" is not defined in the Income Tax Act 2011, it is necessary to revert to the general source criteria. Thus, other activities are activities

509. R. Offermanns, *The Entrepreneurship Concept in a European Comparative Law Perspective* p. 41 (Kluwer Law International 2002).
510. Van Raad, *supra* n. 452, at sec. 9.1.
511. Kavelaars, *supra* n. 465, at sec. 3.2.8c; Stevens, *supra* n. 454, at sec. 6.4d.
512. HR, February 24, 1960, no. 14197, BNB 1960/84.
513. HR, December 7, 1966, no. 15657, BNB 1967/37.
514. H. Mobach, *Cursus belastingrecht: Inkomstenbelasting, supra* n. 490, at sec. 3.2.17.A.a.
515. Stevens, *supra* n. 454, at sec. 6.4a.
516. G. Spenke & M. de Vries, *Taxation in the Netherlands,* sec. 3.3.13 (Kluwer Law International 2011).
517. These are, *inter alia*, fines, representation expenses, entertainment costs, home office (which cannot be separated from the rest of the house) and telephone fees for a telephone connection at home.
518. Stevens, *supra* n. 454, at sec. 11.1a.

carried out in economic life, aimed at deriving profits and not seen as business or employment.[519] In order to obtain other income, labor must be performed although its scope and frequency is irrelevant.[520] A one-time insignificant activity is sufficient.[521] Moreover, there must be a causal connection between one's labor and the benefit obtained.[522] Examples of other activities include income from the following sources: incidental lecturing, writing articles for a magazine, operating a lodging house, patents and copyrights (but in case of heirs, such intangible rights become an asset taxable under Box 3), consultancy work or any other freelance activity.[523] A "*werkzaamheid*" can also exist if a taxpayer tolerates or refrains from an activity.[524]

The criteria used to distinguish business from other activities are: the permanence of the activities, the extent of investments, the time involved, the scope of advertising, proceed- or debtor risk, and work for more than one principal.[525] The Supreme Court decided that business activities must have a minimum scope and substance.[526] However, no precise time and monetary thresholds are set in the statutory income tax law and case law, and it has to be determined on the basis of the facts of an individual case whether business income or income from other activities has been generated.

As income from other activities has less strict substance and scope requirements than income from business activities, it may seem that income derived from disposals of virtual currency could fall within this category. However, the aim of this provision is to capture all benefits derived from one's labor exercised outside the framework of an employment contract or business enterprise. It is questionable whether income from a sales transaction can be seen as a "benefit derived from one's labor." Income from other activities includes considerations received from making property profitable by means of extensive efforts, which are generally not present in the case of simple currency disposals. Trading in virtual currency does not require more intensive activity than normal wealth management that may give rise to Box 3 income.

[4] Income from Savings and Investment

Wealth is taxed in the Netherlands for two reasons. The first one is that wealth improves one's position in society by increasing his ability to pay (*draagkracht*). The

519. Kavelaars, *supra* n. 465, at sec. 3.4.2a; Stevens, *supra* n. 454, at sec. 11.1.a.
520. Kavelaars, *supra* n. 465, at sec. 3.4.2d.
521. Rechtbank Zwolle, January 30, 1953, BNB 1953/116 (the case concerned a lawyer who wrote a note for his colleague and received remuneration for it); HR, June 20, 2003, 37974, BNB 2003/306 (the case involved the sale of a horse by a private individual).
522. H. Mobach, *Cursus belastingrecht: Inkomstenbelasting, supra* n. 490, at sec. 3.4.3.B.b2. There is no causal connection in the case of money transfer to the bank account of a taxpayer (without an underlying business reason). The benefit cannot be considered as an outcome of his own work (Hof 's-Hertogenbosch, April 8, 2008, no. 06/00160, V-N 2008/51.15).
523. H. Mobach, *Cursus belastingrecht: Inkomstenbelasting, supra* n. 490, at sec. 3.4.1.A.
524. HR, October 3, 1990, no. 26142, BNB 1990/329. The case concerned a person who took part in a medical experiment where the participants were obliged to abstain from eating certain food and to undergo regular medical checks.
525. Stevens *supra* n. 454, at sec. 6.3.a.
526. HR, November 20, 1968, BNB 1969/13.

other is that accumulated resources can be used to finance future expenses.[527] From 1892 to 2001, a separate wealth tax was levied on net assets of individuals. The legislator chose a global approach: all wealth (with a few explicitly mentioned exceptions) was subject to tax and not only its certain categories.[528] The tax was estimated to generate around 1% of the total tax revenue and to affect 600,000 taxpayers.[529]

As from 2001, wealth taxation has been partially integrated into the income tax system (although officially the wealth tax has been abolished). Under Box 3, income tax is levied on net wealth, i.e., the value of tangible or intangible assets (*bezittingen*) reduced by the value of associated liabilities (*schulden*). Net assets of a taxpayer are deemed to produce a fictitious yield which is taxed at a flat rate of 30%. The deemed yield cannot be negative. Capital gains on disposal of Box 3 assets are not taxes as such. In the author's view, the main flaw of the current taxation system is its incompatibility with the ability-to-pay principle: taxing fictitious income leaves the real income untaxed.

The Income Tax Act contains a list of assets which are taxable under Box 3. These are: real estate (second home, let property), rights in immovable property (for example, leasehold estate),[530] movable property with the exception personal items (furniture, clothes), savings, securities and other property rights.[531] The last category is a residual one covering all rights not included in the previous groups. Examples of other property rights are: membership in the homeowner association, interests in trusts, cultivation rights, inherited patents and copyrights.[532] Mere expectations (*verwachtingen*) cannot be considered as taxable assets.[533] Certain assets (nature areas, woods, assets of scientific nature, art collection) are explicitly excluded from Box 3.[534]

To be able to produce deemed investment income, an asset must have an economic value. Assets without any economic value are not subject to tax. The economic value exists if the asset itself or its transfer may yield revenue, or the possession of the asset enables its owner to save expenses that otherwise would be incurred.[535] Assets which cannot be alienated (for example, a cultivation permit) are nonetheless considered to have economic value.[536] The economic value is the price that a third party would be willing to pay for the asset under normal market conditions. Any personal interests that the owner may have in his asset (affection value) are not taken into account.[537] For valuation purposes, it is important whether an asset is

527. H. Mobach et al., *Cursus Belastingrecht, Vermogensbelasting*, sec. 0.0.2 (Deventer Gouda Quint May 1999).
528. *Id.*, at sec. 2.4.0.
529. *Id.*, at sec. 0.0.2.
530. Rental rights are considered assets; however, their value is set at nil (sec. 5.19 (4) of the IB).
531. Section 5.3 (2) IB.
532. Kavelaars, *supra* n. 465, at sec. 5.3.2f.
533. Stevens, *supra* n. 465, at sec. 13.5.a.
534. Section 5.7—5.12 IB.
535. Mobach, *Cursus belastingrecht: Inkomstenbelasting, supra* n. 490, at sec. 5.1.4.B.
536. *Id.*, at sec. 5.1.4.B.
537. *Id.*, at sec. 5.1.4.B.

transferable, fully owned or subject to any other legal restrictions.[538] The decisive date for establishing whether certain assets and liabilities are to be taken into account is the beginning of a calendar year.

Accumulated virtual currency could constitute "other property rights" within the meaning of Box 3. Such currency has economic value and can be used to generate revenue for the taxpayer. The fact that there is no absolute certainty as to whether virtual currency can be converted into legal currency (for example, because it may become worthless) is irrelevant, since Box 3 includes assets that are not able to generate any monetary income at all. Even a conditional claim to an uncertain amount can form a taxable asset.[539] Legal restrictions on alienability do not preclude an item from belonging to one's wealth. In such a situation, it is necessary to determine whether an asset can actually be disposed of. The factual possibility of doing so prevails over the legal entitlement.[540] Thus, in the Netherlands, the value of the accumulated virtual currency is subject to income tax under Box 3. Capital gains on disposals of virtual currency that is treated as a Box 3 asset are not subject to tax as such.

[D] Conclusions

The Dutch income tax law has a schedular nature. Income tax is levied on receipts falling within one of the three categories referred to as boxes. A different method of income calculation and a different tax rate apply to each of the boxes. It does not matter whether income is generated in a monetary or non-monetary, tangible or intangible form. Non-monetary receipts are subject tax based on to the rules on benefits in kind (their fair market value is recorded as revenue). Income from virtual currency transactions may fall within either Box 1 (income from labor and owner-occupied dwelling) or Box 3 (income from savings and investment).

A common characteristic of income sources in Box 1 is that income must be derived through market participation and a reasonable profit expectation must be present. This requirement is not met in the case of currency mining where the miner has not made any significant investments in the mining equipment as without proper equipment the likelihood of success is extremely low and no reasonable profit expectation can be assumed.

Income from virtual currency disposals and currency mining may be treated as business income within the meaning of Box 1 if the taxpayer has a permanent organization of labor and capital. Neither the statutory law not the case law provides precise monetary thresholds for business income. A case-by-case analysis is necessary.

538. HR, April 19, 1967, no. 15714, BNB 1967/135.
539. Hof 's-Gravenhage, December 22, 1976, BNB 1978/161.
540. Hof Amsterdam, October 14, 1992, no. 551/90, V-N 1993, p. 449. The case concerned a Dutch person who inherited some assets abroad. The assets were subsequently taken over by the foreign government, except for a few ones that were rescued by his relatives from nationalization. The court decided that the rescued assets constituted assets within the meaning of the wealth tax (currently: Box 3) and were subject to tax, despite the fact that the taxpayer could not dispose of them.

The qualification as business income means that the progressive taxation applies, with the maximum tax rate as high as 52%.

If a taxpayer's activity does not qualify as business, Box 3 taxation may apply. Under Box 3, income tax is levied on the net value of qualifying assets, which are broadly defined and include among others "other property rights." The qualifying assets are deemed to produce a fictitious yield which is taxed at a flat rate of 30%, resulting in the effective tax rate ranging from 0.6% to 1.6%. Accumulated virtual currency may be regarded as "other property rights" since it has economic value. Capital gains on disposals of virtual currency that is treated as a Box 3 asset are not subject to tax as such.

The Dutch Finance Ministry has clarified the fundamental income tax questions raised by virtual currencies and reached the same conclusions as the analysis in this chapter. The Dutch tax authorities indicate on their website that virtual currency may be regarded as Box 3 asset and taxed accordingly.

CHAPTER 6
Income Taxation: Recommendations

This chapter draws conclusions based on the analysis in Chapters 4 and 5. It seeks to make recommendations for the improvement of certain characteristics of the existing tax systems that currently struggle with the imposition and enforcement of tax compliance obligations regarding transactions in virtual currency. The aim of this chapter is also to develop a methodology for creating an effective regulatory framework for the taxation of virtual currencies, taking into the characteristics of the optimal legal framework established in Chapter 4 and best practices identified during the examination of the tax systems of selected countries. An effective regulatory framework will ensure that the revenue raising objective of taxation is achieved but at the same time it will be able to address the unique features of a volatile and rapidly-changing environment, such as the virtual currency market.

§6.01 OPTIMAL REGULATORY FRAMEWORK

Chapter 4 established that an optimal legal framework for taxing transactions in virtual currency must meet the generally accepted principles of (1) equity (fairness), (2) certainty and flexibility, (3) administrative feasibility (which combines efficiency, effectiveness, simplicity and convenience) and (4) neutrality. The principle of equity requires the establishment of a fair relationship between the resources available to the taxpayer and the amount of tax paid by him: people with similar tax capacity should face similar tax liabilities, whereas people with more resources should pay higher tax than those with fewer resources. In the evaluation of the taxpayer's positions, the nature of virtual currency (price volatility and the fact that virtual currency cannot be used to meet tax obligations) should be taken into account. Tax law should consider the possibility that the value of virtual currency may change significantly between the moment the tax liability is computed and the tax needs to be paid.[541]

541. *See* §4.02[A] Equity.

Certainty requires a tax system be clear so that the taxpayer can understand and anticipate the tax consequences of his actions. In the context of virtual currency, the principle of certainty requires that taxpayers are well-informed about, and can predict, the tax consequences of their dealings in virtual currencies. This, in turn, requires (1) enacting legislation or administrative guidelines about the tax implications of virtual currency transactions, and (2) communicating these guidelines to taxpayers in a clear and unambiguous manner. The principle of legal certainty must be balanced against the ability of a tax system to respond to changes in economic circumstances. In other words, tax rules (especially those applicable to evolving phenomena, such as virtual currency) should exhibit a certain degree of adaptability to the changing circumstances.[542]

Administrative feasibility is a key concern for tax policy. Since the primary purpose of a tax system is to raise revenue, all rules should be capable of practical operation. Tax legislation should not be too burdensome for tax authorities to enforce and for taxpayers to apply. There is no point in taxing a source of income if the costs of tax collection exceed the revenue collected or if large amounts of tax due remain uncollected.[543]

The principle of neutrality requires the design of a tax system be influenced only by tax considerations and not result in the adaptation of a taxpayer's behavior. Taxpayers' decisions should be motivated by economic rather than tax considerations.[544]

These principles will form the basis for developing a regulatory framework for the taxation of virtual currencies. Each element of the framework that will be developed will seek to take account of these principles.

§6.02 CURRENT REGULATORY FRAMEWORK

Chapter 5 examined whether income from transactions in virtual currency and virtual currency mining is subject to tax in four selected countries: the United States, the United Kingdom, Germany and the Netherlands. These countries were selected on the basis of their different approaches to income taxation (global versus schedular) and the different treatment of capital gains and accumulated wealth. The following conclusions were reached.

As the United States levies income tax on "all income from whatever source derived," all receipts of virtual currency (both through mining and exchange transactions) are considered taxable income that is subject to progressive taxation. The IRS stipulated that virtual currency should be treated as property for federal income tax purposes, meaning that every time a person spends virtual currency, no matter how small the amount, there is a taxable transaction. Disposals of virtual currency may result in a capital gain or loss if virtual currency is considered capital asset in the hands

542. *See* §4.02[B] Certainty and Flexibility.
543. *See* §4.02[C] Administrative Feasibility.
544. *See* §4.02[D] Neutrality.

of the taxpayer. If transactions in virtual currency (mining and disposals) qualify as a trade or business, the taxpayer has to follow the rules for the self-employed.[545]

In the United Kingdom, transactions in virtual currency and currency mining may give rise to trading income if all the requirements of trade (the six badges of trade) are met. If the requirements of trade are not met, income from transactions in virtual currency may be covered by the miscellaneous income provision provided that virtual currency is not considered a capital asset in the hands of the taxpayer. Both miscellaneous income and trading income are subject to progressive taxation, with the maximum rate of 45%. A profit on the sale of virtual currency held for investment purposes constitutes a capital gain that is taxed by means of a separate CGT at the rate of 10% or 20% (depending on the taxpayer's income tax brackets).[546]

In Germany, transactions in virtual currency and currency mining that require a commercial business operation may result in business income. If a taxpayer's activity does not qualify as business, it may give rise to miscellaneous income that includes short-term private capital gains (that are taxable if the time period between the purchase and sale of the asset does not exceed one year and the total gain from disposals of private assets has exceeded EUR 600 in a calendar year) and other income (i.e., income not covered by any other income category that exceeds EUR 256 per year). Income from all sources is aggregated and taxed at the progressive rates ranging from 0% to 45%, plus a solidarity surcharge of 5.5%. Additionally, business income is subject to business tax that varies per municipality.[547]

In the Netherlands, transactions in virtual currency and currency mining may give rise to business income if the taxpayer has a permanent organization of labor and capital. Business income is subject to progressive taxation, with the maximum rate of 52%. If a taxpayer's activity does not qualify as business, income tax may be levied on the net value of the taxpayer's virtual currency. In such a case, capital gains on disposals of virtual currency are not subject to tax.[548]

Out of these four countries, the United States has provided the most comprehensive guidance on the tax treatment of virtual currency.[549] The UK tax authorities limited their guidance to the statement that the general rules apply.[550] The German Ministry of Finance issued a circular on the VAT implications of virtual currency transactions and shed some light on the income tax treatment of virtual currency when responding to questions posed by some members of the German parliament.[551] The Dutch Ministry of Finance addressed some fundamental income tax implications of virtual currency in a letter to the upper house of parliament.[552]

545. *See* §5.01 The United States.
546. *See* §5.02 The United Kingdom.
547. *See* §5.03 Germany.
548. *See* §5.04 The Netherlands.
549. IRS, *Virtual Currency Guidance, supra* n. 245.
550. HMRC, *Brief 09/14, supra* n. 306.
551. BMF, *Umsatzsteuerliche Behandlung von Bitcoin und anderen sog. virtuellen Währungen, supra* n. 418; Deutsche Bundestag—19. Wahlperiode, Drucksache 19/370, question 24 and 25; BMF, *Letter to Frank Schäffler* (June 20, 2013); BMF, *Letter to Frank Schäffler* (August 7, 2013).
552. Finance Ministry, *Beantwording vragen vaste CIE Financiën fiscale aspected cryptovaluta* (May 28, 2018).

The lack of comprehensive guidance means that taxpayers transacting in virtual currency may not be aware of their tax obligations or may calculate their tax liability incorrectly.[553] The problems faced by taxpayers transacting in virtual currency may fall within three broad categories: income classification, income determination and compliance obligations (recordkeeping and reporting).

The first problem that taxpayers may encounter is to determine the applicable income tax category. In schedular tax systems, income is divided into separate categories. There are frequently different rules to calculate the taxable income within each category and different tax rates apply. To properly classify income from transactions in virtual currencies, the circumstances of an individual case must be examined. As the range of potential income-generating situations is broad (there are Bitcoin miners who treat their currency as stock in trade, occasional sellers who transact in virtual currency from time to time and professional entrepreneurs who accept virtual currency as a means of payment), taxpayers may not be able to determine whether their activity can be categorized as trade or business, investment, a for-profit activity or a non-taxable hobby. As countries generally do not provide for transaction-based or monetary thresholds below which occasional sales may still be considered a non-taxable hobby, taxpayers may generate taxable income but incorrectly assume that it stems from a non-taxable leisure activity. Similarly, frequently, no thresholds (for example, number of transactions, revenue, and profit) are provided to indicate when business activity is deemed to exist.

Even if taxpayers correctly classify their receipts from transactions in virtual currency, they may struggle with calculating the taxable income. In countries where virtual currency is treated as property, exchanges of goods or services for virtual currency constitute barter transactions. For an average taxpayer, the tax treatment of barter transactions is complex since taxpayers must know how to determine an objective (market) value of the transaction objects in order to calculate the taxable gain. This may be difficult if taxpayers engage in a large number of low-value barter transactions or if the objects of barter transactions are subject to significant price fluctuations. Taxpayers may also be unsure which expenses qualify for deduction. This question is particularly difficult to answer in the case of activities that result in losses or very little income (i.e., there is a risk that tax administration may assume a non-taxable hobby and deny all deductions).

Even if taxpayers are aware of the tax implications of transacting in virtual currencies, the complexity of recordkeeping requirements may prevent them from voluntarily complying with their tax obligations. In the United States, the IRS stipulated that virtual currency should be treated as property, meaning that when virtual currency is used to make a purchase (even in small everyday transactions, such as purchasing a cup of coffee), taxpayers will have to treat the transaction as property exchange, determine their tax basis for the virtual currency spent and keep a record of each transaction so that the gains or losses from their transactions can be properly reported. This is further complicated by the fact that taxpayers will rarely use the whole units of

553. For examples of virtual currency regulations in other countries, *see* Annex: Virtual Currency Regulation in Selected Jurisdictions.

virtual currency in everyday low-value transactions. As bitcoins are divisible to eight decimal places, each bitcoin can be divided up into 100 million pieces. Since taxpayers need to determine what portion of the bitcoin is used to make the purchase, the recordkeeping of each transaction can become onerous for people who use virtual currencies in everyday purchases. Notice 2014-21 does not provide taxpayers with guidance on what records should be kept and how the records should be maintained.

§6.03 DEVELOPING A NEW REGULATORY FRAMEWORK

This section proposes a four-step methodology to develop a sound regulatory framework for the taxation of virtual currencies. First, it argues that regulation of any activities makes sense only if these activities and the environment in which they take place are properly understood. Therefore, it suggests that, as a first step, legislators and tax administrations should gather and analyze data on virtual currency usage and transactions. Second, once the scope of virtual currency transaction has been estimated and the relevant risks have been assessed, lawmakers can start considering what regulatory method is most suitable for virtual currency transactions. In general, legal commands can be promulgated as rules or standards. Rules are precise and *ex ante* in nature, whereas standards are general and imprecise. Third, once regulation (in the form of rules or standards) has been enacted, it needs to be properly communicated to taxpayers so that they become aware of the content of the law. Finally, tax administration must possess tools to monitor taxpayer compliance, detect cases of non-compliance and enforce the legal obligations. To sum up, the methodology for the development of a regulatory framework for the taxation of virtual currencies consists of the following four steps, which are described in more detail in the following sections: (1) data-driven assessment; (2) choice of the method of regulation; (3) communication; (4) monitoring.

[A] Data-Driven Assessment

Before legislators and governments embark on designing a regulatory framework for the taxation of virtual currencies, they need to have a good understanding of the concept of virtual currency, its potential applications and the underlying technology. Otherwise, there is a risk that regulation will capture only certain activities, leaving a large part of the virtual money sector unintentionally unregulated.

Any attempt to regulate virtual currency transactions should begin with defining the conceptual framework. In discussions about virtual currency, it is quite common to use the terms "tokens," "cryptocurrency," "coins" and "digital currency" interchangeably.[554] However, these terms do not mean the same. The use of the correct methodology is important to ensure that legislators will not leave out a virtual currency scheme that they intended to cover or that they include a virtual currency scheme that they sought to exclude.

554. For the definitions of these terms, *see* §3.02 Definitions.

Governments should develop a methodology to capture data needed to determine the scope of virtual currency usage and the magnitude of virtual currency transactions. Without any data, governments would not be able to analyze the risk of intentional and unintentional taxpayer non-compliance. Data about virtual currency transactions can be obtained from two sources. The first source is records maintained by the exchange platforms for non-tax regulatory purposes. In many countries, exchange platforms fall within the scope of anti-money laundering (AML) regulation and are obliged to comply with the relevant AML legislation on the identification and investigation of suspicious transactions and customers. The second source of data could be the exiting third-party reporting obligations for tax purposes. For example, in the United States, virtual currency transactions are subject to the standard reporting obligations, such as Form W-2 (Wage and Tax Statement), Form 1099-MISC (Miscellaneous Income), and Form 1099-K (Payment Card and Third Party Network Transactions). However, currently, these methods do not separately identify transactions in virtual currency and do not provide the IRS with any means to identify that the transaction amounts being reported are specifically related to virtual currencies. Revising the existing information reporting obligations to require employers, businesses, and third-party settlement organizations to identify virtual currency transaction amounts would provide the tax authorities with data that allows determining the scope of virtual currency transactions.

[B] Method of Regulation

Legal commands can be promulgated as rules or standards.[555] Rules are precise and ex ante in nature. They indicate to an individual whether certain behavior will violate or comply with the law. When a rule is enacted, effort must be undertaken by lawmakers to give full and precise content to the law before the individual acts. In contrast, standards are imprecise when they are enacted. The exact content of the law comes after an individual acts, as judges and adjudicators determine whether the individual's specific behavior in a particular context violates the standard.[556] The problem of choosing between rules and standards is one concerning how lawmakers should enact and disseminate information about the content of law.

Rules are more costly to promulgate because they involve advance determinations of the law's content, whereas standards are more costly for legal advisors to predict or enforcement authorities to apply because they require later determinations of the law's content. To enact rules, lawmakers must consider a myriad of different scenarios and take into account various contingencies some of which may not even arise. They must gather substantial information before individuals act to minimize the risk of rules being over-or under-inclusive. This difference in promulgation costs favors

555. Kaplow, *supra* n. 182; McGinnis & Wasick, *supra* n. 182; F. Schauer, *The Tyranny of Choice and the Rulification of Standards*, 14 Contemp. Legal Issues 803 (2005); C.R. Sunstein, *Problems with Rules*, 83 California Law Review 953 (1995); Casey & Niblett, *supra* n. 182; J. Braithwaite, *Rules and Principles: A Theory of Legal Certainty*, 27 Australian Journal of Legal Philosophy, pp. 47–82 (2002).
556. Casey & Niblett, *supra* n. 182, at p. 7.

standards, whereas that in enforcement costs favors rules. However, promulgation costs are incurred once. In contrast, enforcement costs may be incurred repeatedly or never. Therefore, for frequent activities with common characteristics, rules tend to be desirable. When frequency is low, standards tends to be preferable.[557]

In an ideal rule-based legal system, no loopholes should exist. New rules are added over time to take account of the experience in implementation, and the regulations tend to grow in size and complexity in a continuous search for clarity and completeness. To address a problem, legislators respond by enacting a set of rules, which may require a further subset of rules. Tax legislation is sometimes described as a never-ending process of closing one loophole to create another one. Although the creation of a fully comprehensive and detailed rule-based legal framework is not possible, any attempts to do so run the risk of overregulation and complexity that endangers legal certainty as the law becomes so complex that people who cannot afford sophisticated legal advice cannot understand it.[558]

As economy, society and technology change over time, so should the content of law. Rules are ill-suited for evolving phenomena where it is difficult to specify all potential scenarios in advance. If one cannot foresee what developments will occur, one cannot determine how to address them before they arise. It is generally believed that standards are easier to keep up-to-date as they are given content in a definitive way only when they are applied to a particular conduct. A standard enacted many years ago may continue to apply in a present situation as it will be interpreted in the present context.[559] In contrast, rules must be changed, which may require more law-making effort. Moreover, the use of detailed rules runs the risk that such legislation may be easily circumvented by taxpayers structuring their transactions in a way not foreseen by the lawmaker.[560] Thus, where conditions change fast, rules seem to be an infeasible option.

From the perspective of the principle of legal certainty, rules seem to be preferable as they reduce room for interpretation and are easier for individuals to understand and follow. Individuals may be better guided by rules since the content of law can be more easily ascertained. However, this only applies if rules are formulated and communicated in a clear way. Rules will result in improved compliance only if individuals choose to learn about the law before they act. Learning about the law may take various forms: legal advice may be acquired through self-study, from lawyers or by other means. If the costs of learning about the law are substantial (for example, because the rules are too complex and taxpayers must consult a wide variety of sources before they understand the legal consequences of their actions), individuals may not conform to the law's commands and they will act based upon their best guesses about the content of law. Thus, an obscure or overly complex rule may be even more difficult to apply than a simple but vague standard.

557. Kaplow, *supra* n. 182, at p. 562, 572-573, 621.
558. Braithwaite, *supra* n. 555, at p. 14.
559. Kaplow, *supra* n. 182, at p. 616.
560. Braithwaite, *supra* n. 555, at p. 13.

Virtual currency is an evolving phenomenon. Although it can be divided into some categories (for example, coins and tokens, convertible and non-convertible currency), each virtual currency scheme has its unique characteristics. New schemes with yet unknown features may appear and replace the existing ones. When the first decentralized virtual currency scheme (Bitcoin) was invented in 2008, it was hardly predicted that in ten years there would be over 1,600 types of virtual currency in circulation. Also, the types of transactions that taxpayers engage in may change significantly. Ten years ago, initial coin offerings were completely unknown, whereas now they are a very popular means of raising capital. For these reasons, legal instruments used to regulate virtual currencies should exhibit a certain degree of flexibility and adaptability to changing circumstances.

Braithwaite (2002) suggested that with complex phenomena in changing environments where large economic interests are at stake, principles regulate with greater certainty than rules. However, to achieve regulatory consistency, a mix of binding principles and non-binding rules should be used.[561] If the application of a rule produces a clearly unreasonable result when viewed from the perspective of the purpose of law, the rule can be abandoned in favor of some more profound principle.[562]

Following Braithwaite's reasoning and to strike a balance between legal certainty and the need to adapt to changing circumstances, a combination of general legislation (equivalent to standards in the rules-versus-standards debate) and more detailed interpretative rules seems to be the right regulatory method in the context of virtual currency. The most fundamental aspects of virtual currency transactions should be regulated by legislation to provide taxpayers with some level of legal certainty about the tax consequences of their actions. What can be considered "a fundamental aspect" varies per jurisdiction. This term covers the qualification of virtual currency for tax purposes (does virtual currency constitute money, property, security?), its eligibility for inclusion in certain income categories (for example, is virtual currency a Box 3 asset for Dutch tax purposes?), or the applicable reporting and recordkeeping obligations. Virtual-currency specific legislation should follow the principle of technology neutrality, i.e., to avoid regulating specific technology types but only activities these technology types facilitate and taxpayers carrying out the activities. Such approach is designed to accommodate innovation and follows the principle of neutrality as it does not influence the choice of a particular type of technology.

To facilitate and promote compliance, the tax administration should be tasked with enacting interpretative rules in the areas where taxpayers need more detailed guidance to apply the legislation correctly. Tax administration can issue rules faster than the legislator as it does not need to follow the lengthy legislative procedure. Thus, it is in a better position to respond swiftly to changing circumstances. Administrative rules could also be issued by the tax administration to fix unintended or too burdensome consequences that result from the application of tax legislation before the legislation itself is amended. Tax administration is in a good position to do so as it generally interacts with taxpayers more often than the legislator. It may receive

561. *Id.*, at p. 37.
562. *Id.*, at p. 25.

feedback from taxpayers and enforcement officials about some general problems they face in complying with certain laws. Rather than wait until the law in question is amended by parliament, tax administration could issue rules that would mitigate the difficulty of meeting the compliance requirements established by legislation. For example, both in Australia and in the United States, virtual currency is treated as property for direct tax purposes. In Australia, there are no income tax implications if the person is not in business or carrying on an enterprise and uses virtual currency to make everyday purchases.[563] Any capital gain or loss realized from the disposal of virtual currency is disregarded provided the acquisition cost of virtual currency is AUD 10,000 or less. In contrast, there are no similar rules in the United States, meaning that taxpayers need to keep track of all everyday retail transactions that involve virtual currency. Imposing too burdensome compliance requirements reduces the likelihood that they will be adhered to. The US IRS could follow the Australian example and provide similar relief for virtual currency used in everyday transactions.

In drafting the legislation and interpretative rules, the volatile nature of virtual currency should be taken into account. In many countries, the fair market value of virtual currency as at the day of transaction is taken into account when calculating taxable income. The existing tax rules fail to recognize that if a taxpayer makes a profit on a transaction and his profit exists solely in the form of virtual currency (for example, the taxpayer sold bitcoins for units of other virtual currency), the profit may be wiped out in case the currency price drops. As taxes cannot be paid in any virtual units, the taxpayer must convert his "virtual profit" into legal currency to meet this tax liability. Generally, the taxpayer bears the risks of value loss between the time of transaction and the time of tax payment. He can eliminate such risk by converting his "virtual profits" into legal currency immediately after the transaction takes place. However, to help taxpayers who failed to monetize their "virtual profits" before the virtual currency's decline in value and are not able to meet their tax liabilities, countries may consider implementing a provision similar to section 24(2) of the UK TCGA. According to this provision, if an asset becomes of negligible value, the taxpayer is deemed to have disposed of and immediately acquired the asset at its market value (nil), enabling him to claim loss relief. Should the value of the asset subsequently increase, the result will be that on a later disposal, the base value will be nil so that all the consideration received will be treated as gain. According to the HRMC, negligible value should be less than 5% of the original value.[564]

[C] Information and Communication

Tax administration should provide comprehensive guidance to help taxpayers comply with their tax obligations resulting from the use of virtual currency. The current approaches to disseminating information about the tax consequences of virtual

563. ATO, *Tax treatment of cryptocurrencies* (last modified: March 16, 2018).
564. Tiley, *UK Tax Guide, supra* n. 290, sec. 27.22.

currency transactions fall into the following categories: (1) no guidance; (2) incomplete and fragmented guidance; and (3) comprehensive guidance.

The first category (no guidance) includes situations where the tax administration has not made any statements on the tax consequences of virtual currency transactions or where it limited its guidance to the statement that the general rules apply. Such a statement is insufficient as it presupposes that individuals know precisely what those general rules are. An individual who is only familiar with, for example, taxes on employment income may not know what rules apply to entrepreneurs. The general rules apply by default and there is no need to communicate this fact explicitly. In the absence of official guidance, taxpayers may apply the law based on their best guesses or seek advice online. If taxpayers turn to the Internet for tax help, they may find a lot of misinformation. There are a number of websites, wikis, and blogs that provide differing opinions on the tax treatment of virtual currency, including some that could lead taxpayers to believe that transacting in virtual currencies relieves them of their responsibilities to report and pay taxes.

Incomplete guidance means that the tax administration has clarified only selected aspects of virtual currency transactions. Fragmented guidance means that guidelines and clarifications were produced by different government bodies and there is no single document or online portal providing an overview of all the relevant statements. For example, in Germany, the only official statement on virtual currency and taxation issued by the Ministry of Finance is the circular explaining the VAT treatment of virtual currency transactions. The Ministry of Finance also clarified the income tax consequences of virtual currency transactions when it provided answers to questions posed by some members of the German parliament. These clarifications were not issued in the form of a circular and are only available in the parliamentary documents or letters sent to the person posing the question.[565] Additionally, some German state authorities began to clarify issues that were not addressed by the Ministry of Finance. For example, the Finance Ministry of Hamburg confirmed the application of the FIFO method to calculate gains from private virtual currency disposals.[566]

Comprehensive guidance means that the tax authorities have provided a detailed explanation of the tax consequences of various uses of virtual currency and the associated reporting requirements. The most clear and informative guidance has been provided in Australia.[567] In 2017, the Australian GST law was amended to align the GST treatment of virtual currency and legal money. At that time, a legal definition of virtual currency was inserted into the legislation.[568] To explain the legislative changes and their consequences for taxpayers, ATO issued comprehensive guidance on the GST treatment of virtual currency.[569] The GST guidance explains in simple terms what the GST consequences of using virtual currency in a wide variety of scenarios are, and provides numerous examples and links where additional information can be obtained.

565. *See supra* n. 551.
566. Finance Ministry of Hamburg, *supra* n. 449.
567. ATO, *supra* n. 563.
568. Treasury Laws Amendment (2017 Measures No. 6) Act 2017.
569. ATO, *GST and digital currency* (last modified: March 16, 2018).

The ATO followed the same approach when it issued guidelines on the income tax treatment of virtual currency.[570] Both guidance documents are interlinked so that taxpayers can easily obtain a comprehensive picture of all tax implications of transacting in virtual currency.

IRS Notice 2014-21 meets the characteristics of comprehensive guidance to a large extent. This notice takes the form of answers to frequently asked questions. It describes the tax consequences of various activities involving virtual currency (for example, mining or acceptance as consideration for sales of goods and services) and answers several questions regarding virtual currency valuation, classification and reporting obligations. Taxpayers are provided with short clear answers to those questions and with references to additional explanatory documents where further information can be found. Although the IRS put significant effort into understanding and clarifying compliance obligations related to virtual currency transactions, the US Treasury Inspector General for Tax Administration (TIGTA) considered the guidance provided in Notice 2014-21 to be insufficient and suggested additional actions that the IRS should take to address income produced through virtual currencies.[571] According to the TIGTA, since virtual currency is treated as property, the public may not understand that each purchase of consumer goods with virtual currency could result in a reportable transaction. Due to the potential complexity of reporting simple retail purchase transactions related to virtual currencies, further guidance is needed to help taxpayers voluntarily comply with their tax obligations. To assist taxpayers in determining their tax obligations, the IRS should provide more detailed guidance about recordkeeping requirements to track a realized gain or loss from virtual currency transactions.

While the provision of administrative guidance is a positive development, the way in which some countries provide information to taxpayers about the tax implications of virtual currency transactions raises concerns. Administrative guidelines will only guide taxpayers if (1) they can be found and (2) they are drafted in a clear and simple language that an average taxpayer can understand. In some countries, the administrative guidance seems to be well hidden from taxpayers. The German Ministry of Finance expressed its views on the income tax treatment of virtual currency when replying to questions posed by some members of parliament. The Ministry's statements can be found in parliamentary documents or on the websites of individual members of parliament who asked the questions but not on the websites of the tax administration where taxpayers are expected to search for information. Another example of how not to communicate with taxpayers is the notice on the tax treatment of virtual currency (*Steuerliche Behandlung von Kryptowährungen*) issued by the Austrian Ministry of Finance (*Bundesministerium für Finanzen*).[572] The two-page notice uses a complex legal language and is full of tax technical terms (for example,

570. ATO, *supra* n. 563.
571. TIGTA, *supra* n. 247.
572. Bundesministerium für Finanzen, *Steuerliche Behandlung von Kryptowährungen (virtuelle Währungen)* (July 25, 2017).

"deemed interest bearing investment") that an average taxpayer can hardly understand. It assumes that a taxpayer has a very good knowledge of the existing tax system and does not provide any references to any additional sources where taxpayers can find more information on selected unfamiliar aspects of the Austrian tax system that are briefly mentioned in the notice.

To promote tax compliance, tax administration should produce comprehensive and detailed guidance that would explain how virtual currency fits within the existing legislative framework. The guidance should take the form of one or more interlinked documents that would address issues, such as income characterization, income determination, allowable deductions, recordkeeping and reporting obligations. The guidance should be drafted in a simple language that can be understood by an average taxpayer[573] and should not assume that taxpayers are familiar with the general rules of a tax system. The explanations of the law should be supplemented by practical examples and references to resources providing additional information on selected aspects of a country's tax system. The guidance issued by the ATO and IRS can serve as a good example of how information could be communicated to taxpayers.

Comprehensive guidance can help taxpayers understand their tax obligations but it does not solve all problems. Given the variety of virtual currency schemes and different personal situations of taxpayers, advice on the taxpayer's individual circumstances would be greatly appreciated. Taxpayers would like to have certainty that the chosen income characterization and the method of income calculation will not be challenged by the tax administration. For these reasons, taxpayers should have the possibility to ask for advice on their personal circumstances by means of an advance ruling request.

Tax rulings are offered in many countries but their characteristics vary significantly depending on the legal system.[574] In the majority of countries, rulings are governed by formal written procedures. Legal or administrative provisions describe the circumstances in which a ruling may be obtained, the duration of the procedure, the responsibilities of the taxpayer and the competent authority, the binding effect and the ruling fees. The law usually specifies the situations in which rulings can be requested. Alternatively, a negative list provides for cases in which rulings cannot be issued (for example, to answer questions of fact or hypothetical questions). Commonly excluded tax matters are those related to tax rates, administrative sanctions, tax calculation and tax returns. The terms of a ruling may be relied upon by the taxpayer, provided that the facts on which the ruling is based have been accurately presented and the taxpayer abides by the terms of the ruling. Rulings are usually provided against a fee. Taxpayers who request a special service from the tax administration (that is of no use to other

573. A good example of how a complex situation is translated in a simple rule is the operation of traffic lights. Traffic lights generate very simple commands: if the light is red you must stop, if the light is green, you may go. However, from the perspective of traffic regulators, the underlying rules are complex: the time intervals when cars have to stop may vary by time of day or intensity of traffic (some traffic lights contain sensors that analyze traffic flow and adjust the timing of the red and green lights accordingly).

574. For a comparison of the main characteristics of tax rulings in the major economies, *see* Compliance Tables, Quick Reference Tables IBFD.

taxpayers) should be prepared to pay for it. Fees act as a deterrent against asking for rulings on issues that are only of theoretical interest. They also contribute towards the cost of issuing rulings, enabling the tax authority to hire more and better qualified personnel.[575]

Tax rulings provide the taxpayer with certainty regarding the tax consequences of his future transactions. A well-executed system of tax rulings contributes to good relations between the tax administration and taxpayers. It also contributes to a consistent and transparent application of the law as tax authorities will express their views on significantly more issues that would arise in court proceedings.

[D] Monitoring

Educating taxpayers may improve tax compliance but it falls short of addressing one of the main difficulties that virtual currencies pose, i.e., the low likelihood of detection and enforcement of the incurred tax liabilities. The main threat to tax compliance is anonymity (tax enforcement cannot be secured if the identity of the taxpayer is not known) and asymmetric information (the taxpayer knows the facts regarding the transactions he engages in, but the government is forced to obtain that information either from the taxpayer or from third parties). Taxpayers who are well aware of their obligations to report income and to pay taxes may purposely choose not to do so if they know that tax authorities are not aware of the existence of such profits.

Activities of individuals are difficult to track. Tax authorities are frequently not aware that someone sells virtual currency until the story is remarkable enough to receive media coverage. Monitoring individuals is nearly impossible and excessive surveillance would raise civil liberty concerns. Traditional anti-tax-evasion mechanisms cannot successfully address virtual currency-based tax evasion. For example, agreements on exchange of information are irrelevant since Bitcoin's operation is not dependent on the existence of a sovereign jurisdiction. There is no jurisdiction to exchange information with. Although tax authorities may employ complex statistical analysis to try to associate virtual currency transactions with external information allowing the identification of taxpayers, such an approach is labor intensive and time-consuming. It can only be used in particular cases but not to address the problem systematically.[576]

Enforcement and monitoring measures by tax authorities should not target an infinitely large number of unidentified individuals but a much smaller number of operators providing exchange services and wallet providers. Companies are easier to regulate as they are smaller in number, have known locations and incentives to comply with the law. Their core business activity is to facilitate trade in virtual currencies and they obtain benefits from it. No real value can be obtained without their involvement: while virtual currencies are valuable, it is their conversion into legal currency that allows the taxpayer to fully enjoy their benefits. If intermediaries were subject to

575. M.J. Ellis, *General Report, IFA Cahiers de Droit Fiscal International* p. 33 (1999).
576. Marian, *supra* n. 112, at p. 45.

reporting requirements, online marketplaces would cease to support anonymous transactions. Properly implemented information reporting can significantly reduce opportunities for tax evasion. It is no surprise that tax compliance is highest if a third-party reporting is present.[577] According to the IRS, "misreporting of income amounts subject to substantial information reporting and withholding is 1%; of income amounts subject to substantial information reporting but not withholding, it is 7%; and of income amounts subject to little or no information reporting (...), it is 63%."[578] The Taxpayer Attitude Survey from the IRS Oversight Board, issued in December 2014, found that personal integrity and third-party reporting are the top two factors having a "great deal of influence" on whether taxes are reported and paid honestly.[579]

In many countries, the existing third-party reporting obligations already apply to transactions in virtual currency. For example, in the United States, taxpayers transacting in virtual currency need to comply with Form W-2, Form 1099-MISC, and Form 1099-K (Payment Card and Third Party Network Transactions). The latter instrument is relevant in the context of virtual currency exchange platforms. Starting from the 2011 tax year, the IRS began the implementation of a new reporting requirement designed to make auditing and compliance of online sellers easier. Any individual selling over USD 20,000 and engaging in over 200 transactions has his gross revenue reported to the IRS by the third-party settlement organization.[580] That organization has to track the payment volume of an individual's accounts to check whether his payment volume goes above both of the above-mentioned thresholds in a calendar year. The amount of USD 20,000 is calculated by looking at a seller's gross payment volume for sales of goods or services, i.e., any adjustments for credits, cash equivalents, discounts, fees, refunded amounts or any other amounts are not netted out.[581] The affected sellers have to provide the settlement organization with their tax identification and social security numbers. The implementation of section 6050W of the IRC was estimated to raise USD 9.5 billion over the ten years following its implementation.[582] The main advantage of this reporting requirement is that of centralization: one middleman files reports for many sellers. Its principal drawback is that the reporting entities cannot provide all of the information necessary for the tax authorities to match the report with the amounts on the taxpayer's return because the reporting entity generally has no reliable way of knowing the taxpayer's basis in the property sold.

In many countries, virtual currency exchange platforms and wallet providers are subject to anti-money laundering (AML) legislation. In 2015, the FATF, an intergovernmental body whose purpose is to develop and promote an international response to combat money laundering, published *Guidance for a Risk-Based Approach—Virtual Currencies*.[583] The 48-page document aims to clarify the application of the relevant

577. Lederman, *supra* n. 188, at p. 1737.
578. TIGTA, *supra* n. 247.
579. *Id.*
580. Section 6050W IRC.
581. IRS, *IRC Section 6050W—Frequently Asked Questions.*
582. E. Roscoe, *Taxing Virtual Worlds: Can the IRS PWN You?* 12 Pittsburgh Journal of Technology Law and Policy, p. 29. (2011).
583. FATF, *Guidance for a Risk-Based Approach—Virtual Currencies* (June 26, 2015).

FATF recommendations to convertible virtual currency exchangers and help national authorities develop regulatory responses to address money-laundering and terrorist-financing risks associated with the use of virtual currency. The report recommends adopting regulations and guidelines similar to those applicable to traditional financial institutions and money transfer businesses. Institutions providing exchange services should be registered and keep adequate records of senders and beneficiaries.

In the European Union, the AMLD5 brought providers of exchange services between virtual currencies and fiat currencies and custodian wallet providers (CWPs) within the scope of the anti-money laundering legislation. It included them in the definition of "obliged entities," giving them the same responsibilities as banks and requiring them to apply customer due diligence (CDD) controls and to conduct ongoing monitoring of transactions in order to report suspicious activity to government entities.

The US Financial Crimes Enforcement Network (FinCEN) published guidance entitled *Application of FinCEN's Regulations to Persons Administering, Exchanging, or Using Virtual Currencies*,[584] which addressed the applicability of the Bank Secrecy Act (BSA)[585] to persons creating, obtaining, distributing, exchanging, accepting, or transmitting virtual currency. The guidance provides information to help taxpayers determine whether their activities with virtual currencies may classify them as an MBS, which are types of non-bank financial institutions that are regulated by the BSA. The FinCEN guidance states that an administrator[586] or exchanger[587] that (1) accepts and transmits a virtual currency, or (2) buys or sells virtual currency for any reason is a MSB under FinCEN's regulations and is subject to the BSA monitoring and reporting requirements unless a limitation to or exemption from the definition applies.

When designing third-party reporting requirements, two approaches can be distinguished: a rule-based or a risk-based approach. The differences between those two approaches have essential implications for the extent and nature of compliance obligations (such as reporting or CDD) and controls performed by supervisory authorities.

A rule-based approach provides precise rules, covering all instances in which measures have to be applied and determining the content of such measures. There is no or little room to apply different methods, even though the mandatory ones may prove inadequate or ineffective in a particular case. Although the rule-based approach is less costly and simpler to implement, it is also less flexible and less effective since it may provide similar rules to different situations and encourage formalistic over-reporting.

A risk-based approach relies on the general assumption that compliance and control obligations should be designed by taking into account the risks they are

584. FinCEN, *Application of FinCEN's Regulations to Persons Administering, Exchanging, or Using Virtual Currencies*, *supra* n. 249.
585. The Bank Secrecy Act (BSA) creates a number of reporting obligations upon financial institutions and money services businesses (MSB). MSBs include check cashers, issuers and redeemers of travelers' checks and money orders, and money transmitters.
586. An administrator is a person who is engaged as a business in using (putting into circulation) a virtual currency and who has the authority to redeem (to withdraw from circulation) such virtual currency.
587. An exchanger is a person engaged as a business in the exchange of virtual currency for real currency, funds, or other virtual currency.

intended to tackle and mitigate. Risk-based systems are more effective since they take into account particular circumstances in a more targeted manner and encourage convergence towards common practices that have proven effective in tackling particular risks in specific circumstances. Risk-based systems need ongoing maintenance to make sure that the understanding of the risks is always up-to-date and require the evaluation of the effectiveness of the applied measures. This is a more complex task than the application of predetermined rules. Risk-based systems also provide less legal certainty.

For the purposes of a third-party reporting regime for virtual currency transactions for tax purposes, the author would support a reporting framework that combines the rule-based and risk-based approaches and builds upon the existing compliance obligations for AML proposes. All users of exchange platforms and online wallets should be subject to a CDD process and their basic data should be collected. CDD should ensure that the intermediary keeps records with the basic data of all users even if such information does not need to be reported to any authorities. As virtual currency exchange platforms and wallet providers are already obliged to perform CDD for AML purposes, the same checks could be used to collect data for tax purposes. Exchange platforms and wallet providers should be required to maintain user data and transaction records for a fixed period of time that could be equivalent to the document retention period for tax purposes. Upon a taxpayer's request, intermediaries should provide him with his transaction records as this information could assist the taxpayer in computing his tax liabilities.

To keep the volume of reportable information manageable, only transactions above predetermined thresholds (just as in the case of the US Form 1099-K reporting obligation) and those with suspicious patterns should be reported to the tax authorities. In determining which transactions are suspicious, intermediaries would have to carry out their own risk assessments, based on their own policies and taking due account of any available guidance from regulatory bodies. It is essential that these policies and guidance are updated and improved in an ongoing manner to take account of changing circumstances and evolving risks. The reporting thresholds would very per country and would be set taking into account any relevant thresholds in domestic tax legislation. Although the principle of equity would require that all income is reported, tax authorities are unlikely to have the administrative capacity to process such a large set of data and enforce the payment of low-value amounts.

Moreover, it should not be forgotten that exchange platforms are global marketplaces visited by users from all over the world. The business activity of intermediaries would be negatively affected if they had to comply with a patchwork of inconsistent and very detailed country-specific reporting and documentation obligations. The imposition of reporting requirements may affect the fundamental freedoms of intermediaries since they bear liability risks and have additional compliance costs.[588] It is therefore important that their fundamental rights are protected by the proportionality principle. Intermediaries should not be held responsible for anything which occurs

588. Seer, *supra* n. 188, at sec. 5.

outside their business relationships with taxpayers. Nor do they have to examine facts occurring beyond the scope of such relationships. Furthermore, intermediaries need a cost-free means of requesting a ruling from the tax authorities if they are in doubt about the scope of their reporting requirements. If the tax authorities do not respond in a timely manner, intermediaries should not be held liable for making a discretional decision.

Technological advances could reduce compliance costs for virtual currency intermediaries in the future. The use of distributed ledger technology (blockchain) can provide numerous benefits and cost reductions where a group of companies needs to use the same information. Currently, companies perform "know your customer (KYC)" checks themselves or outsource them to a third party. If virtual currency intermediaries operated on the same distributed ledger network, the KYC process could be executed more efficiently. Due to the shared nature of the ledger, a database of all customer activity and background information would be available to all companies on the network. Any updates or changes in a customer's status could be communicated and updated in near real time.

Finally, it is clear that every third-party reporting and monitoring system has its limitations. It will not prevent all violations. Determined offenders will find ways to circumvent the rules or sometimes even the institution itself (the trading platform) may be the source of the wrongdoing. However, the inability to achieve perfect compliance should not stand in the way of some improvements. There is a tendency to think that the creation of an unflawed income tax system is possible. That thought is wrong. It is possible to mitigate some of the problems of income tax law as they manifest themselves in some cases or to make some aspects of income tax law work well in certain situations. However, tax authorities cannot guarantee tax enforcement in every single case. Such an expectation is not only unrealistic in fact but also not acceptable under the primacy of law. A 100%-tax enforcement would require administrative forces that would lead to a police state and violate the basic individual freedoms.[589]

§6.04 CONCLUSIONS

This section proposed a four-step methodology to develop an effective regulatory framework for the taxation of virtual currency: (1) data-driven assessment; (2) choice of the method of regulation; (3) communication; and (4) monitoring. This framework originated from the well-established principles of taxation, such as equity, certainty, administrative feasibility and neutrality. The first step involves a thorough examination of the virtual currency concept and the types of transactions in the virtual currency sector. Once these phenomena and the associated risks are properly assessed, lawmakers should determine the applicable method of regulation. This chapter advocates the use of legislation to clarify the fundamental aspects of virtual currency transactions together with more detailed interpretative guidance that can be quickly adapted to the changing circumstances. To promote compliance, tax administration should draft

589. *Id.*, at sec. 5.

guidance in a clear and simple language and make it easily accessible to taxpayers. Enforcement and monitoring measures by tax authorities should not target an infinitely large number of unidentified individuals but a much smaller number of operators providing exchange services and wallet providers. A third-party reporting regime for virtual currency intermediaries should be aligned with the existing reporting obligations for AML purposes. There should be CDD procedures in place to ensure that all basic user data is properly captured. Intermediaries should be required to report transactions above predetermined thresholds (that would very per country) and those with suspicious patterns to the tax authorities. The existing US Form 1099-K reporting obligation could serve as a good example for implementing third-party reporting requirements for virtual currency transactions.

Part III Consumption Taxation

CHAPTER 7

Consumption Taxation: General Considerations

Chapter 7 provides a general introduction to the topic of consumption taxation. First, it describes various consumption tax systems and provides a brief history of consumption taxation (focusing on the digital economy and electronic commerce). Second, it describes the principle underlying an optimal consumption tax system that will be used as a benchmark in the evaluation of the consumption tax treatment of transactions involving virtual currencies in two selected jurisdiction—the European Union and the United States—which is undertaken in the next chapter of this book. Finally, Chapter 7 lists the most important consumption tax questions raised by the emergence of virtual currencies that the next chapter seeks to answer.

§7.01 SYSTEMS OF CONSUMPTION TAXATION

The objective of consumption tax is to tax expenditures made by persons for their private purposes. It is the final consumer who should bear the tax burden. Consumption taxes vary in coverage, systematic approach and name. Some are of general nature, whereas others are levied only on certain products (for example, alcohol, tobacco and petroleum). The latter are not discussed in this thesis due to their irrelevance for virtual currencies.

Consumption taxes are an increasingly important revenue source. In the OECD member countries, the share of taxes on general consumption as a percentage of the GDP rose from 3.2% in 1965 to 7% in 2014. In 2014, the consumption tax revenue comprised about 20.7% of the total tax revenue, with VAT accounting for the largest part.[590] In the United States, retail state taxes yield almost a third of state tax

590. OECD, *Consumption Tax Trends*, Ch. 1 (2016).

revenues.[591] In the European Union, consumption tax revenues accounted for 28.7% of the total tax revenues of the Member States in 2015.[592]

Consumption taxes can be imposed at all stages of the manufacturing and distribution chain or only at one stage (*see* Diagram 2). An all-stage tax may be either cumulative or non-cumulative. Tax accumulation occurs when an amount of tax paid at a previous stage is again subject to tax at a later stage and, as a result, the same amount is subject to multiple taxation, the magnitude of which is determined by the length of the chain of transactions. The longer the chain, the higher the tax. As there is no deduction for tax incurred on purchases, the tax cascading effect favors integrated businesses and leads to distortion of competition. The most frequently applied form of cumulative tax is gross receipt tax (GRT).[593]

In contrast, a non-cumulative tax takes into account the tax paid at an earlier stage, i.e., it applies only to the value added by the business. Three distinct approaches are available to determine the added value. The first one (subtraction method) relies on aggregative data over a fixed period and taxes the difference between the total sales and purchases. Under the second one (addition method), all elements of the turnover (wages, interest, royalties, profit and subsidies) are taxed, provided that they have not been taxed at previous stages of the distribution chain. Both methods cannot accommodate multiple rates and exemptions because they do not distinguish different product categories within the sales. The third method (invoice credit method) calculates the tax on a transaction-by-transaction basis. Tax liability is determined by subtracting tax paid on the purchases (input) from tax due on the sales (output). This method is most frequently used to assess the tax.[594] The most widespread non-cumulative consumption tax is the value added tax (VAT), also called goods and services tax (GST). Limited to fewer than ten countries in the late 1960s, it has now been implemented by over 150 jurisdictions, where it often accounts for a large part of the total tax revenue.

Single-stage taxes are classified according to the stage of the production and distribution chain at which the tax is applied: such tax can take the form of a manufacturer tax, a wholesaler tax or a retailer tax. The main advantage of the first two types is that there is a relatively low number of taxpayers. However, single-stage taxes do not guarantee legal neutrality: as the basis of the tax is not the retail price, identical goods are not taxed equally when sold to final consumers. The degree of integration of a certain business influences the effective tax rate borne by the final consumer, which may lead to distortions of competition. If a production process includes several manufacturers, tax accumulation occurs, which in itself creates an incentive to vertical integration. A drawback of a wholesale tax is complexity that arises when services are integrated in the system: although services should be exempt at the wholesale stage,

591. US Census Bureau, *State Government Tax Collections Summary Report: 2013* (April 8, 2014).
592. European Commission, *Taxation Trends in the European Union*, p. 22 (2017).
593. R.F. van Brederode, *Systems of General Sales Taxation*, Ch. 3.2. (Wolters Kluwer 2009).
594. *Id.*, at Ch. 3.2.2; B. Terra & J. Kajus, *Introduction to European VAT (Recast)*, sec. 7.5.3. (2012), Online Books IBFD.

unless they are rendered to final consumers, it is difficult for a supplier to determine in what capacity a buyer is purchasing a service.[595]

A retail sales tax (RST) is applied to all supplies to final consumers, including those made by manufacturers and wholesalers. The basis of taxation is the retail price. RST does not discriminate between different forms of distribution channels and has the advantage of simplicity. However, it makes it necessary to distinguish between taxable business-to-consumer (B2C) and exempt business-to-business (B2B) transactions, which may be problematic especially in the case of services. In many situations, the service provider has no means to verify for what purpose a transaction is carried out. Although the application of retail sales taxes is retreating because of the growing popularity of VAT, they still remain persistent in the United States.[596]

Although an ideal RST and an ideal VAT should be economically equivalent, the differences between those two types of taxes, especially the remittance method, may affect their economic impact and administrative efficiency. Proponents of VAT argue that it is more resistant to losses because of the incremental collection method. On the other hand, a VAT system which offers input tax deductions all the way up an economic chain may actually be more susceptible to fraud.[597]

Figure 7.1 Systems of Consumption Taxation

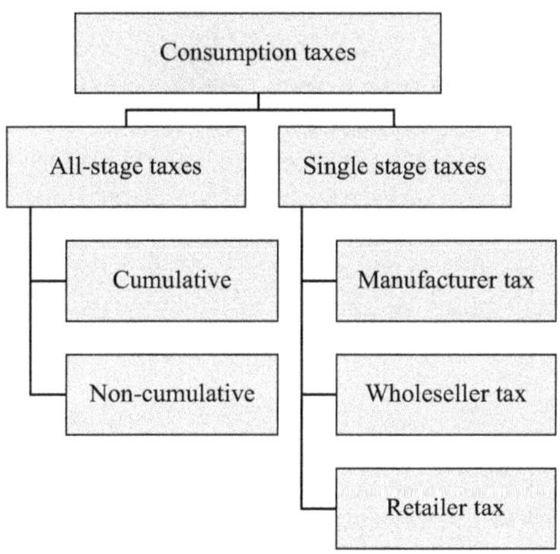

595. Van Brederode, *Systems of General Sales Taxation*, *supra* n. 593, at Ch. 3.1; Terra & Kajus, *Introduction to European VAT (Recast)*, *supra* n. 594, at sec. 7.4.1.
596. Van Brederode, *Systems of General Sales Taxation*, *supra* n. 593, at Ch. 3.1.3.
597. R. de la Feria & R. Krever, *Ending VAT Exemptions: Towards a Post-Modern VAT*, sec. 1.02, in: *VAT Exemptions* (R. de la Feria ed., Wolters Kluwer 2013).

§7.02 BRIEF HISTORY OF CONSUMPTION TAXATION

The rise to prominence of consumption taxation occurred in the 20th century. Gross receipt and sales taxes became a popular instrument to pay for the World War II expenses and to compensate for reduced revenues from other taxes after the Great Depression in Europe and the United States. Although US sales taxes were introduced as temporary measures, they have been maintained as a reliable revenue source for much longer than initially anticipated.[598]

The theoretical origins of VAT are attributed to Thomas S. Adams and Wilhelm von Siemens. German Industrialist Wilhelm von Siemens proposed the tax under the name "ennobled turnover tax" (*veredelte Umsatzsteuer*) in 1919.[599] American economist Thomas S. Adams suggested VAT in the form of a business tax as a replacement for US corporate income tax in 1921.[600] Initially, the suggestions of both writers yielded little influence. In Europe, France was the first country to adopt VAT in 1954 by gradually modifying its gross receipt tax.[601] The spread of VAT can be credited to the European integration process, which required the establishment of a common market and the harmonization of indirect taxation.[602] At the time the European Economic Community (EEC) was created, all of the six original Member States (except France) levied gross receipts taxes. Shortly after the creation of the EEC, a commission headed by Professor Fritz Neumark was established and charged with determining "whether and to what extent the present differences between the financial systems of the Member States impede, or even render impossible, the establishment of a common market," and "what possibilities exist to eliminate those differences."[603] The Neumark Commission investigated both RST and VAT, and rejected the former in favor of the latter. The retail sales tax was not considered a suitable alternative on the practical grounds, especially due to the large number of small retailers, most of whom were thought to be unable to keep adequate books.

In the First VAT Directive of April 11, 1967,[604] the ECC declared that all Member States should adopt VAT. The Second VAT Directive of the same date[605] set out the common VAT system. However, the VAT system based on those Directives permitted

598. R.F. van Brederode, *Introduction to the US State Sales and Use Taxes*, 18 Intl. VAT Mon. 4, sec. 1 (2007).
599. C. von Siemens, *Veredelte Umsatzsteuer* (Siemensstadt 1919), who cites his brother Wilhelm von Siemens as originator of the proposal.
600. T.S. Adams, *Fundamental Problems of Federal Income Taxation*, 35 Quarterly Journal of Economics, pp. 527-556 (1921).
601. Van Brederode, *Systems of General Sales Taxation*, *supra* n. 593, at Ch. 2.
602. For the history of harmonization of indirect taxation in the European Union, *see* B.J.M. Terra & P.J. Wattel, *European Tax Law*, 6th ed., sec. 4 (Kluwer Law International 2012).
603. Report of the Financial and Fiscal Committee (1963) (the "Neumark Report").
604. *First Council Directive 67/227/EEC of 11 April 1967 on the Harmonization of Legislation of Member States Concerning Turnover Taxes*, OJ 71 of April 14, 1967 (hereinafter: the "First VAT Directive").
605. *Second Council Directive 67/228/EEC of 11 April 1967 on the Harmonisation of Legislation of Member States Concerning Turnover Taxes—Structure and Procedures for Application of the Common System of Value Added Tax*, OJ 71 of April 14, 1967 (hereinafter: the "Second VAT Directive").

Member States such discretion that in practice nine different and separate national systems existed. The Directives laid down only the general features and left it to the Member States to determine the VAT coverage and the rate structure. On May 17, 1997, the Sixth Directive[606] was enacted with the aim to harmonize various national laws. As this new VAT legislation became part of the *acquis communautaire*, the introduction of a VAT system became pre-condition for accession of any countries subsequently joining the ECC and its successors (the European Community and the European Union). After its implementation, the Sixth Directive underwent many changes, and those amendments were often contained in separate documents. In order to improve the quality of the EU VAT rules and bring together various provisions into one piece of legislation, the VAT Directive[607] (recasting the Sixth Directive) was adopted on November 28, 2006 and entered into force on January 1, 2007. With later modifications and derogations, it still forms the basis of the EU VAT system today.

Despite the large extent of harmonization, the VAT rules applicable in the Member States are far from uniform. It has proved difficult to achieve political consensus among Member States because of countries' resistance to changes in the domestic tax systems. As unanimity is required for indirect tax measures,[608] the policy-making process was driven by the need of compromise to satisfy demands of particular countries. To achieve support for VAT, controversial decisions were pushed into the future, national derogations accepted, and a wide range of exemption and reduce-rated supplies introduced.

Attempts to enact VAT outside the European Union revealed some shortcomings of the EU VAT model, especially multiple rates and various exemptions, the administration of which was beyond the capabilities of tax authorities in many countries. In 1984, New Zealand enacted what has become known as the modern VAT—a system that significantly improves the European model by applying a single rate, limited exemptions and a comprehensive base. The modern VAT showed that it was possible to apply VAT to many types of supplies that are classified as too difficult to tax in the European Union. From the mid-1980s onwards, many non-European countries have introduced the modern VAT model.

606. *Sixth Council Directive 77/388/EEC of 17 May 1977 on the Harmonization of the Laws of the Member States Relating to Turnover Taxes—Common System of Value Added Tax: Uniform Basis of Assessment*, OJ L145 of June 13, 1977 (hereinafter: the "Sixth Directive").
607. *Council Directive 2006/112/EC of 28 November 2006 on the Common System of Value Added Tax*, OJ L 347 of December 11, 2006 (hereinafter: the "VAT Directive").
608. Article 113 of the Treaty on the Functioning of the European Union (TFEU) of December 13, 2007, OJ C115 (2008), reads as follows: "The Council shall, acting unanimously in accordance with a special legislative procedure and after consulting the European Parliament and the Economic and Social Committee, adopt provisions for the harmonisation of legislation concerning turnover taxes, excise duties and other forms of indirect taxation to the extent that such harmonisation is necessary to ensure the establishment and the functioning of the internal market and to avoid distortion of competition."

§7.03 RISE OF ELECTRONIC COMMERCE

[A] Introductory Remarks

The birth of electronic commerce in the 1990s marked the beginning of a period of rapid change, creating areas of uncertainty. As consumption taxes were conceived at the time when commerce meant local traders selling products to consumers in their brick-and-mortar shops, technological advances and the emergence of new distribution models did not fit within the existing legal scheme any more. Governments and legislators recognized that consumption taxes should be adapted in a coherent manner to the borderless world of global trade and a cooperative approach was required to solve common problems.

The first policy statements on electronic commerce were made in the United States and provided a stimulus for further debates on this new phenomenon. The US Treasury was the first tax administration to set out its views on tax policy implications of global electronic commerce. In its White Paper, published in November 1996, it concluded that the existing tax concepts had to be modified to address the problems raised by this new form of business.[609] As the White Paper was officially labeled a "discussion paper," and given the state of the scholarship on this issue in those days, it provided more questions than answers.[610]

[B] OECD

The international debate in respect of taxation issues arising from electronic commerce was largely driven by the OECD's Committee on Fiscal Affairs (CFA). The OECD work can be traced back to November 1997 when a major international conference *Dismantling the Barriers to Global Electronic Commerce* was organized in Turku, Finland. Following the Turku Conference, the OECD prepared a framework for the taxation of electronic commerce that was presented at the Ottawa Conference in October 1998.[611] The Ottawa Report (1998) concluded that the same principles that governments apply to the taxation of conventional commerce should apply to electronic commerce. These principles included the well-known tax policy concepts of neutrality, efficiency, certainty, simplicity, effectiveness, fairness and flexibility. New legislative measures were not precluded, provided that they were intended to assist in the application of the existing taxation principles and not to impose a discriminatory tax treatment of electronic commerce transactions.[612] The Ottawa Report (1998) recommended to treat the supply of digitized products as a supply of services and to tax it in the country of consumption. International consensus had to be sought on the circumstances under

609. US Treasury, *Selected Tax Policy Implications of Global Electronic Commerce* (November 22, 1996). The White Paper was quite conservative, rejecting the need for any radical rethinking of traditional tax concepts.
610. For a discussion of the White Paper, *see* R.S. Avi-Yonah, *International Taxation of Electronic Commerce*, 52 Tax L. Rev. 507 (1996/1997).
611. OECD, *supra* n. 167.
612. *Id.*, at sec. 2.

which supplies were held to be consumed in a jurisdiction. Countries were advised to examine the use of reverse charge, self-assessment or other equivalent mechanisms for digital supplies acquired from suppliers outside the country.[613]

Following the Ottawa Conference, five Technical Advisory Groups (TAG), consisting of government representatives from both OECD member and non-member countries and business participants, were established to investigate policy solutions to the challenges raised by electronic commerce.[614] The results of the work undertaken by the OECD and TAGs were published in the Implementation Report (2001).[615] As regards consumption taxation, an important element of this Report was *Guidelines of the Definition of the Place of Consumption of Cross-Border Services and Intangible Property*.[616] These guidelines acknowledged that although electronic supplies should be taxed at the place of their actual consumption, this place might not be easily identifiable by the supplier. To prevent administrative difficulties and unnecessary compliance burdens, such services should be deemed to be supplied where the recipient had established his business (for B2B transactions) or where the person had his usual residence (for B2C transactions). However, it was recognized that there were no reliable means of verification of that place.[617] Another important part of the Implementation Report (2001) was *Guidelines on Tax Collection Mechanisms for Electronic Commerce*.[618] These guidelines recommended the application of the reverse charge mechanism for cross-border B2B transactions. For B2C trade, it was recognized that no option was without significant difficulty. The registration of non-resident suppliers was suggested as an interim solution. However, countries wishing to apply this option had to ensure simplified registration procedure and the use of electronic declarations.

In 2013, the OECD and the G20 initiated a project on base erosion and profit shifting (BEPS).[619] The fundamental idea behind this project was concerns about MNEs being able to avoid tax by artificially separating income from activities that generate it.

613. *Id.*, at sec. 5.
614. The TAG on Treaty Characterization of Electronic Commerce Payments considered the application of the definition of royalties in the context of electronic commerce. The Business Profits TAG examined how the current tax treaty rules for the taxation of business profits apply in the context of e-commerce and elaborated proposals for alternative rules. The Consumption Tax TAG advised on the practical implementation of the principle of taxation in the place of consumption. The Technology TAG provided expert technological input into the work of the other TAGs. The Professional Data Assessment TAG focused on the examination of the feasibility and practicality of developing internationally compatible information and record-keeping requirements and tax collection arrangements.
615. OECD, *Taxation and Electronic Commerce: Implementing the Ottawa Taxation Framework Conditions* (2001).
616. *Id.*, at p. 44.
617. *Id.*, at p. 27. The Technology TAG found credit card-related information to be inaccurate as evidence of jurisdiction of the customer. The use of IP number also had limits in terms of its reliability and capacity to be manipulated. Finally, the Technology TAG pointed out increasing consumer sensitivity about personal privacy and data protection, which resulted in businesses being reluctant to seek to collect more information from customers than they needed for their commercial purposes.
618. *Id.*, at p. 46.
619. OECD, *Action Plan on Base Erosion and Profit Shifting* (2013) and OECD, *Addressing Base Erosion and Profit Shifting* (2013).

The BEPS Action Plan set out 15 Actions to counteract commonly employed BEPS strategies and designated tax challenges of the digital economy as Action 1. On March 24, 2014, the OECD published a discussion draft on Action 1[620] and, on September 16, 2014, a follow-up report was released.[621] The "2015 final" report was presented in October 2015.[622] In the context of consumption taxation, this report identified as the main policy concerns the ability of private consumers to acquire goods, services and intangibles from remote suppliers, and the use of exemptions for imports of low-value goods. The report recommended that countries apply the principles of the International VAT/GST Guidelines and consider introducing the tax collection mechanisms included in those guidelines. Despite publishing the "final" report in 2015, the OECD announced the work on the taxation of the digital economy was still underway and the real "final" report on BEPS Action 1 would be released in 2020.

The Consolidated International VAT/GST Guidelines were adopted by the OECD member countries in November 2015.[623] They set the international standards for the VAT treatment of cross-border transactions in remote services and intangibles by making recommendations regarding their place of supply and tax collection mechanisms. The OECD recommends that where it is not necessary for the supplier and customer to be in the same location when the services are supplied, the jurisdiction in which the customer has his usual residence should have taxing rights. In order to collect VAT on these supplies, non-resident suppliers providing services to private individuals should be required to register and file VAT returns in the jurisdiction where their customer usually reside.

On October 24, 2017, the OECD published its Implementing Guidance on the efficient and effective collection of VAT/GST on supplies of services and intangibles by foreign suppliers.[624] This Implementing Guidance follows up on the Consolidated OECD International VAT/GST Guidelines. According to the OECD, the reverse charge mechanism is the preferred regime for B2B transactions due to its enforceability and to the fact that business customers can comply with domestic regulations at lower compliance costs. For B2C supplies, the OECD recommends that countries follow the traditional supplier collection model (where the supplier is required to register in the destination country) and implement a simplified registration regime. The OECD also believes that intermediaries may be able to support foreign suppliers with the collection and reporting of VAT. The relationship between the foreign supplier and the intermediary can be established either based on a contract or a legal presumption (deemed supplier approach). The OECD envisages that for the future automated

620. OECD, *BEPS Action item 1: Address the Tax Challenges of the Digital Economy* (Public Discussion Draft) (2014).
621. OECD, *Addressing the Tax Challenges of the Digital Economy. Action item 1: 2014 Deliverable* (2014).
622. OECD, *Addressing the Tax Challenges of the Digital Economy, Action 1—2015 Final Report* (2015).
623. OECD, *International VAT/GST Guidelines* (2015).
624. OECD, *Mechanisms for the Effective Collection of VAT/GST When the Supplier Is Not Located In the Jurisdiction of Taxation* (2017).

systems will also assist in the collection of VAT in the case of cross-border supplies of services and intangibles.

On March 16, 2018, the OECD presented an interim report on the tax challenges arising from digitalization.[625] The lengthy report (2,018 pages) was prepared by the OECD's Task Force on the Digital Economy at the request of G-20 finance ministers. Initially, it was scheduled to be released mid-April 2018. However, the OECD released its report a month earlier than planned, responding to the European Union's announcement that it would present its own digital taxation plans in March 2018.[626] The interim report builds heavily on the previous reports and is focused on direct taxation. It examines the two key fundamental concepts in international taxation—profit allocation and nexus rules—and expresses the commitment to undertake a coherent and concurrent review of those concepts, considering the impact of digitalization on the economy. An update on this work will be provided in 2019 and a consensus-based solution on how to tackle the challenges arising from digitalization is expected by 2020. The OECD indicated that at the time the report was issued there was no consensus among countries on whether and to what extent changes to the current tax regime are needed.

[C] European Union

The European Union participated in the electronic commerce debate from the very beginning. In June 1998, the European Commission issued a *Communication on Electronic Commerce and Indirect Taxation*,[627] which intended to be the EU contribution to the Ottawa Conference. The Communication concluded that VAT, as opposed to any new form of tax, was appropriate to electronic commerce. All supplies of goods and services within the European Union should be subject to the same tax, irrespective of the means of communication or commercial mode used to perform transactions. The

625. OECD, *Tax Challenges Arising from Digitalisation: 2018 Interim Report* (2018). For a summary of the content of the report, *see* A.M. Bal, *Halfway towards Consensus or Chaos? Taxation of the digital economy at the crossroads*, IBFD White Paper (March 26, 2018).
626. On March 21, 2018, the European Commission presented two legislative proposals. The first proposal involves a comprehensive reform of corporate taxation in the European Union and introduces the concept of significant digital presence (the long-term solution). A taxable digital presence (virtual permanent establishment) will be deemed to exist if an online business meets one of the following criteria: (i) it exceeds a threshold of EUR 7 million in annual revenues in a Member State; (ii) it has more than 100,000 users in a Member State in a taxable year; and (iii) over 3,000 business contracts for digital services are concluded between the company and business users in a taxable year. The second proposal responds to calls from several Member States for an interim measure and includes a 3% tax on gross revenue resulting from selling online advertising space, digital intermediary activities, and sale of data generated from user-provided information. This tax would be collected by the Member States where the users are located and would apply to companies with total annual worldwide revenues of EUR 750 million and EU revenues of EUR 50 million. It is estimated that only around 150 companies would be covered by the proposed rules.
627. European Commission, *Communication on Electronic Commerce and Indirect Taxation*, COM(1998)374 final (June 17, 1998).

Communication provided a set of guidelines which were to be used as a starting point for further discussions. The guidelines were as follows:[628]

- VAT must be adapted to the developments of electronic commerce. No new or additional taxes are to be considered.
- Supplies of digital products are considered to be supplies of services.
- Digital supplies made for consumption should be taxed in the European Union, irrespective of their origin. Similarly, services supplied by EU operators in third countries should be not subject to VAT.
- Compliance should be made as easy as possible, for example, through the use of electronic invoices and VAT returns. At the same time, tax authorities must have sufficient tools for control and prevention of abuse.

In June 2002, the European Council adopted a directive which aimed at the implementation of some of the above-mentioned guidelines.[629] The main features of the Electronic Services Directive (2002/38) were: new place-of-supply rules and a special regime for third-country suppliers of electronic services. Electronic services supplied by non-EU taxable persons to EU customers followed the destination principle. So did services supplied by an EU taxable person to another EU taxable person or a non-EU private person. However, the origin principle was maintained for supplies made by an EU business to an EU private person. To reduce the compliance burden of third-country suppliers who were obliged to charge VAT of their customer's country of residence, the Directive allowed them to register and submit their VAT returns by electronic means in only one Member State (the OSS arrangement).

Although the Electronic Services Directive (2002/38) improved the existing VAT system, it failed to provide a level playing field for taxable persons supplying electronic services to private individuals resident in the European Union. Whereas an EU taxable person supplying electronic services to private individuals needed to charge and remit VAT in the country where it was established (regardless of where the customer is resident), a non-EU business had to identify the customer's country of residence and charge VAT at the rate applicable there (although such VAT can be remitted to only one tax authority). To remove this disparity between EU and non-EU suppliers, new rules had to be implemented by the Member States by January 1, 2015.[630] According to those rules, all providers of electronic services have to charge VAT at the rate of the customer's country and apply the OSS regime for B2C supplies.

---

628. *Id.*
629. *Council Directive 2002/38/EC of 7 May 2002 Amending and Amending Temporarily Directive 77/388/EEC as regards the Value Added Tax Arrangements Applicable to Radio and Television Broadcasting Services and Certain Electronically Supplied Services*, OJ L 128 of May 15, 2002 (hereinafter: the "Electronic Services Directive (2002/38)"). Originally the Electronic Services Directive (2002/38) was intended to apply for a period of three years, starting from July 1, 2003. This period was extended many times and, finally, in 2008, the arrangements became permanent.
630. *Council Directive 2008/8/EC of 12 February 2008 Amending Directive 2006/112/EC as regards the Place of Supply of Services*, OJ L 44 of February 20, 2008.

On May 6, 2015, the European Commission announced its Strategy for the EU Digital Single Market.[631] In this context, the Commission committed to make legislative proposals to modernize the VAT rules for cross-border e-commerce and to reduce the administrative burden arising from different VAT regimes by the end of 2016. In particular, the Strategy recommended: (1) extending the current single electronic registration and payment mechanism to intra-EU and third country online sales of tangible goods; (2) introducing a common EU-wide simplification measure (VAT threshold) to help small e-commerce businesses; (3) allowing for home country controls, including a single audit of cross-border businesses for VAT purposes; and (4) removing the VAT exemption for the importation of low-value consignments. The Commission's commitment to remove VAT obstacles to electronic commerce in the EU Single Market was repeated in the VAT Action Plan, published on April 7, 2016.[632]

On December 1, 2016, the European Commission unveiled plans to simplify the VAT rules for cross-border electronic commerce. The Commission's proposals ("E-commerce VAT package") seek to make it easier for businesses to carry out online sales in other Member States and reduce compliance costs. The "E-commerce VAT package" was adopted during the 5 December 2017 meeting of the ECOFIN Council and should be transposed into the national legislations of the Member States by 2019 and 2021.[633] The main measures included in the package are as follows: (1) expansion of the OSS scheme to include cross-border online supplies of physical goods to non-taxable customers,[634] (2) simplification of the VAT rules for small businesses (companies with annual turnover up to EUR 10,000 from supplies of intra-EU B2C electronic services will be able to account for VAT on these sales under their home country rules and companies with annual turnover up to EUR 100,000 from supplies of intra-EU B2C

631. European Commission, *Communication from the Commission to the European Parliament, the Council, the European Economic and Social Committee and the Committee of the Regions: A Digital Single Market Strategy for Europe*, COM(2015) 192 final (May 6, 2015).

632. European Commission, *Communication from the Commission to the European Parliament, the Council, the European Economic and Social Committee on an action plan on VAT: Towards a single EU VAT area—Time to decide*, COM(2016) 148 final (April 7, 2016).

633. The "E-commerce VAT package" consists of one directive and two regulations. See *Council Directive (EU) 2017/2455 of December 5, 2017 amending Directive 2006/112/EC and Directive 2009/132/EC as regards certain value added tax obligations for supplies of services and distance sales of goods*; *Council Implementing Regulation (EU) 2017/2459 of December 5, 2017 amending Implementing Regulation (EU) No. 282/2011 laying down implementing measures for Directive 2006/112/EC on the common system of value added tax*; and *Council Regulation (EU) 2017/2454 of December 5, 2017 amending Regulation (EU) No. 904/2010 on administrative cooperation and combating fraud in the field of value added tax.*

634. In the European Union, there is currently a special VAT regime for distance sales of goods. The place of taxation of those supplies depends on the supplier's turnover from distance sales in the customer's country. VAT of the Member State of destination is applied if sales in that Member State exceed a certain threshold (EUR 100,000, EUR 35,000 or the equivalent in national currency). Distance sales below the threshold are taxed in the Member State of origin. However, even if the threshold is not exceeded, suppliers have an option to select the country of destination as the place of taxation. The consequence of the fact that distance sales are taxed at destination is that the supplier must register in the country of the customer. There is no simplification option similar to the OSS scheme to prevent multiple registrations. Registration is required in each country where the sales volume has exceeded the applicable threshold. This significantly increases the operating costs of businesses engaged in intra-EU sales of goods.

electronic services will be able to rely on one piece of evidence to identify the place of supply), (3) abolition of the exemption for the importation of low-value consignments[635] and (4) a deeming provision to make platforms liable for the payment of tax.

§7.04 EVALUATION MODEL

This chapter describes the principles underlying an optimal consumption tax system. Such a system is used as a benchmark in the evaluation of the treatment of transactions involving virtual currencies in two selected jurisdiction—the European Union and the United States—which is undertaken in Chapter 8. By comparing these two different jurisdictions with each other and against the benchmark, best practices for virtual currencies will be identified and recommendations for the modifications of the existing tax systems made.

The fundamental characteristic of an optimal consumption tax system is the ability to raise revenue in a neutral manner. In their origins, consumption taxes were not designed to meet social or redistributive objectives but to raise revenue.[636] How much revenue they generate depends on several factors: the size of the economy, the tax rate and tax base structure, the tax administration and the degree of compliance. All these elements interact with each other. The broader the base, the more activities are subject to tax and the higher the revenue. A single rate is easier for tax authorities to administer and for businesses to comply with. Multiple rates often lead to misclassifications of goods and services and create high compliance and administrative burdens. Exemption by sectors of activity may create distortions and incentives for evasion, which require additional administrative capacities to detect and prevent abuse. Reasonably high registration or collection thresholds may ease the work of tax authorities by allowing them to concentrate on larger taxpayers. The degree of voluntary compliance mainly depends on the probability of detection of non-compliance and possible sanctions. Regular tax audits, penalties and third-party reporting are likely to boost taxpayers' honesty. Burdensome administrative requirements and complex tax structure may result in involuntary non-compliance.

The revenue-raising potential of a consumption tax system depends on the extent to which this system meets the generally accepted principles of:[637]

- efficiency (compliance costs for taxpayers and administrative costs for the tax authorities should be minimized. The key role of businesses in tax collection must be properly recognized since consumption taxes are intended to be borne by consumers and not by businesses);

635. The importation of goods of a total value not exceeding EUR 10 (or EUR 22, if a Member State decides so) is currently exempt from VAT. The VAT exemption for the importation of low-value consignments enables EU customers to purchase third-country goods VAT free, whereas the same goods supplied within the European Union would be subject to tax. It creates distortions of competition since it gives preferential treatment to supplies of low-value goods from third countries.
636. Due to its regressive nature, VAT does not seek to ensure vertical equity.
637. OECD, *supra* n. 167.

- simplicity and certainty (tax rules should be clear and simple to understand, so that taxpayers can anticipate consequences of a transaction in advance, including knowing when, where and how the tax is to be accounted. A simple tax system reduces the operational costs to taxpayers and tax administrations, thereby increasing the net benefit for the state revenue);
- fairness (the potential for tax evasion and avoidance should be minimized. All tax that is due should actually be collected. In the context of tax collection, the concepts of substantive and enforcement jurisdiction developed by *Hellerstein* (2003) can be useful.[638] Substantive jurisdiction concerns the state's right to levy tax, whereas enforcement jurisdiction is related to the state's power to compel tax collection. Ideally, rules should be designed so that a state has either both types of jurisdiction or neither. If a state lacks enforcement jurisdiction, it will have difficulty collecting the right amount of tax. The state's ability to enforce tax laws and penalize non-compliance acts as a deterrent and discourages taxpayers from "hiding" their tax liabilities);
- flexibility (tax systems should be flexible and dynamic to ensure that they keep pace with technological and commercial developments).

Furthermore, tax revenue should be raised in a neutral manner. Neutrality generally means that taxes should not have distortive effects on the economy. They should neither influence business decisions nor affect consumer choices. Neutrality can be divided into external neutrality and internal neutrality.[639]

External neutrality is concerned with cross-border transactions and means a neutral functioning of the tax borders. In a conceptually ideal tax system, it should not make any difference whether expenditure is related to goods imported or locally produced. The total amount of tax collected should not be influenced by the geographical structure of the value chain.[640] Such an ideal tax system should follow the destination principle, according to which the total tax paid in relation to a supply is determined by the rules applicable in the jurisdiction of consumption (exports are exempt with refund of input taxes, and imports are taxed on the same basis and with the same rates as local production). The correct application of the destination principle requires that the place where goods or services are to be consumed is known to the supplier. However, the increasing global nature of businesses and the use of modern communication technologies may make it difficult to apply a pure consumption test. Thus, consumption tax systems use various proxies to predict the expected place of consumption (for example, the place where services are used and enjoyed, the permanent address or the usual residence of a customer). The benefit principle of taxation also advocates taxation according to the place of consumption: if VAT is seen as a compensation for benefits a consumer receives, the right to tax should be allocated to the jurisdiction that facilitates use and enjoyment of such consumption.

638. W. Hellerstein, *Jurisdiction to Tax Income and Consumption in the New Economy: A Theoretical and Comparative Perspective* (2003), http://digitalcommons.law.uga.edu/fac_artchop/124.
639. Terra & Kajus, *Introduction to European VAT (Recast)*, *supra* n. 594, at sec. 7.3.
640. *Id.*, at sec. 7.3.2.

The opposite of the destination principle is the origin principle, which means that in cases where the value chain crosses several jurisdictions, each jurisdiction where a value is added collects the tax on this value at the local rate. The application of the origin principle does not achieve neutrality as the total tax amount reflects the various rates applicable in countries where a value is added, clearly favoring production in low tax jurisdictions.[641]

Internal neutrality refers to the national aspects of levying a consumption tax. It can be divided into economic, competition and legal neutrality. First, economic neutrality implies that taxation should not be influenced by the technology and commercial channels used for the supply of goods and services. It should not interfere with (favor or penalize) a particular form of trade (interstate, international or domestic). The market mechanism should determine the means of production and distribution. Second, in a neutral tax system, the tax burden is borne exclusively by consumers (competition neutrality). This can be achieved by either exempting supplies to businesses or granting the full right of deduction of input tax throughout the supply chain. A business that cannot shift the tax burden forward cannot remain competitive. Third, the principle of neutrality requires that the equal is treated equally (legal neutrality). Therefore, it is necessary that the amount of tax is the same for identical products. The fact whether consumption tax is levied on particular products should not depend on the type of the person performing a supply or the probability of tax enforcement.[642]

Finally, it is necessary to mention that the existence of basic principles underlying a tax does not mean that each consumption tax provision must reflect all those principles. As the application of principles sometimes leads to contradictory results, a trade-off in their practical implementation may be required for enforcement or practical reasons. In such a case, the principles have to be weighed against each other.

§7.05 QUESTION RAISED BY VIRTUAL CURRENCIES

The emergence of virtual currencies has posed several consumption tax questions. As consumption taxes are levied on transactions, the following events involving virtual currency may have consumption tax implications:

- exchanges of goods and services for virtual currency;
- exchanges of legal currency for virtual currency (including ICOs);
- exchanges of virtual currency for another virtual currency (including ICOs);
- currency mining;

For each of the following events, a number of questions must be answered in order to determine its treatment for consumption tax purposes. As virtual currencies are frequently bought and sold by private individuals who are not registered for

641. If all countries had identical VAT systems, the origin and destination principles would become equivalent.
642. Terra & Kajus, *Introduction to European VAT (Recast)*, *supra* n. 594, at sec. 7.3.1.

consumption tax purposes, the first question that arises is under which circumstances transacting in virtual currency results in acquiring the status of an entrepreneur (taxable person) or retailer, and triggers a registration obligation. Second, it needs to be clarified what is the status of virtual currency for consumption tax purposes (i.e., does it qualify as digital products, securities, legal currencies, ... etc?) and whether all types of virtual currency can have the same qualification. The classification of virtual currency for consumption tax purposes is crucial for the determination where transactions in virtual currency take place and whether they can benefit from an exemption. If trade in virtual currencies results in taxable transactions, the traders must be aware of their compliance obligation and the tax authorities must have effective methods to monitor and enforce compliance. Chapter 8 seeks to answer these questions by examining the relevant parts of the US sales tax system and the EU VAT system.

CHAPTER 8
Consumption Taxation: Selected Jurisdictions

As consumption taxes are levied on transactions, the following events may have consumption tax implications:

- exchanges of goods and services for virtual currency;
- exchanges of legal currency for virtual currency (including ICOs);
- exchanges of virtual currency for virtual currency (including ICOs);
- currency mining.

This chapter examines the consumption tax treatment of these transactions in two selected jurisdictions, the European Union and the United States, focusing on the following questions:

- Under which circumstances transacting in virtual currency requires the person to charge consumption tax?
- How to classify virtual currency for consumption tax purposes (digital products, securities, legal currencies ... etc.)?
- Can all types of virtual currency be treated in the same manner for consumption tax purposes?
- What sourcing rules apply to virtual currency transactions (i.e., where do transactions in virtual currency take place)?
- Can transactions in virtual currency benefit from a VAT exemption?
- What are the compliance obligations of virtual currency traders and miners?

In Chapter 9, the outcome of the analysis carried out in this chapter is evaluated against the principles underlying an optimal tax system that were identified in Chapter 7. On this basis, recommendations the improvement of the existing EU and US systems are made.

§8.01 THE EUROPEAN UNION

[A] The EU VAT System: Introduction

VAT is an important pillar in the tax and economic system of the European Union. Apart from being a significant revenue source, it contributes to a non-distortive trade policy and respects the fundamental freedoms. VAT legislation in the European Union has been harmonized to a large extent to ensure the proper functioning of the internal market. This process started in 1967, when the First and the Second VAT Directive were enacted. Currently, the VAT Directive lays down the fundamental concepts of the VAT system. The majority of its provisions is straightforward and leaves no discretion with regard to their implementation; however, some allow certain leeway in adopting national rules.[643] To ensure uniform application of the VAT Directive, the VAT Implementing Regulation[644] was enacted.[645] However, the large number of VAT cases referred to the Court of Justice of the European Union (CJEU) indicates that the EU VAT system is far from being clear and uniform.

CJEU decisions play a fundamental role in the application of the EU VAT rules. The CJEU is "the supreme court" in EU VAT matters, since it has the main responsibility for ensuring that VAT law is interpreted and applied in the same way in all EU countries. The CJEU makes sure that national courts do not give different rulings on the same issue and that Member States and EU institutions do what the law requires. Most matters brought before the Court are either references for preliminary rulings or direct actions. Preliminary rulings result from requests by Member States' national courts for the CJEU to give guidance on the interpretation of EU law. Direct actions are usually brought by the European Commission against Member States that have failed to fulfill their obligations under EU law. The CJEU is acknowledged to have been the driving force in the emergence of a distinctive "European Union law," separate from both national and traditional international law. The CJEU proclaimed this law to be "a new legal order" in *NV Algemene Transporten Expeditie Onderneming van Gend en Loos v. Nederlandse Administratie der Belastingen* (26/62).[646] Moreover, this new legal order was accorded supremacy over the national laws of the Member States in *Flaminio Costa v. ENEL* (6/64).[647]

643. For example, Member States may decide about the applicable VAT rates. The VAT Directive only lays down the minimum standard rate (15%) and the minimum reduced rate (5%).
644. *Council Implementing Regulation (EU) No 282/2011 of 15 March 2011 Laying Down Implementing Measures for Directive 2006/112/EC on the Common System of Value Added Tax*, OJ L77 of March 23, 2011 (hereinafter: the "VAT Implementing Regulation").
645. Regulations are binding in their entirety and are directly applicable in all Member States. In contrast, a directive is binding as to the result to be achieved, allowing each Member State to choose the method and form of implementing it.
646. CJEU, February 5, 1963, 26/62, *NV Algemene Transport- en Expeditie Onderneming van Gend & Loos v. Netherlands Inland Revenue Administration.*
647. CJEU, July 15, 1964, 6/64, *Flaminio Costa v. ENEL.*

In simple terms, the functioning of the VAT system can be described as follows. All supplies of goods and services carried out for consideration by a taxable person in the EU territory are subject to VAT, unless a specific exemption applies. VAT charged by the supplier to his customers is known as "output VAT." The supplier is generally responsible for the remittance of output VAT to the tax authorities. VAT paid by the supplier to other businesses on goods and services that he receives is known as "input VAT." A taxable person is generally able to recover input VAT attributable to his taxable transactions by setting it off against the output VAT in his VAT return, provided that all the requirements for an input VAT deduction are met.

[B] EU VAT and Virtual Currency

This section provides a brief summary of the official statements on the VAT treatment of virtual currency made by various EU institutions. To date, there have not been any legislative proposals in the form of a directive or a regulation on this topic. The VAT Committee[648] provided some guidance on the VAT treatment of virtual currency transaction in its three working papers. In 2015, the CJEU issued its first and so far the only one judgment concerning virtual currency transactions. In its judgment, the CJEU ruled that exchanges of bitcoins into national currency benefit from the exemption for "banknotes and coins used as legal tender" as bitcoins have no other purpose than to be a means of payment. The following sections examine the VAT Committee working papers and the CJEU judgment in more detail.

[1] VAT Committee Working Paper No. 811

In 2014, the VAT Committee presented its first opinion on the VAT treatment of virtual currency in its Working Paper No. 811.[649] Although the Committee's paper focused on Bitcoin, the conclusions it reached should apply to any other form of virtual currency with the same characteristics except virtual currencies whose use is restricted to online computer gaming environments and social networks.

First, the Committee observed that the VAT treatment of Bitcoin depends on its legal nature. While it seems unlikely that Bitcoin could be seen as e-money,[650] a

648. The VAT Committee was set up to promote the uniform application of the provisions of the VAT Directive. Because it is an advisory committee only and has not been attributed any legislative powers, the VAT Committee cannot take legally binding decisions. It can however give some guidance on the application of the VAT Directive.
649. VAT Committee, *Working Paper No. 811* (July 29, 2014).
650. Electronic money is defined in Article 2 of Directive (2009/110/EC) as monetary value as represented by a claim on the issuer, which is issued on receipt of funds for the purpose of making payment transactions and which is accepted by persons other than the issuer.

currency,[651] a security[652] or a voucher,[653] it could meet the characteristics of a digital product (i.e., an electronically supplied service) or a negotiable instrument.

Next, the Committee examined the VAT implications of the following transactions: (1) supplies of goods and services remunerated by means of bitcoins; (2) services concerning the arrangement of transactions in bitcoins (i.e., the provision of digital wallets); (3) services concerning the verification of transactions in bitcoins (mining activities); and (4) services concerning the exchange of bitcoins.

Regarding the first category, the Committee considered the transfer of bitcoins in exchange for goods or services to constitute a means of payment and, therefore, to fall outside the scope of VAT as for VAT purposes payments are not a form of consumption but a measure of consumption. If Bitcoin was seen as a negotiable instrument, the three other types of transactions (i.e., the provision of digital wallets, mining activities and services related to the exchange of bitcoins into other currencies) would be exempt under Article 135(1)(d) of the VAT Directive (exemption for transactions involving deposit accounts, payment, transfers and other negotiable instruments). If Bitcoin was regarded as a digital product, these three types of transactions would be subject to VAT as electronically supplied services and an exemption could not be applied.

[2] VAT Committee Working Paper No. 854

Given the divergence of views among Member States on the VAT treatment of virtual currency transactions, the VAT Committee revisited the issue in 2015. In its Working Paper No. 854,[654] the VAT Committee stressed again that the VAT treatment of Bitcoin transactions[655] depends on the legal status of virtual currency and examined the challenges that would arise if Bitcoin was treated as a negotiable instrument or digital product (i.e., an electronically supplied service).

The Committee observed that although Bitcoin operates in a similar way to traditional currencies, it should not be given the same VAT treatment as a legal tender

651. The Committee observed that traditional currencies have three different functions: (1) medium of exchange used as an intermediary in trade; (2) unit of account for the measurement of value and costs of goods or services; and (3) store of value as money can be saved and retrieved in the future. It concluded that it is doubtful whether Bitcoin can be considered a safe storage of value due to the lack of supervision, potential technical problems and, above all, high volatility.

652. According to the CJEU, an instrument would only qualify as a security for the purposes of Article 135(1)(f) of the VAT Directive if the acquisition of the instrument implied a transfer of rights related to the issuer of the instrument or a claim against the issuer. *See* CJEU, June 12, 2014, Case C-461/12, *Granton Advertising BV v. Inspecteur van de Belastingdienst Haaglanden/kantoor Den Haag*.

653. According to the Committee, Bitcoin lacks the fundamental characteristic of a voucher; i.e., the obligation for the supplier to provide goods or services in exchange for the voucher.

654. VAT Committee, *Working Paper No. 854* (April 30, 2015).

655. Again, the VAT Committee stressed that although its Working Paper No. 854 focused on Bitcoin, the views expressed there should apply to any other form of virtual currency with the same characteristics except virtual currencies whose use is restricted to online computer gaming environments and social networks.

currency; i.e., Article 135(1)(e) of the VAT Directive exempting "transactions, including negotiations, concerning currency, bank notes and coins" should not be applied.[656]

If Bitcoin was seen as a digital product, the following challenges could arise: (1) the use of bitcoins for payment for goods or services could be seen as a barter, increasing the costs for participating businesses; (2) individuals using bitcoins on a continuing basis could be seen as taxable persons carrying out an economic activity; (3) it could be difficult to identify the place where the customer is located, which is the place of supply for electronically supplied services; and (4) there would be a risk that fraudulent schemes could be designed in order to embezzle collected VAT.

Treating Bitcoin as a negotiable instrument would require determining the scope of the exemption contained in Article 135(1)(d) of the VAT Directive (i.e., which activities performed in relation to Bitcoin may be covered by this provision). Irrespective of the Bitcoin classification as a digital product or negotiable instrument, it would be challenging to determine the applicable exchange rate: under the VAT invoicing rules, the amount of tax to be paid must be expressed in the national currency of the Member State where the supply takes place. Article 91(2) of the VAT Directive provides that if "factors used to determine the taxable amount (...) are expressed in a currency other than that of the Member State in which assessment takes place, the exchange rate applicable shall be the latest selling rate recorded, at the time VAT becomes chargeable, on the most representative exchange market or markets of the Member State concerned." Since Bitcoin is traded on multiple exchange platforms, its value in other currencies varies and depends on the exchange platform. However, the VAT Committee admitted that variations in the price of Bitcoin among several exchange platforms are negligible.

Taking into consideration the above-mentioned analysis, the VAT Committee was of the opinion that treating Bitcoin as a negotiable instrument represented the most suitable solution from a VAT perspective.[657]

[3] Hedqvist (Case C-264/14)

On October 22, 2015, the CJEU gave its decision on the VAT treatment of bitcoin exchange services in *Skatteverket v. David Hedqvist* (Case C-264/14)—the first and the only case concerning virtual currencies that has been referred to it so far.[658] The facts of the case are as follows: a Swedish national, David Hedqvist, intended to open a Bitcoin trading platform where bitcoins would be exchanged for Swedish kroner. His company would purchase bitcoins form other individuals and companies and subsequently resell them. The price of bitcoins would be based on an exchange rate shown on an exchange rate portal, adjusted by a percentage charged by him as a transaction fee. He asked the Swedish Board for Advanced Tax Rulings (*Skatterättsnämnd*) whether the proposed service would attract VAT. According to the ruling issued by the

656. The opposite conclusion was reached by the CJEU in *Hedqvist*. *See* §8.01[B][3] *Hedqvist* (Case C-264/14).
657. In *Hedqvist*, the CJEU rejected this classification. *See* §8.01[B][3] *Hedqvist* (Case C-264/14).
658. CJEU, October 22, 2015, Case C-264/14, *Skatteverket v. David Hedqvist*.

Board, the buying and selling of bitcoins is a service performed for consideration, but not subject to VAT, as bitcoins are used as a legal means of payment. The Swedish tax authorities (*Skatteverket*) appealed the ruling and on June 2, 2014 the Swedish Supreme Administrative Court (*Högsta förvaltningsdomstol*) referred the following questions to the CJEU: (1) do exchanges of means of payment without legal tender status, such as Bitcoin, into a national currency constitute a supply of services for consideration; and (2) are such exchanges are exempt from VAT under Article 135(1) of the VAT Directive?

The CJEU answered the first question in the affirmative, following the opinion of the Advocate Generale Kokott delivered on July 16, 2015.[659] The CJEU observed that bitcoins have no other purpose than to be a means of payment. As they serve the same purpose as national currencies, the principle of fiscal neutrality requires that they be treated in the same way. In line with previous CJEU case law, the mere transfer of legal tender or other means of payment should not attract VAT. The function of legal tender is to facilitate transactions rather than to be consumed as goods or services. However, the activities envisaged by David Hedqvist go further than transferring a means of payment. They constitute currency exchange services, which constitute supplies of services for consideration, as was already clarified by the CJEU in *First National Bank of Chicago* (Case C-172/96).[660]

With regard to the second question, the CJEU examined the requirements of Article 135(1)(d), (e) and (f) of the VAT Directive. First, the CJEU examined whether the exemption for transactions involving "deposit and current accounts, payments, transfers, debts, cheques and other negotiable instruments" could be applicable. On that matter, it concluded that this provision concerns services or instruments that operate as a way of transferring money but not transactions that involve money itself, which are the object of a specific provision, namely Article 135(1)(e) of the VAT Directive.

In considering Article 135(1)(e) of the VAT Directive, which exempts transactions "concerning banknotes and coins used as legal tender," the CJEU observed that the wording of the VAT Directive is unclear on this matter. Various language versions of Article 135(1)(e) of the VAT Directive do not allow determining without ambiguity whether that provision applies only to transactions involving traditional currencies or whether, on the contrary, it is also intended to cover transactions involving another currency. Given this ambiguity, the question needs to be answered by taking into account the purpose of the VAT exemption. The CJEU observed that the purpose of the VAT exemption is to allow for the free exchange of means of payment, which would benefit the internal market insofar as cross-border services require currency conversions. Although Bitcoin is not legal tender, it serves the same purpose as national currencies, i.e., it functions as a medium of exchange. Therefore, the purpose of Article 135(1)(e) justifies the application of VAT exemption to exchanges of bitcoins for national currencies.

---

659. AG Opinion, July 16, 2015, Case C-264/14, *Skatteverket v. David Hedqvist*.
660. CJEU, July 14, 1998, Case C-172/96, *Commissioners of Customs & Excise v. First National Bank of Chicago*.

Finally, the CJEU looked at Article 135(1)(f) of the VAT Directive, which applies to transactions in "shares, interests in companies or associations, debentures and other securities," i.e., to items that represent property rights in corporations, debt instruments and rights related thereto. As neither bitcoins nor Swedish kroner could be regarded as such, the CJEU concluded that Article 135(1)(f) cannot be applied.

Therefore, the CJEU answered the questions referred by the Swedish Court as follows:

- exchanges of means of payment without legal tender status, such as Bitcoin, into a national currency, at an exchange rate that takes into account the commission by the service provider, constitute a supply of services for consideration under Article 2(1)(c) of the VAT Directive; and
- such exchanges are exempt from VAT under Article 135(1)(e) of the VAT Directive.

[4] Working Paper No. 892

Following the CJEU decision in *Hedqvist*, the VAT Committee revisited the VAT treatment of Bitcoin, taking into account the interpretation and reasoning of the Court in that judgment.[661] The VAT Committee acknowledged that the CJEU judgment departed from the analysis presented in the Committee's previous working papers: neither of the two options considered by the VAT Committee—bitcoins treated as a negotiable instrument or as a digital product—was accepted by the CJEU. In practical terms, however, the conclusion reached by the CJEU seemed to entail the same consequences (exemption of transactions concerning Bitcoin) as the Committee's analysis but based on a different legal provision (Article 135(1)(e) rather than Article 135(1)(f) of the VAT Directive).

The VAT Committee observed that since *Hedqvist* was limited to transactions concerning the exchange of bitcoins for traditional currencies, it was necessary to examine the implications of the judgment on the VAT treatment of other Bitcoin transactions, such as: (1) supplies of goods and services remunerated by way of Bitcoin; (2) services concerning the arrangement of transactions in Bitcoin (the provision of digital wallets); (3) mining activity; and (4) services related to intermediation provided by exchange platforms (in *Hedqvist*, the CJEU examined only one type of exchange transactions where Mr Hedqvist's company was buying and selling bitcoins; i.e., it was acting as the owner of bitcoins).

The conclusions reached by the VAT Committee were as follows:

- the use of bitcoins for acquiring goods or services is outside the scope of VAT (as Bitcoin acts as a means of payment) and no VAT should be levied on the value of the bitcoins used in a transaction;

661. VAT Committee, *Working Paper No. 892* (February 4, 2016).

- services supplied by digital wallets providers are either outside the scope of VAT (if there is no consideration) or exempt based on Article 135(1)(e) of the VAT Directive;
- mining activity is out of the VAT scope if miners receive no transaction fee in return for their verification activities. However, if mining activity is done for a fee, it would be exempt.[662]
- services related to intermediation supplied by exchange platforms for consideration are taxable services and cannot benefit from any exemption.[663]

[C] Personal Scope

This section seeks to answer the question under which circumstances mining activities and trading in virtual currency may result in acquiring the status of a taxable person and trigger a VAT registration obligation. "Taxable person" is an autonomous VAT concept. It does not exist in civil or trade law. Under Article 9 of the VAT Directive, a taxable person is anyone who independently carries out in any place any economic activity, whatever the purpose or result of that activity. Article 9(2) provides a non-exhaustive list of economic activities ("any activity of producers, traders, person supplying services, including mining and agricultural activities and activities of the professions"), and notes that "exploitation of tangible or intangible property for the purposes of obtaining income therefrom on a continuing basis" should also be taxable.

Thus, the definition of the taxable person is very broad: it is not limited to EU residents ("any person in any place") or to persons acting for profit motives ("whatever the purpose"). This is in line with the objective of VAT as a general consumption tax. The characterization as a taxable person depends on two factors: the existence of economic activities and the independent pursuit of such activities. The former requirement is examined in the next sections. The latter is not discussed further as persons trading in virtual currencies generally do not perform these activities in an employment relationship.[664] Thus, they act independently.

[1] Beginning of Economic Activities

A person may acquire the status of a taxable person long before he first performs a taxable transaction. The CJEU ruled in *Rompelman* (C-268/83) that the exploitation of

662. Miners will have to rely on transaction fees from around 2040 as the ceiling of 21 million bitcoins will have been reached by then and no new bitcoins will be created. Transaction fees will be the only incentive for mining activity.

663. An exchange platform makes available the infrastructure that allows exchanges to take place. Thus, it does not supply exchange services but services consisting in the provision of technical infrastructure that cannot benefit from an exemption for financial services.

664. Under Article 11 of the VAT Directive, "the condition in Article 9(1) that the economic activity be conducted 'independently' shall exclude employed and other persons from VAT in so far as they are bound to an employer by a contract of employment or by any other legal ties creating the relationship of employer and employee as regards working conditions, remuneration and the employer's liability."

property generally begins "with the first preparatory act, i.e., with the first transaction on which input tax may be charged."[665] Any other view would be contrary to the purpose of the VAT system since in the period between the remittance of VAT which is payable on the first transaction and the refund of that VAT, the person would bear the tax burden; however, the intention of the VAT system is precisely to relieve the trader entirely of that burden.[666] Thus, preparatory activities, such as the acquisition of operating assets, must be treated as economic activities. Nevertheless, the tax authorities may require that the declared intention to perform taxable supplies is supported by objective evidence.[667]

It is not relevant that the acquired assets are immediately used for taxable transactions.[668] The immediate use of goods for taxable supplies does not constitute a condition for the existence of an economic activity. As the CJEU observed in *Lennartz* (C-97/90), the use to which the goods are put, or intended to be put, merely determines the extent of the initial deduction to which the taxable person is entitled. However, it is the acquisition of the goods by a taxable person acting as such that gives rise to the application of the VAT system and the deduction mechanism.[669] To determine whether a person acquires goods in his capacity as a taxable person, all relevant circumstances, such as the nature of the goods concerned and the period which elapsed between their acquisition and their use for the taxable person's economic activities, must be taken into account.[670]

The analysis presented above shows that a person may acquire the status of a taxable person long before he starts selling virtual currency or making a profit from his transactions. This means that a person who intends to mine or sell virtual currency may benefit from input VAT deductions in a very early stage of his activities. However, according to the settled CJEU case law, the intention to perform taxable transactions must be confirmed by objective evidence. What kind of evidence can qualify as sufficient depends on a case-by-case situation. It is clear that some activity must be carried out: the mere intention to become a virtual currency miner or trader is not sufficient. Registering with a virtual currency exchange platform or downloading the mining software from the Internet does not seem to be sufficient evidence that taxable transitions will be carried out in the future. However, activities aimed at establishing one's own exchange platform or purchases of specialized hardware to mine bitcoins may indicate that a person prepares to carry out economic activity.[671]

665. CJEU, February 14, 1985, C-268/83, *D. A. Rompelman and E. A. Rompelman-Van Deelen v. Minister van Financiën*, para. 13.
666. *Id.*
667. *Id.*, at para. 25.
668. CJEU, July 11, 1991, C-97/90, *H. Lennartz v. Finanzamt München III*, para. 14.
669. *Id.*, at para. 15.
670. *Id.*, at para. 20.
671. It is assumed here that a person does not already qualify as a taxable person due to other circumstances.

[2] Purpose and Result of Economic Activities

Under Article 9 of the VAT Directive, an activity may be considered an economic one, irrespective of its purpose or result. According to the Advocate General (AG) opinion in *Hong Kong Trade Development* (C-89/81), the expression "whatever the purpose or result" ("whether or not for gain")[672] is only explanatory and of secondary importance. It merely intends to clarify that not the aim but the nature of the activities in question is relevant.[673]

An activity does not cease to be an economic one because it is loss-making or carried out for a charitable or philanthropic purpose. The CJEU held in *Hotel Scandic Gåsabäck AB* (C-412/03) that the fact that the price paid for an economic transaction is higher or lower than the cost price is irrelevant.[674] In *Enkler* (C-230/94), the CJEU stated that the hiring out of the caravan could be an economic activity despite that fact that it resulted in losses.[675] The indifference towards profit generation is consistent with the nature of VAT: whether a profit is made is irrelevant, it is the private expenditure made for consumption what counts.

In *SPÖ Landesorganisation Kärnten* (C-267/08), the question was whether public relation activities and supply of advertising material carried out by a section of a political party could be viewed as economic activities. The CJEU answered the question in the negative. In the judgment, it referred to the fact that "the exploitation does not allow the generation of revenue on a continuing basis" and income from other sources (party members' contributions and public funding) had to be raised "to cover losses made by the activity at issue."[676] However, this statement cannot be used to conclude that a loss-making activity cannot be an economic activity. The decisive argument for the CJEU was that SPÖ did not participate in any market. Its task was to spread ideas as a political organization.

In contrast to the income tax legislation of many European countries, VAT does not require a profit motive. The argument that no profits are or will be made cannot be used to deny the status of a "taxable person." However, the statement "whatever purpose or result" cannot be interpreted as meaning that a hobby purpose is sufficient. According to the settled CJEU case law, the economic nature of the activities is decisive. The next sections try to shed more light on the interpretation of this concept.

672. The case was decided on the basis of the Second VAT Directive. Article 4 of that Directive defines the taxable person as "any person who independently and habitually engages in transactions pertaining to the activities of producers, traders or persons providing services, whether or not for gain."
673. AG Opinion, March 2, 1982, C-89/81, *Staatssecretaris van Financiën v. Hong Kong Trade Development Council*, para. 33.
674. CJEU, January 20, 2005, C-412/03, *Hotel Scandic Gåsabäck AB v. Riksskatteverket*, para. 22.
675. CJEU, September 26, 1996, C-230/94, *R. Enkler v. Finanzamt Homburg.*
676. CJEU, October 6, 2009, C-267/08, *SPÖ Landesorganisation Kärnten*, paras. 21 and 25.

[3] Duration of Economic Activities

It is apparent from the settled case law that the term "economic activities" is very broad and objective in character.[677] From Article 12 of the VAT Directive, it may be deduced that economic activities should be carried out on more than an occasional basis since occasional transactions *may* be included in the concept of a taxable person if Member States decide so. This same continuity requirement is found in Article 9(2) of the VAT Directive regarding the exploitation of tangible and intangible property.

However, this should not be understood as meaning that one needs to enter into several transactions to qualify as a taxable person. The Advocate General clarified this matter in the case *Wellcome Trust* (C-155/94). The Wellcome Trust Ltd was the sole trustee of a charitable trust. It sold a large amount of shares that it had held for several years and reclaimed input tax on expenses incurred in relation to that sale. The transaction took place on one day; however, it required extensive preparatory work and assistance of investment advisors. The question was whether the company's investment activities constituted economic activities. The AG observed that the fact that the shares were sold during one day had no bearing on the assessment of that sale. If an activity is treated as an economic activity within the meaning of the VAT Directive, it will remain so even if completed in a single day. The AG concluded that "it is neither the scope nor the duration which is conclusive, but solely the question whether that activity is an economic activity."[678] The CJEU followed the AG's reasoning in its judgment.

There seems to be some inconsistency between the CJEU case law and the wording of the VAT Directive. Under the former, a one-time transaction is sufficient, whereas under the latter, occasional activities may be regarded as economic ones only if a Member State decides so.

The decisive element for the characterization as a taxable person is the economic nature of activities. The term "economic" literally means "considered in relation to trade, industry" or "justified in terms of profitability."[679] Thus, a literal interpretation of this concept suggests that several transactions must be carried out. A person is not considered to be a trader by making a single sale. The fact that there are no guidelines what number of transactions is required or during what period they must occur to qualify as economic ones creates significant legal uncertainty. What if the activities are related but there is a large time break between them? For example, a person sells five bitcoins during one week and then makes another five sales during another week six months later as he wishes to benefit from a favorable exchange rate. As continuity is not required, such time breaks should be irrelevant. However, adding up several occasional sales seems to contradict the wording of the VAT Directive, which excludes such transactions from the VAT scope.

677. CJEU, October 6, 2009, C-267/08, *SPÖ Landesorganisation Kärnten*, para. 17 with further references.
678. AG Opinion, December 7, 1995, C-155/94, *Wellcome Trust Ltd v. Commissioners of Customs & Excise*.
679. Oxford Dictionary, http://oxforddictionaries.com/definition/english/economic?q = economic.

[4] Exploitation of Property

Under Article 9 of the VAT Directive, a person exploiting tangible or intangible property must act with the purpose of obtaining income from such activities on a continuing basis. The term "exploitation" refers to all transactions, irrespective their legal form.[680] However, to be subject to VAT, the exploitation must meet two requirements: its purpose must be to obtain income (condition one) on a continuing basis (condition two).[681] The CJEU shed more light on the interpretation of those requirements in *Ainārs Rēdlihs* (C-263/11),[682] *Enkler* (C-230/94), *Słaby* (C-180/10) and *Kuć* (C-181/10).[683]

Mr. Rēdlihs carried out 12 supplies of timber in April 2005 and 25 transactions of the same type between May 2005 and December 2006. He was not as registered as a taxable person and did not declare any economic activity to the tax authorities, as, in his view, his transactions were non-systematic, of an exceptional nature and not made for profit (he supplied timber to alleviate the damage caused by a storm).

Mrs. Enkler was employed in her husband's tax consultancy firm. She notified her local tax authorities that she was also carrying on the business of hiring out motor caravans. During three fiscal years, she hired out the vehicle, which was mainly used for private purposes, only twice to third parties. Mrs. Enkler did not advertise that the motor caravan was available for hire. When it was not out on hire, the vehicle was kept in a covered parking area near the building where the Enklers lived.

Mr. Słaby purchased, as a natural person not carrying out any economic activity, land designated under the urban management plan for agricultural purposes. He used that land accordingly. When the plan was changed and the land in question was earmarked for a holiday home development. Mr. Słaby divided the land into 64 plots and began to sell them to private individuals. Mr. and Mrs. Kuć purchased land not permitted for development and used it for agricultural purposes. Following a change to the urban management plan, according to which the land in question was henceforth earmarked for residential and service development, they began to sell plots on an occasional and non-organized basis. In both cases, the question was whether the sale of land plots could be regarded as an economic activity or whether it was merely a non-taxable sale of private property.

In all the cases, the CJEU held that the question of whether an activity (the exploitation of a private forest, land or hiring out of a caravan) is designed to obtain income on a continuing basis is an issue of fact which must be assessed having regard to all the circumstances of the case, including, *inter alia*, the nature of the property concerned. The fact that property is suitable only for economic exploitation will normally be sufficient for a finding that its owner is exploiting it for the purposes of economic activities. However, if property is capable of being used for both economic

680. CJEU, December 4, 1990, C-186/89, *W.M. van Tiem v. Staatssecretaris van Financiën*, para. 18.
681. If the latter requirement is not fulfilled, the exploitation of property on an occasional basis may nevertheless qualify the person as a taxable person based on Article 12 of the VAT Directive.
682. CJEU, July 19, 2012, C-263/11, *Ainārs Rēdlihs v. Valsts ieņēmumu dienests*.
683. CJEU, September 15, 2011, joined cases C-180/10 *Jazrosław Słaby v. Minister Finansów* and C-181/10 *Emilian Kuć and Halina Jeziorska-Kuć v. Dyrektor Izby Skarbowej w Warszawie*.

and private purposes (just as in the case of virtual currency), all the circumstances in which it is used must be examined in order to determine whether it is actually being used for the purpose of obtaining income on a continuing basis. One way of ascertaining that is to compare circumstances in which the person concerned actually uses the property with the circumstances in which the corresponding economic activity is usually carried out.

The CJEU repeated that the mere exercise of the right of ownership by its holder cannot, in itself, be regarded as an economic activity. The number and scale of the sales are not decisive for distinguishing between activities in a private capacity and those of a taxable person. A large volume of sales may also be carried out by private individuals. Similarly, the fact that, prior to the disposal, the party concerned proceeded to divide the land into plots in order to obtain a higher overall price from that land, the period of time over which those transactions took place and the level of income derived therefrom are not decisive for the existence an economic activity as all those circumstances could also fall within the scope of the management of the personal property. The occurrence of such activities may only be a useful indication that one is acting a taxable person.

The CJEU held that a person may be assumed to carry out economic activities in the situation where he takes active steps to market property by mobilizing resources similar to those deployed by a producer or trader. Since those initiatives do not normally fall within the scope of the management of personal property, they cannot be regarded as the mere exercise of the right of ownership by its holder. However, the CJEU ruled in *Wellcome Trust* (C-155/94) that whether an investor is in a position to carry out his investment activity himself or whether he requires the assistance of one or more advisers in that regard is not relevant. Otherwise, the characteristics and skills of the investor would determine whether an economic activity ought to be assumed. In *Wellcome Trust*, the CJEU concluded that the activity of the trust was similar to that of a private individual managing its own assets. Neither the scale of the sale of shares nor support from consultancy firms could change that.

Form the above-mentioned case law, it can be concluded that also in the case of exploitation of property there are no clear-cut criteria for identifying the taxable person: the scope and volume of transactions are not decisive. Instead, the requirement of economic nature, which should be established on a case-by-case basis, is used. This approach may result in divergent interpretations of "economic nature," which will finally lead to turning this (intended as objective) concept into a subjective one.[684]

Under EU VAT, the mere acquisition and holding of shares in a company is not regarded as an economic activity, conferring on the holder the status of a taxable person. The holding of shares does not amount to the exploitation of property for the purpose of obtaining income therefrom on a continuing basis because any dividend yielded from these shareholdings is merely the result of ownership of property and is

684. The CJEU held on various occasions that the terms "taxable person" and "economic activities" must be objective in character. CJEU, February 21, 2006, C-255/02, *Halifax plc, Leeds Permanent Development Services Ltd and County Wide Property Investments Ltd v. Commissioners of Customs & Excise*, para. 55.

not consideration for any economic activity. The same holds true for the sale of shares. The CJEU clarified in *Kretztechnik* (Case C-465/03)[685] that the issuing of shares is not an economic activity as it is made with the aim of raising capital and not providing services. The same applies to the issuance of other securities, such as bonds. This principle may have important implications for virtual currency transactions. The main objective of ICOs is to raise capital. Were equity and debt tokens to be considered similar instruments to shares and bonds respectively, an ICO could be treated in the same way as a share or bond issue. Although there are many differences between initial public offerings and ICOs, the purpose of both activities is the same: to obtain funds to finance business activity. As the issuance of shares and bonds is outside the scope of VAT, it would seem discriminatory if an alternative way of financing, such as an ICO, was subject to VAT.

[5] Acting as Such

It is clear from the wording of Article 2(1) of the VAT Directive that a taxable person must act "as such" for a transaction to be subject to VAT. When a taxable person makes a supply which is not part of his economic activity, the supply is not taxable. The taxable person may choose whether to retain an item among his private assets, excluding it from the VAT system or to integrate it into his business.[686] However, the taxable person must, throughout his period of ownership of the property in question, demonstrate an intention to retain it amongst his private assets.[687] The CJEU declared in *Galin Kostov* (C-62/12)[688] that a natural person who already qualifies as a taxable person for his normal activities (as a self-employed bailiff) may also qualify as such in respect of any other economic activity carried out occasionally.

[6] National Case Law

The term "taxable person," as the fundamental VAT concept existing since the introduction of the common EU VAT legislation, should be sufficiently clear and unambiguous. However, it is far from that. Numerous CJEU judgments have not helped to clarify this concept either. The lack of precision in the definition of the taxable person at EU level translates into uncertainty at national level and to unexpected consequences for taxpayers. The following three German cases (car collector, eBay seller and card player) concerning the distinction between an economic activity and a non-economic activity illustrate this.

685. CJEU, May 26, 2005, Case C-465/03, *Kretztechnik AG v. Finanzamt Linz.*
686. CJEU, October 4, 1995, C-291/92, *Finanzamt Uelzen v. Dieter Ambrecht,* paras. 16-20.
687. *Id.* at para. 21.
688. CJEU, June 13, 2013, C-62/12, *Galin Kostov v. Direktor na Direktsia "Obzhalvane i upravlenie na izpalnenieto"—Varna pri Tsentralno upravlenie na Natsionalnata agentsia za prihodite.*

[a] Car Collector

A car enthusiast established a limited liability company, the aim of which was the purchase of classic automobiles and their resale after 20 years (to profit from their increase in value). From 1986 to 1991, the company purchased 126 cars and stored them in an underground garage. Two of the cars were sold during that time. The company also planned to develop a roadster. For this purpose, it hired an engineer and had the model name protected by intellectual property rights. When it turned out that the use of the roadster would not be allowed under road traffic regulations, only one copy of the car was produced.

The contentious issue was the right to input VAT deduction. The tax authorities claimed that the company did not carry out any economic activity, but was used to create a private car museum.[689] They pointed out that neither a sound business plan (showing the expected profits or turnover) was developed nor the market investigated. The Tax Court of Hessen (*Finanzgericht Hessen*) rejected the claim of the tax authorities and confirmed the existence of economic activities.[690] Based on the examinations of all the relevant circumstances of the case, it concluded that the company had developed a unique business concept and followed it consequently.

The Federal Tax Court (*Bundesfinanzhof*, BFH) reversed the decision of the Tax Court.[691] To determine whether the activity in question was designed to obtain income on a continuing basis, the Court referred to the *Enkler* (C-230/94) case, in which the CJEU stated that this issue must be assessed having regard to all the circumstances of the case including, *inter alia*, the nature of the property concerned. The Federal Tax Court concluded that the concept of economic activities required that the taxpayer acted as an entrepreneur (taxable person) while building up his car collection. In the case in question, the company planned to sell the cars after 20 years. Thus, during those years, it did not act as an entrepreneur but as a private person. The idea to construct a roadster was, according to the Court, very risky and of speculative nature and, for that reason, it was not likely to constitute economic activities either. Moreover, no detailed calculations of production costs and revenues were made. Another fact that was used to deny the performance of economic activities was that the company did not have business premises. The underground garage was not considered as such as it was merely used to store the cars and not to perform sales and marketing activities. No sign with the company name was present there either. Thus, the intention of the company to perform taxable activities in the future could not be confirmed by objective evidence.

In the "car collector" case, two courts reached a different conclusion based on the examination of the same facts and following the same CJEU guidelines of the *Enkler* (C-230/94) case. The Federal Tax Court denied the existence of economic activities as "no resources similar to those deployed by a trader" were used. It was not important

689. Under sec. 2 of the German VAT Act (*Umsatzsteuergesetz*), each activity carried out on a continuing basis for the purposes of generating income therefrom shall be regarded as an economic activity, even where the intention of generating a profit is absent.
690. FG Hessen, April 22, 2009, 6 K 2821/02.
691. BFH, January 27, 2011, V R 21/09.

that: there were sound reasons for the sale to occur after 20 years, the cars were acquired and properly stored, the name of the roadster was registered as a trade mark and professionals were hired to assist with its development. Instead, the Court focused on the existence of business premises and the risky nature of the enterprise (criteria not directly mentioned by the CJEU). Surprisingly, it did not refer to the CJEU judgment in *Lennartz* (C-97/90), according to which the acquired assets do not have to be immediately used for taxable transactions. Nor did it comment how the findings from the *Rompelman* (C-268/83) case would impact the case in question.

[b] EBay Seller

In 2012, the German Federal Tax Court had to answer the question when a private individual selling goods on eBay becomes a taxable person.[692] The facts of the case were as follows: from November 2001 to June 2005, a married couple sold 1,200 goods (stamps, coins, carpets and cutlery) on eBay and achieved total revenue of more than EUR 110,000.[693] The tax authorities considered this an economic activity as the transactions were carried out to obtain income on a continuing basis. The couple claimed that they just wanted to get rid of some items that they did not need any more. Those items were acquired without the intention of resale. The sales did not require any organizational effort: items were simply put on eBay without being advertised or marketed in any way. The couple used their private eBay account and did not register any commercial activity.

The Federal Tax Court held that the transactions in question constituted taxable economic activities. First, the Court pointed out that the concept of economic activities is very broad. Second, it recalled that under the settled CJEU case law, a person may be assumed to carry out economic activities in the situation where he takes active steps to market property by mobilizing resources similar to those deployed by a producer or trader. Those initiatives do not normally fall within the scope of the management of personal property, so they cannot be regarded as the mere exercise of the right of ownership by its holder. The Court ruled that the assessment of the activity in question must be made on the basis of the overall circumstances of the case. To distinguish private asset management from economic activity, the following factors are of vital importance: duration and frequency of the transactions, turnover, market participation, structured and planned performance of the activity. However, it is not possible to set a monetary threshold below which transactions are considered to be private asset management. The fact that the items were not purchased for resale cannot be decisive for denying economic activities. The Court pointed out that the couple used a commercial distribution system (eBay) and that the activities required considerable

692. BFH, June 26, 2012, V R 2/11.
693. The amounts of revenue were as follows: DM 2,600 (2001), EUR 25,000 (2002), EUR 28,000 (2003), EUR 21,000 (2004) and EUR 35,000 (2005). In Germany, the special regime for small enterprises applies if the total turnover did not exceed EUR 17,500 in the preceding calendar year and will not be higher than EUR 50,000 in the current year (sec. 19 of the German VAT Act).

organizational effort: the couple had to describe each item, put it in the correct category and provide a photo of it. Moreover, the sellers had to monitor the website to respond to any enquiries of potential customers. When an item was sold, it had to be packed and sent to the recipient.

The reasoning of the Federal Tax Court in the eBay case can be criticized on several grounds. The sale of items on eBay was motivated by private needs (to give away obsolete personal items). The decisions on which item to sell were made spontaneously, without prior plan and irrespective of the situation on the market. It must be recalled from the *Wellcome Trust* (C-155/94) case that "neither the scope nor the duration" is decisive for the presence of economic activities.

In the car collector case, the lack of a detailed business plan and business premises was an indication that no economic activities took place. However, it did prevent the Federal Tax Court from concluding that eBay sellers acted as taxable persons. For the Federal Tax Court, spontaneous sales of old personal items on eBay apparently require more effort than the purchase and storage of 126 cars since it held that only in the eBay case "resources similar to those deployed by a producer or trader" were mobilized. This reasoning is hard to follow.

[c] Card Player

The Federal Tax Court had to answer the question whether a card player was a taxable person.[694] The case concerned a person who frequently visited casinos during the period 1982-1985 and played different card games there. The player was present at the casino during fixed times which were known to people who were interested in playing cards with him. He usually played with the same group of people. The tax authorities considered his activity to be an economic one and required him to remit VAT on the services he provided. They estimated the player's turnover to be DM 49,500 (1984) and DM 54,000 (other years).[695]

The Federal Tax Court first observed that the player provided services consisting of playing cards with others according to the agreed rules. The consideration was performance-dependent and consisted of money that was at stake. Based on the duration and frequency of the activity, the Court concluded that the player was a taxable person.

This decision shows that for the Federal Tax Court, the fact that an activity is generally regarded as a hobby does not have any influence on its VAT treatment. A hobby card player may turn into a professional player (taxable person) if his activity has certain intensity and frequency. Unlike in the car collector case, the Court did not pay any attention to the nature of the activities and to the fact that the outcome of card games could be speculative and dependent on factors beyond the player's control. From the analysis of the three German cases, it can be concluded that turnover and

694. BFH, August 26, 1993, V R 20/91.
695. Approximately EUR 25,000.

frequency of transactions are the decisive criteria in determining whether a person becomes a taxable person.

[7] Compliance Obligations

Taxable persons face numerous administrative obligations. First, they must register their economic activity with the competent tax authorities. Under Article 213 of the VAT Directive, every taxable person shall state when his economic activity commences, changes or ceases. Detailed rules on the registration of taxable persons are laid down in the domestic legislation of the Member States. In most countries, registration thresholds are used to relieve taxpayers with low turnover ("small enterprises")[696] from levying and collecting tax.[697] If the turnover is equal to or higher than the threshold, VAT registration is required. Taxable persons with a turnover below the threshold can opt for registration. The registration thresholds vary significantly among Member States. They can be as low as EUR 3,145 (Sweden) or reach EUR 97,490 (the United Kingdom).[698] However, it is important to keep in mind that small enterprises have to register irrespective their turnover if they render services to taxable persons established in other Member States and those services are deemed to be supplied in the customer's country or if they receive services from abroad that are subject to VAT under Article 44 of the VAT Directive. No monetary thresholds apply to supplies of these cross-border services.

A high threshold reduces the number of taxpayers that must register and fulfill administrative obligations. It means less frequent audits and less work for the tax administration. The main reason for excluding small businesses from the scope of VAT is that tax revenue from their activity is not likely to exceed the related administrative and compliance costs. However, a high threshold may be regarded as giving an advantage to small enterprises and creating distortion of competition with larger ones. Thus, the level of the threshold is often a compromise between the desire to save compliance and collection costs and the desire not to jeopardize tax revenue and not to distort competition.

A failure to observe the obligation to register may result in penalties. According to the CJEU, those penalties must not go further than is necessary to attain the objectives of the correct tax levying, tax collection and fraud prevention. In order to assess whether the penalty at issue is consistent with the principle of proportionality, the nature and the degree of seriousness of the infringement which that penalty seeks to sanction must be taken into account.[699] As the registration obligation constitutes

696. Articles 281-292 VAT Directive.
697. Some countries use only collection thresholds: all taxable persons are required to register for VAT, but those with supplies below the threshold are relieved from collecting the tax.
698. For an overview of the registration thresholds in Europe, *see* F. Annacondia, *VAT Options Exercised by the Member States*, Topical Analyses IBFD (January 1, 2017).
699. CJEU, July 19, 2012, Case C-263/11, *Ainārs Rēdlihs v. Valsts ieņēmumu dienests.*

only a formal requirement, the penalty must not seek to ensure recovery of the tax from the party liable for it.[700]

Taxable persons must issue VAT invoices to their customers. The detailed rules on the invoice content and form are laid down in the VAT Directive.[701] For a long time, the invoicing rules in the European Union were far from uniform, which caused administrative burdens and considerable uncertainty for companies engaged in cross-border activity. This lack of uniformity led to the adaptation of the Invoicing Directive[702] on July 13, 2010. This Directive, which entered into force on January 1, 2013, simplified and harmonized the invoicing rules, and implemented the freedom of choice regarding the invoicing method: paper and electronic invoices are now treated equally.[703] Suppliers may use any invoicing method provided that it ensures the authenticity of the origin and the integrity of the invoice content. Invoicing is governed by the national legislation of the Member State in which the supply of goods or services is deemed to be made. The exception to that rule, i.e., the requirement that the invoices must be drawn up in accordance with the rules applicable in the service provider's Member States, is limited to situations in which the customer must account for VAT under the reverse charge mechanism on the value of the B2B services received from abroad.[704]

Taxable person must file VAT returns and remit VAT within the prescribed deadlines.[705] Those engaged in the provision of cross-border services to other EU taxable persons must additionally submit recapitulative statements (EU sales lists).[706] EU sales lists show the details of all service recipients and the value of supplies made to them during the reporting period.

[8] Interim Conclusions

Giving the wrong answer to the question of whether or not a natural or legal person acts as a taxable person for VAT purposes, i.e., whether or not that person is engaged in economic activities, may have dramatic financial consequences because the tax authorities normally check a person's VAT liability retrospectively over a period of several years and, if it exists, the VAT liability is a substantial percentage of the person's total gross proceeds. Where a person registers for VAT under the assumption

---

700. CJEU, October 21, 2010, C-385/09, *Nidera Handelscompagnie BV v. Valstybinė mokesčių inspekcija prie Lietuvos Respublikos finansų ministerijos*, para. 50.
701. Articles 220-249 VAT Directive.
702. *Council Directive 2010/45/EU amending Directive 2006/112/EC on the Common System of Value Added Tax as regards the Rules on Invoicing*, L 189/1 of July 22, 2010. For a description of the invoicing rules applicable as from January 1, 2013, *see* A.M. Bal, *Recent EU VAT Changes—The Invoicing Directive*, 52 Eur. Taxn. 9 (2012).
703. Although paper and electronic invoices shall be treated equally, one important difference remains between those two types: the use of electronic invoicing should be accepted by customers. The acceptance may also occur by tacit agreement, for instance by processing or payment of the received e-invoice (Article 232 of the VAT Directive).
704. Article 219a VAT Directive.
705. Articles 250-261 VAT Directive.
706. Articles 262-271 VAT Directive.

that he is engaged in economic activities but the tax authorities (and the national courts) take a different position, that person will be liable for repayment of the amount of VAT that he has claimed as refundable input tax, especially where the initial output tax liability is nil or relatively low. On top of having to repay to the tax authorities the incorrectly claimed input tax, the person may incur a penalty for having fraudulently reclaimed tax. By contrast, where a person does not register for VAT under the assumption that he is not engaged in economic activities but the tax authorities take a different position, that person will be liable for payment of the VAT that he has not declared and remitted on the output transactions, especially where the initial input tax claim is nil or relatively low. On top of having to pay the unpaid tax, without having the possibility to recharge the tax to his customers, the person may incur a penalty for having committed tax fraud. To a certain extent, the VAT registration threshold should prevent unexpected VAT assessments in a large number of situations but it does not solve all problems as small businesses have to register irrespective their turnover if they render or receive B2B cross-border services that are subject to the default place-of-supply (Article 44 of the VAT Directive).

Reliance on vague legal concepts that must be interpreted, firstly, by the tax authorities and, subsequently, by national courts and, in the final instance, by the CJEU, gives rise to legal uncertainty, especially when the concepts must be interpreted taking into account "all facts and circumstances of the case at hand." The outcome largely depends on the emphasis that the tax authorities and the national courts put on specific aspects of a scenario under consideration. The more aspects must be taken into account, the larger the risk of different conclusions.

Taxpayers should have certainty about the legislation applicable to them: they should be able to foresee whether an intended activity may give rise to disputes in court. An evaluative statement that the existence of economic activities depends on all the facts of the case is susceptible to diverging interpretations. The use of CJEU case law as the sole interpretation guidance is questionable. There is a risk that taxpayers and tax authorities will take bits and pieces of individual judgments that best fit their reasoning and that they will ignore decisions which are less favorable to their views. It may also happen that decisions are mainly motivated by budgetary considerations: if the VAT remittance is at issue, a person will be regarded as a taxable person, if the case concerns input VAT deductions, the status of the taxable person will be denied.

[D] Taxable Transactions

[1] Supplies of Goods and Services

Taxable transactions are defined in articles 14 to 30 of the VAT Directive. These are: supplies of goods and services, intra-Community acquisitions and importation.[707] A

707. Importation and intra-Community acquisitions are not discussed further due to their irrelevance to the exchange of virtual currencies. Both taxable events involve goods, whereas transactions in virtual currencies are characterized as supplies of services for EU VAT purposes.

supply of goods is defined as the transfer of the right to dispose of tangible property as owner.[708] The transfer does not have to take place in accordance with the procedures prescribed by the applicable national private law. It is sufficient that the transaction empowers the other party to actually dispose of the goods as if he were the owner of the property.[709] This view is in accordance with the purpose of the VAT Directive, which is designed to base the common system of VAT on a uniform definition of the taxable transactions. This objective might be jeopardized if the preconditions for a supply of goods varied from one Member State to another, as do the conditions governing the transfer of ownership under private law.[710]

The supply of services is defined residually as any transaction which is not a supply of goods.[711] Under Article 25 of the VAT Directive, the supply of services may include: assignments of intangible property, obligations to refrain from an act or to tolerate an act or situation, and performances of services in pursuance of an order made in the name of a public authority or in pursuance of the law. This list is not meant to be exhaustive. The characterization as goods or services is important as it determines the applicable rates, exemptions and place of supply rules. Moreover, services cannot be imported or subject to an intra-Community acquisition.

Given their intangible nature, all supplies of virtual currency should be classified as supplies of services. However, in *Hedqvist*, the CJEU observed that bitcoins (and other coins similar to bitcoins) have no other purpose than to be a means of payment. As they serve the same purpose as legal currencies, the principle of fiscal neutrality requires that they be treated in the same way. In line with previous CJEU case law, the mere transfer of legal tender or other means of payment should not attract VAT. The function of legal tender is to facilitate transactions rather than to be consumed as goods or services. Based on the CJEU judgment, coins that intend to act as a means of exchange should be classified as items similar to legal currency and follow the same tax treatment as legal currency.

The CJEU judgment and the statements made by the VAT Committee apply to Bitcoin and other types of virtual currency with the same characteristics. This would imply that these statements cannot be applied to tokens as tokens and coins differ in both their structure and purpose. In contrast to coins, tokens do not intend to act as a means of payment. Tokens serve as a means of financing: they are issued during ICOs to collect funds to finance future projects of their offerors.

An interesting question arises as to whether, based on an extensive interpretation of the CJEU judgment, utility tokens could be considered to be similar to bitcoins and thus similar to legal currency. Although utility tokens serve a means of raising capital, they also function as a means of exchange as they entitle their holders to goods and services provided by the company that issued the tokens. In other words, they act as a means of payment for these goods and services. In the author's opinion, utility tokens

708. Article 14(1) VAT Directive.
709. CJEU, February 8, 1990, C-320/88, *Staatssecretaris van Financiën v. Shipping and Forwarding Enterprise Safe BV*, para. 7.
710. *Id.*, para. 8.
711. Article 24 VAT Directive.

should be treated according to their primary objective, which is to raise capital. At the time the tokens are issued, it is frequently not clear whether the token issuer will succeed in developing the envisaged goods or services.

To sum up, all transfers of virtual currency should be regarded as supplies of services. Based on the CJEU judgment, an exception should apply to virtual currency that is designed to act as means of payment (coins). Such virtual currency should be treated as "something similar to legal tender" and follow the VAT treatment of legal currency.

[2] Consideration

To fall within the scope of VAT, the supply must be carried out for consideration. In *Hong Kong Trade Development Council* (C-89/81), the CJEU held that that a person who habitually provides services free of charge is not a taxable person at all. Such a person must be assimilated to a final consumer.[712]

The consideration is a subjective concept. It does not have to reflect the actual value of the supply or a value estimated according to objective criteria. Moreover, it must be capable of being expressed in money.[713]

There must be a direct link between the service provided and the consideration received.[714] A supply is taxable only if there is a legal relationship between the service provider and the recipient (a reciprocal performance).[715] However, VAT liability does not depend on the existence of an enforceable and binding obligation according to domestic law of a Member State. This would be contrary to the principle of VAT neutrality. Decisive is the mutual agreement, i.e., that the parties agree to exchange some items and not a valid legal relationship between them.[716]

It cannot be disputed that a bilateral legal relationship exists between the parties who exchange virtual currencies for goods, services, legal tender and other virtual currency. The transaction is performed in order to obtain consideration from the other party. However, a link between services provided and consideration received cannot be assumed in the case of Bitcoin mining. Although it may appear that Bitcoin miners perform a service (solving cryptographic algorithms to verify Bitcoin transactions) for which they get paid in bitcoins, not every miner is rewarded with new bitcoins. As

712. CJEU, April 1, 1982, C-89/81, *Staatssecretaris van Financiën v. Hong Kong Trade Development Council*, para. 10.
713. CJEU, 5. February 1981, C-154/80, *Staatssecretaris van Financiën v. Association coopérative "Coöperatieve Aardappelenbewaarplaats GA,"* para. 13; CJEU, October 16, 1997, C-258/95, *Julius Fillibeck Söhne GmbH & Co. KG v. Finanzamt Neustadt*, para. 13; CJEU, November 23, 1988, C-230/87, *Naturally Yours Cosmetics Limited v. Commissioners of Customs and Excise*, para. 16.
714. CJEU, March 8, 1988, C-102/86, *Apple and Pear Development Council v. Commissioners of Customs and Excise*, paras. 11 and 12; CJEU, March 3, 1994, C-16/93, *R. J. Tolsma v. Inspecteur der Omzetbelasting Leeuwarden*, para. 13.
715. CJEU, October 6, 2009, C-267/08, *SPÖ Landesorganisation Kärnten*, para. 19 with further references.
716. CJEU, September 17, 2002, C-498/99, *Town & County Factors Ltd v. Commissioners of Customs & Excise*, para. 24.

more and more miners compete for a limited supply of blocks to verify, it is becoming less and less likely to get a reward for one's mining efforts. Thus, mining activities are outside the scope of VAT.

The same conclusion applies to mining in return for bitcoin miner fees. Bitcoin miner fees are small amounts of bitcoin given to incentivize miners to confirm Bitcoin transactions.[717] Miners use the fees attached to transactions to decide which transactions to confirm first. A large enough miner fee makes it more likely that a transaction will be confirmed in a short period of time. However, a miner fee is not given to a particular miner but it is communicated to all miners within the network who compete be the first one to verify the transaction. Therefore, in the case of miner fees, there is no legal reciprocal relationship between the service provider (miner) and the service recipient (person carrying out the transaction).

When virtual currency is exchanged for legal currency, the consideration is easily identifiable. It is more difficult to determine the amount of consideration in barter transactions that do not involve legal currency. Barter transactions occur when virtual currency that does not intend to act as a means of payment (and therefore cannot be seen as "something similar to legal currency") is exchanged for other virtual currency that also does not intend to act as a means of payment or for goods or services. For example, the exchange of utility tokens for goods or services provided by the company that issued the tokens constitutes a barter transaction.

Barter consists of two different transactions and their VAT treatment differs depending whether they are performed between two taxable persons or whether there is a private person involved. In the B2B case, VAT applies to both transactions. In the B2C case, the B2C part is subject to VAT but the C2B part is not. Barter transactions follow the general VAT rules. The main problem that they present is how to determine the value of the consideration. In *Empire Stores* (C-33/93), the CJEU held that consideration may also consist in a provision of services and its value must correspond to the value which the recipient of the services constituting the consideration for the supply of goods attributes to the services which he is seeking to obtain and to the amount which he is prepared to spend for that purpose.[718] In *First National Bank of Chicago* (C-172/96), the CJEU observed that any technical difficulties which exist in determining the amount of consideration cannot by themselves justify the conclusion that no consideration exists.[719]

Although some virtual currency transactions can be seen as barter for VAT purposes, the valuation problems identified while discussing the income tax consequences of virtual currency transactions are not equally relevant in the VAT context. For VAT purposes, it is not necessary to establish the objective value of an item since the consideration is a subjective concept. It is decisive what value is attributed to the transaction by the individual person.

717. For the amounts of miner fees, *see* https://bitinfocharts.com/comparison/bitcoin-transactionfees.html#1y.
718. CJEU, June 2, 1994, Case C-33/93, *Empire Stores Ltd v. Commissioners of Customs and Excise.*
719. CJEU, July 14, 1998, C-172/96, *Commissioners of Customs & Excise v. First National Bank of Chicago*, para. 31.

Since VAT is a tax on private expenditure, the value that the consumer has to sacrifice (i.e., the value of the object disposed of by him) should be relevant. The consumer is the person who pays, his expenditure is taxed and what he "sacrifices" can only be judged by him. However, this theoretically correct result cannot be applied in practice since the supplier must account for VAT. If the value determined by the customer was decisive, the taxable person would have to ask the other party about that value in order to calculate the VAT due, which would be rather impractical. Thus, the subjective value that the taxable supplier attaches to his supply should be the basis of assessment.[720] The question of the value in barter transactions between two taxable persons is irrelevant if both have the full right to input VAT deduction. If one party is not fully entitled to deduction, the rule outlined in this section for B2C transactions should be applied.

[3] Unlawful Activities

Based on the wording of Article 9(1) of the VAT Directive ("whatever the purpose or result of that activity"), the illegality or even immorality of certain activities should not play any role in a tax that aims to apply to private expenditure. However, certain illegal transactions fall outside the scope of VAT. It is necessary to examine whether the fact that trade in some virtual currencies is considered illegal due to violations of anti-money laundering and banking regulations could have an impact on the VAT treatment of these transactions.

The VAT Directive does not explicitly mention unlawful activities. The CJEU established rules for the VAT treatment of such activities on basis of the principle of neutrality. According to the settled CJEU case law, import and supplies of goods which are totally prohibited in the European Union are outside the VAT scope.[721] However, illegal supplies that may compete with lawful ones should be taxed according to the general rules.[722] If the corresponding lawful supplies are exempt, the unlawful supplies should be exempt too. Such treatment is in line with the principle of fiscal neutrality, which would be violated if unlawful supplies were treated more favorably than lawful ones.

Supplies of certain virtual currency may be unlawful since they violate the existing laws. However, such virtual currency is not prohibited from entering economic channels due to its characteristics. A ban on marketing and selling does not exclude competition between the legal and illegal market. Thus, illegal trade in virtual currency cannot be removed from the scope of the VAT Directive.

Another question that must be discussed in connection with unlawful activities is whether theft may give rise to VAT liability. The CJEU shed more light on this issue in

720. B. Terra & J. Kajus, *A Guide to the Recast VAT Directive*, sec. 7.3.1.3 (2012), Online Books IBFD.
721. CJEU, February 28, 1984, 294/82, *Senta Einberger v. Hauptzollamt Freiburg* (illegal import of drugs (morphine) into Germany), CJEU, July 5, 1988, 269/86, *W.J.R. Mol v. Inspecteur der Invoerrechten en Accijnzen* (sale of amphetamines).
722. CJEU, August 2, 1993, C-111/92, *Wilfried Lange v. Finanzamt Fürstenfeldbruck*. Later CJEU case law follows the same line of argumentation.

Newman Shipping (C-435/03).[723] It held that a theft of goods does not give rise to any financial counterpart for the victim of the theft, and, following the reasoning in *Tolsma* (C-16/93), it cannot be considered a supply of goods for consideration.[724] The CJEU also observed that, as a result of the supply of goods, the recipient should be empowered to actually dispose of the property as if he were its owner. A theft of goods does not fulfill these criteria since it merely sets the thief as the possessor of the goods and does not empower him to dispose of them as if he were their owner.[725]

Virtual currency is characterized as services for VAT purposes. For services, the criterion of empowering the purchaser with the right to dispose over the received content as if he was its owner is not required. A thief or other unlawful possessor of virtual currency can actually dispose of them and transfer them in competition with legal transfers. Therefore, theft of virtual currency meets the criteria of a supply of services; however, it is not taxable due to the lack of consideration.

[E] Sourcing Rules

[1] Introductory Remarks

The EU VAT rules are based on the concept of territoriality: only transactions taking place within the territory of the Member States are subject to VAT. The VAT Directive contains a number of rules that determine where transactions are deemed to occur (these provisions are commonly referred to as "place-of-supply rules").

Originally, many supplies of services were subject to VAT at origin, i.e., in the Member State where the service provider was established. This was a logical solution at the time when most services were provided domestically. However, due to the rapid increase in the volume of cross-border services, it was recognized that the origin-based approach distorted competition in favor of business activity in low-tax countries.[726] To increase the application of the destination principle, which is regarded as the conceptually ideal approach to taxing consumption, the European Union introduced a major amendment to the place-of-supply rules in 2008.[727] This reform, commonly referred to as the "VAT Package," phased in changes to the rules on the place of taxation of services between 2010 and 2015. The last stage of the "VAT Package" took effect on January 1, 2015. It affected the supply of telecommunications, broadcasting and electronic (TBE) services by EU service providers to final consumers.

723. CJEU, July 14, 2005, C-435/03, *British American Tobacco International Ltd, Newman Shipping & Agency Company NV v. Belgian State.*
724. *Id.*, at para. 32.
725. *Id.*, at paras. 35-36.
726. Many suppliers of electronic services chose to provide such services from Luxembourg to benefit from the lowest VAT rate of the European Union (15%).
727. *Council Directive 2008/8/EC of 12 February 2008 Amending Directive 2006/112/EC as regards the Place of Supply of Services*, OJ L 44 of February 20, 2008.

[2] General Rules

Since 2010, the general rule for B2B services is that they follow the destination principle and take place where the recipient has established his business, has a permanent address or usually resides.[728]

A permanent address of a natural person is the address entered in the population or similar register, or the address indicated by that person to the relevant tax authorities, unless there is evidence that this address does not reflect reality.[729] The place where a natural person usually resides is the place where that natural person usually lives as a result of personal and occupational ties. Where the occupational ties are in a country different from that of the personal ties, or where no occupational ties exist, the place of usual residence shall be determined by personal ties which show close links between the natural person and a place where he is living.[730] If a non-taxable person is established in more than one country or has his permanent address in one country and his usual residence in another, priority must be given to the place where he usually resides, unless there is evidence that the service is used at his permanent address.[731]

Within the European Union, the supplier may regard his customer as a taxable person and apply the general B2B rule when the customer has communicated his VAT identification number to him and the supplier has checked its validity.[732] Logically, if no VAT identification number has been communicated, the customer will be regarded as a non-taxable person.

Cross-border B2B services are subject to the reverse charge mechanism.[733] The VAT liability is shifted to the customer who accounts for VAT on the supply in his VAT return. Thus, once received a valid VAT identification number, the supplier will not have to deal with the VAT law of a foreign country, as the liability to remit VAT will be shifted to the customer. The supplier only has to report the service in his VAT return and recapitulative statement.

The general rule for the place of supply of services to non-taxable persons (B2C scenarios) is the origin principle.[734] Such supplies take place where the supplier has established his business, has a permanent address or usually resides. There are many exceptions to the general rules.[735] Once a transaction falls under a specific rule, the latter prevails and the general rule no longer applies. In the virtual currency context, a specific rule for the place of supply of electronic services could be relevant.

728. Article 44 VAT Directive.
729. Article 12 VAT Implementing Regulation.
730. Article 13 VAT Implementing Regulation.
731. Article 24 VAT Implementing Regulation.
732. Article 18(2) VAT Implementing Regulation.
733. Article 196 VAT Directive.
734. Article 45 VAT Directive.
735. For example, there are special rules for services related to immovable property, transport services, cultural, artistic, sporting and entertainment activities. *See* Articles 46 to 59b VAT Directive.

[3] Electronically Supplied Services

Electronically supplied services (commonly referred to as "digital supplies" or "online services") are defined as services delivered over the Internet or an electronic network, the nature of which renders their supply essentially automated, involving minimum human intervention and impossible in the absence of information technology.[736] A non-exhaustive list of those services provided in the VAT Implementing Regulation includes, *inter alia*, the supply of digitized products (movies, music, games), services automatically generated from a computer via the Internet or an electronic network, in response to specific data input by the recipient, Internet Service Packages (ISP) of information in which the telecommunications component forms an ancillary and subordinate part, website hosting, remote systems administration, online data warehousing, accessing the digitized content of books and other electronic publications, the provision of advertising space, use of search engines and Internet directories and automated distance teaching (except where the Internet or similar electronic network is used as a tool for communication between the teacher and student).[737]

Virtual currencies are intangible by nature and their transfers occur via the Internet. Therefore, the most intuitive view would be to classify all types of virtual currencies as electronically supplied services. This classification was considered by the VAT Committee in its Working Paper No. 811.[738] The VAT Committee rejected it as it would give rise to many practical challenges (e.g. individuals using virtual currency on a continuing basis could be seen as taxable persons carrying out an economic activity). In other words, a theoretically correct solution would cause immense practical difficulties. Apart from the practical difficulties, there seem to be hardly any reasons why all types of virtual currencies should not be considered electronically supplied services. Both coins and tokens meet the definition of a digital asset (which is anything that exists in a binary format and comes with the right to use). In *Hedqvist*, the CJEU failed to address the question of classifying bitcoins as digital products. A discussion to that effect would be necessary, given that in some countries with similar VAT systems (Norway, Singapore and Australia) transfers of bitcoins were regarded as supplies of electronic services at the time of the judgment. Therefore, in the author's view, all transfers of virtual currency should be considered electronically supplied services.[739]

As from January 1, 2015, all supplies of electronic services follow the destination principle, i.e., they are taxed at the place where the customer is established, has a

736. Article 7(1) VAT Implementing Regulation.
737. Article 7(2) and Annex 1 VAT Implementing Regulation.
738. In the view of the VAT Committee: "Due to its digital character, it might seem bitcoins fall within the definition of electronically supplied services. Indeed, bitcoins are delivered over the Internet or an electronic network, and they are generated from a computer via the Internet or an electronic network in response to specific data input by the recipient." *See* VAT Committee, *Working Paper No. 811*, p. 10 (July 29, 2014).
739. As shown in this chapter, the practical difficulties resulting from the classification of virtual currency transactions as electronically supplied services can be avoided by the application of VAT exemptions. *See* §8.01[G] Exemptions.

permanent address or usually resides, which means that the supply (and the invoicing requirements) are governed by the VAT legislation of the customer's country.

Since all supplies of electronic services (both B2B and B2C transactions) are deemed to be made at the location of the customer, the status of the customer is relevant to establish who has to remit VAT to the tax authorities. Cross-border B2B supplies are subject to the reverse charge mechanism and the recipient of such supplies is responsible for VAT remittance, whereas in a B2C situation the supplier will remit VAT under the OSS scheme.

In a B2C situation, one of the biggest challenges for suppliers of electronic services is to establish the permanent address or usual residence of their customers. Since electronic services can be provided at a distance, suppliers may not obtain enough information to identify the location of their customers. Given the multitude of low-value transactions in the electronic services sector, the determination of the customer's location on a transaction-by-transaction basis may result in a large compliance burden for suppliers. To assist suppliers with the identification of the location of their non-taxable customer, the Commission has issued a detailed regulatory framework consisting of the provisions of the VAT Implementing Regulation, which establish a number of rebuttable presumptions and an evidence rule, supplemented by more detailed explanations in the non-binding Explanatory Notes.[740] The rebuttable presumptions are as follows:

- If the physical presence of the recipient is required for the provision of electronic services (for example, a telephone box, a Wi-Fi hot spot or an Internet café), such services will be taxable at the location where the recipient effectively uses and enjoys them.[741]
- If electronic services are provided on board a ship, aircraft or train during an intra-Community passenger transport operation, the customer is presumed to be resident in the Member State of departure of the passenger transport.[742]
- If electronic services are provided to a customer through a fixed land line connected with a residential building, the customer is presumed to be located at the place where the fixed land line is located.[743]
- For services supplied via mobile networks, the customer is presumed to be established in the country identified by the mobile country code of the SIM card used for receiving such services.[744]
- For electronic services consisting of the transmission of signals for which a device or viewing card is needed, the customer is presumed to be located at the

740. European Commission, *Explanatory Notes on the EU VAT Changes to the Place of Supply of Telecommunications, Broadcasting and Electronic Services That Enter into Force in 2015* (April 3, 2014).
741. Article 24a(1) VAT Implementing Regulation.
742. Article 24a(2) VAT Implementing Regulation.
743. Article 24b(a) VAT Implementing Regulation.
744. Article 24b(b) VAT Implementing Regulation.

place where the device is installed or, if that place is not known, the place to which the viewing card is sent with the purpose of being used there.[745]

The service provider can rebut the above-mentioned presumptions on the basis of three items of non-contradictory evidence indicating that the customer is resident elsewhere.[746] Tax authorities may rebut the presumptions if there are indications of misuse or abuse by the supplier.[747] If none of the rebuttable presumptions is applicable, it is assumed that the customer is established at the place identified on the basis of two of the following items of non-contradictory evidence (the "evidence rule"):[748]

- customer details, such as the customer' s billing address;
- the customer's Internet protocol (IP) address or any method of geolocation;
- bank details, such as the place where the bank account used for payment is and the billing address of the customer held by that bank;
- the mobile country code (MCC) of the international mobile subscriber identity (IMSI) stored on the subscriber identity module (SIM) card used by the customer;
- the location of the residential fixed land line through which the service is supplied to the customer; and
- other commercially relevant information obtained by the supplier.

The items of evidence used to identify the location of the customer must be different and should not duplicate each other. For example, the fact that the customer gives his bank details and those details are confirmed by a payment service provider is considered one piece of evidence.[749] The supplier must verify the collected evidence items by normal commercial security measures, such as those relating to identity or payment checks.[750] Since the correct determination of the place of supply remains with the supplier, verifications made by third parties (for example, payment service providers) do not relieve the supplier of his responsibility in cases of abuse or misuse.[751] It is unclear what to do if two non-contradictory pieces of evidence cannot be found. The Explanatory Notes issued by the European Commission simply recommend the supplier to "continue to seek" them.[752]

A simplified registration framework (the OSS arrangement) applies to suppliers of electronic services to EU private individuals. The OSS scheme was introduced on July 1, 2003 to avoid a situation in which, for the purpose of having to account for VAT on

745. Article 24b(c) VAT Implementing Regulation.
746. Article 24d(1) VAT Implementing Regulation.
747. Article 24d(2) VAT Implementing Regulation.
748. Articles 24b(d) and 24f VAT Implementing Regulation. As from January 1, 2019, one piece of evidence will be sufficient for companies with the total annual turnover from the supplies of electronic, broadcasting, radio and telecom services not exceeding EUR 100,000.
749. *Explanatory Notes*, *supra* n, 740, at sec. 9.5.5.
750. Article 23 VAT Implementing Regulation.
751. *Explanatory Notes*, *supra* n. 740, at sec. 9.5.9.
752. *Id.*, at sec. 9.5.7.

B2C electronic services in a maximum of 28 Member States, non-EU suppliers had to be registered in all of those Member States. Under this scheme, the non-EU supplier can register and account for VAT in a single Member State, but must apply the VAT rate of the customer's Member State.[753] As from January 1, 2015, EU suppliers of electronic services to EU final consumers have the option to use a similar arrangement (the Mini One Stop Shop scheme, MOSS), i.e., to register and remit VAT only in the Member State of their establishment. The MOSS regime is optional; however, a taxable person that chooses to use the scheme must apply it in all relevant Member States. The scheme cannot be applied to supplies of electronic services in the Member State where the taxable person is established and such supplies must be declared in the domestic VAT return.

[4] Interim Conclusions

Under the EU VAT system, the general place-of-supply rule for B2B services is the place where the recipient has established his business, has a permanent address or usually resides, whereas the general rule for services supplied to private individuals is the place where the supplier has established his business, has a permanent address or usually resides. An exception applies to electronically supplied services—they always follow the destination principle.

If transactions involving virtual currency are treated as electronically supplied services, they are deemed to take place at the location of their recipient. Cross-border B2B transactions are subject to the reverse charge mechanism, whereas in a B2C situation the supplier has to determine the location of the customer and remit VAT under the OSS scheme.

[F] Tax Liability and Chargeable Event

Under the general rules, VAT must be remitted by the taxable person carrying out the supply.[754] However, to simplify the tax collection process, the reverse charge system has been introduced. It means that the obligation to remit VAT is shifted to the recipient of the supply, provided that he is a taxable person. If the recipient uses the services or goods for carrying out taxable transactions, the amount of tax to be paid is immediately deductible, so there is no actual payment to the tax authorities. The main benefit of the reverse charge mechanism is that foreign suppliers do not have to register and account for VAT in the customer's country. Apart from the simplification objective, the reverse

753. The OSS Scheme cannot be used by non-EU suppliers that are already registered in the European Union (e.g., because they receive services that are effectively used and enjoyed in a Member State or perform intra-Community supplies of goods). *See* Art. 358a VAT Directive. However, this will change from January 1, 2019 as a result of the "E-commerce VAT package," which will allow taxable persons not established in the European Union but having an EU VAT number to use the OSS.

754. Article VAT Directive.

charge is also used as a means of combating VAT fraud. The reverse charge rule applies to all supplies of electronic services to taxable persons.

For the purposes of VAT liability, it is important to distinguish between the concepts "tax chargeable" and "tax due." VAT becomes chargeable when tax authorities become entitled to claim it from the person liable to pay it although the time of payment may be deferred.[755] VAT becomes due when it must be remitted to the tax authorities. VAT liability arises as soon as an item is supplied.[756] However, it does not have to be settled immediately but by the deadline provided by the domestic legislation. This deadline usually coincides with the deadline for the submission of the VAT return.

In terms of the time when tax liability arises, special rules apply to supplies of vouchers.[757] Article 30a of the VAT Directive defines voucher as "an instrument where there is an obligation to accept it as consideration or part consideration for a supply of goods or services and where the goods or services to be supplied or the identities of their potential suppliers are either indicated on the instrument itself or in related documentation, including the terms and conditions of use of such instrument." It further divides vouchers into single-purpose vouchers and multipurpose vouchers and sets rules to determine the tax treatment of voucher transactions in both cases. Single-purpose vouchers are defined as vouchers where the place of supply of the goods or services to which the voucher relates and VAT due on those goods or services is known at the time of issue of the voucher. A multipurpose voucher is any voucher which is not a single-purpose voucher. A transfer of a single-purpose voucher will be treated as a supply of goods or services to which the voucher relates and VAT should be accounted for accordingly. Multipurpose vouchers will only be subject to VAT when the voucher is redeemed, i.e., no VAT will be due when the voucher is transferred through the supply chain. The value on which VAT should be accounted for is either the consideration paid by the consumer, or if that is not known, the face value of the voucher, less the amount of VAT relating to the goods or services supplied.

When issuing utility tokens, the offeror promises to exchange them for goods and services in the future. Just as in the case of multipurpose vouchers, tokens can be redeemed for goods or services that are not precisely identified at the time of the sale of the token. Thus, utility tokens seem to meet the definition of multipurpose vouchers. Treating utility tokens as vouchers would mean that ICOs and sales of utility tokens are not subject to VAT. The taxable event would occur when utility tokens would be redeemed for goods or services.

755. Article 62(2) VAT Directive.

756. Article 63 VAT Directive.

757. On June 27, 2016, the European Union adopted *Council Directive (EU) 2016/1065 of 27 June 2016 amending Directive 2006/112/EC as regards the treatment of vouchers*, OJ L 177/9 of July 1, 2016, which harmonized the VAT treatment of vouchers in the European Union. The provisions of this Directive were subsequently included in the VAT Directive.

[G] Exemptions

[1] Introductory Remarks

The term "exempt supplies" describes supplies that do not bear output tax: the supplier does not have to collect and remit any tax in respect of the supply and the recipient is not entitled to any input tax deduction. However, this terminology is misleading: from the point of view of taxable persons and their right to deduct input VAT, exempt supplies are actually "taxable" and taxable supplies are actually "exempt." A taxable person performing taxable supplies can recover input VAT, whereas there is no right to recover input tax for a taxable person performing exempt supplies. The cost of the tax included in the price of taxable inputs must be borne by the person that makes the exempt supply unless the tax is passed onto consumers in the price.[758]

There is an extensive use of VAT exemptions across the European Union.[759] Member States exempt some categories of goods and services considered as essential for social reasons: health care, education and supplies by charities. In addition, they also use exemptions for practical reasons (for example, in the case of financial and insurance services due to the difficulties in assessing the taxable amount). Exemptions beyond these core items cover a wide variety of sectors, such as culture, legal aid, passenger transport, public cemeteries, waste and recyclable material, water supply, precious metals and certain agricultural inputs.

In the context of virtual currency, the following two questions need to be examined: (1) whether the qualification of virtual currency transactions as electronically supplied services for the place-of-supply purposes precludes the application of the exemptions; and (2) whether the exemptions for financial transactions apply to virtual currency transactions.

[2] Electronically Supplied Services and VAT Exemptions

The first question was examined by the VAT Committee in its Working Paper 843.[760] The VAT Committee first observed that the EU VAT system has its own logic which requires that when identifying the correct tax treatment of a supply certain steps need to be taken in a certain order as reflected by the structure of the VAT Directive itself. Before discussing the question whether a given supply is taxed or exempt, its place of supply has to be identified. In order to do that, a service has to be categorized for the use of the place-of-supply purposes. In other words, it has to be assessed whether a service is covered by one of the specific place-of-supply rules and, if not, then it falls under the general rules. It is only after establishing the correct place of supply that a given supply may be assessed from the point of view of applying the correct VAT rate or exemption. In the place of supply rules, there is an explicit reference to electronically supplied services while financial services are not mentioned there at all. At the same

758. De la Feria & Krever, *supra* n. 597, at sec. 1.02.
759. Article 131 VAT Directive.
760. VAT, *Working Paper No. 843* (February 12, 2015).

time, the provisions dealing with VAT exemptions refer extensively to financial services but they are silent with regard to electronically supplied services. The VAT Committee concluded that a service may be qualified as an electronically supplied service for the place of supply rules and afterwards it may be assessed in accordance with the rules of the relevant Member State whether it is VAT exempt.

[3] VAT Exemptions for Financial Services

Having established that the qualification as electronically supplied services does not preclude the application of VAT exemptions for financial transactions, the scope of the exemptions and their applicability to virtual currency transactions is examined in this section.

Article 135(1)(e) of the VAT Directive exempts transactions "concerning banknotes and coins used as legal tender." In *Hedqvist,* the CJEU observed that the applicability of this provision to virtual currency transactions needs to be answered by taking into account the purpose of this VAT exemption. The CJEU observed that the purpose of the VAT exemption is to allow for the free exchange of means of payment, which would benefit the internal market insofar as cross-border services require currency conversions. The CJEU concluded that although Bitcoin is not legal tender, it serves the same purpose as national currencies, i.e., it functions as a medium of exchange. Therefore, the purpose of Article 135(1)(e) of the VAT Directive justifies the application of VAT exemption to exchanges of bitcoins for national currencies. Based on the CJEU reasoning, exchanges of virtual currencies having similar characteristics to those of Bitcoin into legal currency should be covered by the exemption of Article 135(1)(e) of the VAT Directive.

Article 135(1)(d) of the VAT Directive exempts "transactions, including negotiation, concerning deposit and current accounts, payment, transfers, debts, cheques and other negotiable instruments." The term "other negotiable instruments" is not defined in the VAT Directive. In *Granton Advertising* (Case C-461/12), the Advocate Generale explained that other negotiable instruments mean "only those rights which—in the absence of a debt or a cheque—confer an entitlement to a particular sum of money." It concluded that a Granton card did not constitute a negotiable instrument as it was "neither concerned with a right to a particular sum of money, nor it was likely to be regarded in the course of trade as similar to money." Thus, the concept of "other negotiable instruments" is closely linked to payment instruments acting as a way of transferring money. This provision does not cover transactions that involve money itself. In *Hedqvist*, the CJEU concluded that Bitcoin is a direct means of payment and does not operate as a way of transferring money. Thus, Article 135(1)(d) could not be applied to bitcoin transactions. In contrast to Bitcoin (which, so the CJEU, has no other purpose than being a means of payment), tokens are not designed to serve as a direct means of payment. It could be argued that they operate as a way of transferring money as the ultimate objective of the offeror is to obtain funds to finance future projects. Nevertheless, certain concerns may arise as regards the negotiability of tokens: they do not give their holder an unconditional right to be paid in currency. They can be exchanged for currency (i.e., sold on secondary markets) only to the extent that another party is willing to buy them.

Article 135(1)(f) of the VAT Directive exempts "transactions, including negotiation but not management or safekeeping, in shares, interests in companies or associations, debentures and other securities." The term "other security" is not defined in the VAT Directive. In *Granton Advertising*, the CJEU pointed out that an instrument would only qualify as a security if the transfer of the instrument implied the acquisition of a right of ownership over the issuer or claim against the issuer and the instrument could be exchanged for money or goods. In other words, "other securities" have to be comparable in nature to the securities explicitly mentioned in the provision. The holder of a utility token is entitled to exchange it for goods and services supplied by the issuer provided that those goods and services will be marketed. He does not acquire any right against the offeror but merely access to products and services provided by the offeror. Thus, utility tokens cannot be seen as securities. However, the purchaser of debt or equity tokens assumes a position similar to that of a debt- or shareholder. He acquires some rights in respect of the offering company. Thus, debt and equity tokens could be seen as having the same functions as securities. Should debt and equity tokens be treated as "other securities," all transactions involving these categories of tokens would be exempt.

[4] Interim Conclusions

The VAT Committee concluded that the qualification of transactions as electronically supplied services does not preclude the application of the exemption for financial transactions. Thus, an electronically supplied service may be exempt under Article 135 of the VAT Directive. Based on the CJEU reasoning in *Hedqvist*, transfers of virtual currencies having similar characteristics to those of Bitcoin into legal currency should be covered by the exemption for transactions "concerning banknotes and coins used as legal tender." Equity and debt tokens could be seen as having the same functions as securities and fall under the exemption for "transactions (...) in shares, interests in companies or associations, debentures and other securities."

[H] Taxable Amount and Tax Rate

VAT liability is calculated by applying the VAT rates to the taxable amount. The taxable amount includes everything that constitutes consideration obtained or to be obtained for the supply from the supplier or a third party.[761]

Member States are bound by the common rules regarding VAT rates. These rules provide that supplies of goods and services are generally subject to a standard rate of at least 15%. There are differences in the standard rates between the Member States, with rates ranging from 15% (Luxembourg) to 27% (Hungary).

761. Article 73 VAT Directive. A list of the items included into and excluded from the taxable amount is provided in Arts. 78 and 79 VAT Directive.

Reduced rates of no less than 5% may be applied to goods and services enumerated in Annex III of the VAT Directive.[762] They usually apply to basic essentials, such as medical and hospital care, food and water supplies, and to activities that are considered socially desirable. One of the reasons for the introduction of a differentiated rate structure is the promotion of equity (ensuring a fairer distribution of aggregate income). It is considered desirable to alleviate the tax on goods and services that form a larger share of expenditure of the poorest households. Such a policy is partly based on the assumption that consumption taxes have a regressive impact on the income distribution. However, the effectiveness of the reduced VAT rates to achieve distributional objectives is questionable in that the wealthier members of the population also benefit from them. Moreover, rate differentiation increases administrative and compliance costs, legal uncertainty and opportunities for fraud through deliberate misclassification of items. An important limitation on the use of reduced rates is that they cannot apply to electronically supplied services.[763] Should virtual currency transactions be treated as non-exempt electronic services, they would not qualify for the application of the reduced rate.

[I] Tax Deduction

The right to deduct input VAT is what mainly distinguishes an all-stage consumption tax from a single stage retail sales tax. Under the EU VAT system, VAT is charged on all transactions, irrespective of the status of the customer. However, taxable persons who perform taxable transactions are relieved from the tax burden by deducting, from their VAT liability, VAT invoiced to them by other taxable persons.[764] The right to deduct input VAT arises as soon as the deductible tax becomes chargeable.[765] To exercise it, the taxable person must hold an invoice drawn up in accordance with the applicable rules.[766]

Taxable persons who incur VAT in connection with their business activities in a Member State in which they do not make taxable supplies of goods or services are also entitled to deduct the VAT charged in that Member State. This "deduction" occurs by means of a refund of VAT from the Member State in which the VAT was paid. EU taxable persons may use an electronic procedure by submitting a refund application to the tax authorities in their country of residence.[767] Third-country suppliers have to

762. On January 18, 2018, the European Commission made a proposal to introduce more flexibility for Member States to change the VAT rates they apply to different products. *See* European Commission, *Proposal for a Council Directive amending Directive 2006/112/EC as regards rates of value added tax*, COM(2018) 20 final.
763. Article 98(2) VAT Directive.
764. Articles 167-192 VAT Directive.
765. Article 167 VAT Directive.
766. Article 178(a) VAT Directive.
767. *Council Directive 2008/9/EC of 12 February 2008 Laying Down Detailed Rules for the Refund of Value Added Tax, Provided for in Directive 2006/112/EC, to Taxable Persons Not Established in The Member State of Refund but Established in Another Member State*, OJ L 44/23 of February 20, 2008.

contact the Member State in which input VAT was incurred.[768] They must provide the competent tax authorities with a certificate of entrepreneurial status and original invoices.

The right to deduction or refund of VAT is restricted to goods and services used for the purposes of taxed transactions.[769] No deduction is permitted if the supplier performs exempt transactions or uses goods or services for non-business purposes. However, an exception applies to certain exempt financial transactions where the customer is established outside the European Union.[770] In other words, if virtual currency (coins, debt and equity tokens) is supplied to customers outside the European Union in exchange for other types of virtual currency or for legal currency and the transaction benefits from the VAT exemption, the supplier is entitled to reclaim VAT on costs and expenses incurred in connection with such supplies. However, persons performing exempt supplies of virtual currency frequently do not have enough information about the location of the recipients. If the supplier does not have evidence that the recipient is established outside the European Union, an input VAT deduction cannot be claimed.

A taxable person who performs transactions that both permit and preclude the right to input VAT deduction may deduct only the (proportion of the) tax that is attributable to the former transactions.[771] If attribution is not possible, the VAT Directive provides for apportionment ("pro rata calculation") to determine the deductible proportion.[772]

[J] Conclusions

This chapter examined the EU VAT treatment of virtual currency transaction following the internal logic of the EU VAT system, which requires that when identifying the correct tax treatment of a supply certain steps be taken in a certain order as reflected by the structure of the VAT Directive itself.

First, this chapter examined the question under which circumstances transacting in virtual currency may result in acquiring the status of a taxable person. A taxable person is anyone who independently carries out an economic activity, irrespective of the purpose or result of this activity. The chapter concluded that the concept of taxable person lacks clarity. The definition contained in the VAT Directive is very broad. The CJEU gives general guidelines and recommends a case-by-case analysis. Thus, an individual case may be interpreted differently by tax authorities and courts. VAT registration thresholds help prevent unexpected assessments, but they do not solve all the problems as small businesses are required to register irrespective of their turnover

768. *Thirteenth Council Directive 86/560/EEC of 17 November 1986 on the Harmonization of the Laws of the Member States relating to Turnover Taxes—Arrangements for the Refund of Value Added tax to Taxable Persons Not Established in Community Territory*, OJ L 326 of November 21, 1986.
769. Article 168 VAT Directive.
770. Article 169(c) VAT Directive.
771. Article 173 VAT Directive.
772. Article 174 VAT Directive.

if they perform certain cross-border services. This chapter observed that the issuing of shares or bonds is not an economic activity granting the status of a taxable person. If equity or debt tokens are to be considered similar instruments to shares or debt instruments, the sale of equity tokens during an ICO would be outside the VAT scope.

Second, this chapter looked at the concept of taxable transactions. As virtual currency is intangible, transfers of virtual currency should be viewed as supplied of services. However, as virtual currency is not a uniform category, virtual currency transactions cannot be treated in a one-fits-all manner. According to the CJEU, coins (similar to Bitcoin) serve the same purpose as national currencies and should be treated as such. Therefore, when goods and services are paid for with coins, no VAT should be due on the transfer of bitcoins as the mere transfer of legal tender or other means of payment outside the VAT scope. To be considers a taxable transaction, a supply must be carried out for consideration. There is no consideration in the case of currency mining as there is no bilateral legal relationship between the miner and the person carrying out taxable transactions (this also applies if miner fees are available). Thus, currency mining is outside the VAT scope.

Third, the chapter examined the place of supply rules. In the author's view, all virtual currency types that are within the scope of VAT should be classified as electronically supplied services and follow the place-of-supply rule applicable to such services.[773] Electronically supplied services are deemed to be supplied at the place where the recipient has established its business, has a permanent address or usually resides. Cross-border B2B transactions are subject to the reverse charge mechanism, whereas in a B2C situation the supplier has to determine the location of the customer and remit VAT under the OSS scheme.

Fourth, this chapter looked at the time of taxation. In this context, it observed that utility tokens seem to meet the definition of multipurpose vouchers. Therefore, exchanges of utility tokens for legal currency or coins should not attract VAT and VAT may only be due when utility tokens are redeemed.

Fifth, this chapter examined the application of VAT exemptions to virtual currency transactions after noting that the qualification of a transaction as a supply of electronic services does not preclude the application of the exemption for financial transactions. Based on the CJEU reasoning in *Hedqvist*, exchanges of coins into legal currency should be covered by the exemption for transactions "concerning banknotes and coins used as legal tender." Equity and debt tokens could be seen as having the same functions as securities and fall under the exemption for "transactions (...) in shares, interests in companies or associations, debentures and other securities."

Based on the analysis presented in the chapter, the VAT treatment of the virtual currency transaction is as follows.

- *Exchanges of virtual coins for goods and services*: as coins act like legal currency, the transfer of coins should not attract VAT. Exchanges of virtual

773. This would be the most logical and intuitive approach. The negative practical consequences of this approach that the VAT Committee mentioned in its Working Paper would not occur due to the application of VAT exemption, which was discussed in §8.01[G] Exemptions.

coins for goods or services are not barter transactions. The supply of goods or services that is paid for with coins follows the general rules and may attract VAT.

- *Exchanges of virtual coins for legal currency*: according to the CJEU, such exchanges are covered by the exemption for transactions "concerning banknotes and coins used as legal tender."
- *Exchanges of coins for coins*: based on the CJEU reasoning in *Hedqvist*, such exchanges should be exempt as coins have the same function as legal currency.
- *Exchanges of coins for debt or equity tokens:* as transactions involving debt and equity tokens are either out of scope (ICOs) or exempt, no VAT is due.
- *Exchanges of coins for utility tokens*: if utility tokens are treated as vouchers, no VAT applies to sales of utility tokens for legal tender or coins.
- *Exchanges of utility tokens for goods and services*: if utility tokens are treated as vouchers, the exchange of utility tokens for goods or services has the same consequences as redemption of a multipurpose voucher.
- *Exchanges of debt or equity tokens for legal currency*: the sale of debt or equity tokens during an ICO should be exempt or outside the VAT scope. Subsequent sales should be exempt based on the exemption for "transactions (...) in shares, interests in companies or associations, debentures and other securities."
- *Exchanges of utility tokens for legal currency*: if utility tokens are treated as vouchers, no VAT applies to sales of utility tokens for legal tender or coins.
- *Virtual currency mining*: as their no consideration, mining (both for a fee and without a fee) is outside the VAT scope.

§8.02 THE UNITED STATES

[A] State Sales Taxation: Introduction

The United States is the only OECD member country that does not apply a nationwide federal consumption tax. Instead, sales taxes are levied at the state level. Although in their design and scope, state sales taxes follow a similar pattern, their rates and scope vary considerably. The following sections will focus on the common elements of these taxes while highlighting some deviations.

Sales taxes may also be imposed by local jurisdictions (counties, cities and districts). About 7,500 local governments levy local sales tax as a supplement to the state sales tax. Local sales taxes are commonly administered by the state and collected together with the state sales tax. However, they are frequently subject to different rules with regard to the tax base and exemptions, which highly complicates tax compliance.[774]

774. R.F. van Brederode, *Introduction to the US State Sales and Use Taxes*, 18 Intl. VAT Mon. 4, sec. 10 (2007).

State sales taxes were introduced in the 1930s to compensate the effects of the Great Depression on state finances. In view of the decline in income and property values, coupled with the increased demand for social services, state legislators saw the sales tax with its broad coverage and relatively simple compliance as the solution to their financial needs. Although intended as a temporary measure, sales taxes have turned out to be enduring in nature.[775] Currently, 45 states and the District Columbia have sales taxes.[776] In fiscal year 2014, sales taxes were responsible for 23.3% of state and local tax revenue, and tend to feature more prominently in state than in local tax collections, yielding 31.4% of state and 12.1% of local tax revenue.[777]

[B] Due Process and Commerce Clause

The US Constitution allows the states enormous latitude in taxation. It explicitly prohibits import and export duties, but beyond that it is largely silent on the taxing powers of the states. Constitutional restraints on the nature and scope of state taxation have resulted from judicial interpretations of two broad constitutional provisions: the Due Process Clause and the Commerce Clause.

The Due Process Clause relates to the fairness of the tax burden.[778] Due process can be procedural, which is concerned with how the government acts (administrative fairness), or substantive, which is concerned with whether or not it has the right to act.[779] With respect to sales and use tax, due process refers to links and contacts, both qualitative and quantitative, between the state and the person over which the state attempts to assert jurisdiction. The Supreme Court has provided two tests for the due process. In its view, under the Due Process Clause, state taxation requires (1) a minimal connection (nexus) between the interstate activities and the taxing state; and (2) a rational relationship between the income attributed to the state and the interstate values of the enterprise.[780]

The Commerce Clause reserves to Congress the power to regulate international and interstate commerce.[781] Historically, the Commerce Clause restrictions on state

775. *Id.*, at sec. 1.
776. Sales taxes are not levied in: Alaska, Delaware, Montana, New Hampshire and Oregon.
777. Tax Foundation, *Unpacking the State and Local Tax Toolkit: Sources of State and Local Tax Collections* (June 20, 2017).
778. The 14th Amendment to the US Constitution states: "[Nor] shall any State deprive any person of life, liberty, or property, without due process of law."
779. B.M. Nelson et al., *Sales and Use Tax Answer Book*, sec. 2:1 (CCH 2013).
780. *Exxon Corp. v. Wisconsin*, 447 US 207, 219-20 (1980).
781. The Commerce Clause reads: "The Congress shall have the power ... to regulate commerce with foreign Nations, and among the several States, and with the Indian Tribes." Congress made use of its power to regulate interstate commerce by enacting the Internet Tax Freedom Act (ITFA) in 1998. The Act was enacted for a limited period of three years, which was extended later several times. The Act became permanent law when President Obama signed the Trade Facilitation and Trade Enforcement Act of 2015 (Pub.L. 114-125) on February 24, 2016. The Act forbids any tax on Internet access and any multiple or discriminatory taxes on electronic commerce (such as a bit or bandwidth tax). However, it does not exempt from taxation sales made via the Internet.

and local taxation were ambiguous or even contradictory.[782] In *Complete Auto Transit* (1977), the Supreme Court provided a four-element test to determine whether or not a state tax on interstate commerce is constitutional. A tax that satisfies the *Complete Auto Transit* test must (1) apply to an activity with a substantial nexus with the taxing state; (2) be fairly apportioned; (3) not discriminate against interstate commerce; and (4) be related to the services provided by the state.[783]

The first prong is by far the most important component of the *Complete Auto Transit* test. It simply asks whether the tax applies to an activity with a substantial nexus within the taxing state. Such nexus is established when the taxpayer "avails itself of the substantial privilege of carrying business in that jurisdiction."[784] The second prong (fair apportionment) ensures that multistate economic activity is not subject to taxation in two different states. The third element is satisfied as long as the tax rate does not exceed that which would apply to an intrastate sale. The fourth prong is closely connected to the first element of the test. Additionally, it requires the measure of the tax be reasonably related to the extent of the taxpayer's contact with the state. The Supreme Court has repeatedly interpreted this fourth prong as being met when a tax is measured as a percentage of some proxy for the value of the taxpayer's economic activity occurring within the state. As long as this is the case, the Court has declined to inquire into the appropriate tax rate, ruling that determinations about the appropriate levels of taxation must be made by the political process.[785]

Both the Due Process and the Commerce Clause serve as protection against states' aggressive taxing policy. However, their purpose is different: the former is concerned with the circumstances and procedures under which a jurisdiction can impose tax, while the latter—with the impact of a tax upon interstate commerce.[786]

[C] *National Bellas Hess* (1967) and *Quill* (1992)

Two judgments are of fundamental importance in interpreting the Due Process and Commerce Clause limitations on state taxation: *National Bellas Hess* (1967)[787] and *Quill* (1992).[788]

782. For more information, *see* W. Hellerstein, *State Taxation of Interstate Business: Perspectives on Two Centuries of Constitutional Adjudication*, 41 Tax L. 37 (1987); J. Hellerstein, *State Taxation under the Commerce Clause: An Historical Perspective*, 29 Vand. L. Rev. 335 (1976).
783. *Complete Auto Transit Inc. v. Brady*, 430 US 274 (1977). The taxpayer (a Michigan corporation) was a transporter of motor vehicles. The vehicles were shipped to Jackson, Mississippi, and were transported by the taxpayer to Mississippi dealers. Mississippi imposed a tax on "the privilege of doing business" in the state. The taxpayer argued that the transportation was a part of an interstate movement and the tax was unconstitutional as it applied to operations in interstate commerce. The Supreme Court ruled that a "privilege tax" can be applied to an out-of-state corporation's activities in the state without violating the Commerce Clause.
784. *Polar Tankers, Inc. v. City of Valdez*, 557 US 1, 11 (2009).
785. D. Gamage & D.J. Heckman, *A Better Way forward for State Taxation of E-commerce*, 92 B.U.L. Rev. 483, pp. 493 et seq. (2012).
786. Nelson et al., *supra* n. 779, at sec. 2:5.
787. *National Bellas Hess v. Illinois*, 386 US 753 (1967).
788. *Quill Corp. v. North Dakota*, 504 US 298 (1992).

National Bellas Hess was a Missouri mail-order seller whose only contacts with the state of Illinois were through the mail and commercial carriers. It did not have any property, employees or agents there. Customers sent their orders to Belles Hess' Missouri facility, and the goods were shipped to them either by mail or by common carrier. The tax authorities of Illinois argued that Bellas Hess was regularly and continuously exploiting the consumer market in Illinois and this should give rise to sufficient nexus in that state.

The Supreme Court found that the Illinois tax collection obligation violated both the Due Process and the Commerce Clause. It held that remote sellers could be required to collect tax only if they had a physical presence in the state. The reason for the restriction on the taxing power of the states was that, in the Court's view, the states' exercise of fiscal sovereignty had produced a sales tax system of such complexity that it was necessary to restrict the states' taxing powers by the physical presence test. The Supreme Court ruled that:

> the many variations in rates of tax, in allowable exemptions, and in administrative and record-keeping requirements could entangle [the taxpayer]'s interstate business in a virtual welter of complicated obligations to local jurisdictions with no legitimate claim to impose "a fair share of the cost of the local government."
>
> The very purpose of the Commerce Clause was to ensure a national economy free from such unjustifiable local entanglements. Under the Constitution, this is a domain where Congress alone has the power of regulation and control.[789]

Quill, a Delaware corporation, sold office equipment to North Dakota customers by soliciting sales through catalogues, flyers, advertisements in periodicals and telephone calls. It did not have any property, employees or agents in North Dakota. The goods were shipped to North Dakota from out-of-state locations either by email or by common carrier. The question was whether there was a sufficient nexus to warrant taxation in North Dakota.

In the *Quill* judgment, the Supreme Court distinguished between the Due Process nexus (minimum contacts) and the Commerce Clause nexus (substantial presence). As these two tests were not identical, it was possible that a taxpayer's activities could satisfy one and fail the other:

> The State contends that the nexus requirements imposed by the Due Process and Commerce Clauses are equivalent and that if, as we concluded above, a mail order house that lacks a physical presence in the taxing State nonetheless satisfies the due process "minimum contacts" test, then that corporation also meets the Commerce Clause "substantial nexus" test. We disagree. Despite the similarity in phrasing, the nexus requirements of the Due Process and Commerce Clauses are not identical. The two standards are animated by different constitutional concerns and policies.[790]

The Supreme Court agreed that Quill's exploitation of the North Dakota market satisfied the Due Process test but not the nexus under the Commerce Clause. As the taxpayer purposely directed its activities towards North Dakota residents, its

789. *National Bellas Hess v. Illinois*, 386 US 759 (1967).
790. *Quill Corp. v. North Dakota*, 504 US 312 (1992).

"economic presence" (solicitation of business) was sufficient to create some minimum connection with the state. However, Quill did not have a physical presence in North Dakota and thus lacked the substantial nexus with the state.

The physical presence test was justified based on *stare decisis*[791] and on the concern that allowing states to impose use tax compliance obligations on remote sellers could burden interstate commerce by entangling remote sellers in a "'virtual welter of complicated obligations' imposed by the "nation's 6,000-plus taxing jurisdictions":

> North Dakota's use tax illustrates well how a state tax might unduly burden interstate commerce. On its face, North Dakota law imposes a collection duty on every vendor who advertises in the State three times in a single year. Thus, absent the Bellas Hess rule, a publisher who included a subscription card in three issues of its magazine, a vendor whose radio advertisements were heard in North Dakota on three occasions, and a corporation whose telephone sales force made three calls into the State, all would be subject to the collection duty. What is more significant, similar obligations might be imposed by the Nation's 6,000-plus taxing jurisdictions. See National Bellas Hess, Inc. v. Department of Revenue of Ill., 386 U.S. 753, 759-760 (noting that the "many variations in rates of tax, in allowable exemptions, and in administrative and recordkeeping requirements could entangle [a taxpayer] in a virtual welter of complicated obligations").[792]

The *Quill* decision was widely criticized and even nominated for "the most maligned Supreme Court tax decision."[793] It created a sales tax loophole that gave remote sellers a competitive advantage as sellers without physical presence in a state could make tax-free supplies of goods and services to that state's residents. Numerous commentators called for the Court to revisit the decision or for Congress to pass legislation enabling states to tax out-of-state sellers.

Although the *Quill* decision created market distortions by putting local businesses and many interstate businesses with physical presence at a competitive disadvantage relative to remote sellers, it was not based on any notion that out-of-state sellers ought to be placed in a tax-advantaged position as compared to local retailers. The Supreme Court recognized that interstate commerce may be required to pay its fair share of state taxes when it held in *Commonwealth Edison* (1981) that:

> To accept appellants' apparent suggestion that the Commerce Clause prohibits the States from requiring an activity connected to interstate commerce to contribute to the general cost of providing governmental services (...) would place such commerce in a privileged position. But as we recently reiterated, "[i]t was not the purpose of the commerce clause to relieve those engaged in interstate commerce from their just share of state tax burden even though it increases the cost of doing business."[794]

791. The invocation of *stare decisis* was important because the North Dakota State Supreme Court had previously determined that *Bellas Hess'* physical presence rule no longer applied due to the evolution of the US Supreme Court's Commerce Clause jurisprudence.
792. *Quill Corp. v. North Dakota*, 504 US 313 (1992).
793. P.L. Caron, *Pepperdine Hosts Symposium on the Most Maligned Supreme Court Decisions*, Tax Prof. L. Blog (April 1, 2011).
794. *Commonwealth Edison*, 453 US 623-624 (1981).

In *Quill*, the Supreme Court was concerned about increased reporting and remittance obligations resulting from participation in interstate trade. Whereas a seller operating exclusively within a single state must only bear the tax collection costs imposed by that state's sales or use tax, in the absence of the physical presence nexus, a seller operating in many states would bear tax collection costs of the use tax of each state to which he ships goods.

A common misinterpretation of the physical presence test is that it requires either the presence of tangible property or employees within a state to establish nexus. In *Scripto Inc. v. Carson* (1960), the Supreme Court held that agents soliciting on behalf of a corporation satisfied the nexus requirement under both the Due Process and Commerce Clause.[795] Similarly, in *Tyler Pipe Industries v. Washington* (1987),[796] the Supreme Court held that the corporate taxpayer had substantial nexus in Washington based on activities performed in the state on behalf of the corporation. The Court reached this result even though the corporation had no office, property or employees in the state. Therefore, *Scripto* and *Tyler Pipe* indicate that the physical presence requirement may be satisfied by the in-state activities of others taken on behalf of an out-of-state retailer. Nexus based on the activities of another is referred to as attribution nexus because the in-state activities are attributed to the out-of-state seller. Attribution nexus disregards certain formal distinctions, such as whether the in-state activities are performed by an employee or an independent agent, and, instead, focuses on the nature and extent of the activities themselves, in particular, whether they allow the taxpayer to establish and maintain a market in the state.[797]

Finally, it is important to note that the fact that a taxpayer has nexus for sales tax purposes does not imply that he will also have nexus for income tax purposes. Both approaches are similar and both are heavily rooted in the Commerce and Due Process Clause. However, different levels of activity within a state may trigger one type of nexus but not the other. The federal legislator passed Public Law 86-272, according to which states cannot collect income tax from corporations whose only activity within the state is the solicitation of orders for tangible personal property.

[D] "Amazon" Laws

The reliance on physical presence nexus has created planning opportunities for taxpayers in mail-order and online businesses. As the electronic commerce grew, the potential loss of revenue became a serious concern for the states. In 2015, sales from e-commerce for US retailers were USD 340.4 billion—a 14% increase from USD 298.7 billion in 2014.[798]

Frustrated by the *Quill* decision and desperate for revenues, a number of states have passed legislation, commonly referred to as "Amazon" laws, which aggressively

795. *Scripto Inc. v. Carson*, 362 US 207 (1960).
796. *Tyler Pipe Industries v. Washington*, 483 US 232 (1987).
797. A. Haile, *Affiliate Nexus in E-Commerce*, Elon Univ. Sch. of Law, Legal Studies Research Paper No. 2011-04, sec. I.C (2011).
798. US Census Bureau, *E-Stats 2015: Measuring the Electronic* Economy (May 24, 2017).

interprets the physical presence requirement in an attempt to tax interstate e-commerce.[799] Although there is a considerable variation in the content of "Amazon" laws, they generally try to assert nexus through affiliation (affiliate nexus), referral (click-through nexus) or the number of sales (economic nexus).[800]

Click-through nexus legislation triggers use tax liability for remote sellers who solicit sales through state residents. The remote supplier must have an agreement with state residents according to which the latter refer to him potential customers (for example, by a link on a website) and gross receipts from sales in that state must exceed a certain threshold. New York was the first state to enact click-through nexus legislation in 2008.[801] In 2009, Rhode Island and North Carolina adopted identical laws. As of April 2018, click-through nexus legislation has been enacted in the following states: Arkansas, California, Colorado, Connecticut, Georgia, Idaho, Illinois, Kansas, Louisiana, Maine, Michigan, Minnesota, Missouri, Nevada, New Jersey, New York, North Carolina, Ohio, Pennsylvania, Rhode Island, Tennessee, Vermont, Washington.[802]

Affiliate nexus exists if the remote seller and the state business are under common control or if the remote seller and a state business use a similar name or trademark to promote and maintain sales. This kind of nexus attempts to circumvent the Commerce Clause prohibitions by disregarding the corporate structure and treating related business entities as though they were a single unitary business.[803] In 2010, Colorado adopted a law under which if a "controlled group of corporations" had at least one member with physical presence in Colorado, all the retailers in the group had nexus with Colorado.[804] In 2011, California amended the definition of a "retailer engaged in business in California" to include certain affiliates of in-state companies and to require them to collect use taxes.[805] The affiliate nexus provision was reportedly targeted at Amazon, which has a research and development facility (operated by an Amazon subsidiary) in the state. As of April 2018, click-through nexus legislation has been enacted in the following states: Alabama, Arkansas, California, Colorado, Georgia, Illinois, Iowa, Kansas, Louisiana, Maine, Michigan, Missouri, Nevada, New York,

799. For detailed discussion of Amazon Laws and their constitutionality, *see* T. Cavanaugh, *Iowa Can Do Better than the Affiliate Tax: A Proposal for an Intermediary Tax*, 97 Iowa L. Rev. 567 (2012); D. Cowan, *New York's Unconstitutional Tax on the Internet: Amazon.com v. New York State Department of Taxation and Finance and the Dormant Commerce Clause*, 88 N.C. L. Rev. 1423 (2010); S.W. Gaylord & A. Haile, *Constitutional Threats in the E-Commerce Jungle: First Amendment and Dormant Commerce Clause Limits on Amazon Laws and Use Tax Reporting Statutes*, 89 N.C. L. Rev. 2011 (2011); T.S. Steele et al., *The "Amazon" Laws and the Perils of Affiliate Advertising*, 59 St. Tax Notes 939 (March 28, 2011); Haile, *supra* n. 797; J. Henchman, *Amazon Taxes*, The Tax Foundation (July/August 2012).
800. Sales Tax Institute, *Remote Seller Nexus Chart* (accessed: June 1, 2018).
801. Gamage & Heckman, *supra* n. 785, at pp. 518 et seq.
802. Sales Tax Institute, *supra* n. 800.
803. Gamage & Heckman, *supra* n. 785, at pp. 520 et seq.
804. Henchman, *supra* n. 799, p. 36.
805. Assembly Bill No. 155, passed by the California State Legislature on September 9, 2011 and signed by Governor Brown into law on September 23, 2011.

Ohio, Oklahoma, Pennsylvania, Rhode Island, South Dakota, Tennessee, Taxes, Utah, Virginia and West Virginia.[806]

Affiliate nexus is similar to attribution nexus, but those two concepts are not exactly the same. Attribution nexus means that the actions of an in-state representative establish and maintain a market for an out-of-state entity. Affiliate nexus applies if the in-state and out-of-state entity satisfy a common ownership requirement. These two theories overlap when an in-state affiliate is performing services for an out-of-state retailer, those services are essential to establishing and maintaining a market for the retailer and they are part of a unitary business between the affiliate and the retailer.[807]

Economic nexus means that if the in-state activity of an out-of-state seller exceeds a certain sales threshold, the seller is considered to have sufficient nexus in the state and can be required to collect and remit sales and use taxes. In 2016, economic nexus legislation took effect in South Dakota. It required remote sellers without a physical presence in the state to collect and remit South Dakota sales and use tax on sales in the state if the retailer made in-state sales exceeding USD 100,000 or made 200 or more separate sales transactions in the previous or current calendar year. On June 21, 2018, the Supreme Court confirmed the validity of South Dakota's economic nexus legislation.[808]

Some states have chosen to impose additional reporting requirements on marketplace operators ("marketplace nexus") or out-of-state retailers in addition to, or instead of, expanding the nexus definition. Arizona was the first state that implemented "marketplace nexus" through an administrative ruling rather than a legislative change. In 2016, the Arizona Department of Revenue has issued a ruling stating that a business that operates an online marketplace and makes online sales on behalf of third-party merchants is a retailer conducting taxable sales.[809] In some other states, reporting requirements have been imposed on retailers: they become obliged to inform buyers about their use tax obligations, to send the buyers an annual statement of all of their purchases and to provide this information to the local tax authorities.

"Amazon laws" (especially, click-through and affiliate nexus) do not seem to offer an effective solution for taxing interstate electronic commerce. These laws have been described as unconstitutional and they have been the subject of litigation across the country. Courts are extremely reluctant to disregard the separate legal status of distinct entities, even if those entities are affiliates. This reluctance is based on the fundamental principle of corporate law that the parent company and its subsidiary are treated as separate and distinct legal persons, even though the parent owns all the shares in the subsidiary and the two enterprises have identical directors.[810] Moreover, since the use tax is imposed on the consumer's act of using personal property, it has no relation to the corporate structure of the retailer selling the property.

806. Sales Tax Institute, *supra* n. 800.
807. Haile, *supra* n. 797, at sec. I.C.
808. *See* §8.02[G] *South Dakota v. Wayfair* (2018).
809. Sales Tax Institute, *Arizona Issues Ruling on Marketplace Nexus* (October 28, 2016).
810. *SFA Folio Collections, Inc. v. Bannon*, 585 A.2d 673 (1991) (quoting H. Henn and J. Alexander, Laws of Corporations (3d ed. 1983) sec. 148, p. 355).

Remote suppliers found a way of circumventing "Amazon" laws by moving their subsidiaries or suspending their relationships with marketing organizations from the states that passed such laws. Amazon responded to the New York law establishing the click-through nexus by terminating its affiliate programmes in the state and filing a lawsuit in state court. Thus, the first "Amazon" taxes did not result in more revenue. Rhode Island actually saw revenue loss due to reduced income tax collections from terminated affiliate's relationships.[811]

[E] Streamlined Sales and Use Tax Agreement

The US Constitution does not provide a nationwide forum in which the states can meet to seek uniformity in policies or rules that govern cooperative arrangements between them. On the contrary, the US Constitution imposes restrictions on the ability of the states to collaborate with each other on tax administration. The Compact Clause[812] generally prohibits interstate agreements without the consent of Congress. Thus, congressional approval is required for a state to enter into an agreement to collect sales taxes on a uniform basis.

In an effort to simplify and to gain consistency on the structure of sales taxes, a group of states established the Streamlined Sales Tax Project (SSTP).[813] The result of this work was the adoption of the Streamlined Sales and Use Tax Agreement (SSUTA) in November 2002. The SSUTA focuses on improving sales and use tax administration systems by developing uniform definition and sourcing rules for taxable transactions and by simplifying compliance matters, thereby minimizing costs and administrative burdens on retailers operating in multiple states. It encourages remote sellers to collect tax on sales to customers living in the streamlined states to ensure a level playing field between online shops and local "brick-and-mortar" stores. The governance of the SSUTA is in the hands of the Governing Board, which has the form of a non-profit entity. All full and associate Member States have a seat on the Board. The ultimate goal of the SSTP is to persuade the federal government to allow tax collection on interstate trade by demonstrating the desirability of uniformity in taxation.

Under the SSUTA, all local sales and use taxes must be administered by the state. Sellers are only required to register and file returns with the state, which redistributes the revenues to the local governments. The tax base for state and local jurisdictions must be identical. Participating states agree to reduce compliance burden for sellers by making a reasonable effort:

- to notify sellers of legal changes in the tax base, rate and other rules and regulations;
- not to apply multiple tax rates;
- to maintain a database that describes the boundaries of all taxing jurisdictions according to the five and nine-digit zip code.

811. Haile, *supra* n. 797, at sec. I.C.
812. Article 1 (10) US Constitution.
813. Streamlined Sales Tax Governing Board, http://streamlinedsalestax.org.

The participating states must provide monetary compensation for the implementation of new technology in the case of voluntary registration, i.e., registration in a state where the seller lacks sufficient nexus. The SSUTA provides for four compliance models. In Model 1, sellers employ a Certified Service Provider (CSP) to perform all their sales and use tax functions.[814] A CSP is designed to allow a business to outsource most of its sales tax administration responsibilities and is liable to the tax authorities for any errors made. The services rendered by CSPs are paid for by the participating states in the case of "volunteer sellers." If registration in a particular state is mandatory, for example because the seller has sufficient physical presence (nexus) there, no compensation will be paid under the terms of the CSP contract in respect of taxes due to that particular state.[815] In Model 2, sellers retain their responsibility in respect of sales and use taxes and use Certified Automated Systems (CAS) software to perform compliance functions. The CAS identifies which products are taxable, applies the appropriate tax rate and can be linked to the company's accounting system. The costs of the CAS software are borne by the businesses employing them. A seller that uses a CAS is responsible for filing the tax returns, paying the taxes dues to each of the streamlined states, and resolving any notices or audits by any of the streamlined Member States. Model 3 sellers use their own systems to make their tax calculations on the basis of performance standards determined in a performance agreement with the streamlined states. Finally, a Model 4 seller is any seller that is registered under the SSUTA but does not qualify as Model 1, 2 or 3 seller.

Until February 2018, 24 states have passed the conforming legislation. Those states represent about 31% of the country's total population.[816] However, some important states, like California and New York, have not joined the project yet.

[F] Proposed Legislation

[1] Marketplace Fairness Act

The dubious constitutionality of "Amazon laws" and their lack of success in raising revenue has shifted attention to the federal level where there have been several attempts to adopt a new nexus standard. Almost every year since the *Quill* decision in 1992, new legislation that would grant states the authority to compel remote sellers to collect state sales and use taxes has been proposed.[817]

814. For a list of CSPs, *see* Streamlined Sales Tax Governing Board, *Certified Service Providers* (accessed: June 3, 2018).
815. *See* Streamlined Sales Tax Governing Board, *Certified Service Provider (CSP) and Certified Automated System (CAS)* (accessed: June 3, 2018).
816. *See* Streamlined Sales Tax Governing Board, *About Us*.
817. For example, the Main Street Fairness Act (S. 1452/H.R. 2701) introduced on July 29, 2011 and the Marketplace Equity Act (H.R. 3179) introduced on October 13, 2011.

The Marketplace Fairness Act has made the greatest progress so far.[818] On May 6, 2013, the Senate of the 113th Congress passed the 2013 version of the bill.[819] Despite its popularity in the Senate, the bill never gained much traction in the House of Representatives: it never came out of committee to a vote on the House floor. On March 10, 2015, the Marketplace Fairness Act of 2015 was introduced in the Senate of the 114th Congress.[820] Just like its predecessors, this bill did not become law. On April 27, 2017, a bipartisan group of senators introduced the Marketplace Fairness Act of 2017.[821]

The Marketplace Fairness Act grants the states the authority to compel remote sellers to collect sales tax at the time of a transaction just as local retailers are already required to do. However, before states are allowed to start collecting tax from remote sellers, they must simplify their sales tax laws. The Act provides for two simplification options. The first one is to join the SSTP and the other—to introduce simplification measures listed in the proposed bill. For states which do not participate in the SSTP, the minimum simplification requirements are as follows:

(1) there must be a single entity within the state to administer all state and local sales and use taxes;
(2) the state must provide for a single audit for all taxing jurisdictions within the;
(3) a single return must be filed with the single entity responsible for tax administration;
(4) the state cannot require a remote seller to file sales and use tax returns more frequently than it is required for non-remote sellers or impose requirements on remote sellers that the state does not impose on non-remote sellers;
(5) there must be a uniform sales and use tax base among the state and local taxing jurisdictions;
(6) remote sales must be sourced in accordance with the sourcing definition provided in the Marketplace Fairness Act;[822]

818. For more information on the Marketplace Fairness Act, *see* www.marketplacefairness.org/what-is-the-marketplace-fairness-act/.
819. The Marketplace Fairness Act of 2013 was introduced in the Senate as S. 743 (formerly S. 336) on April 16, 2013, and in the House of Representatives as H.R. 684 on February 14, 2013. The 2013 version was not the first version of the Marketplace Fairness Act. An earlier version of the Marketplace Fairness Act (S. 1832) was introduced on November 9, 2011 in the 112th Congress.
820. www.congress.gov/bill/114th-congress/senate-bill/698.
821. www.congress.gov/bill/115th-congress/senate-bill/976.
822. According to sec. 4(7) of the Marketplace Fairness Act of 2017, the sourcing rules are as follows: "the location to which a remote sale is sourced refers to the location where the product or service sold is received by the purchaser, based on the location indicated by instructions for delivery that the purchaser furnishes to the seller. When no delivery location is specified, the remote sale is sourced to the customer's address that is either known to the seller or, if not known, obtained by the seller during the consummation of the transaction, including the address of the customer's payment instrument if no other address is available. If an address is unknown and a billing address cannot be obtained, the remote sale is sourced to the address of the seller from which the remote sale was made."

(7) the state must provide remote sellers with information about the taxability of goods and services and the rates;
(8) the state must provide free software for remote sellers to calculate and file sales and use tax returns and hold them harmless for any errors and omissions resulting from relying on state-provided systems and data;
(9) the state must provide certification procedures for persons to be approved as certified software providers.

Sellers whose nationwide remote sales did not exceed USD 1 million in the preceding year are not required to collect sales and use taxes on those sales (the small seller exemption). As the exemption threshold refers to "gross annual receipts in remote sales," remote sellers that primarily sell non-taxable items may also be subject to collection and remittance obligations. By way of example, a seller with remote sales of non-taxable items of USD 950,000 who also sold taxable items in the value of USD 55,000 would still be required to collect tax on the USD 55,000 of remote sales of taxable items since he would not qualify as an exempt small seller. For the purposes of determining the threshold of USD 1 million, the sales made by related persons (as defined by section 267 or 707 of the Internal Revenue Code) are aggregated. In addition, aggregation is required if relationships were designed with a principal purpose of avoiding the application of these rules.

The Marketplace Fairness Act intends to provide some level of sales tax simplification in an effort to make it easier for remote sellers to comply with the collection and remittance process. Although it does not address one of the main concerns of the remote sellers, i.e., significant variance among the states as to which goods and services are taxable, it provides remote sellers with free-of-charge software that calculates sales and use taxes due on each transaction and it holds them harmless for any errors or omissions that result from relying on state-provided systems and data.

[2] Remote Transactions Parity Act

The Remote Transaction Parity Act (H.R. 2775) was first introduced in the 114th House of Representatives on June 15, 2015 and then reintroduced in the 115th Congress on April 27, 2017.[823]

Just like the Marketplace Fairness Act, it also creates sales and use tax collection obligations for remote sellers that do not have physical presence within the state. The Remote Transaction Parity Act authorizes each member of the SSUTA and non-members that comply with certain minimum simplification requirements to require remote sellers to remit sales and use tax.

Although the content of both Acts is very similar, some fundamental differences can be observed. The Remote Transaction Parity Act has a different definition of a small seller—there is a phased-in threshold of gross annual receipts, staring at USD 10 million in year one, then USD 5 million in year two and USD 1 million in year three. In year

823. www.congress.gov/bill/115th-congress/house-bill/2193.

four, there is no threshold. In addition to the monetary thresholds, the Remote Transaction Parity Act excludes businesses that "utilize an electronic marketplace for the purpose of making products or services available for sale to the public" from the small seller exemption. Another difference is that the Remote Transaction Parity Act puts more onus on the certified software providers (CSPs). If a remote seller utilizes a certified software provider, a state requesting an audit is first obliged to contact the CSP unless there is a reasonable suspicion that the seller has engaged in intentional representation. The CSP must provide the state with all the records, represent the vendor during an audit and will be held responsible for the audit findings. Remote sellers are relieved of liability for the incorrect collection or remittance of tax if the liability is the result of an error or omission made by the CSP unless the remote seller misled or provided inaccurate information to the CSP.

[3] No Regulation Without Representation Act

On July 14, 2016, Rep. Jim Sensenbrenner (R-WI) introduced into Congress the No Regulation Without Representation Act of 2016. The proposed legislation took the opposite approach of the Marketplace Fairness Act and the Remote Transactions Parity Act, and sought to codify the physical presence nexus requirement established by the Supreme Court in *Quill*. As the bill failed to pass during the 114th Congressional Session, a slightly modified version of the bill was re-introduced on June 12, 2017 as the No Regulation Without Representation Act of 2017 (H.R. 2887).[824] Under the proposed legislation, a state may tax or regulate a person's activity in interstate commerce only when such person is physically present in the state during the period in which the tax or regulation is imposed. The bill lists activities that constitute a physical presence and provides a list of specific *de minimis* activities that are excluded from this concept. If enacted, the bill would prohibit all the remote seller legislation (click-through nexus, affiliate nexus, reporting requirements) that has been enacted by states so far.

[G] *South Dakota v. Wayfair* (2018)

Under the Supreme Court's decisions in *National Bellas Hess* and *Quill*, South Dakota was not allowed to require a business to collect its sales tax if the business lacked a physical presence in the state. Instead, it had to rely on its residents to pay the use tax owed on their purchases from out-of-state resellers. Given the very low consumer compliance rates, the South Dakota Department of Revenue estimated revenue loss at USD 48 to 58 million annually. Concerned about the erosion of its sales tax base and the corresponding loss of critical funding for state and local services, South Dakota passed a law requiring out-of-state sellers to collect the state's sales tax based on their

824. www.congress.gov/bill/115th-congress/house-bill/2887.

economic connection to the state.[825] Under the new law, sellers exceeding a threshold of USD 100,000 in sales or having 200 separate transactions in South Dakota were obliged to charge and remit the local sales tax. South Dakota's main argument supporting its newly enacted law was that changes in technology rendered *Quill*'s physical presence rule harmful and unfair. The complexity of state sales taxation was no longer an issue as tax filing software had significantly reduced tax compliance costs for multistate sellers. Moreover, when deciding *Quill*, the Supreme Court could not foresee the exponential rise of online trade that had magnified the revenue losses resulting from the physical presence rules. Thus, in South Dakota's view, the physical presence rule posed a serious threat to the fiscal stability of state and local governments.

Prior to the enactment of the new law, large online retailers (Wayfair, Overstock and Newegg) with no employees or real estate in South Dakota had not been collecting South Dakota sales tax. As they easily met the minimum sales or transactions requirements imposed by the new law, South Dakota filed a declaratory judgment action against them, seeking a declaration that the requirements of the new law were valid and applicable to the remote online retailers. The retailers sought summary judgment, arguing that the new law was unconstitutional. The trial court granted their motion and the South Dakota Supreme Court affirmed on the ground that *Quill* was a controlling precedent. As the matter concerned the interpretation of the Commerce Clause and its limitations on interstate collection of sales taxes, the South Dakota Supreme Court asked the Supreme Court for declaratory judgment on the validity of the new law. On January 12, 2018, the Supreme Court agreed to hear the case *South Dakota v. Wayfair.* (No. 17-494). The question presented to the Court was: "Should this Court abrogate *Quill*'s sales-tax-only physical-presence requirement?"

On June 21, 2018, the Supreme Court made its highly anticipated decision in *South Dakota v. Wayfair.* The Supreme Court held that the physical presence standard in *Quill* was "unsound and incorrect" and should be overturned. The majority opinion was authored by Justice Anthony Kennedy, who was joined by Justices Samuel A. Alito Jr., Neil Gorsuch, Ruth Bader Ginsburg and Clarence Thomes. Four justices dissented, agreeing that *National Bellas Hess* and *Quill* were wrongly decided but arguing that Congress should fix it.

In the Supreme Court's view, the *Quill* decision was flawed on its own terms. First, the physical presence rule was not a necessary interpretation of the *Complete Auto Transit* requirement that a state tax must be "applied to an activity with a substantial nexus with the taxing state." Thus, it was an incorrect interpretation of the Commerce Clause. As the Supreme Court wrongly assumed in *Quill* that physical presence was necessary to create a substantial nexus, it was the job of the Court and not Congress to correct this error. The Court should not ask Congress to address a false constitutional premise of the Court's own creation.

825. An Act to provide for the collection of sales taxes from certain remote sellers, to establish certain Legislative findings, and to declare an emergency, S. 106, 2016 Leg. Assembly, 91st Sess. (S.D. 2016)(S.B. 2016).

Second, *Quill* created rather than resolved market distortions. It put local businesses and many interstate businesses with physical presence at a competitive disadvantage relative to remote sellers that could offer *de facto* lower prices by avoiding the regulatory burden of tax collection. The physical presence test resulted in treating economically identical actors differently for arbitrary purposes. For example, a business that maintained a few items of inventory in a state was required to collect and remit tax on all of its sales in that state, while a seller with a pervasive Internet presence was not subject to the same tax for the sale of the same items. In effect, *Quill* came to serve as a judicially created tax shelter for businesses that decide to limit their physical presence and sell their goods to a state's consumers. By giving online retailers an arbitrary advantage over their competitors who collect sales taxes, the physical presence rule prevented market participants from competing on an even playing field.

The Supreme Court observed that Quill's physical present rule was artificial not just "at its edges" but in its entirety as modern electronic commerce does not align analytically with a test that "relies on the sort of physical presence" and "ignores substantial virtual connections" to the state. The technology progress "made Quill's original error all the more egregious and harmful." Each year, the physical presence rule become further removed from economic reality and resulted in significant revenue losses to the states. Thus, it must give way "far-reaching and structural changes" in the economy caused by the Internet's prevalence and the growth of the e-commerce retail sector. In the modern economy, nexus should be established based on economic and virtual contacts that retailers have with a state.

Finally, the Supreme Court addressed the question of constitutionality of the South Dakota's new law. It declared the law to be constitutionally valid as it included several features that were designed to prevent discrimination against, or undue burdens upon, interstate commerce (such as a safe harbor for businesses with limited transactions or no obligation to remit sales tax that may be applied retroactively). Moreover, South Dakota joined the SSUTA to standardize its sales tax system and reduce administrative and compliance costs. In the Supreme Court's view, the substantial nexus requirement of *Complete Auto Transit* was satisfied as the large retailers maintained an extensive virtual presence in South Dakota.

The Supreme Court's decision in *South Dakota v. Wayfair* will undoubtedly have a huge impact on sellers who found shelter under the *Quill* standards as they will be faced with increased compliance obligations. Being no longer constrained by the *Quill* standards, states may enact legislation requiring remote sellers to collect and remit their sales taxes. However, the *Wayfair* ruling did not give them *carte blanche* to design their remote sales tax laws as they deem fit. While the Supreme Court confirmed the constitutional validity of South Dakota's law, observing that it was "designed to prevent discrimination against or undue burdens upon interstate commerce," it left the threshold issue open to interpretation. It is not clear whether a lower threshold than that used by South Dakota (USD 100,000 of remote sales or 200 such transactions) is also compatible with the *Complete Auto Transit* substantial nexus requirement. It is generally expected that other states will model their nexus requirements after South Dakota's law to ensure that their laws cannot be challenged at court. However, states may also choose to experiment with lower thresholds to see if their versions could survive under the *Complete Auto Transit* framework.

Congress has pending bills (the Remote Transactions Parity Act and the Marketplace Fairness Act) that specify what simplifications a state must make to be able to require online sellers to collect taxes. Such laws would be compatible with the Court's ruling as they provide more protections for remote sellers. It remains to be seen whether states will focus on their own legislation and slow their push for federal legislation or continue to support a federal solution. Depending on how states will act, there might be a need for congressional action to codify seller protections in federal law. If states enact remote sales tax laws without the necessary simplifications and protections for remote sellers, which were a prominent feature of South Dakota's laws, there will be more litigation and a higher potential for action by Congress.

The Supreme Court's decision in *South Dakota v. Wayfair* will also affect non-US businesses that make sales to the United States but do not have physical presence there. Under the *Quill* rule, non-US businesses without physical presence in the United States were able to avoid state sales taxation. Now states are no longer constrained by the *Quill* standards and may enact legislation requiring remote sellers to collect and remit their sales taxes.

[H] Basic Characteristics of Sales Taxes

[1] Personal Scope

The sales tax does not know the concept of a taxable person, similar to that under EU VAT law. The seller or retailer is responsible for sales tax collection and remittance, provided that he has sufficient nexus with the state.

As regards the liability for the payment of tax, a distinction must be made between seller privilege tax (SPT) and consumer tax (CT) states. In SPT states, the tax is imposed on the privilege of doing business in the state. The tax subject is the retailer who must remit the tax whether or not it is collected from the customer. In CT states, the tax is imposed on the privilege of consuming the goods and services purchased. The tax subject is the consumer, but the responsibility for tax collection rests on the retailer.[826]

The retail sales tax and the EU VAT employ different techniques to avoid taxing business purchases. The US retail tax system does not know the concept of input tax. Sales and use taxes are only imposed on the ultimate consumer. Retailers, manufacturers and wholesalers are exempt on their sales under the resale/manufacturing exemption. Despite this, it is estimated that more than 40% of sales tax revenues are derived from business purchases, which results in tax cascading effect that distorts choices among productive techniques.[827]

826. D.L. Yetter, *United States—VAT & Sales Tax*, sec. 2.1., Topical Analyses IBFD.
827. C.E. McLure Jr. & P. Merrill, *Why Doesn't the United States Use a VAT for Deficit Reduction? Political Impediments and Fiscal Coordination Issues*, sec. 4.2., 67 Bull. Intl. Taxn. 4/5 (2013).

The sales tax administration is decentralized and handled at the state level, which means that persons seeking to register, collect and remit taxes are confronted with different rules in each state. Creating nexus in a state or a local jurisdiction generates the responsibility for a retailer or service provider to register, collect and remit sales and use tax. Registration to collect and remit sales tax can typically be administered online by completing an application form. Once an application has been processed and approved and the necessary certification is sent to the taxpayer, the taxpayer can legally initiate the collection and remittance of the sales tax. This is often referred to as the "retailer's permit."[828]

Once a taxpayer is registered to collect or remit sales and/or use taxes in a jurisdiction, the jurisdiction will notify the taxpayer of their filing frequency and due date. Filing frequencies can change based on a taxpayer's level of sales activities. The due date applies to both the filing of the return and the payment of the tax.[829]

There are neither registration thresholds nor simplifications measures for small businesses. Any company, regardless of its size or turnover, which establishes nexus in a taxing jurisdiction and makes taxable sales is required to register to collect and remit sales tax. The filing frequency can be lower if the average tax liability is low.[830]

[2] Taxable Transactions

[a] General Remarks

In general, all sales of tangible personal property are taxable.[831] A "sale" is defined as any transfer of title or possession, exchange or barter of tangible personal property for consideration.[832] Some states have expanded their definition of tangible personal property to include items such as electronically delivered software and digital products, as well as some commodities, such as natural gas and electricity.[833]

As sales taxes are leveled only on sales of taxable items for consideration, mining activity is outside the scope of US sales taxation. There is no bilateral relationship between miners and other users in a virtual currency network. Although some miners receive rewards in the form of new virtual currency or fees for their activities, the receipt of this reward is generally a matter of chance.[834]

Intangibles are excluded from the RST scope in the majority of states. However, there are some states (for example, Hawaii, New Mexico and South Dakota) that tax almost all services and in those states, the sale of intangibles is taxable to the extent

828. Yetter, *supra* n. 826, at sec. 11.1.1.1.
829. *Id.*, at sec. 11.4.1.
830. *Id.*, at sec. 12.1.
831. Sales tax statutes do not distinguish between legal and illegal supplies, both of which are subject to tax. *See Greer v. Department of the Treasury*, 145 Mich. App. 248, 377 N.W.2d 836 (1985).
832. Yetter, *supra* n. 826, sec. 3.1.2.
833. *Id.*, at sec. 3.1.1.
834. *See also* §8.01[D][2] Consideration.

that the intangibles are considered services.[835] Intangible property is treated as tangible property if it is transferred in a tangible format, for example, software delivered on a data carrier.[836]

Most states tax only a few enumerated services. When sales taxes were enacted, services accounted for a substantially smaller fraction of national output than now. Thus, the failure to tax them did not cause a serious loss of revenue. Over time, the economic landscape of the United States has changed, but sales taxes have not reflected those changes. Although now services comprise a larger share of national output than goods, service providers have been able to defeat proposals to extend the tax to the service sector. There is an understandable reluctance for the states to apply sales taxes to services. The main reason is the lack of uniformity in the definition of what may constitute a service and in the rules to determine which state may tax interstate services. In the absence of such rules, a service contracted in one state, performed in another and used by the customer in several other states may be subject to multiple taxation.[837]

A retailer or service provider is required to charge, collect and remit sales or use tax on all transactions subject to tax in a given jurisdiction, except when the provisions in that jurisdiction allow for a sale to be exempt. The states apply exemptions to certain categories of goods and services, for example, food, medical supplies and educational materials. The determination of which goods are taxable or exempt varies among the states.

Many states allow an exemption for occasional or casual sales as these types of transactions are generally not made in the regular course of business. The states vary on what types of transactions qualify for this type of exemption. The exemption is sometimes limited to a certain number of sales or a specified dollar amount. If a taxpayer exempts a transaction believing that the threshold will not be exceeded, but within the specified time period the sales value does exceed the threshold, all past sales are subject to tax. New York only exempts occasional sales of property sold by individuals at a residence (i.e., garage sales). California does not consider sales by anyone holding a retail permit to qualify for a casual sale. In Alabama, an exemption applies to items sold outside the normal course of business (for example, a publishing company selling computers).[838]

[b] Classification of Digital Goods

When digital goods first entered the marketplace, the existing statutes and regulations focused on the taxation of supplies of tangible personal property and specifically enumerated services. In the absence of statutory or administrative provisions imposing tax on digital goods, sales of such goods were generally not considered taxable because the consumer did not receive any tangible personal property. Over the last few years,

835. Nelson et al., *supra* n. 779, at sec. 6:52.
836. Yetter, *supra* n. 826, at sec. 3.1.1.
837. Van Brederode, *Introduction to the US State Sales and Use Taxes*, *supra* n. 774, at sec. 6 and 7.
838. Yetter, *supra* n. 826, at sec. 2.3.

as states have been looking for ways to expand their sales tax bases in order to increase revenues, new statues and regulations have appeared to address the taxation of digital goods. Those rules generally follow one of the three trends.

First, there are states that still have not addressed the issue of taxation of digital goods. As they tax only tangible personal property, digital goods escape taxation due to their intangible nature. Second, there are states that tax digital goods because such goods are considered to be tangible property. The Texas Tax Code provides the following definition of a taxable item:[839]

> "Taxable item" means tangible personal property and taxable services. Except as otherwise provided by this chapter, the sale or use of a taxable item in electronic form instead of on physical media does not alter the item's tax status.

The Louisiana Revised Statute defines tangible personal property as property which may be seen, weighed, measured, felt or touched, or is in any other manner perceptible to the senses.[840] However, the Administrative Code provides examples of tangible property, including:[841]

> digital or electronic products such as "canned" computer software, electronic files, and "on demand" audio and video downloads.

Relying on prior case law according to which electricity constituted tangible personal property,[842] the Alabama Department of Revenue (Administrative Law Division) ruled that a photographer's sale of digital images transmitted electronically was subject to sales tax because the digital images constituted tangible personal property:[843]

> Whether sales tax applies to the sale of digital goods delivered electronically is an emerging issue in state taxation. Admittedly, treating the sale of digitized photographs delivered electronically as a taxable sale of tangible personal property pushes the bounds of what has traditionally been viewed as the sale of tangible goods. But Alabama's broad definition of tangible personal property, which the Alabama Supreme Court has construed to include electricity, is sufficiently broad to include digital goods transmitted by electrical impulses. I also see no principled reason why the retail sale of goods that can now be delivered electronically due to advances in technology, i.e., photographs, music, movies, books, etc., should be taxed any differently than the sale of those goods delivered by traditional means.

The third approach includes states that have enacted a definition of digital goods and impose tax on them. The majority of those states are members of the SSUTA. Under

839. Texas Tax Code 151.010.
840. Louisiana Revised Statute 47:301(16)(a).
841. Louisiana Administrative Code 61:I.4301(C) (Definition of Tangible Personal Property).
842. In *Curry v. Alabama Power Co.*, 8 So.2d 521 (Ala. 1942), the Alabama Supreme Court held that electricity, i.e., the flow of electrons, constituted tangible personal property for sales and use tax purposes. The Court later confirmed that holding in *State v. Television Corp.*, 127 So.2d 603 (Ala. 1961), and *Sizemore v. Franco Distributing Co., Inc.*, 594 So.2d 143 (Ala. Civ. App. 1991).
843. *Robert Smith d/b/a FlipFlopFoto v. State Department of Revenue*, Admin. L. Div. Dkt. No. S051240.

the SSUTA, Member States must not include "any products transferred electronically"[844] in the definitions of "tangible personal property," "computer software,"[845] "telecommunication services" or "ancillary services."[846] A Member State may choose to tax products transferred electronically by enacting special rules but not by including those products within one of the categories specified above. For states that impose a tax on products transferred electronically, section 332(D) of the SSUTA provides that, unless the statute specifically states otherwise, a tax on such products shall be construed as being imposed on a sale which grants the right of permanent use to an end user and which is not conditioned upon continued payment to the seller by the purchaser.[847] A person that purchases products "transferred electronically" for the purpose of giving away such products shall not be considered to have engaged in the distribution or redistribution of such products and shall be treated as an end user.[848] Athough the SSTUTA lays down conditions under which the sale of products transferred electronically should be taxable, many SSUTA Member States have deviated in their statutes from the SSUTA provisions. Some states consider a sale of digital products taxable even if the right to use a digital item is not permanent or the purchaser is obliged to make continuous payments. North Dakota exempted sales of digital products from taxation.[849] On the other side of the spectrum is South Dakota, which has taken the broadest approach to taxing digital products: all sales, leases and rentals of electronically transferred products are taxable.[850] Thus, even among the SSUTA Member States—where one might expect some consistency—a taxpayer must study each statute individually and cannot make a determination regarding the taxability of digital goods in one state based upon its knowledge of the taxability of digital goods in another one.

To date, state tax authorities have published very limited guidance on the classification and taxation of virtual currencies for sales tax purposes. The State of New York classified convertible virtual currency as intangible property.[851] The Michigan

844. The term "transferred electronically" means obtained by the purchaser by means other than tangible storage media (sec. 333 SSUTA).
845. According to the definition in Appendix C Part II of the SSUTA, "computer software" means a set of coded instructions designed to cause a computer or automatic data processing equipment to perform a task.
846. Sections 332A and 333 SSUTA. Before January 1, 2010, the restriction applied only to "specified digital products" defined as digital audio-visual works, digital books and digital audio works.
847. Section 332D SSUTA.
848. Section 332D(1) SSUTA. However, this provision excludes a person who receives by contract a product transferred electronically for further commercial broadcast, rebroadcast, transmission, retransmission, licensing, relicensing, distribution, redistribution or exhibition of the product, in whole or in part, to another person or persons.
849. Sales Tax Handbook, *North Dakota: Sales Tax Handbook—Are Software and Digital Products subject to sales tax?* www.salestaxhandbook.com/north-dakota/sales-tax-taxability/software-and-digital-products.
850. South Dakota Department of Revenue, *Factsheet "Products Transferred Electronically"* (March 2011).
851. New York State Department of Taxation and Finance, *Tax Department Policy on Transactions Using Convertible Virtual Currency*, Technical Memorandum TSB-M-14(5)C, (7)I, (17)S (December 5, 2014).

Department of Treasury announced that virtual currency is not tangible personal property.[852] The result of this classification is that purchases of virtual currency are not subject to sales and use tax in both states. Under the SSUTA, virtual currency would fall within the category of "products transferred electronically."[853] Therefore, it seems that there is general agreement among the states to consider virtual currency to be intangible property. However, the tax treatment resulting from this classification varies per state.

[c] Barter Transactions

The concept of sale includes barter transactions. The two parties to a barter transaction function as both "buyer" and "seller" and the goods and services exchanged serve, in turn, as both the items sold and the consideration paid. Barter is subject to the general sales tax rules. Barter rules apply to exchanges of virtual currencies only in the states that include electronically transferred products in the scope of their retail sales taxes.

The following example explains the tax treatment of a barter transaction under the RST rules. If the "seller" of taxable goods sold in a barter transaction is a New Jersey vendor (i.e., a vendor who has sales tax nexus with New Jersey or a vendor without nexus who has voluntarily chosen to register as a vendor in this state), the seller should collect and remit sales tax calculated on the normal retail value of the item sold, assuming that the purchaser cannot claim a valid statutory exemption (for example, resale, exempt organization, production equipment). The normal retail value is the price at which merchandise or services of the same kind are offered for sale by him to retail customers paying by traditional means (money). If the seller is an out-of-state vendor, not registered in New Jersey, who delivers taxable merchandise to a New Jersey customer in a barter transaction, the New Jersey customer will be liable for compensating use tax. The New Jersey customer will owe the tax on the value of the consideration that he paid. This consideration will consist of the goods or services that it gave to the seller in lieu of money.[854]

In one of the very few state guidance documents on the tax treatment of virtual currency, the State of New York clarified that the use of convertible virtual currency by a customer to pay for goods or services delivered in New York is treated as a barter transaction. Since the purchase or use of intangible property is not subject to sales tax, any convertible virtual currency received by a party to a barter transaction is not subject to sales tax.[855]

852. Michigan Department of Treasury, *Treasury Update* (November 2015).
853. Sec. 332G of the SSUTA clarifies that the tax treatment of a "digital code" shall be the same as the tax treatment of the "specified digital product" or product "transferred electronically" to which the "digital code" relates.
854. New Jersey Treasury, *New Jersey State Tax News*, vol. 30, no. 1 (Spring 2007).
855. New York State Department of Taxation and Finance, *supra* n. 851.

[3] Sourcing Rules

In the United States, the sales tax applies only to domestic (i.e., intra-state) supplies, which means supplies that originate and end within the boundaries of the same state. States have no authority over out-of-state suppliers because interstate trade is the exclusive domain of the federal government. Under the current judicial interpretation of the Commerce Clause, only sellers with adequate nexus (which no longer amounts to physical presence) are required to register as use tax collectors. In an interstate scenario, the obligation to calculate and remit the tax is shifted to the customer. However, the customer will have little incentive to fulfill his obligations knowing that the probability that the tax authorities will find out about the transaction is very low.[856]

The determination of whether a transaction takes place within a state jurisdiction depends on where the transfer of title or possession occurs. This is generally the location where the goods are shipped to the customer by the retailer. The place of taxation for services is usually the location where the service is performed or where the benefit of the service is enjoyed or where the customer makes first use of the service.[857]

The sourcing rules for digital goods depend on their characterization for state sales tax purposes. States that treat digital goods as tangible property follow the sourcing provisions applicable to other tangible goods. Given the intangible nature of digital goods and the characteristics of the electronic means of delivery, the application of rules for sales of tangible property may give rise to significant difficulty. For example, it is unclear where the place of supply is if person A permanently residing in State A, but currently staying temporarily in State C, buys digital goods from entrepreneur B from State B and mentions a billing address in State D where he has his holiday home.[858] Thus, both taxpayers and tax administrators face uncertainty in this area.

Under the SSUTA, the sourcing of digital goods follows the general provisions of section 310A. If the digital good is "received" by the purchaser at a location of the seller, the sale takes place at that location.[859] The term "received" means taking possession or making first use of digital goods, whichever comes first.[860] If the product is not received at the location of the seller, the sale occurs where the purchaser receives the product, as long as that location is known to the seller.[861] If neither of the above applies, the place of supply is the location of the purchaser available from the seller's business records[862] or an address of the purchaser obtained during the consummation of the sale.[863] If none of the above applies, the seller is to source the transaction to the location from which the digital product delivered electronically was first available for transmission by the seller.[864]

856. *See* §8.02[H][5] Use Taxes.
857. Yetter, *supra* n. 826, at sec. 4.
858. It is assumed that entrepreneur B has nexus in States A, C and D, and that digital goods are subject to sales tax in all those states.
859. Sec. 310A.1 SSUTA.
860. Sec. 311C SSUTA.
861. Sec. 310A.2 SSUTA.
862. Sec. 310A.3 SSUTA.
863. Sec. 310A.4 SSUTA.
864. Sec. 310A.5 SSUTA.

Some states are unwilling or unable to adopt the destination-based sourcing approach of the SSUTA. Origin-based taxation is a critical issue for states that permit local jurisdictions to tax intrastate sales that originate in their territory. The origin principle benefits not only local businesses that are required to collect tax for only one jurisdiction but also municipalities that are home to large retailers. To encourage those states to join the SSTP, the Governing Board amended the SSUTA to permit origin-based sourcing for intrastate sales of tangible personal property and digital goods.[865] While the destination principle remains the rule for interstate sales, Member States with local jurisdictions that impose or receive sales or use taxes may elect origin-based sourcing.

Just like in the case of the characterization of digital goods, there are no uniform sourcing rules among the SSUTA Member States. A taxpayer must study each state statute individually and cannot make a determination regarding the sourcing of digital goods in one state based upon its knowledge of the laws of another one.

[4] Tax Rate

The sales tax rates vary from 2.9% to 7.25%.[866] The applicable combined rate for a taxable sale is the state sales tax rate plus any local rates. The differences in tax rates result in cross-border shopping, i.e., consumers making their purchases in a state with a lower tax.

Contrary to the situation in the European Union, where VAT is included in the listed retail sales price, the US sales tax is an addition to the price. There is a dual rationale for separating the price and tax. First, by stating the tax separately, customers are made aware of what they are paying for public services. Second, it makes it easier for suppliers to shift the tax forward to their customers and it prevents loss in sales volume when prices increase upon the introduction of the tax or when the existing rates are increased since the listed price is never affected by the tax.[867]

[5] Use Taxes

Use tax is defined as a tax on the storage, use or consumption of taxable items on which no sales tax has been paid. It applies to purchases made outside the taxing state but used within that state. Its aim is to prevent competitive disadvantage for domestic sellers.[868]

Use taxes were initially enacted in the 1930's, shortly after states started passing sales tax laws. The original purpose of use taxes was to prevent residents from crossing

865. Sec. 310.1 SSTUA (effective January 1, 2010).
866. For a list of state sales tax rates, *see* Sales Tax Institute, *State Sales Tax Rates*, http://salestaxinstitute.com/rates.html.
867. Van Brederode, *Introduction to the US State Sales and Use Taxes*, *supra* n. 774, at sec. 2.
868. *Id.*, at sec. 8.

state borders and purchasing goods in neighboring states which had not yet enacted sales taxes.[869]

Use taxes must be remitted by the customer unless the seller has sufficient nexus in the state of destination. Thus, there are two types of use taxes: consumer use tax (CUT) and seller use tax (SUT). The former is self-assed by the customer on items on which no tax was collected by the retailer, whereas the latter applies to sales made by a retailer to a consumer located in another state if the retailer has nexus and is registered to collect tax there.[870]

In practice, use tax compliance is drastically lower than sales tax compliance. Due to ignorance or intentional tax evasion, consumers rarely self-report transactions. The California State Board of Equalization estimates that only 0.4% of individual taxpayers actually pay the use taxes they owe the state. Non-compliance with the use tax resulted in an estimated revenue loss of USD 1.2 billion in California in 2011.[871] An empirical study on the sales tax compliance by eBay sellers showed that cross-border activity amounts to 92% of the total eBay activity. Coupled with a low level of use tax compliance, this creates a large threat to state tax revenues.[872]

If state residents paid the use taxes they owe on e-commerce purchases, there would be no problem of taxation of interstate transactions since the states' inability to levy sales or use taxes on remote sellers would be remedied by the state residents paying use taxes on these purchases.

[I] Conclusions

In the United States, the scope of sales taxation varies from state to state. When digital goods first entered the marketplace, the existing statutes and regulations focused on taxing sales of tangible personal property and specifically enumerated services, leaving digital products untaxed. As the importance of the digital sector and electronic commerce grew, states started looking for ways to subject digital goods to taxation. The result of these efforts is a very inconsistent and complex set of rules that further complicates the multistate sales tax system. In many states, digital products escape taxation due to its intangible nature. In others, they are considered to be tangible property and are taxed accordingly. Although the SSUTA provides rules on the classification of digital products, SSUTA Member States attach different consequences to this classification.

The taxation of digital products is further complicated by the sourcing rules. As most states have not explicitly addressed sourcing with respect to digital products, taxpayers and tax administrators face uncertainty in this area. The SSUTA failed to create uniformity in that matter either.

869. Haile, *supra* n. 797, at sec. I.A.
870. Yetter, *supra* n. 826, at sec. 2.1.
871. Haile, *supra* n. 797, at sec. I.A.
872. J. Alm & M.I. Melnik, *Do Ebay Sellers Comply with State Sales Taxes?* 63 National Tax Journal 2 (2010).

Based on the Supreme Court's decisions in *National Bellas Hess* and *Quill*, interstate suppliers of digital products were effectively exempt from state sales and use taxes for over 50 years. Although consumers are expected to pay use taxes in situations where no sales tax is charged, there is ample evidence to show that consumers rarely comply with their use tax obligations, causing huge revenue losses for the states. The recent Supreme Court's decision in *Wayfair* overturned the physical presence nexus standard and allowed states to enact legislation requiring remote sellers to collect and remit sales taxes. Although the physical presence rule has been abolished, it is not clear what the current requirements of substantial nexus are. The Supreme Court confirmed the constitutional validity of South Dakota's law but it is not clear whether a lower threshold than that used by South Dakota (USD 100,000 of remote sales or 200 such transactions) is also compatible with the Commerce Clause.

Uniformity in consumption taxation seems to be more easily achieved in the European Union than in the United States. While the VAT Directive allows Member States some latitude in defining their tax bases, that latitude is nowhere as great as that found in the sales taxes. This development is easy to explain: at the time the European Community was created, it had only six Member States. As other countries joined, they were required to levy VAT based on the Sixth Directive and its successors. By comparison, the US states were already there when the first sales tax was levied. The EU Member States chose to limit their fiscal sovereignty in the field of indirect taxation at the outset in order to create conditions for the establishment of a single market. The VAT imposed in the European Union is a result of rational design and politics (especially in the case of exemptions and differential rates). The system was explicitly chosen to avoid the distortions inherent in the turnover taxes that preceded it. By comparison, in the United States, fiscal sovereignty has prevailed over uniformity. The US sales taxes "just grew" with little purpose or design other than to raise revenue. Each state went its own way with no efforts at coordination until the past few years.[873]

To summarize, the answer to the question on how to tax virtual currency transactions will vary from state to state. Currency mining generally remains outside the scope of sales taxation as it does not constitute a sale for consideration. In states that do not tax intangible products, all virtual currency transactions (including ICOs) are exempt. In states that tax intangible (digital) products, virtual currency transactions may still be tax free as (1) occasional sales that are not made in the course of business can be exempt; and (2) in the case of inter-state transactions, the seller may lack nexus in the state where the recipient is located (although, in theory, in such circumstances, use tax should be paid by the recipient, the general non-compliance with use tax obligations amounts to a *de facto* exemption for inter-state trade).

873. C.E. McLure Jr., *EU and US Sales Taxes in the Digital Age: A comparative Analysis*, 56 Bull. Intl. Fisc. Doc. 4, sec. 6.2. (2002).

CHAPTER 9

Consumption Taxation: Recommendations

§9.01 INTRODUCTORY REMARKS

Chapter 7 established that an optimal consumption tax system must be able to raise revenue in a neutral manner. This can occur if a tax system meets the generally accepted principles of efficiency (compliance costs for taxpayers and administrative costs for the tax authorities should be kept as low as possible), simplicity and certainty (the tax rules should be clear and simple to understand, so that taxpayers can anticipate consequences of a transaction in advance, including knowing when, where and how the tax is to be accounted for), fairness (all tax due should be collected) and flexibility (the tax system should be flexible and dynamic to ensure that it keeps pace with technological and commercial developments). Neutrality can be divided into external and internal neutrality. External neutrality requires the tax system to be indifferent between expenditure related to goods imported or locally produced. Internal neutrality means that the tax burden is borne exclusively by consumers, taxation does not differ depending on the technology used for the supply of goods and services, and identical goods are taxed in the same way.

Chapter 8 described the basic features of the EU VAT system and the US retail sales tax systems and applied them to transactions in virtual currencies. Although it was focused only on two jurisdictions, the issues identified in those jurisdictions may also be encountered in a wide range of other countries around the world that are trying to find the best way to tax virtual currency transactions.

In the European Union, all supplies of goods and services made by a taxable person acting as such are subject to VAT unless a specific exemption applies. The examination of the VAT treatment of virtual currency transactions in the European Union followed the internal logic of the EU VAT system, which requires that when identifying the correct tax treatment of a supply the following concepts are considered: (1) taxable person, (2) taxable transaction, (3) place of supply, (4) time of taxation and (5) exemption. Chapter 8 concluded that the concept of taxable person lacks clarity.

The definition contained in the VAT Directive is very broad. The CJEU gave general guidelines and recommended a case-by-case analysis. Thus, an individual case may be interpreted differently by tax authorities and courts. VAT registration thresholds help prevent unexpected assessments, but they do not solve all the problems as small businesses are required to register irrespective of their turnover if they perform certain cross-border services. As the concept of taxable person requires the performance of economic activities, non-economic activities, such as the issuance of shares and bonds (and similar activities, such as the issuance of debt or equity tokens during an ICO) are outside the VAT scope. When examining the concept of taxable transactions, Chapter 8 concluded that transfers of virtual currency should generally be viewed as supplies of services due to their intangible nature. This should not apply to coins that serve the same purpose as national currencies and should be treated as such. As the concept of supply requires transactions be performed for consideration, currency mining is outside the scope of VAT. For the purposes of the place-of-supply rules, all virtual currency transactions that are within the scope of VAT should be classified as electronically supplied services and should follow the place-of-supply rule applicable to such services. Electronically supplied services are deemed to be supplied at the place where the recipient has established its business, has a permanent address or usually resides. Cross-border B2B transactions are subject to the reverse charge mechanism, whereas in a B2C situation the supplier has to determine the location of the customer and remit VAT under the OSS scheme. The qualification of a transaction as a supply of electronic services does not preclude the application of the exemption for financial transactions. Exchanges of coins into legal currency are covered by the exemption for transactions "concerning banknotes and coins used as legal tender." Equity and debt tokens could be seen as having the same functions as securities and fall under the exemption for "transactions (...) in shares, interests in companies or associations, debentures and other securities." Utility tokens could also be viewed as multi-purpose vouchers and follow the VAT consequences applicable to transactions involving multiple-purpose vouchers.

Having examined the VAT treatment of virtual currency transactions in the European Union, Chapter 8 looked at how virtual currency is treated for US state sales tax purposes. There is no uniform sales tax system: the scope of tax, tax rates and sourcing rules vary from state to state. There is a general consensus among the states to consider virtual currency to be intangible property. Many states exempt intangible property, whereas others subject it to taxation. Currency mining is outside the sales tax scope as it does not constitute a sales transaction for consideration. Out-of-state retailers are not allowed to collect sales taxes without substantial nexus with the state where the consumption takes place. For the last 50 years, substantial nexus was said to be equivalent to having a physical presence in a state. In *South Dakota v. Wayfair*, the Supreme Court held that economic nexus is sufficient; however, the Court left open what the minimum number of transactions or sales revenue to satisfy the economic nexus test is. Purchases made outside but used within the state are subject to use tax. However, there is ample evidence to show that consumers rarely comply with their use tax obligations, causing huge revenue losses for the states. Therefore, Chapter 8 concluded that transactions in virtual currencies generally escape taxation in the United Sates.

This Chapter draws conclusions based on the analysis in Chapter 8. It examines to what extent the existing rules meet the characteristics of an optimal consumption system, identifies best practices for virtual currency transactions and makes recommendations for the improvement of the existing tax systems. It goes without saying that the general recommendations about the design of an effective regulatory framework for taxing virtual currencies that were made in Chapter 6 in the context of income taxation also apply to consumption taxation. An effective regulatory framework for taxing consumption of virtual currency requires (1) data-driven assessment, (2) choice of the method of regulation; (3) clear communication of the content of laws and regulations, and (4) monitoring taxpayer compliance. To avoid repetition and overlaps with Chapter 6, this chapter will focus only on recommendations specific to consumption taxation.

§9.02 PERSONAL SCOPE

The personal scope of the EU VAT system depends on the concept of the taxable person, which is independent of similar concepts that may exist in commercial or civil law. Given its importance for the functioning of the VAT system, the definition of the taxable person should be clear and unambiguous as required by the principle of legal certainty. However, despite numerous CJEU judgments on its interpretation, the concept of the taxable person still appears to lack clarity and continues to give rise to controversial decisions of national courts. Inconsistent case law results in uncertainty, which in turn undermines one of the most fundamental constitutional values: the predictability of law.

In the digital age, the line between taxable persons and consumers becomes blurred. Anyone can become a professional trader in virtual currency. Websites, such as eBay, have demonstrated that millions of people can be e-retailers without even having their own webpage. VAT registration thresholds should prevent unexpected VAT assessments in a large number of situations but they not solve all problems as businesses are required to register irrespective of their turnover if they provide certain cross-border services. The situation is even more complicated when one realizes that a taxpayer can be an entrepreneur for income tax purposes but not a taxable person (entrepreneur) for VAT purposes.

In the United States, sales tax may be charged by sellers who hold a sales tax permit. In general, states require a person to obtain a sales tax permit if the person is engaged in business in the state and intends to sell personal property or provide taxable services to customers in that state. The term "engaged in business" is usually defined in broad terms. For example, in California, it means:

- having an office, sales room, warehouse, or other place of business in this state (even if the location is only temporary);
- having a sales representative, agent, or canvasser operating in this state;

- receiving rental payments from the lease of tangible personal property in this state.[874]

Sales tax collection must commence with a business' first taxable sale. There are no turnover thresholds below which retail sales are not subject to tax.

There are no straightforward answers to the question how to determine who falls within the personal scope of VAT or sales tax. On the one hand, it is obvious that the principle of legal certainty is best served with a detailed legislation, in which clear and quantified rules are stated for clearly described series of cases.[875] Although the US Supreme Court acknowledged in the *Quill* decision (with regard to the physical presence rule) that any bright-line tests appear artificial at their edges, the majority of the judges concluded that "this artificiality (...) is more than offset by the benefits of a clear rule." By adopting clear, bright-line rules, it was hoped to reduce litigation and to avoid confusion that might otherwise arise in the absence of "precise guides to the States in the exercise of their indispensable power of taxation."[876] However, there are no principled ways to set turnover thresholds. The use of thresholds seems to violate the principle of equity: taxpayers in very similar situations are treated differently because their turnovers are just below or just above a certain monetary amount.

One solution that could help taxpayers determine whether they qualify as a taxable person/retailer is the possibility to obtain advanced opinions from the tax administration.[877] Taxpayers would describe their individual circumstances to the tax authorities and the latter would give their opinion on whether the activity in question triggers VAT or sales tax obligations. There should be a low- (or no) cost possibility to request such a ruling in an administrative-friendly procedure, using electronic forms and e-mail communication. Tax authorities should be obliged to respond to those requests within a short predefined time limit.

§9.03 TAXABLE TRANSACTIONS

In the European Union, supplies of virtual currency can be classified as supplies of (electronic) services due to the intangible nature of virtual currency. However, supplies of virtual currency used as a means of payment are outside the scope of VAT as they follow the rules applicable to legal currency. In the Unites States, virtual currency is generally treated as products transferred electronically or intangible property. The sales tax treatment of these two categories varies per state. Many states exempt intangible property, whereas others subject it to taxation.

874. California Department of Tax and Fee Administration, *Obtaining a Seller's Permit*.
875. B. Peeters, *European Supervision on the Use of Vague and Undetermined Concepts in Tax Laws*, EC Tax Review 3 (2013).
876. *Quill Corp. v. North Dakota*, 504 US 315 (1992).
877. The European Commission recognizes the fact that taxpayers need certainty with regard to the VAT consequences of their transactions. In June 2013, it introduced a pilot scheme under which the participating Member States provided taxable persons with an advance opinion regarding the VAT treatment of complex cross-border transactions.

As the principle of neutrality requires all consumption be taxed, digital products should generally be included in the scope of VAT or sales tax. No general exemption should apply to digital products since, from a tax policy point of view, no reasons for such an exemption can be found. The current policy of the US states, which involves taxing digital products on a selective basis or not taxing them at all, gives rise to competitive inequalities and violates the principle of neutrality. Distinctions are made that neither have economic sense nor serve useful purpose. Sales taxes discriminate the goods and few services that are subject to them in favor of the large sectors of the economy that remain untaxed. There is no rational reason for the way different goods and services are currently treated under sales tax law and for the fact that tax policy favors content delivered online over that in tangible forms. The failure to tax all consumption complicates tax compliance and administration, and leads to losses of revenue or to higher income and sales tax rates for supplies that do not escape taxation.

However, it seems reasonable to remove means of payment from the scope of consumption taxation. The function of legal tender is to facilitate transactions rather than to be consumed as goods or services. Therefore, if virtual currency acts like legal currency, it should receive the same treatment as the latter. Exchanges of goods and services for coins should not be treated as barter transactions. For the purposes of legal certainty, it would be reasonable to include, in the legislation, a statement that transfers of virtual currency that serves as a means of payment are outside of the scope of consumption tax.

Australia has been the first country to introduce such legislation. The Treasury Laws Amendment (2017 Measures No. 6) Act 2017, which amended the Australian GST law, made it clear that the use of virtual currency to pay for goods and services has the same consequences as using money. The Act amended section 9-10(4) as follows:

> (4) However, *supply* does not include:
> (a) a supply of money unless the money is provided as consideration for a supply that is a supply of money or digital currency; or
> (b) a supply of digital currency unless the digital currency is provided as consideration for a supply that is a supply of digital currency or money.

In other words, the new section 9-10(4) provides that a transfer of digital currency is outside the GST scope unless it is made in a currency exchange transaction (which is exempt under the Australian GST law). The new Act amended multiple sections of the GST law by inserting "or 'digital currency'" after the term "money" to make sure that both means of payment enjoy the same treatment.

§9.04 SOURCING RULES

Currently, there is a widespread consensus that the destination principle is the proper way to tax international trade.[878] Since the object of consumption taxation is to tax consumption, the country where consumption takes place should have the right to

878. *International VAT/GST Guidelines*, *supra* n. 623, at p. 27; A. Schenk & O. Oldman, *Value Added Tax: A Comparative Approach* p. 35 (Cambridge University Press 2007).

assert jurisdiction to tax. In theory, in a destination-based VAT system, the place-of-supply rules should identify the place of actual consumption. However, in most cases, the supplier is not able to identify such a place at the time of the supply since the person who will "consume" the goods or services may not necessarily be the purchaser or at the time of the supply it may not be sure where the goods will actually be consumed. Consumption taxes are imposed as transaction taxes, meaning that the amount of tax must be determined as soon as the consumer makes the expenditure, irrespective of when and how the goods will be used later on. The term "consumption" merely indicates who bears the tax burden. As the decision about the place of taxation must be made at the time of the transaction, all destination-based VAT systems use various proxies (for example, the place where services are used and enjoyed, the permanent address or the usual residence of the customer) to predict with reasonable accuracy the place where goods and services are likely to be consumed.

In the context of digital products, the application of the destination principle triggers two important questions: first, whether it is possible (at least in theory) to determine the destination of digital products (i.e., the place where the consumption of digital products occurs); and, second, what proxies can be used to identify that place.

[A] Destination Principle as the Main Rule

Identifying the place where digital products are actually consumed is not an easy task. Digital products bear no relationship with a particular geographical location. They can be moved and consumed many times without delay or transport costs. The consumer can access them everywhere (although sometimes access to the Internet is necessary). Digital products follow the consumer: he can use them both at the place of his usual residence and during his trips abroad. Thus, consumption of digital products cannot be pinned down to one particular place.

However, even though digital products can be consumed multiple times and at multiple locations and thus do not have a single destination, for the correct application of tax, a place of taxation needs to be determined. There must be mechanisms in place to identify where a transaction takes place and those mechanisms should aim to identify a location where a digital good is most often likely to be consumed. In this context, a question arises whether the use of multiple proxies and presumptions to establish the place of taxation (for example, place of performance, place of use of enjoyment, customer's residence) is preferable or one simple rule would be sufficient.

[B] Proxies to Establish the Place of Taxation

In the European Union, the place of taxation of electronic services supplied to a non-taxable person should be the place where the customer is established, has his permanent address or usually resides.[879] In order to determine that place, the VAT

879. Article 58 VAT Directive.

Implementing Regulation has introduced a number of presumptions, which unfortunately often contradict the main rule rather than clarify its application.[880] For example, electronic services supplied at a location, such as a wi-fi hot spot, an internet café, a restaurant or a hotel lobby shall be presumed to take place at that location.[881] Similarly, for services provided through mobile networks, it shall be presumed that the place where the customer is located is the country identified by the mobile country code of the SIM card used when receiving those services.[882]

Both presumptions (which can be rebutted on the basis of three non-contradictory evidence items)[883] aim at identifying a location that does not seem to bear any relationship to the main rule mentioned in the VAT Directive (i.e., permanent address or usual residence). For services not covered by a specific presumption, the customer is deemed to belong at the place identified by the supplier on the basis of two items of non-contradictory evidence (such as the customer's billing address, the IP address of the device used by the customer or any method of geo-location, bank details or other commercially relevant information). The application of some of the evidence items may also lead to a different result than the main legislative rule. For example, the IP address indicates the place where the customer is located at the time of the transaction and which may be different from the customer's usual residence. In other words, the customer's IP address is a way to identify the computer used to perform a particular transaction, but not the residence of a person participating in the transaction. Despite this inconsistency, the VAT Explanatory Notes state that all presumptions should be interpreted consistently with the rules set by the VAT Directive.[884] It remains unclear how to achieve that.

The VAT Explanatory Notes admit the possibility of a clash between presumptions and provide that in order to determine which one should prevail a factual assessment of the supply should be made and the supplier should collect all available information.[885] If there is a conflict among the items of evidence collected, priority is to be given to the place that best ensures taxation at the place of actual consumption of the services. In cases where items of evidence are contradictory, verification by the supplier on a regular basis is more needed.[886]

In the author's view, the European Union have constructed an impressive regulatory framework that seeks to tax electronic services at the place of their actual consumption although as shown earlier in this section there is hardly ever a single place where a digital good is consumed. By introducing a number of presumptions whose application may lead to a different result that that of the main legislative rule,

880. For a critical evaluation of the presumptions, *see* A.M. Bal, *The Myth of Taxing Cloud Computing under EU VAT*, 25 Intl. VAT Monitor 6 (2014).
881. Article 24a VAT Implementing Regulation.
882. Article 24b VAT Implementing Regulation.
883. A supplier is not obliged to rebut a presumption. Even though there can be evidence to the contrary, the supplier may, for determining the place where the customer belongs, decide to rely on the presumption and disregard evidence to the contrary.
884. Explanatory Notes, *supra* n. 740, at p. 54.
885. Explanatory Notes, *supra* n. 740, at p. 62.
886. Explanatory Notes, *supra* n. 740, at p. 72.

the VAT system for taxing electronic services became more complex and less transparent. The rules for identifying the place of supply are difficult to comply with and their application cannot be effectively checked by the tax authorities. Thus, the complex regulatory framework fails to adhere to the principles of efficiency, simplicity and certainty, which the rules on the taxation of electronic commerce should follow.[887]

Since there is rarely a single place of consumption of digital products, it makes little sense to use a wide variety of proxies and presumptions to seek to determine one. The example of the European Union shows that the application of multiple presumptions does not guarantee correct results and adds to the complexity of the regulatory framework. The requirement to use a large number of proxies is based on the assumption that suppliers can verify information provided by their customers on a transaction-by-transaction basis. Whereas this may work for conventional supplies, this assumption does not hold true in a digital context where suppliers usually cannot obtain all relevant information to carry out transaction-based assessments in a timely fashion. For this reason, the use of a single rule rather than a large number of different proxies seems to be a superior alternative. As consumers most often consume digital products in their country of residence, the consumer residence should be used to determine the place of taxation of digital products. For suppliers, it will be easier to comply with one rule than a multitude of presumptions that may give rise to conflicting results. Such a rule may not identify correctly the place of actual consumption in all cases, but provides a good approximation. As suppliers use different business models, they should be allowed to identify the place of residence based on the information they usually collect or that which is available in their commercial records (such as billing address, mailing address, bank details, web-based country selection, location detected through geolocation software, IP address).

[C] Origin Principle as a Last Resort

Although the destination principle is the theoretically correct way to tax consumption and to create a level playing field for cross-border supplies, the difficulty of its practical application should not be underestimated in practice. For example, EU suppliers of electronic services to private individuals in other Member States have to be aware of the relevant VAT legislation in other Member States where they make taxable supplies of electronic services. Thus, service providers having customers in 28 Member States will have to comply with 28 national VAT laws. Second, the location of their customer is not easy to identify when services are provided at a distance, payment intermediaries are involved and no physical shipments take place. It is not clear what is considered to be sufficient verification of the customer status. Suppliers' efforts can be evaluated differently by different tax authorities and the question of liability inevitably arises. Another element that should not be underestimated is the average sales price of digital products and the high number of daily transactions. Many digital products are cheap and they can be easily and fast moved across the globe. This means that imposing

887. OECD, *A Borderless World: Realizing the Potential of Global Electronic Commerce* (OECD 1998).

transaction-based verifications is likely to cause costs equal to or even exceeding the benefit of most online transactions.

As shown above, the application of the destination principle may give rise to uncertainty and high compliance burden, both of which are absent when digital products are taxed at origin. Under the origin approach, suppliers assess and collect VAT in accordance with their local legislation. Moreover, they only have to satisfy administrative formalities required by their own tax authorities. However, the origin principle was rejected by the European Commission for the following reasons. First, origin-based taxation would make it necessary to harmonize the VAT rates to prevent rate differences from influencing decisions on where to buy and to locate business activity.[888] Second, a clearing system would be needed to ensure that VAT receipts accrue to the Member State of consumption. Third, Member States would have to rely on each other to collect a substantial part of their VAT revenue.[889] As destination-based taxes can be avoided only by changing the place of consumption, which generally means changing the place of residence, they do not give rise to serious competition issues. Consumers have little inclination to change their location only to benefit from a lower VAT rate. Thus, differences in destination-based taxes are not likely to distort decisions of where to live and consume.[890]

The author agrees with the merits of using the destination principle. However, in the author's view, the compliance burden placed upon suppliers of cross-border electronic services would lessened if an option to apply the origin principle to such supplies was available in circumstances in which no information on the usual residence of the customer could be obtained. Such a rule would eliminate suppliers' potential liability for an incorrect determination of the customer's location. If it is impossible to identify the customer's location, the supplier should be allowed to charge consumption tax in accordance with his own domestic legislation. The US SSTP, the Marketplace Fairness Act of 2017 and the Remote Transactions Parity Act of 2017 prescribe a hierarchy of sourcing rules depending on information that is available to sellers: taxation should follow the destination principle, but if the seller cannot determine the place of consumption, origin-based taxation may apply. Section 310(A)(5) of the SSUTA states that "when none of the previous rules (...) apply, including the circumstance in which the seller is without sufficient information to apply the previous rules, then the location will be determined by the address from which tangible personal property was shipped, from which the digital good or the computer software delivered electronically was first available for transmission by the seller, or from which the service was provided." Similarly, the Marketplace Fairness Act of 2017 and the Remote Transactions Parity Act of 2017 provide that "if an address is unknown and a billing address cannot be obtained, the remote sale is sourced to the address of the seller from which the remote sale was made."

888. Under the EU origin regime applicable to supplies to private individuals until December 31, 2014, there was a clear incentive to provide digital products from Luxembourg, which had the lowest VAT rate in the European Union (15%).
889. European Commission, *Green Paper on the Future of VAT: Towards a Simpler, More Robust and Efficient VAT System*, sec. 4, COM(2010) 695 final (December 1, 2010).
890. C.E. McLure Jr., *Tax Competition in a Digital World*, 57 Bull. Intl. Fisc. Doc. 4, sec. 2.1, (2003).

Taxation according to the origin principle in a limited number of cases would be less distortive than non-taxation resulting from the application of the destination principle (non-taxation occurs if the customer pretends to be resident in a third country and the supplier has no means to verify this). It would make the tax system workable and would not punish businesses which have chosen certain distribution channels by placing on them too burdensome and difficult to fulfil compliance obligations.

[D] Inter-jurisdictional Transactions

In the United States, interstate commerce is the exclusive domain of the federal government: the US Constitution grants Congress the power to regulate international and interstate commerce ("the Commerce Clause"). The US Supreme Court explained the application of the Commerce Clause to state sales taxation in its decision in *Complete Auto Transit*. In this decision, the Supreme Court developed a four-element framework to determine whether or not a state tax on interstate commerce is constitutional. A tax that satisfies the *Complete Auto Transit* test must: (1) apply to an activity with a substantial nexus with the taxing state; (2) be fairly apportioned; (3) not discriminate against interstate commerce; and (4) be related to the services provided by the state.

The Supreme Court shed more light on the requirement of substantial nexus in its decisions in *Quill v. North Dakota* and *National Bellas Hess*. It held that a seller was deemed to have a substantial nexus with the state if he maintained a physical presence there. If the seller had no physical presence in the state, the state could not impose tax collection and remittance obligations. The physical presence rule, so the Supreme Court, was necessary to prevent undue burden on interstate commerce. The Supreme Court did not consider that remote sellers ought to be placed in a tax-advantaged position as compared to local retailers. Rather, it was afraid that "variations in rates of tax, in allowable exemptions, and in administrative and recordkeeping requirements" could create "a virtual welter of complicated obligations" for taxpayers engaged in interstate business.

While the nexus rules provided in *Quill* reduced complexity, they were a highly defective way to deal with avoidable complexity. The physical presence standard was unfair to local merchants since it distorted interstate commerce: not by impeding it but by favoring it at the expense of intrastate commerce. The *Quill*'s bright-line presence test made no economic sense and violated the principle of neutrality: consumers escaped taxation because the seller lacks physical presence in the state although the seller's physical presence had nothing to do with the process of consumption. Since consumers ordinarily do not remit use tax on purchases from remote sellers, despite the legal obligation to do so, the physical presence standard amounted to a *de facto* exemption of B2C remote sales.

In its recent highly anticipated decision in *South Dakota v. Wayfair*, the Supreme Court admitted that the physical presence standard was "unsound and incorrect" and should be overturned. In the Court's view, the *Quill* decision was flawed on its own terms. First, physical presence was not necessary to create a substantial nexus. Second,

Quill created rather than resolved market distortions. By giving online retailers an arbitrary advantage over their competitors who collected sales taxes, the physical presence rule prevented market participants from competing on an even playing field.

As a result of the *Wayfair* judgment, states are no longer constrained by the *Quill* standards and may enact legislation requiring remote sellers to collect and remit their sales taxes. *Way*fair made it clear that economic connections are sufficient to create substantial nexus and that the physical presence rule no longer applies. However, it is not clear what number of transactions or sales revenue may create substantial nexus. Although the Supreme Court confirmed the constitutional validity of South Dakota's law, it is not clear whether a lower threshold than that used by South Dakota (USD 100,000 of remote sales or 200 such transactions) is also compatible with the Commerce Clause.

Pending federal legislation that seeks to subject remote sellers to state sales taxation (the Marketplace Fairness Act of 2017 and the Remote Transactions Parity Act of 2017) also follows an economic nexus approach. Both pieces of proposed legislation provide protections for small businesses. Under the Marketplace Fairness Act 2017, sellers whose gross annual receipts in remote sales do not exceed USD 1 million fall under the small seller exemption and are not required to collect sales and use taxes on those sales. The Remote Transactions Parity Act of 2017 introduces a phased-in threshold of gross annual receipts.

It is a positive development that the United States has started embracing the economic nexus approach for indirect tax purposes. This approach is economically sensible and clear. It renders irrelevant issues, such as whether placing advertisement on a website constitutes nexus. The turnover threshold relieves sellers who derive negligible revenue from remote sales from the obligation to comply with the local rules. It remains to be seen how the United States will define the minimum requirements for substantial nexus. The *Wayfair* decision and the pending federal legislative proposals imply that the United States will not (at least not in the near future) follow the EU model which requires remote sellers supplying electronic services to private individuals to charge local VAT, irrespective of any turnover they generate from remote sales.

[E] Interim Conclusions

As the destination principle is the correct way to tax consumption, consumption taxes should be levied in the country where the recipient is located. Whereas in cross-border situations tax liability can be shifted to business customers, the US use tax example has shown that shifting the tax liability to private individuals is not a workable solution. In the case of B2C supplies, suppliers should be required to register and collect tax in the jurisdiction of their non-taxable customers. In order to do so, they must be able to determine the customer's location at the time of the transaction. This chapter recommends digital products (including virtual currency) be deemed to be supplied at the customer's usual residence, which should be determined on the basis of information that is available in the supplier's business systems. If no such information is available and the seller cannot reasonable obtain it, the seller should be allowed to apply the origin principle and charge his local VAT. Charging consumption tax should not be dependent on the seller's presence in the customer's jurisdiction as the location of the seller is not a factor affecting consumption. To lessen the seller's compliance burden in respect of cross-jurisdictional transactions, economic nexus (for example, a small seller exemption) should be used rather than a nexus based on physical presence.

§9.05 EXEMPTIONS

The EU VAT system applies exemptions to a wide range of activities which are said to be difficult to tax (for example, financial and insurance services and gambling). There seems to be no scholarly argument that supports exemption for those activities, except the one that accurately calculating the tax base is too complicated (for example, in the case of gambling, under the credit-invoice method, casinos would be required to report the bets as outputs and the winning paid out as inputs on a transaction-by-transaction basis). Preparatory work to the Sixth Directive confirms this reasoning.[891] From a legal perspective, exemptions give rise to definitional and interpretative problems and create difficulties in calculating the proportion of deductible input VAT. Taxpayers who sell both taxable and exempt outputs are faced with complex tax calculations. If taxpayers carry out both exempt and taxed transactions, the right to input tax deduction has to be allocated between the two kinds of supplies either by the assessment of a global proportion of the taxable outputs by comparison with total outputs or on the basis of the actual use of inputs or some other method that is acceptable to the tax administration. This increases the compliance burden and introduces further complexities into an already complex tax system.

However, the use of exemption is supported by practical considerations. Regarding virtual currency, the VAT Committee mentioned some practical problems that would occur if transfers of virtual currency were considered taxed transactions: "private individuals could become taxable persons for VAT purposes where the annual turnover exceeded the allowed thresholds. Anonymity of traders would represent an added difficulty in identifying taxable persons and the place of supply."[892]

Therefore, a balance needs to be struck between practical considerations supporting the application of exemptions and the lack of legal arguments for their use. From the point of view of simplicity, making virtual currency transactions tax free would eliminate many practical problems. As VAT exemptions are already a permanent element of the VAT Directive, the principle of neutrality supports the application of exemptions to transactions involving similar items to those explicitly mentioned as exempt in the VAT Directive or to transactions having the same purpose as exempt transactions. However, to ensure legal certainty, the author would recommend the application of exemptions to virtual currency transactions be clarified by legislation.

---

891. European Commission, *Proposal for a Sixth VAT Directive on the Harmonization of Legislation of Member States Concerning Turnover Taxes—Common System of Value Added Tax: Uniform Basis of Assessment*, COM(73) 95 (June 20, 1975).
892. VAT Committee, *Working Paper No. 811*, p. 14 (July 29, 2014).

§9.06 ENFORCEMENT AND COMPLIANCE

The ability to collect the tax due is part of a country's sovereignty. The question "how to collect the tax due?" is as important as "which country has the right to levy tax?" Enacting legislation that requires remote suppliers to charge local consumption tax seems to be a relatively easy task compared to the challenge of how to collect the tax due.

There is a widespread consensus that the most effective approach to ensure collection of VAT on supplies of digital products by non-residents is to require the non-resident supplier to register and account for VAT in the jurisdiction of taxation.[893] A number of such systems are already in operation around the world.[894] Other mechanisms for tax collection on cross-border supplies, such as VAT self-assessment by final consumers, have proven ineffective. In the absence of effective enforcement mechanisms, consumers are unlikely to comply.

One of the main disadvantages of simplified registration systems is that they rely on voluntary compliance. If the supplier does not register and remit VAT, the tax administration will hardly ever know that a taxable supply took place. To encourage voluntary compliance by non-residents, the simplified registration systems should strive to be as user-friendly and as easy to apply as possible. They should rely on electronic communication and electronic payment facilities and the information requested from foreign suppliers (for both registration and filing purposes) should be limited to the absolutely necessary data. To facilitate compliance, all information necessary to register, calculate tax liability and submit tax returns should be available online in multiple languages.[895] A good incentive to foster compliance by remote sellers is the provision of free-of-charge software, which is recommended by the SSUTA, the Marketplace Fairness Act of 2017 and the Remote Transactions Parity Act of 2017. According to the provisions of these Acts, remote sellers can outsource most of their sales tax compliance responsibilities to certified service providers or employ certified automated systems to perform compliance functions. In terms of liability, remote sellers are held harmless for any errors or omissions resulting from relying on these systems and providers. Under the Remote Transactions Parity Act of 2017, certified software providers are even obliged to represent the remote seller during an audit and may be responsible for the audit findings.

An important question is whether a registration threshold should be introduced for non-resident suppliers using the simplified registration mechanism. The OECD VAT/GST Guidelines do not contain a clear recommendation on that matter but recommend striking a balance between the compliance costs for non-residents and the need to level the playing field between resident and non-resident businesses. Relieving suppliers from the obligation to register in countries where their sales are of negligible value is not likely to cause net losses of revenue in light of the offsetting expenses. In countries, such as New Zealand and Australia, non-resident businesses are obliged to

893. *International VAT/GST Guidelines*, *supra* n. 623, at. p. 50.
894. For example, in the European Union, Norway, South Africa, Korea (Rep.).
895. *International VAT/GST Guidelines*, *supra* n. 623, at p. 53.

register only if they exceed certain monetary thresholds (NZD 60,000 and AUD 75,000). Both the Marketplace Fairness Act of 2017 and the Remote Transactions Parity Act of 2017 introduce small seller exemptions under which sellers whose nationwide turnover from remote sales remains below certain thresholds are relieved from the obligation to collect sales and use taxes on those sales. However, currently, there is no "small seller exemption" for supplies of cross-border electronic services in the European Union.[896] This means that foreign suppliers must be aware of the local VAT rules even if they perform a single transaction in another Member State. The lack of thresholds puts EU businesses engaged in cross-border EU sales at a disadvantage compared to businesses carrying out purely domestic transactions. For the purposes of domestic transactions, no VAT needs to be charged if the supplier's turnover remains below the registration threshold. However, businesses engaged in cross-border trade cannot rely on domestic registration thresholds. The author supports an equal treatment of all businesses, irrespective of the type of their activity, and recommends extending the application of registration thresholds to cross-border trade. Consequently, businesses with a turnover below the national registration threshold of the consumer's country would not have to charge VAT when selling digital products in that country.

It is questionable whether the fact that tax collection in cross-border scenarios is reliant on voluntary compliance by non-resident suppliers is acceptable from a neutrality and competition perspective in the long term. Without effective supervision and enforcement, there is a risk of non-taxation that threatens to distort competition. If tax rules are not linked to a real possibility of enforcement, taxpayers are unlikely to comply. To ensure tax collection in the country of destination, the enforcement capacity of tax authorities needs to be reinforced through enhanced international cooperation. In the European Union, a supranational legal framework for exchange of VAT information is already in place.[897] Data on cross-border B2B supplies of services is stored and made available through the electronic VAT Information Exchange System (VIES): the supplier has to submit, to the tax authorities of his country of establishment, a recapitulative statement containing information on his intra-EU supplies and their recipients and this information becomes automatically available to the tax authorities of the country of his recipients. However, no similar system is in place in relation to B2C supplies, which rely on voluntary compliance by non-resident suppliers.

Both EU and non-EU countries can make use of the existing instruments on exchange of information and assistance in tax collection, such as the Convention on

896. However, according to the European Commission's proposals presented on December 1, 2016, online companies with annual cross-border sales up to EUR 10,000 will be able to account for VAT on these sales under their home country rules as from January 1, 2019. Thus, they will benefit from the familiar VAT rules of their home country, such as invoicing requirements and record-keeping.

897. *Council Regulation (EU) No 904/2010 of 7 October 2010 on administrative cooperation and combating fraud in the field of value added tax and Council Directive 2010/24/EU of 16 March 2010 concerning mutual assistance for the recovery of claims relating to taxes, duties and other measures.*

Mutual Administrative Assistance in Tax Matters (as amended by the 2010 protocol), tax information exchange agreements, and tax treaties based on the OECD or UN Model Convention (articles 26 and 27 apply to all taxes, including VAT). Countries would be more willing to exchange information and answer requests of other jurisdictions if a revenue-sharing mechanism was introduced. This would mean that the country of supplier would be entitled to retain a proportion of the VAT revenues collected for the country where the final consumer is resident. Revenue sharing is well established in the European Union in respect of customs duties, and is also provided for in the initial period of the MOSS operation (30% in 2015 and 2016, and 15% in 2017 and 2018).

Digital products are traded on the global marketplace. Such a market can never be subject to full control by the tax authorities. If the collection of tax on the supplies of digital products is to be reliant on voluntary compliance by non-resident suppliers without the presence of effective domestic enforcement mechanisms, suppliers must be provided with incentives to comply and countries must be encouraged to cooperate. The former could be achieved by simple registration and reporting mechanisms, whereas the latter by revenue sharing system.

§9.07 CONCLUSIONS

This chapter identified best practices for taxing virtual currency transactions and made recommendations for the improvement of the existing tax systems of the European Union and the United States, which were examined in detail in Chapter 8. The outline of this chapter followed the logical structure of consumption tax systems and discussed the following elements: personal scope, taxable transactions, scouring rules, exemptions and tax compliance.

Regarding the personal scope, the principle of certainty requires that taxpayers can easily determine when they are required to collect tax. This could be achieved by introducing monetary thresholds below which there is no obligation to charge consumption tax irrespective of the type of activity (domestic or cross-border). If such thresholds are not provided, taxpayers should have the possibility to request advance opinions from the tax authorities on whether their activities may have any consumption tax implications.

When discussing taxable transactions, this chapter observed that the principle of neutrality requires all consumption (including that of intangible property and digitally transferred products) fall within the scope of consumption tax. However, transfers of means of payment should be removed from the scope of consumption taxation as the function of legal tender is to facilitate transactions rather than to be consumed as goods or services. For the purposes of legal certainty, it would be reasonable to include, in the legislation, a statement that transfers of virtual currency that serves as a means of payment are outside of the consumption tax scope. The Australian GST law serves as a good example.

There is a widespread consensus that the destination principle is the correct way to tax consumption. However, the place-of-taxation rules should take into account that there is rarely a single place of consumption of digital products that can be used by consumers multiple times and at multiple locations. The application of multiple proxies and presumptions will not guarantee the correct determination of the place of taxation. Therefore, this chapter advocates the use of a simple rule that provides a good approximation of the place of actual consumption and is relatively easy to apply by non-resident suppliers: the place of taxation should be the consumer's usual residence, which should be determined on the basis of information that is available in the supplier's business systems. If no such information is available and the seller cannot reasonable obtain it, the seller should be allowed to apply the origin principle and charge his local VAT. Charging consumption tax should not be dependent on the seller's presence in the customer's jurisdiction as the location of the seller is not a factor affecting consumption. To lessen the seller's compliance burden in respect of cross-jurisdictional transactions, economic nexus (for example, a small seller exemption) should be used rather than a nexus based on physical presence.

In the EU VAT system, the application of VAT exemptions to virtual currency is supported by practical considerations. The principle of neutrality supports the application of exemptions to transactions involving similar items to those mentioned explicitly as exempt in the VAT legislation or to transactions having the same purpose as exempt transactions. To ensure legal certainty, the author recommends the application of exemptions to virtual currency transactions be clarified by legislation.

The most effective approach to collect VAT on supplies of digital products by non-residents is to require the non-resident supplier to register and account for VAT in the jurisdiction of taxation. To ensure that the tax due is actually collected, suppliers must be provided with incentives to comply (such as free-of-charge software) and countries must be encouraged to cooperate (for example, by using a system of revenue sharing). The author supports an equal treatment of all businesses, irrespective of the type of their activity, and recommends extending the application of registration thresholds to cross-border trade. Consequently, businesses with a turnover below the national registration threshold of the consumer's country would not have to charge VAT when selling digital products to private individuals of that country.

Annex

Virtual Currency Regulation in Selected Jurisdictions

This annex provides an overview of legislation, regulations and court decisions on the tax treatment of virtual currency in selected countries.

AUSTRALIA

The Australian Taxation Office (ATO) has provided very comprehensive guidance on the tax treatment of virtual currency. This guidance is regularly updated to take account of new developments. All documents are published on the ATO website and contain multiple examples and references to sources where additional information on specific topics can be found.

In its notice *Tax treatment of cryptocurrencies*, the ATO clarified that any disposal of virtual currency constitutes a taxable event for CGT purposes.[1] If a digital wallet contains different types of cryptocurrencies, each cryptocurrency is a separate CGT asset. The income tax treatment of cryptocurrency transactions depends on whether the currency is held for business, investment or private purposes.

Cryptocurrency may be a personal use asset if it is kept mainly to purchase items for personal use or consumption. Capital gains that one makes from personal use assets acquired for less than AUD 10,000 are disregarded for CGT purposes. Also, all capital losses on personal use assets are disregarded. If cryptocurrency is held as an investment, one is not entitled to the personal use asset exemption.

If cryptocurrency is acquired as an investment, the taxpayer has to pay tax on any capital gain he makes on disposal of the cryptocurrency. Changes in the market value of cryptocurrency do not result in a capital gain or loss until the currency is disposed of.

1. ATO, *Tax treatment of cryptocurrencies* (last updated: June 29, 2018). The notice applies to Bitcoin and other digital currencies that have the same characteristics as Bitcoin.

If a disposal of virtual currency is part of a business activity, the profits one makes on the disposal will be assessable as ordinary income and not as a capital gain.

The ATO notice also clarifies the tax consequences of chain splits (forks)[2] and contains a separate section on recordkeeping obligations. If one holds cryptocurrency as an investment, and receives a new cryptocurrency as a result of a chain split, one does not derive ordinary income or make a capital gain. A new cryptocurrency received as a result of a chain split in relation to cryptocurrency held in a business will be treated as trading stock and must be brought to account at the end of the income year. The section on recordkeeping obligations lists records that a taxpayer needs to maintain in relation to his cryptocurrency transactions.

For goods and services tax (GST) purposes, the tax treatment of virtual currency was aligned with that of legal currency as from July 1, 2017. The relevant legislation was included in Treasury Laws Amendment (2017 Measures No. 6) Act 2017, which received royal assent on October 30, 2017. Before the law was amended, virtual currency was treated in a similar way to property for GST purposes, meaning that consumers who used digital currencies as payment effectively paid GST twice: once on the purchase of the digital currency and again on its use in exchange for other goods and services subject to GST.

The amending law provided a definition of virtual currency that was added to the Australian GST Act (A New Tax System (Goods and Services Tax) Act 1999), making Australia the first country with a legal definition of virtual currency for tax purposes. According to this definition, virtual currency is a digital unit of value that has all of the following characteristics: (1) fully interchangeable with another unit of the same digital currency for the purpose of its use as payment, (2) can be provided as payment for any types of purchases, (3) generally available to the public free of any substantial restrictions, (4) not denominated in any country's currency, (5) the value is not derived from or dependent on anything else, and does not give an entitlement or privileges to receive something else. The amending law made it clear that the following was not covered by the virtual currency definition: (1) loyalty points provided by retailers that can only be redeemed for products and services specified by that loyalty scheme, (2) "currency" used in online multiplayer games that cannot be used outside the game under which the "currency" is made available; and (3) "digital currency" with value based on something else or that gives an entitlement or privileges to something else (such as, ICO tokens).

The ATO issued a notice *GST and digital currency* providing a detailed explanation of the legislative amendments and their consequences for taxpayers.[3] The notice made it clear that sales and purchases of virtual currency are not subject to GST as from July 1, 2017. This means that no GST is charged on supplies of virtual currency and there is no entitlement to GST credits for purchases to make these supplies. For businesses that receive digital currency as payment for their sales of goods and services, the normal GST rules apply. If they make a taxable sale of goods, they are

2. For a definition of a fork, *see supra* n. 59.
3. ATO, *GST and digital currency* (last modified: March 16, 2018).

required to remit one-eleventh of the payment received for that taxable sale. In addition, they need to comply with the standard tax invoice requirements.

In its notice explaining the legislative changes, the ATO also commented on the GST treatment of ICOs. According to the ATO, the GST treatment of token sales will depend on the particular features of tokens. Some ICOs may be designed to be a payment method, while others may offer a share of profits in a product, or provide access to a software application.

AUSTRIA

On July 25, 2017, the Austrian Ministry of Finance (*Bundesministerium für Finanzen*) published a notice on the tax treatment of virtual currency (*Steuerliche Behandlung von Kryptowährungen*).[4] The Ministry does not provide a definition of virtual currency but classifies it as a non-depreciable intangible business asset (*nicht abnutzbare unkörperliche Wirtschaftsgüter*). In its view, virtual currency does not constitute a financial instrument.

The Ministry confirmed that exchanges of legal currency into virtual currency should be exempt based on the CJEU decision in *Hedqvist* and held that Bitcoin mining is not a taxable transaction because it is not possible to determine the recipient of the transaction.

If virtual currency is held for business purposes, it should be allocated to either fixed or current assets. If the currency constitutes a current asset, it should be valued annually. Sales and purchases of bitcoins will result in a capital gain or loss. For the calculation of the gain or loss, the values of the virtual currency as at the date of purchase and sale should be used.

Virtual currency used for business purposes should be generally treated as other business assets (*sonstige betriebliche Wirtschaftsgüter*) and subject to the general income tax rules. However, it can also constitute a deemed interest-bearing investment (*zinsbringend veranlagte Kryptowährung)*, meaning that any realized gains will be subject to a special tax rate of 27.5%. Bitcoin mining and the operation of online exchange platforms should be seen as business activity (*gewerbliche Tätigkeit*) and be treated for tax purposes as such. If virtual currency is held for private purposes, any gains from its sale are not subject to tax if the currency is sold after one year from its purchase. Sales of virtual currency within one year from its purchase will be taxed as a speculative gain.

CANADA

The Canada Revenue Agency defines virtual currency as "virtual money that can be used to buy and sell goods or services on the Internet."[5] In a statement posted on its

4. Ministry of Finance (*Bundesministerium für Finanzen*), *Steuerliche Behandlung von Kryptowährungen (virtuelle Währungen)* (July 25, 2017).
5. Canada Revenue Agency, *What you should know about digital currency* (March 17, 2015).

website, it clarified that the use of virtual currency to pay for goods or services is subject to the rules for barter transactions.[6] The Revenue observed that when virtual currency is bought or sold like a commodity, any resulting gains or losses could be taxable income or capital for the taxpayer. The general rules should be used to determine whether transactions are income or capital in nature. In other words, if a taxpayer engages in the business of trading or investing in cryptocurrency, gains or losses therefrom should be treated as being on account of income; however, if the taxpayer acquires cryptocurrency for a long-term growth, any gain or loss generated from the disposition of cryptocurrency should be treated as on account of capital).[7]

The mining of cryptocurrencies can be undertaken for profit (as a business) or as a personal hobby (which is non-taxable). If a taxpayer mines cryptocurrencies as a business, any income from the business will be included in his income at the end of the year based on the value of the inventory (i.e., the cryptocurrencies), and any thefts or losses are deductible from your income if they are an inherent risk to carrying on the business.[8]

CHINA

Although China is a key market for cryptocurrency mining and transactions, the Chinese government has taken a series of regulatory measures to crack down on activities related to cryptocurrencies for purposes of investor protection and financial risk prevention. Those measures include announcing that initial coin offerings are illegal, restricting the primary business of cryptocurrency trading platforms, and discouraging Bitcoin mining.

China has not passed any legislation on the tax treatment of cryptocurrencies yet. The State Administration of Taxation clarified that income from virtual currency transactions is subject to individual income tax as income from transfers of property. It remains unclear whether this tax treatment should apply only to exchanges of virtual currency into legal currency or also to exchanges of virtual currency for real goods and services.[9]

6. Canada Revenue Agency, *Interpretation Bulletin IT-490, Barter Transactions* (January 1, 1995).
7. Canada Revenue Agency, *Interpretation Bulletin IT-479R, Transactions in Securities* (January 1, 1995).
8. Wildeboer Dellelce, *Cryptocurrencies and Tax: Five Things Every Canadian Needs to Know* (December 12, 2017); www.wildlaw.ca/resource-centre/legal-updates/2017/cryptocurrencies-and-tax-five-things-every-canadian-needs-to-know/.
9. Sheppard Mullin Richter & Hampton LLP, *Taxation on virtual currency income in China* (December 9, 2008), www.lexology.com/library/detail.aspx?g=87cd4685-3e8f-4571-83ec-66987 3ff7942.

DENMARK

On March 25, 2014, the Danish Tax Board (*Skatterådet*) gave its ruling in the case of SKM2014.226.SR.[10] The Board ruled that bitcoins are not considered an official currency for tax and VAT purposes. Consequently, neither the Danish tax return nor invoices can be prepared in bitcoins. Fluctuations in the value of bitcoins are not taxable as gains or losses on currency covered by the Tax Act on Capital Gains and Losses on Debt Claims and Financial Instruments (*Kursgevinstloven*). The ruling also stated that the traditional trading with bitcoins is not considered a financial contract for tax purposes and payments made to a bitcoin exchange platform are non-deductible. Finally, the tax authorities explained that the taxable value of goods and services purchased and sold in bitcoins should not be affected by the exchange rate adjustments as the Bitcoin system is considered an unnecessary and an unrecognized payment system that is not needed to complete a money transfer.

In another ruling issued on April 3, 2018, the Danish Tax Board explained that gains and losses from trade in bitcoin and ether cryptocurrencies should be included in taxable income as income from capital.[11] The acquisition price of virtual currency should be calculated using the "First-in, First-out" principle. The ruling request was made by a taxpayer who earned DKK 450,000 from trading transactions on the Kraken platform in two months and planned to use these earnings to purchase an apartment. The Board also ruled that the trading and administrative fees relating to speculating in digital assets on the Kraken Platform are deductible.

ESTONIA

On March 13, 2014, the Estonian Tax and Customs Board provided its opinion on Bitcoin transactions.[12] In a document entitled *Taxation of Trade in Bitcoin* (*Maksustamine Bitcoin'idega Kauplemisel*), the Tax and Customs Board clarified that under Estonian law Bitcoin is neither e-currency nor security. Under the Money Laundering and Terrorist Financing Prevention Act, Bitcoin could be considered an alternative means of payment. Accordingly, the purchase, sale and intermediation of bitcoins are considered to be the provision of services of alternative means of payment.

For individual income tax purposes, Bitcoin is treated as property and disposal of bitcoins gives rise to capital gains. Income from trading in bitcoins is taxed as business income that, in addition to individual income tax, is also subject to social security contributions.

The Tax and Customs Board was of the opinion that the provision of service of alternative means of payment is not a financial service which would be VAT exempt under EU or Estonian VAT legislation. However, the opinion of the Board was

10. K.J. Dyppel, *Assessment Board: Bitcoin currency fluctuations not taxable—details* (April 14, 2014), News IBFD.
11. J.P. Finet, *Bitcoin Trade gains Are Personla Income, Danish Tax Board Says* (April 4, 2018), Tax Analyst 2018 WDT 65-3.
12. M. Herm, *Taxation of bitcoin transactions* (April 8, 2014), News IBFD.

expressed before the CJEU clarified the application of VAT exemptions to Bitcoin transactions in the *Hedqvist* judgment.

FRANCE

On July 11, 2014, the French tax administration issued guidelines on the tax treatment of Bitcoin transactions.[13] According to these guidelines, income resulting from sales of bitcoins must be reported as (i) industrial and commercial profits (*bénéfices industriels et commerciaux*) when it results from a regular activity; or (ii) as non-commercial profits (*bénéfices non commerciaux*) when it is derived from a non-regular activity. Determining when an activity is regular or occasional requires a case-by-case examination of the factual circumstances. In addition, units of virtual currency stored electronically are subject to net wealth tax (*impôt de solidarité sur la fortune*) and must therefore be included in the annual net wealth tax declaration.

Several taxpayers sought to annul the administrative guidelines, arguing that gains from the sale of bitcoins should be taxed as capital gains from movable property (*plus-values de biens meubles*). On April 26, 2018, the French Administrative Supreme Court (*Conseil d'État*) issued a judgment in joint cases Nos. 417809, 418030, 418031, 418032 and 418033, agreeing with the litigants' general proposition that profits on disposals of bitcoins may be reported as a capital gain on movable property under Article 150UA of the French Tax Code (*Code général des impôts*).[14] Such gains will be taxed at a flat rate of 19% plus social contributions of 17.2%. However, the Court also ruled that the capital gains regime will not apply if the transaction, based on its factual circumstances, falls within another category of income. Thus, gains resulting from a regular activity exercised in the course of a commercial profession must be reported as industrial and commercial profits. Similarly, gains from occasional non-investment transactions must be reported as non-commercial profits.

FINLAND

In August 2013, the Finnish Tax Authority (*Vero Skatt*) issued the first notice on the tax treatment of Bitcoin for income tax purposes.[15] This notice was replaced by another notice published on May 28, 2018.[16] In the opinion of the Finnish Tax Authority, virtual currency should not be regarded as currency, security or any other financial product. The notice provides a very comprehensive overview of the tax treatment of virtual currency for individual income, corporate income and VAT purposes, and contains

13. A. Pascual, *Tax regime applicable to bitcoins* (July 14, 2014), News IBFD.
14. E. Joannard-Lardant, *Administrative Supreme Court rules on Bitcoin gains* (April 30, 2018), News IBFD. The decision (in French) is available at www.conseil-etat.fr/Decisions-Avis-Publications/Decisions/Selection-des-decisions-faisant-l-objet-d-une-communication-particuliere/Conseil-d-Etat-26-avril-2018-M.-G-et-autres.
15. Tax Administration (*Vero Skatt*), *Income Taxation of Virtual Currencies* (*Inkomstbeskattning av virtuella valuator)* (August 28, 2013).
16. Tax Administration (*Vero Skatt*), *Taxation of Virtual Currencies* (*Beskattning av virtuella valutor*) (May 28, 2018).

numerous examples on how to calculate the taxable income from virtual currency transactions.

Income from virtual currency transactions derived by individuals may be categorized as business income or personal income (which includes income from employment and capital). Different rules (in particular, on the deductibility of losses) apply to each category. If transactions in virtual currency are carried out by corporations, the general rules of the corporate income tax law apply. Virtual currency may be treated as current or financial assets. For VAT purposes, the Finnish Tax Authority confirmed the application of the VAT exemption to exchanges of virtual currency into legal currency (in line with the CJEU decision in *Hedqvist*). The notice also clarified the tax consequences of forks and ICOs.

The Finnish Central Tax Board (*Keskusverolautakunta*) confirmed, in a ruling CSN: 2014/34, that the VAT exemption for financial services applies to exchanges of bitcoins into legal currency.[17] The ruling was issued at the request of a company providing an Internet platform where sellers and buyers exchanged bitcoins into EUR and concerned the question whether the applicant's intermediary services should be subject to VAT. The Finnish Central Tax Board ruled that bitcoins are considered currency for VAT purposes and the services provided by the applicant constitute VAT exempt financial services.

IRELAND

On May 15, 2018, the Irish Revenue published an eBrief on the tax treatment of cryptocurrency transactions.[18] The eBrief observes that the tax treatment of income received from activities involving cryptocurrencies will depend on the activities and the parties involved, and each case must be considered on the basis of its own individual facts and circumstances.

Businesses that accept payment for goods or services in cryptocurrencies must follow the general rules of corporate income tax. As cryptocurrencies are not a legal currency, accounts for tax purposes cannot be prepared in cryptocurrencies.

The tax treatment of disposals of virtual currency depends on whether an individual or a company is engaged in trade or investment activities. The Irish tax legislation does not set out specific rules to determine when an activity may be considered trade: the answer to this question is heavily fact-dependent. If the buying and selling of cryptocurrencies is not part of trade, it may be liable to corporation tax on chargeable gains at the rate of 33%. Trading profits are subject to the corporation tax at the rate of 12.5%.

In the Revenue's view, Bitcoin and similar cryptocurrencies are regarded for VAT purposes as "negotiable instruments" and exempt from VAT in accordance with section 6(1)(c) of the VAT Consolidation Act 2010. Although the Revenue adopted a different basis on which transactions in cryptocurrencies are VAT exempt, it came to

17. L. Ambagtsheer-Pakarinen, *Central Tax Board rules on VAT treatment of bitcoin services* (November 21, 2014), News IBFD.
18. Revenue, *Taxation of Cryptocurrency Transactions*, eBReif No. 88/2018 (May 2018).

the same result as the CJEU in the *Hedqvist* judgment. Income received from cryptocurrency mining activities will generally be outside the scope of VAT as the activity does not constitute an economic activity for VAT purposes.

ITALY

On September 2, 2016, the Italian Revenue Agency (*Agenzia delle Entrate*) published Resolution No. 72/E, which provides guidance on the VAT treatment of virtual currency transactions.[19] The Resolution follows the CJEU decision in the case *Hedqvist* and clarifies that exchanges of virtual currency for legal currency are exempt from VAT under Article 10(3) of the Italian VAT law. It also mentions that any profits from sales of virtual currency made by an entrepreneur in the context of his business activity are taxed according to the general corporate tax rules.

JAPAN

In Japan, the Payment Services Act defines a virtual currency as property of value, usable for payment to unspecified persons, purchasable from and sellable to unspecified persons and transferable by electronic processing devices.[20]

According to the Cabinet Order for Partial Revision of the Order for Enforcement of the Consumption Tax Act (effective as from July 1, 2017), exchanges of virtual currency into legal currency are exempt from consumption tax. However, the exchange of virtual currency for goods or services is still subject to consumption tax in the same way as transactions that are paid for in traditional currency.[21]

On December 1, 2017, the National Tax Agency (NTA) released a notice *Information about the calculation method etc. of income on virtual currency*. This notice clarifies that income from virtual currency transaction falls within the category of miscellaneous income and is subject to the general income tax rules (including the progressive taxation). Profits from cryptocurrency trading that are less than JPY 200,000 are not subject to tax. Gains/losses from virtual currency transactions are treated differently than gains/losses from foreign currency transactions and stock investments (the latter are taxed at a flat rate). Gains also have to be determined if one type of virtual currency is exchanged for another type of virtual currency or for goods and services. The mere holding of virtual currency does not have any tax implications. The NTA notice also provides guidelines for the calculation of the acquisition cost of virtual currencies, also in the case of a hard fork.[22]

19. Revenue Agency (*Agenzia delle Entrate*), *Risoluzione n. 72/E* (September 2, 2016).
20. M. Kawamura et al., *Japan exempts virtual currencies from consumption tax* (March 31, 2017), www.dlapiper.com/en/netherlands/insights/publications/2017/03/global-tax-news-mar-2017/japan-exempts-virtual-currencies/.
21. *Id.*
22. N. Gehrke, *Japan Income Tax on Virtual Currencies* (January 29, 2018), https://medium.com/tokyo-fintech/japan-income-tax-on-virtual-currencies-8e8c170195a2; K. Nagata, *Cryptoprofits are taxable — have you filed?* (February 18, 2018), www.japantimes.co.jp/news/2018/02/18/business/financial-markets/cryptoprofits-taxable-filed/#.W2GJgNUzbcs.

LUXEMBOURG

On June 11, 2018, the Luxembourg tax administration published Circular No. 787 on the VAT treatment of virtual currency.[23] The Circular confirmed the application of the VAT exemption to virtual currency transactions as set out in the *Hedqvist* judgment. The Circular explained that the only purpose of virtual currencies, such as bitcoins, is to be used as a method of payment. Therefore, virtual currency must be treated in the same manner as legal currency. This means that the VAT exemption for currency transactions as included in Article 135(1)(e) of the EU VAT Directive applies.

On July 26, 2018, the tax administration released Circular 14/5–99/3–9bis/3 on the income tax treatment of virtual currency transactions.[24] According to the circular, virtual currency should be treated as an intangible asset for the purposes of income tax, local business tax and net wealth tax. Profits, gains and expenses denominated in virtual currency must be converted into EUR or any other legal currency, and the exchange rate of the time of the transaction should be used.

Income from virtual currency transactions (including virtual currency mining) is taxed as business profits or miscellaneous income. Business profits are deemed to exist in the case of a permanent participation in economic life (business activity). Indications for the existence of a business activity are the presence of an organization assigned to operations involving virtual currencies, the use of borrowed capital, frequent changes in the inventory of virtual currencies and trading on behalf of third parties. Expenses related to business activities (for example, electricity costs in the case of currency mining, conversion fees, depreciation) are fully deductible. Miscellaneous income includes income from services performed occasionally (if such income does not qualify as business income) and capital gains on disposal of privately-held assets. Miscellaneous income is not taxable if it is lower than EUR 500 per year. For the purposes of determining the taxable profit or gain, the "First-in First-out" (FIFO) or the "Last-in First-out" (LIFO) method may be used.

For net wealth tax (loi relative à l'impôt sur la fortune) purposes, the value of a virtual currency must be assessed in accordance with the provisions of the valuation law (*loi sur l'évaluation des biens et valeur*). The net wealth tax is levied at the rate of 0.5% of the taxable net assets as at January 1. The tax does not apply to individual taxpayers.

NORWAY

In November 2013, the Norwegian Directorate of Taxation (*Skatteetaten*) published a statement explaining that Bitcoin is an asset (not a currency) and income tax can be

23. R. Offermanns, *Circular on digital currency VAT exemption released* (June 18, 2018), News IBFD. For the text of the circular (in French), *see* www.aed.public.lu/actualites/2018/6/Circulaire-787/Circulaires_787.pdf.
24. R. Offermanns, *Circular on virtual currency released* (July 27, 2018), News IBFD. For the text of the circular (in French), *see* https://impotsdirects.public.lu/dam-assets/fr/legislation/legi18/circulaireLIR14-5-99-3-99bis-3du26072018.pdf.

charged on gains from disposals of bitcoins. For VAT purposes, supplies of bitcoins constituted taxable supplies of electronic services that were not subject to the exemption for financial services.[25] Following the CJEU decision in *Hedqvist*, the Norwegian Ministry of Finance asked the Directorate of Taxation to reassess its position of the tax treatment of digital currency. In its renewed assessment, the Directorate of Taxation concluded that exchanges of bitcoins into legal currency are covered by the exception for financial services.[26] In a letter of April 17, 2018, the Directorate of Taxation ruled that Bitcoin mining is also covered by the exemption of financial services.

The Norwegian Directorate of Taxation published some general guidelines on the tax treatment of virtual currency on its website.[27] The guidelines confirm that an exemption applies for VAT purposes. For income tax purposes, the guidelines clarify that bitcoins are not a currency but property and disposals of property may result in a taxable gain. The guidelines also provide some information on recordkeeping obligations.

On January 30, 2018, the Minister of Finance, in a reply to Question No. 777 of the parliamentary debate, confirmed that cryptocurrency is exempt from VAT, and that gains on disposal of virtual currency are taxable and losses are deductible according to the general tax rules.[28]

SINGAPORE

The Inland Revenue Authority of Singapore (IRAS) explained its position on the treatment of virtual currency transactions for goods and services tax (GST) purposes.[29] In its view, virtual currencies do not constitute money, currency or goods but services and do not qualify for GST exemption. When a person uses virtual currencies to pay for goods or services, the transaction will be considered as a barter trade. There are two supplies made—one by the supplier who supplies the goods and services, and another by the person who uses virtual currencies to pay the supplier. GST will need to be charged on each supply if the respective supplier is GST-registered. However, if virtual currency is used to pay a supplier belonging outside Singapore, there is no need to charge GST as the supply will be zero-rated. As a concession, if taxpayers use virtual currencies to buy virtual goods or services within the gaming world, they need not charge GST until those virtual goods and services are exchanged for real money, goods or services. A GST-registered business that sells virtual currencies as a principal has to

25. Directorate of Taxation (*Skatteetaten*), *Use of bitcoins—tax consequences* (*Bruk av bitcoins—skatte- og avgiftsmessige konsekvenser)* (November 11, 2013).
26. Ministry of Finance (*Finansdepartementet*), *Value Added Tax—Except for Financial Services* (*Merverdiavgift—unntaket for finansielle tjenester*) (February 6, 2017).
27. Directorate of Taxation (*Skatteetaten*), *Tax and value-added treatment of bitcoins and other virtual currencies* (*Skatte- og merverdiavgiftsmessig behandling av bitcoins og andre virtuelle valutaer*).
28. Ministry of Finance (*Finansdepartementet*), *Answer to Question No. 777 from Representative Gjelsvik on registration and traceability of bitcoin trade (cryptovaluta) (Svar på spørsmål nr. 777 fra representant Gjelsvik om registrering og sporbarhet av handel med bitcoin (kryptovaluta)*) (January 30, 2018).
29. IRAS, *e-Commerce.*

charge GST on the sale of the virtual currencies unless the sale is made to a person belonging outside Singapore. If the company acts as an agent in the virtual currency trade, then GST is chargeable only on the commission fees received.

Another IRAS notice clarified that businesses that accept virtual currencies as payment for goods or services are subject to the general corporate tax rules and should record the sales based on the open market value of the goods or services in Singapore dollars.[30] The same applies for businesses which pay for goods or services using virtual currencies. If the open market value of the goods or services that would have otherwise been exchanged in Singapore dollars cannot be determined (for example, the goods or services are only traded with virtual currencies), the virtual currency exchange rate at the point of the transaction may be used. Profits derived by businesses that mine and trade in virtual currencies in the ordinary course of their business are subject to tax. Businesses that buy virtual currencies for long-term investment purposes may enjoy a capital gain from the disposal of these virtual currencies. However, as there are no CGTs in Singapore, such gains are not subject to tax. Whether gains from disposal of virtual currencies are trading income or capital gains depends on the facts and circumstances of each case. Factors such as purpose, frequency of transactions, and holding periods are considered when determining whether such gains are taxable.

SLOVENIA

The Finance Ministry of Slovenia issued a comprehensive document addressing the tax implications of transactions in virtual currency.[31] This guidance applies to cryptocoins and clarifies that cryptocoins are not considered "monetary funds" within the meaning of the Slovenian Payment Services and Systems Act. In the Ministry's view, the tax treatment of transactions involving virtual currencies depends on several factors, such as the status of the trader, the type of the transaction, and other individual circumstances.

Income in virtual currency (also from mining activities) received by an individual is taxed as income received in kind under the rules for the taxation of income generated from an independent activity or other income. The income amount in EUR is determined by means of the exchange rate at the time of the receipt of income. Individual income tax is not levied on disposals of virtual currency regarded as capital assets or derivative financial instruments.

For corporate income tax purposes, the possession of bitcoins and other virtual currencies must be reported as financial investments in business ledgers. Virtual currency must be valued at fair market value in the profit and loss statement (the difference between its book and market value must be reported as financial revenue or financial expenses).

30. IRAS, *Income Tax Treatment of Virtual Currencies*.
31. Ministry of Finance, *New version of the document Tax treatment of business operations with virtual currencies as per ZDoh-2, ZDDPO-2, ZDDV-1 and ZDFS (Detailed description)* (June 4, 2018).

For VAT purposes, exchanges of virtual currency into legal currency are exempt from VAT. Virtual currency mining is outside the scope of VAT as it does not involve consideration. However, if users were obliged to pay a miner fee for validating their transactions, virtual currency mining would be within the scope of VAT but exempt as a transaction in connection with payments. There is no right to input VAT deduction on mining software and hardware unless virtual currency mining is treated as an exempt service and transaction validation is performed for users established outside the European Union.

On May 25, 2018, the tax authorities published a clarification on the tax treatment of the ICOs in which individuals receive virtual tokens free of charge.[32] In such as case, the market value of tokens should be recorded as taxable income. The initial nominal value of the tokens is determined by the issuing company. Once the tokens are traded, the market value is determined by supply and demand. Income is earned when the individual becomes the owner of the tokens. This is the moment when the tokens are placed in the digital wallet of the individual. Any limitations in terms of ownership rights that could be set by the issuer of tokens do not interfere with the moment when the income is earned. The relationship between the issuer and recipient determines a type of income earned (salary, dividend, other income) and consequently the method of taxation.

SPAIN

The Spanish General Directorate of Taxation (*Dirección General de Tributos*) issued a number of binding rulings on the tax treatment of virtual currency. On March 30, 2015, the General Directorate issued Binding Rulings V1028-015 and V1029-015 on the VAT treatment of virtual currency transactions.[33] According to the rulings, exchanges of virtual currency for legal currency are exempt from VAT. In contrast to the CJEU, which applied the VAT exemption laid down in Article 135(e) of the VAT Directive, the General Directorate considered exchanges of virtual currency to be exempt based on Article 135(d) of the VAT Directive ("transactions, including negotiation, concerning deposit and current accounts, payments, transfers, debts, cheques and other negotiable instruments"). According to the rulings, virtual currencies operate as a means of payment and should be included in the concept of "other negotiable instruments." The Directorate confirmed this classification in Binding Ruling V2846-15, in which it also dealt with the question whether the buying and selling of virtual currency may be considered economic activity for VAT purposes, conferring on the taxpayer the status of a taxable person.[34] In Binding Ruling V3625-16, the Directorate ruled that virtual

32. A. Majer, *Tax authorities clarify tax treatment of tokens received in Initial Coin Offering* (June 1, 2018), News IBFD.
33. General Directorate of Taxation (*Dirección General de Tributos*), *Consulta vinculante V1028-15, V1029-15* (March 30, 2015).
34. General Directorate of Taxation, *Consulta vinculante V2846-15* (October 1, 2017).

currency mining is outside the scope of VAT as there is no legal reciprocal relationship between the service provider and recipient.[35]

Binding ruling V2908-17 clarified the treatment of virtual currency for the purposes of tax on economic activities (*impuesto sobre actividades económicas*, IAE).[36] The Directorate ruled that the purchase and sale of virtual currencies through a web portal that the taxpayer has developed should be classified as "other financial services" for IAE purposes.

Binding ruling V0590-18 clarified the treatment of virtual currency for the purposes of net wealth tax *(impuesto sobre el patrimonio)*.[37] The Directorate ruled that virtual currency (just like any foreign currency) has to be declared together with other assets and its value as of December 31 should be used.

On April 18, 2018, the Directorate issued Binding Ruling V0999-18 on the individual income tax treatment of gains and losses from virtual currency transactions.[38] The Directorate clarified that exchanges of virtual currency into another type of virtual currency (made outside the performance of a business activity) constitute barter transactions and any profits resulting therefrom are subject to income tax as income from investment (capital gains) according to the Individual Income Tax Law (*Ley del Impuesto sobre la Renta de las Personas Físicas*, LIRPF). In another ruling, the Directorate ruled that the gains are deemed to arise in the period when the currency in question is delivered, irrespective of when the payment is made.[39]

SOUTH AFRICA

On April 6, 2018, the South African Revenue Service (SARS) issued a statement on the tax treatment of virtual currency transactions.[40] According to the statement, virtual currency is considered an intangible asset for income and capital gains tax (CGT) purposes. The SARS announced that it will continue to apply the general income tax rules to virtual currency transactions and will expect affected taxpayers to declare virtual currency gains or losses as part of their taxable income. This means that any revenue received, gains made or losses incurred in respect of virtual currency transactions may be regarded either as revenue in nature and included in the taxpayer's gross income or as capital in nature and subject to CGT in terms of the Eighth Schedule of the Income Tax Act No 58 of 1962. To determine whether a receipt is revenue or capital in nature, the general rules should be followed. Taxpayers are entitled to claim expenses associated with virtual currency accruals or receipts, provided such expenditure is incurred in the production of the taxpayer's income and for purposes of trade. Virtual currency acquired by means of mining is treated as trading stock until it is exchanged for cash or for other goods or services (barter transactions). Taxpayers who

35. General Directorate of Taxation, *Consulta vinculante V3625-16* (August 31, 2017).
36. General Directorate of Taxation, *Consulta vinculante V2908-17* (November 13, 2017).
37. General Directorate of Taxation, *Consulta vinculante V0590-18* (March 1, 2018).
38. General Directorate of Taxation, *Consulta vinculante V0999-18* (April 18, 2018).
39. General Directorate of Taxation, *Consulta vinculante V0808-18* (March 22, 2018).
40. SARS, *SARS's stance on the tax treatment of cryptocurrencies* (April 6, 2018).

are uncertain about specific transactions involving virtual currencies may seek guidance from the SARS through channels such as binding private rulings.

The Budget Review 2018 indicated that the VAT treatment of virtual currencies will be reviewed. The relevant passage read as follows:[41]

> Tax treatment of cryptocurrency transactions: Cryptocurrencies are addressed by existing provisions in South African tax law. Cryptocurrencies pose risks to the income tax system as they are extremely volatile and their sustainability is uncertain. At the same time, the supply of cryptocurrency can cause administrative difficulties in the VAT system. To address these issues, it is proposed that the income tax and VAT legislation be amended.

Pending policy clarity in this regard, the SARS announced that it would not require VAT registration as a vendor for purposes of the supply of virtual currencies.

On July 17, 2018, SARS issued the Draft Taxation Laws Amendment Bill (TLAB) 2018 for public comment before its formal introduction to Parliament. The Draft Bill proposes to include virtual currencies in the definition of financial services for VAT purposes. This means that transactions in virtual currencies will benefit from a VAT exemption. As VAT will not be charged on virtual currency transactions, there will be no right to deduct input VAT on the incurred costs.

SOUTH KOREA

Although South Korea is considered by many to be the world capital of cryptocurrency, there are currently no regulations of the tax treatment of virtual currency transactions. In April 2018, the Ministry of Strategy and Finance announced that it would develop a regulatory framework for taxing cryptocurrencies.[42] Originally, the Ministry planned to unveil its framework in June 2018; however, it failed to meet this deadline. In developing the framework, the Ministry is looking into virtual currency regulations in other countries (the United States, the United Kingdom, Japan and Germany). It is expected that the new rules would be applicable as from 2019.

SWEDEN

In 2015, the Swedish Tax Authority (*Skatteverket*) issued guidelines on the tax treatment of virtual currency mining.[43] Income from the virtual currency mining typically will be characterized for tax purposes as income from services (hobby) rather than from economic activity. The costs associated with hobby activities are deductible

41. Treasury, *Budget Review 2018*, p. 136 (February 21, 2018).
42. M.J. Zuckerman, *South Korean Regulators To Release Crypto Tax Framework By June* (April 1, 2018), https://cointelegraph.com/news/south-korean-regulators-to-release-crypto-tax-framework-by-june; J.A. Lanz, *South Korea Will Announce Crypto Tax Policies in July* (April 2, 2018), https://cryptocurrencynews.com/daily-news/crypto-news/south-korea-crypto-tax-policies/.
43. Tax Authority (*Skatteverket*), *Guidelines on the Taxation of Mining of Bitcoins and Other Virtual Currencies* (*Beskattning vid mining av bitcoin och andra virtuella valutor m.m.*) (April 24, 2015).

for up to five years prior to the year the hobby activity generated a surplus. In the opinion of the Tax Authority, Bitcoin mining is unlikely to be considered economic activity because of the limited potential for profit in light of the cost of the equipment needed. However, if mining is carried out in a professional and cost efficient manner over a longer period with appropriate equipment, the operations can be expected to provide a surplus over the entire economic calculation period and the computing capacity can be expected to generate more than 25 bitcoins a year, mining can be considered economic activity and give rise to income from economic activity. The guidelines also clarify that virtual currency mining is not subject to VAT as the transaction does not involve any consideration.

In a notice addressing virtual currencies and the taxation of income from capital, the Swedish Tax Authority clarified that virtual currency is "basically a data file that can be transferred to another person."[44] Thus, bitcoin represents an asset and disposals of bitcoins may have consequences under the rules on taxing income from capital. Any sale of bitcoins, irrespective of whether compensation is received in legal currency, goods or services, may result in a taxable capital gain.

SWITZERLAND

In June 2015, the Swiss Federal Tax Administration (*Eidgenössische Steuerverwaltung*) decided to treat Bitcoin as a means of payment for VAT purposes.[45] This decision was made in response to a formal request submitted by a group of three Swiss Bitcoin organizations. The Swiss tax authorities confirmed that transfers of bitcoins do not constitute either supplies of goods or supplies of services.

Various canton tax administrations published guidance on the tax treatment of virtual currency.[46] According to the notice by Canton Lutzern, holders of virtual currency are subject to wealth tax (*Vermögenssteuer*) at the rate determined by the federal tax administration on December 31. If the federal tax administration fails to determine an official exchange rate, the exchange rate of the platform that was used to carry out transactions should be used. Capital gains from movable private assets, such as virtual currency, are generally tax exempt in Switzerland. Similarly, losses on cryptocurrency transactions cannot be deducted for tax purposes. However, if someone qualifies as a professional trader, the profits from the virtual currency trade are part of the taxable income and must be reported as income from self-employment. In this case, losses are deductible. Virtual currency mining is also subject to income tax.

---

44. Tax Authority (*Skatteverket*), *Taxation of bitcoin and other virtual currency for capital gains purposes* (*Beskattning av bitcoin och andra s.k. virtuella valutor i inkomstslaget kapital*) (April 23, 2014).
45. G. Prisco, *Swiss Tax Authorities Confirm that Bitcoin is VAT-free in Switzerland* (June 12, 2015), https://bitcoinmagazine.com/articles/swiss-tax-authorities-confirm-bitcoin-vat-free-switzerland-1434140401/.
46. Canton Lutzern, *Bitcoin & Co. und Steuern* (November 15, 2017); Kanton Zug, *Kryptowährungen* (November 30, 2017). For an explanation of both notices in English, *see* Vischer Blog, *Taxation of cryptocurrencies* (December 18, 2017), http://blog.vischer.com/en/taxation-of-cryptocurrencies.

Bibliography

LITERATURE

Abreu, A.G. & R.K. Greenstein, *Defining Income*, 11 Fla. Tax Rev. 295 (2011)

Adams, T.S., *Fundamental Problems of Federal Income Taxation*, 35 Quarterly Journal of Economics, 527 (1921)

Adhami, S. et al., *Why Do Businesses Go Crypto? An Empirical Analysis of Initial Coin Offerings, Working Paper* (October 3, 2017), https://papers.ssrn.com/sol3/papers.cfm?abstract_id = 3046209

Ainsworth, R.T. & M. Alwohaibi, *The first real-time blockchain VAT: GCC solves MTIC fraud*, Tax Notes International (May 22, 2017)

Ainsworth, R.T. et al., *VATCoin: Can a Crypto Tax Currency Prevent VAT Fraud?* 84 Tax Notes International 703 (November 14, 2016)

Ainsworth, R.T. & A.B. Shact, *Blockchain technology might solve VAT fraud*, Tax Notes International (September 26, 2016)

Alm, J. & M.I. Melnik, *Do Ebay Sellers Comply with State Sales Taxes?* 63 National Tax Journal 2 (2010)

Ambagtsheer-Pakarinen, L., *Central Tax Board rules on VAT treatment of bitcoin services* (November 21, 2014), News IBFD

Annacondia, F., *VAT Options Exercised by the Member States*, Topical Analyses IBFD (January 1, 2017)

Avi-Yonah, R.S., *International Taxation of Electronic Commerce*, 52 Tax L. Rev. 507 (1996/1997)

Bal, A.M., *Recent EU VAT Changes – The Invoicing Directive*, 52 Eur. Taxn. 9 (2012)

Bal, A.M., *The Myth of Taxing Cloud Computing under EU VAT*, 25 Intl. VAT Monitor 6 (2014)

Bal, A.M., *Taxation of Virtual Currency*, PhD Thesis (Leiden University 2014)

Bal, A.M., *Blockchain, Initial Coin Offerings and Other Developments in the Virtual Currency Marke*t, 20 Derivs. & Fin. Instrums. 2 (2018)

Bal, A.M., *VAT Treatment of Initial Coin Offerings*, 29 Intl. VAT Monitor 3 (2018)

Bal, A.M., *Does the Tax Sector Need Blockchain?* (April 4, 2018) White Paper IBFD

Bal, A.M., *Halfway towards Consensus or Chaos? Taxation of the digital economy at the crossroads*, IBFD White Paper (March 26, 2018)

Barber, S., X. Boyen, E. Shi & E. Uzun, *Bitter to Better – How to Make Bitcoin a Better Currency*, in *Financial Cryptography and Data Security*, pp. 399-414 (Springer 2012)

Baumach, A. et al., *Handelsgesetzbuch*, (C.H. Beck Verlag 2010)

Bergstra, J.A. & K. de Leeuw, *Bitcoin and Beyond: Exclusively Informational Money* (2013), http://arxiv.org/abs/1304.4758.

Blümich, W., B. Heuermann, P. Brandis et al., *Einkommensteuergesetz. Loseblatt-Kommentar* (C.H. Beck Verlag 2009)

Braithwaite, J., *Rules and Principles: A Theory of Legal Certainty*, 27 Australian Journal of Legal Philosophy 47 (2002)

Braun, N.,*Objektivierung der Gewinnerzielungsabsicht bei der Liebhaberei*, 55 Betriebsberater 6 (2000)

Burns, L. & R. Krever, *Individual Income Tax* in: *Tax law design and drafting* (V. Thuronyi ed. IMF 1998)

Burns, L. & R. Krever, *Taxation of Income from Business and Investment* in: *Tax law design and drafting* (V. Thuronyi ed. IMF 1998)

Casey, A. & A. Niblett, *The Death of Rules and Standards*, Coase-Sandor Working Paper Series in Law and Economics No. 738 (2015)

Cavanaugh, T., *Iowa Can Do Better than the Affiliate Tax: A Proposal for an Intermediary Tax*, 97 Iowa L. Rev. 567 (2012)

CCH, *British Master Guide* (CCH 2012)

CCH, *US Master Tax Guide 2013* (CCH 2013)

Cheng, E., *Structural Laws and the Puzzle of Regulating Behaviour*, 100 Northwestern University Law Review 655 (2006)

Cowan, D., *New York's Unconstitutional Tax on the Internet: Amazon.com v. New York State Department of Taxation and Finance and the Dormant Commerce Clause*, 88 N.C. L. Rev. 1423 (2010)

De la Feria, R. & R. Krever, *Ending VAT Exemptions: Towards a Post-Modern VAT* in: *VAT Exemptions* (R. de la Feria ed., Wolters Kluwer 2013)

Dworkin, R., *Taking Rights Seriously* (Harvard University Press 1978)

Dyppel, K.J., *Assessment Board: Bitcoin currency fluctuations not taxable – details* (April 14, 2014), News IBFD

Eckert, P., *Steuerliche Betrachtung elektronisher Zahlungsmittel am Beispiel sog. Bitcoin-Geschäfte*, Der Betrieb 38 (2013)

Elkins, D., *The Myth of Realization: Market-to-Market Taxation of Publicly-Traded Securities*, 10 Florida Tax Review 5 (2010)

Ellis, M.J., *General Report* in*: IFA Cahiers de Droit Fiscal International* (1999)

Endriss, H. at al., *Steuerkompendium, Band 1: Ertragsteuern* (NWB, 2007)

Epstein, R.A., *Taxation in a Lockean World*, 4 Social Philosophy and Policy 1 (1986)

Finet, J.P., *Bitcoin Trade gains Are Personla Income, Danish Tax Board Says* (April 4, 2018), Tax Analysts 2018 WDT 65-3.

Gamage, D. & D.J. Heckman, *A Better Way forward for State Taxation of E-commerce*, 92 B.U.L. Rev. 483 (2012)

Gaylord, S.W. & A. Haile, *Constitutional Threats in the E-Commerce Jungle: First Amendment and Dormant Commerce Clause Limits on Amazon Laws and Use Tax Reporting Statutes*, 89 N.C. L. Rev. 2011 (2011)

Grashoff, D. & F. Kleinmanns, *Aktuelles Steuerrecht 2012* (C.H. Beck 2012)

Hacker, P. & C. Thomale, *Crypto-Securities Regulation: ICOs, Token Sales and Cryptocurrencies under EU Financial Law*, SSRN Electronic Journal (January 2017)

Haig, R. (ed.), *The Federal Income Tax* (Columbia University Press 1921)

Haile, A., *Affiliate Nexus in E-Commerce*, Elon Univ. Sch. of Law, Legal Studies Research Paper No.2011-04, (2011)

Hayek, F.A., *Denationalization of Money: The Argument Refined*, 3rd ed. (IEA 1990)

Hellerstein, J., *State Taxation under the Commerce Clause: An Historical Perspective*, 29 Vand. L. Rev. 335 (1976)

Hellerstein, W., *Jurisdiction to Tax Income and Consumption in the New Economy: A Theoretical and Comparative Perspective* (2003), http://digitalcommons.law.uga.edu/fac_artchop/124

Hellerstein, W., *State Taxation of Interstate Business: Perspectives on Two Centuries of Constitutional Adjudication*, 41 Tax L. 37 (1987)

Henchman, J., *Amazon Taxes*, The Tax Foundation (July/August 2012)

Herm, M., *Taxation of bitcoin transactions* (April 8, 2014), News IBFD

Herrmann, C., G. Heuer, A. Raupach et al., *Einkommensteuergesetz. Kommentar* (Otto Schmidt Verlag 2008)

Hey, J., *"Taxation Where Value is Created" and the OECD/G20 Base Erosion and Profit Shifting Initiative*, 72 Bull. Intl. Taxn. 4/5 (2018)

Iansiti, M. & Karim R. Lakhani, *The Truth About Blockchain*, Harvard Business Review (Jan. 2017)

Joannard-Lardant, E., *Administrative Supreme Court rules on Bitcoin gains* (April 30, 2018), News IBFD

Kahan, D., *Signaling or Reciprocating? A Response to Erich Posner's Law and Social Norms*, 36 Richmond Law Review 367 (2002)

Kaplow, L., *Rules Versus Standards: An Economic Analysis*, 42 Duke Law Journal 557 (1992)

Kavelaars, P. et al., *Inkomstenbelasting: inclusief hoofdzaken loonbelasting en premieheffing*, 8th ed. (Kluwer 2012)

Kirchhof, P. et al., *Einkommensteuergesetz. Kommentar* (Otto Schmidt Verlag 2011)

Kirkbridge, J. & A.A. Olowofoyeku, *Revenue Law, Principles and Practice*, p. 11 (Tudor Business Publishing 1992)

Kwall, J., *When Should Asset Appreciation Be Taxed?: The Case for a Disposition Standard of Realization*, 86 Indiana Law Journal 77 (2011)

Lederman, L., *Statutory Speed Bumps: The Roles Third Parties Play in Tax Compliance*, 60 Stanford Law Review 695 (2007)

Lederman, L., *Reducing Information Gaps to Reduce the Tax Gap: When Is Information Reporting Warranted?* 78 Fordham Law Review 1733 (2010)

Lee, N., et al., *Revenue Law: Principles and Practice*, 28th ed. (Bloomsbury 2010)

Loy, T., *Umsatzsteuerbetrug im innergemeinschaftlichen Erwerb: Konzept eines Blockchain-basierten Lösungsansatzes*, 22 Deutsches Steuerrecht (2018)

Macintosh, K.L., *How to Encourage Global Electronic Commerce: The Case for Private Currencies on the Internet,* 11 Harvard Journal of Law and Technology 733 (1998)
Majer, A. *Tax authorities clarify tax treatment of tokens received in Initial Coin Offering* (June 1, 2018), News IBFD.
Marian, O., *Are Cryptocurrencies Super Tax Havens?* 112 Michigan Law Review First Impressions 38 (2013)
Maurer, B., T.C. Nelms & L. Schwarz, *"When Perhaps the Real Problem Is Money Itself": The Practical Materiality of Bitcoin*, 23 Social Semiotics 2 (2013)
McGinnis, J.O. & S. Wasick, *Law's Algorithm*, 66 Florida Law Review 991 (2014)
McLure Jr., C.E., *Tax Competition in a Digital World*, 57 Bull. Intl. Fisc. Doc. 4 (2003).
McLure Jr., C.E., *EU and US Sales Taxes in the Digital Age: A comparative Analysis*, 56 Bull. Intl. Fisc. Doc. 4, (2002)
McLure Jr. C.E., & P. Merrill, *Why Doesn't the United States Use a VAT for Deficit Reduction? Political Impediments and Fiscal Coordination Issues,* 67 Bull. Intl. Taxn. 4/5 (2013)
McNulty, K. & D.L. Lathrope, *Federal Income Taxation of Individuals* 8th ed. (West 2002)
Mobach, H et al., *Cursus belastingrecht: Inkomstenbelasting* (Deventer Gouda Quint 2011)
Mobach, H. et al., *Cursus Belastingrecht, Vermogensbelasting* (Deventer Gouda Quint May 1999)
Morse, G.K. & D. Williams, *Principles of Tax Law,* 6th ed. (Sweet & Maxwell 2008)
Musgrave, R.A., *In Defense of an Income Concept*, 81 Harvard Law Rev. 45 (1967)
Nakamoto, S., *Bitcoin: A Peer-to-Peer Electronic Cash System* (2008), http://bitcoin.org /bitcoin.pdf
Nelson, B.M. et al., *Sales and Use Tax Answer Book*, sec. 2:1 (CCH 2013)
Niemeier, G. et al., *Einkommensteuer* (Erich Fleischer Verlag 2009)
Niessen, R.E.C.M. et al., *De Wet inkomstenbelasting 2001 met hoofdzaken loonbelasting* (Sdu 2012)
Niessen, R.E.C.M., *Algemene en bijzondere bronkenmerken*, Weekblad voor Fiscaal Recht 3 (1997)
O'Dwyer, K. J. & D. Malone, *Bitcoin Mining and its Energy Footprint* (June 2014), http://karlodwyer.com/publications/pdf/bitcoin_KJOD_2014.pdf.
Offermanns, R., *Circular on virtual currency released* (July 27, 2018), News IBFD
Offermanns, R., *The Netherlands* in: *Global Individual Tax Handbook* (IBFD 2017)
Offermanns, R., *The Entrepreneurship Concept in a European Comparative Law Perspective* (Kluwer Law International 2002)
Offermanns, R., *Circular on digital currency VAT exemption released* (June 18, 2018), News IBFD
Pareja, S., *Taxation without Liquidation: Rethinking "Ability to Pay"*, Wisconsin Law Review 841 (2008)
Pascual, A., *Tax regime applicable to bitcoins* (July 14, 2014), News IBFD
Peeters, B., *European Supervision on the Use of Vague and Undetermined Concepts in Tax Laws*, EC Tax Review 3 (2013)

Plasschaert, S., *The Definition of Gross Taxable Income in Schedular or Global Income Taxes*, 31 Bull. Intl. Fisc. Doc. 12 (1977)

Plasschaert, S., *First Principles about Schedular and Global Frames of Income Taxation*, 30 Bull. Intl. Fisc. Doc. 3 (1976)

Posner, E., *Law and Social Norms: The Case of Tax Compliance*, 86 Virginia Law Review 1781 (2000)

Reid F., & M. Harrigan, *An Analysis of Anonimity in the Bitcoin System* (2012), http://arxiv.org/abs/1107.4524

Repetti, J.R., *The United States* in: *Comparative Taxation: A Structural Analysis* (H.J. Ault & B.J. Arnold eds., Kluwer Law International 2010)

Roscoe, E., *Taxing Virtual Worlds: Can the IRS PWN You?* 12 Pittsburgh Journal of Technology Law and Policy 29 (2011)

Savelyev, A., *Contract Law 2.0: Smart Contracts as the Beginning of the End of Classic Contract Law*, Working Paper Law WP BRP 71/LAW/2016

Schauer, F., *The Tyranny of Choice and the Rulification of Standards*, 14 Conetmp. Legal Issues 803 (2005)

Schenk, A. & O. Oldman, *Value Added Tax: A Comparative Approach* (Cambridge University Press 2007)

Schmidt-Liebig, A., *Einkommensteuerbarkeit und Einkunftsqualifikation von Spiel- und ähnlichen Gewinnen*, Steuer und Wirtschaft 2 (1995)

Schön, W., *Germany* in *Comparative Income Taxation: A Structural Analysis* (H.J. Ault & B.J. Arnold eds., Kluwer Law International 2010)

Seer, R., *Voluntary Compliance*, 67 Bull. Intl. Taxn. 11 (2013)

Shaviro, D.N., *An Efficiency Analysis of Realization and Recognition Rules Under The Federal Income Tax*, 48 Tax Law Review 1 (1992)

Siekman, P. & N. Luijsterburg, *Personal Income Taxation in the Netherlands*, 60 Bull. Intl. Taxn. 8 (2006)

Simons, H., *Personal Income Taxation – The Definition of Income as a Problem of Fiscal Policy* (University of Chicago Press 1983)

Smith, A., *An Inquiry into the Nature and Causes of the Wealth of Nations*, Book V, Chapter II (1776)

Spenke, G. & M. de Vries, *Taxation in the Netherlands* (Kluwer Law International 2011)

Steele, T.S. et al., *The 'Amazon' Laws and the Perils of Affiliate Advertising*, 59 St. Tax Notes 939 (March 28, 2011)

Stevens, L.G.M., *Elementair belastingrecht voor economen en bedrijfsjuristen – Theorieboek*, 28th ed., (Kluwer 2012)

Sunstein, C.R., *Problems with Rules*, 83 California Law Review 953 (1995)

Tavares, R.J.S. & J.P. Owens, *Human Capital in Value Creation and Post-BEPS Tax Policy: An Outlook*, 69 Bull. Intl. Taxn. 10 (2015)

Terra, B. & J. Kajus, *Introduction to European VAT (Recast)* (2012), Online Books IBFD

Terra, B. & J. Kajus, *A Guide to the Recast VAT Directive* (2012), Online Books IBFD

Terra, B. & P.J. Wattel, *European Tax Law*, 6th ed., (Kluwer Law International 2012)

Tiley, J., *The United Kingdom* in: *Comparative Income Taxation: A Structural Analysis* (H.J. Ault & B.J. Arnold eds. Kluwer Law International 2010)

Tiley, J., et al., *Tiley and Collison's UK Tax Guide* 2012-2012 (LexisNexis 2012)

Tipke, K. & J. Lang, *Steuerrecht*, 21st ed. (Otto Schmidt Verlag 2013)
Thuronyi, V., *The Concept of Income*, 46 Tax Law Review 58 (1990)
Thuronyi, V. et al., *Comparative Tax Law* (Wolters Kluer 2016)
Van Brederode, R.F., *Systems of General Sales Taxation* (Wolters Kluwer 2009)
Van Brederode, R.F., *Introduction to the US State Sales and Use Taxes*, 18 Intl. VAT Mon. 4 (2007)
Van Dijk, J.E.A.M., *Vermogensbeheer*, WFR 1976/5258
Van Raad, K., *The Netherlands* in: *Comparative Taxation: A Structural Analysis* (H.J. Ault & B.J. Arnold eds. Kluwer Law International 2010)
Van Soest, A.J. et al., *Belastingen: inkomstenbelasting, vennootschapsbelasting, besluit voorkoming dubbele belasting 2001*, 23rd ed. (Kluwer 2007)
Von Siemens, C.,*Veredelte Umsatzsteuer* (Siemensstadt 1919)
Waldron, J., *The Concept and the Rule of Law*, Public Law and Legal Theory Research Paper Series, Working Paper No. 08-50 (Nov. 2008)
Westberg, B., *Cross-border Taxation of E-commerce* (IBFD 2002)
Whiteman, P.G. et al., *Whiteman on Capital Gains Tax* (Sweet & Maxwell 2008)
Wueller, P.H., *Concepts of Taxable Income - The German Contribution*, 53 Political Science Quarterly 1 (1938)
Yetter, D.L., *United States - VAT & Sales Tax*, Topical Analyses IBFD

PUBLICATIONS BY INTERNATIONAL ORGANIZATIONS AND THEIR INSTITUTIONS

ESMA, *ESMA highlights ICO risks for investors and firms* (November 13, 2017)
European Central Bank, *Issues Arising from the Emergence of Electronic Money*, ECB Monthly Bulletin (November 2000)
European Central Bank, *Virtual Currency Schemes* (October 2012)
European Central Bank (ECB), *Virtual Currency Schemes - A further analysis* (February 2015)
European Commission, *Communication on Electronic Commerce and Indirect Taxation*, COM(1998)374 final (June 17, 1998)
European Commission, *Green Paper on the Future of VAT: Towards a Simpler, More Robust and Efficient VAT System*, COM(2010) 695 final (December 1, 2010).
European Commission, *Explanatory Notes on the EU VAT Changes to the Place of Supply of Telecommunications, Broadcasting and Electronic Services That Enter into Force in 2015* (April 3, 2014)
European Commission, *Communication from the Commission to the European Parliament, the Council, the European Economic and Social Committee and the Committee of the Regions: A Digital Single Market Strategy for Europe*, COM(2015) 192 final (May 6, 2015)
European Commission, *Communication from the Commission to the European Parliament, the Council, the European Economic and Social Committee on an action plan on VAT: Towards a single EU VAT area – Time to decide*, COM(2016) 148 final (April 7, 2016)

European Commission, *Fact Sheet, Modernising VAT for e-commerce: Questions and Answers* (December 1, 2016), http://europa.eu/rapid/press-release_MEMO-16-3746_en.htm

European Commission, *Taxation Trends in the European Union* (2017)

European Commission, *Proposal for a Council Directive amending Directive 2006/112/EC as regards rates of value added tax*, COM(2018) 20 final.

European Commission, *Authorized Economic Operator*, https://ec.europa.eu/taxation_customs/general-information-customs/customs-security/authorised-economic-operator-aeo/authorised-economic-operator-aeo_en#what_is

European Commission, *VAT Gap*, https://ec.europa.eu/taxation_customs/business/tax-cooperation-control/vat-gap_en

FATF, *Virtual Currencies: Key Definitions and Potential AML/CFT Risks* (July 2014)

FATF, *Guidance for a Risk-Based Approach – Virtual Currencies* (June 26, 2015)

FATF, *FATF Report to the G20: Beneficial Ownership* (September 2016)

FATF, *Concealment of Beneficial Ownership* (July 2018)

OECD, *A Borderless World: Realizing the Potential of Global Electronic Commerce* (1998)

OECD, *Taxation and Electronic Commerce: Implementing the Ottawa Taxation Framework Conditions* (2001)

OECD, *Addressing Base Erosion and Profit Shifting* (2013)

OECD, *Action Plan on Base Erosion and Profit Shifting* (OECD 2013)

OECD, *BEPS Action item 1: Address the Tax Challenges of the Digital Economy* (Public Discussion Draft) (2014)

OECD, *Addressing the Tax Challenges of the Digital Economy. Action item 1: 2014 Deliverable* (2014)

OECD, *Addressing the Tax Challenges of the Digital Economy, Action 1 - 2015 Final Report* (2015)

OECD, *Actions 8-10: Aligning Transfer Pricing Outcomes with Value Creation* (OECD 2015)

OECD, *International VAT/GST Guidelines* (2015)

OECD, *Consumption Tax Trends* (2016)

OECD, *Commentaries on the Articles of the OECD Model Tax Convention* (November 21, 2017)

OECD, *Mechanisms for the Effective* Collection *of* VAT/*GST When the Supplier Is Not Located in the Jurisdiction of Taxation* (2017)

OECD, *Tax Challenges Arising from Digitalisation: 2018 Interim Report* (2018)

OECD, *OECD Secretary-General Report To The G20 Finance Ministers And Central Bank Governors* (March 2018)

Report of the Financial and Fiscal Committee (1963) (the "Neumark Report")

VAT Committee, *Working Paper No. 811* (July 29, 2014)

VAT Committee, *Working Paper No. 854* (April 30, 2015)

VAT Committee, *Working Paper No. 892* (February 4, 2016)

PUBLICATIONS BY NATIONAL TAX ADMINISTRATION AND OTHER REGULATORY BODIES

Germany

Bundesanstalt für Finanzdienstleistungsaufsicht (BaFin), *Hinweise zu Finanzinstrumenten nach § 1 Abs. 11 Satz 1 Nummern 1 bis 7* KWG *(Aktien, Vermögensanlagen, Schuldtitel, sonstige Rechte, Anteile an Investmentvermögen, Geldmarktinstrumente, Devisen und Rechnungseinheiten)* (July 2013), www.bafin.de/SharedDocs/Veroeffentlichungen/DE/Merkblatt/mb_111220_finanzinstrumente.html

BaFin, *Virtual Currency*, www.bafin.de/EN/Aufsicht/FinTech/VirtualCurrency/virtual_currency_node_en.html

BaFin, *Blockchain technology*, www.bafin.de/EN/Aufsicht/FinTech/Blockchain/blockchain_node_en.html

BaFin, *Initial coin offerings: High risks for consumers* (November 15, 2017), www.bafin.de/SharedDocs/Veroeffentlichungen/EN/Fachartikel/2017/fa_bj_1711_ICO_en.html

BaFin, *Initial Coin Offerings: Advisory letter on the classification of tokens as financial instruments* (March 29, 2018), www.bafin.de/SharedDocs/Downloads/EN/Merkblatt/WA/dl_hinweisschreiben_einordnung_ICOs_en.html?nn=8249098

BMF, *Letter to Frank Schäffler* (June 20, 2013), https://www.frankschaeffler.de/wp-content/uploads/2013/08/2013_06_20-Antwort-Bitcoin-Koschyk.pdf

BMF, *Letter to Frank Schäffler* (August 7, 2013), https://www.frankschaeffler.de/wp-content/uploads/2013/08/2013_08_07-Antwort-Koschyk-Bitcoins-Besteuerung-Wirtschaftsgut.pdf

BMF, *Letter to Frank Schäffler* (August 7, 2013), https://www.frankschaeffler.de/wp-content/uploads/2013/08/2013_08_07-Antwort-Koschyk-Bitcoins-Umsatzsteuer.pdf

BMF, *Umsatzsteuerliche Behandlung von Bitcoin und anderen sog. virtuellen Währungen*, III C 3 - S 7160-b/13/10001, 2018/0163969 (February 27, 2018), www.bundesfinanzministerium.de/Content/DE/Downloads/BMF_Schreiben/Steuerarten/Umsatzsteuer/Umsatzsteuer-Anwendungserlass/2018-02-27-umsatzsteuerliche-behandlung-von-bitcoin-und-anderen-sog-virtuellen-waehrungen.pdf?__blob=publicationFile&v=1

Deutsche Bundestag - 19. Wahlperiode, Drucksache 19/370, question 24 and 25, https://dipbt.bundestag.de/doc/btd/19/003/1900370.pdf

Finance Ministry of Hamburg (*Finanzministerium/Finanzbehörde der Freien und Hansestadt Hamburg*), *Ertragsteuerliche Behandlung des Handels mit Bitcoins auf der privaten Vermögenssphäre*, S 2256 - 2017/003-52 (December 11, 2017)

Regional Tax Office North Rhine-Westphalia (*Oberfinanzdirektion Nordrhein-Westfalen*), *Ertragsteuerliche Behandlung von virtuellen Währungen (Kryptowährungen)* (April 20, 2018).

NETHERLANDS

AFM, *Virtuele valuta's*, www.afm.nl/nl-nl/consumenten/themas/producten/betalen-sparen/virtueel-geld; *Wat is blockchaintechnologie?* www.afm.nl/nl-nl/consumenten/themas/waarschuwing/blockchain

AFM, *Reële risico's bij cryptocurrencies* (November 13, 2017), www.afm.nl/nl-nl/nieuws/2017/nov/risico-cryptocurrencies; *AFM waarschuwt voor grote risico's bij Initial Coin Offerings* (November 13, 2017), www.afm.nl/nl-nl/nieuws/2017/nov/risico-ico

Belastingdienst, *Overige Bezittingen*, www.belastingdienst.nl/wps/wcm/connect/bldcontentnl/belastingdienst/prive/vermogen_en_aanmerkelijk_belang/vermogen/wat_zijn_uw_bezittingen_en_schulden/uw_bezittingen/overige_bezittingen/.

Belastingdiesnt, *Wanneer bent u ondernemer voor de inkomstenbelasting?* www.belastingdienst.nl/wps/wcm/connect/bldcontentnl/belastingdienst/zakelijk/winst/inkomstenbelasting/wanneer_bent_u_ondernemer_voor_de_inkomstenbelasting/wanneer_bent_u_ondernemer_voor_de_inkomstenbelasting

Belastingdienst, *Urencriterium*, www.belastingdienst.nl/wps/wcm/connect/bldcontentnl/belastingdienst/zakelijk/winst/inkomstenbelasting/inkomstenbelasting_voor_ondernemers/voorwaarden_urencriterium

Finance Ministry (*Ministerie van Financiën*), *Antwoord van de Minister van Financiën op vragen van het lid Nijboer (PvdA) aan de minister van Financiën over de opkomst van de Bitcoin als digitale betaaleenheid (ingezonden 10 april 2013)*

Finance Ministry, *Beantwording vragen vaste CIE Financiën fiscale aspected cryptovaluta* (May 28, 2018), www.rijksoverheid.nl/documenten/kamerstukken/2018/05/28/beantwoording-vragen-vaste-cie-financien-fiscale-aspecten-cryptovaluta

UNITED KINGDOM

Financial Conduct Authority (FCA), *Discussion Paper on Distributed Ledger Technology*, DP17/3 (April 2017), www.fca.org.uk/publication/discussion/dp17-03.pdf

FCA, *Initial Coin Offerings* (September 12, 2017), www.fca.org.uk/news/statements/initial-coin-offerings

FCA, *Consumer warning about the risks of investing in cryptocurrency* CFDs (November 14, 2017), www.fca.org.uk/news/news-stories/consumer-warning-about-risks-investing-cryptocurrency-cfds

FCA, *Cryptocurrency derivatives* (April 6, 2018), www.fca.org.uk/news/statements/cryptocurrency-derivatives

HMRC, *Residence, domicile and the remittance basis* (October 3, 2013), www.gov.uk/government/publications/residence-domicile-and-remittance-basis-rules-uk-tax-liability

HMRC, *Capital Gains Tax on personal possessions*, www.gov.uk/capital-gains-tax-personal-possessions.

HMRC, *Capital Gains Tax*, www.gov.uk/capital-gains-tax/allowances

HMRC, *Brief 09/14: Tax Treatment of Activities Involving Bitcoin and Other Similar Cryptocurrencies* (March 3, 2014), www.gov.uk/government/publications/revenue-and-customs-brief-9-2014-bitcoin-and-other-cryptocurrencies

HMRC, *Meaning of trade: general: hobbies and artificial trades,*www.gov.uk/hmrc-internal-manuals/business-income-manual/bim20090

HMRC, *VAT Business and Non-Business activities: hobbies*, www.gov.uk/hmrc-internal-manuals/vat-business-non-business/vbnb27000

HMRC, *Athletes: Trade or hobby*, www.gov.uk/hmrc-internal-manuals/business-in come-manual/bim50605

HMRC, *Trade: general: hobbies and artificial trades*, www.gov.uk/hmrc-internal-manuals/business-income-manual/bim20090)

HMRC, *Cash basis*, www.gov.uk/simpler-income-tax-cash-basis/who-can-use-cash-basis

HMRC, *Claim capital allowances*, www.gov.uk/capital-allowances

HMRC, *Miscellaneous income: scope of the provisions: overview*, www.gov.uk/hmrc-internal-manuals/business-income-manual/bim100101

HMRC, *Miscellaneous income: scope of the provisions: isolated sales of assets*, www.gov.uk/hmrc-internal-manuals/business-income-manual/bim100135

HMRC, *Miscellaneous income: scope of the provisions: series of sales of assets*, www.gov.uk/hmrc-internal-manuals/business-income-manual/bim100140

HM Treasury, *Digital currencies: response to the call for information* (March 2015), https://assets.publishing.service.gov.uk/government/uploads/system/uploads/attachment_data/file/414040/digital_currencies_response_to_call_for_information_final_changes.pdf

Royal Commission on the Taxation of Profits and Income, Final Report Cmd 9474 (1955), Comments on what is a trade

UNITED STATES

California Department of Tax and Fee Administration, *Obtaining a Seller's Permit*, www.cdtfa.ca.gov/taxes-and-fees/faqseller.htm

Census Bureau, *State Government Tax Collections Summary Report: 2013* (April 8, 2014), https://www2.census.gov/govs/statetax/2013stcreport.pdf

Customs and Border Protection (CBP), *CTPAT: Customs Trade Partnership against Terrorism*, www.cbp.gov/border-security/ports-entry/cargo-security/ctpat

CBP, *CSI: Container Security Initiative*, www.cbp.gov/border-security/ports-entry/cargo-security/csi/csi-brief

FinCEN, *Application of FinCEN's Regulations to Persons Administering, Exchanging, or Using Virtual Currencies* (March 18, 2013), http://fincen.gov/statutes_regs/guidance/pdf/FIN-2013-G001.pdf.

FinCEN, *FinCEN Publishes Two Rulings on Virtual Currency Miners and Investors* (January 30, 2014), www.fincen.gov/news/news-releases/fincen-publishes-two-rulings-virtual-currency-miners-and-investors

FinCEN, *FinCEN Fines Ripple Labs Inc. in First Civil Enforcement Action against a Virtual CurrencyExchanger* (May 5, 2015), www.fincen.gov/news_room/nr/pdf/20150505.pdf

GAO, *Report to the Committee on Finance, U.S. Senate. Virtual Economies and Currencies. Additional IRS Guidance Could Reduce Tax Compliance Risks* (May 2013), www.gao.gov/assets/660/654620.pdf

IRS, *Virtual Currency Guidance,* Notice 2014-21 (March 25, 2014), www.irs.gov/uac/Newsroom/IRS-Virtual-Currency-Guidance

IRS, *Like-Kind Exchanges Under IRC Code Section 1031*, www.irs.gov/newsroom/like-kind-exchanges-under-irc-code-section-1031

IRS, *Topic Number 307 - Backup Withholding*, www.irs.gov/taxtopics/tc307

IRS, *Comparison of Form 8938 and FBAR Requirements*, www.irs.gov/Businesses/Comparison-of-Form-8938-and-FBAR-Requirements

IRS, *IRC Section 6050W - Frequently Asked Questions*, www.irs.gov/pub/irs-utl/irdm_section_6050w_faqs_7_23_11.pdf

Michigan Department of Treasury, *Treasury Update* (November 2015), https://www.michigan.gov/documents/treasury/Tax-Policy-November2015-Newsletter_504036_7.pdf

National Taxpayer Advocate, *2013 Annual Report to Congress, www.taxpayeradvocate.irs.gov/userfiles/file/2013FullReport/DIGITAL-CURRENCY-The-IRS-Should-Issue-Guidance-to-Assist-Users-of-Digital-Currency.pdf*

New Jersey Treasury, *New Jersey State Tax News*, vol. 30, no. 1 (Spring 2007), available at: www.state.nj.us/treasury/taxation/pdf/pubs/stn/spring07.pdf

New York State Department of Taxation and Finance, *Tax Department Policy on Transactions Using Convertible Virtual Currency*, Technical Memorandum TSB-M-14(5)C, (7)I, (17)S (December 5, 2014), https://www.tax.ny.gov/pdf/memos/multitax/m14_5c_7i_17s.pdf

SEC, *Investor Bulletin: Initial Coin Offerings* (July 25, 2017), www.investor.gov/additional-resources/news-alerts/alerts-bulletins/investor-bulletin-initial-coin-offerings

SEC, *Report of Investigation Pursuant to Section 21(a) of the Securities Exchange Act of 1934:The DAO* (July 25, 2017), www.sec.gov/litigation/investreport/34-81207.pdf

SEC, *SEC Exposes Two Initial Coin Offerings Purportedly Backed by Real Estate and Diamonds* (September 29, 2017), www.sec.gov/news/press-release/2017-185-0

SEC, *Company Halts ICO After SEC Raises Registration Concerns* (December 11, 2017), www.sec.gov/news/press-release/2017-227

SEC, *U.S. Securities Laws May Apply to Offers, Sales, and Trading of Interests in Virtual Organizations* (July 25, 2017), www.sec.gov/litigation/investreport/34-81207.pdf

SEC, *Investor Alert: Public Companies Making ICO-Related Claims* (August 28, 2017), www.sec.gov/oiea/investor-alerts-and-bulletins/ia_icorelatedclaims;

SEC, *Statement on Potentially Unlawful Promotion of Initial Coin Offerings and Other Investments by Celebrities and Others* (November 1, 2017), www.sec.gov/news/public-statement/statement-potentially-unlawful-promotion-icos

SEC, *Statement on Cryptocurrencies and Initial Coin Offerings* (December 11, 2017), www.sec.gov/news/public-statement/statement-clayton-2017-12-11#_ftn3

South Dakota Department of Revenue, *Factsheet "Products Transferred Electronically"* (March 2011), https://dor.sd.gov/Taxes/Business_Taxes/Publications/PDFs/digital.pdf

TIGTA, *As the Use of Virtual Currencies in Taxable Transactions Becomes More Common, Additional Actions Are Needed to Ensure Taxpayer Compliance*, 2016-30-083 (September 21, 2016), www.treasury.gov/tigta/auditreports/2016reports/201630083fr.pdf

Treasury, *Selected Tax Policy Implications of Global Electronic Commerce* (November 22, 1996), www.treasury.gov/resource-center/tax-policy/Documents/Report-Global-Electronic-Commerce-1996.pdf

OTHER COUNTRIES

Austria: Bundesministerium für Finanzen, *Steuerliche Behandlung von Kryptowährungen (virtuelle Währungen)* (July 25, 2017), www.bmf.gv.at/steuern/kryptowaehrung_Besteuerung.html

Australia: ATO, *Tax treatment of cryptocurrencies* (last modified: March 16, 2018), www.ato.gov.au/General/Gen/Tax-treatment-of-crypto-currencies-in-Australia---specifically-bitcoin/

Australia: ATO, *GST and digital currency* (last modified: March 16, 2018), www.ato.gov.au/Business/GST/In-detail/Your-industry/Financial-services-and-insurance/GST-and-digital-currency/

Canada: Canada Revenue Agency, *Interpretation Bulletin IT-490, Barter Transactions* (January 1, 1995), www.canada.ca/en/revenue-agency/services/forms-publications/publications/it490.html

Canada: Canada Revenue Agency, *Interpretation Bulletin IT-479R, Transactions in Securities* (January 1, 1995), www.canada.ca/en/revenue-agency/services/forms-publications/publications/it479r.html

Canada: Canada Revenue Agency, *What you should know about digital currency* (March 17, 2015), www.canada.ca/en/revenue-agency/news/newsroom/fact-sheets/fact-sheets-2015/what-you-should-know-about-digital-currency.html

Finland: Tax Administration (*Vero Skatt*), *Income Taxation of Virtual Currencies (Inkomstbeskattning av virtuella valuator)* (August 28, 2013), www.vero.fi/sv/Detaljerade_skatteanvisningar/anvisningar/48411/inkomstbeskattning_av_virtuella_valuto/

Finland:Tax Administration (*Vero Skatt*), *Taxation of Virtual Currencies* (*Beskattning av virtuella valutor*) (May 28, 2018), www.vero.fi/sv/Detaljerade_skatteanvisningar/anvisningar/48411/beskattning-av-virtuella-valutor/

Ireland: Revenue, *Taxation of Cryptocurrency Transactions*, eBReif No. 88/2018 (May 2018), www.revenue.ie/en/tax-professionals/tdm/income-tax-capital-gains-tax-corporation-tax/part-02/02-01-03.pdf

Italy: Revenue Agency (*Agenzia delle Entrate*), *Risoluzione n. 72/E* (September 2, 2016), www.finaria.it/pdf/bitcoin-tasse-agenzia-entrate.pdf.

Norway: Directorate of Taxation (*Skatteetaten*), *Use of bitcoins - tax consequences (Bruk av bitcoins – skatte- og avgiftsmessige konsekvenser)* (November 11, 2013), www.skatteetaten.no/rettskilder/type/uttalelser/prinsipputtalelser/bruk-av-bitcoins--skatte--og-avgiftsmessige-konsekvenser/

Norway: Ministry of Finance (*Finansdepartementet*), *Value Added Tax - Except for Financial Services* (*Merverdiavgift - unntaket for finansielle tjenester*) (February 6, 2017), www.regjeringen.no/no/dokumenter/merverdiavgift---unntaket-for-finansielle-tjenester/id2538129/

Norway: Directorate of Taxation (*Skatteetaten*), *Tax and value-added treatment of bitcoins and other virtual currencies* (*Skatte- og merverdiavgiftsmessig behandling av bitcoins og andre virtuelle valutaer*), www.skatteetaten.no/bedrift-og-organisasjon/rapportering-og-bransjer/bransjer-med-egne-regler/internett/skatt-mva-virtuell-valuta/

Norway: Ministry of Finance (*Finansdepartementet*), *Answer to Question No. 777 from Representative Gjelsvik on registration and traceability of bitcoin trade (cryptovaluta) (Svar på spørsmål nr. 777 fra representant Gjelsvik om registrering og sporbarhet av handel med bitcoin (kryptovaluta)*) (January 30, 2018), www.regjeringen.no/no/aktuelt/sporsmal-nr.-777-fra-representant-gjelsvik-om-registrering-og-sporbarhet-av-handel-med-bitcoin-kryptovaluta/id2588056/

Singapore: IRAS, *e-Commerce*, www.iras.gov.sg/irashome/GST/GST-registered-businesses/Specific-business-sectors/e-Commerce/

Singapore: IRAS, *Income Tax Treatment of Virtual Currencies*, www.iras.gov.sg/irashome/Businesses/Companies/Working-out-Corporate-Income-Taxes/Specific-topics/Income-Tax-Treatment-of-Virtual-Currencies/

Slovenia: Ministry of Finance, *New version of the document Tax treatment of business operations with virtual currencies as per ZDoh-2, ZDDPO-2, ZDDV-1 and ZDFS (Detailed description)* (June 4, 2018), www.fu.gov.si/en/taxes_and_other_duties/areas_of_work/international_taxation/novica/new_version_of_the_document_tax_treatment_of_business_operations_with_virtual_currencies_a_8164/

South Africa: South African Revenue Service (SARS), *SARS's stance on the tax treatment of cryptocurrencies* (April 6, 2018), www.sars.gov.za/Media/MediaReleases/Pages/6-April-2018---SARS-stance-on-the-tax-treatment-of-cryptocurrencies-.aspx

South Africa: Treasury, *Budget Review 2018* (February 21, 2018), www.treasury.gov.za/documents/national%20budget/2018/review/FullBR.pdf

Spain: General Directorate of Taxation (*Dirección General de Tributos*), *Consulta vinculante V1028-15, V1029-15* (March 30, 2015), https://petete.minhafp.gob.es/consultas/?num_consulta=V1028-15 and https://petete.minhafp.gob.es/consultas/?num_consulta=V1029-15

Spain: General Directorate of Taxation, *Consulta vinculante V3625-16* (August 31, 2017), https://petete.minhafp.gob.es/consultas/?num_consulta=V3625-16

Spain: General Directorate of Taxation, *Consulta vinculante V2846-15* (October 1, 2017), https://petete.minhafp.gob.es/consultas/?num_consulta=V2846-15

Spain: General Directorate of Taxation, *Consulta vinculante V2908-17* (November 13, 2017), https://petete.minhafp.gob.es/consultas/?num_consulta = V2908-17

Spain: General Directorate of Taxation, *Consulta vinculante V0590-18* (March 1, 2018), https://petete.minhafp.gob.es/consultas/?num_consulta = V0590-18

Spain: General Directorate of Taxation, *Consulta vinculante V0808-18* (March 22, 2018), https://petete.minhafp.gob.es/consultas/?num_consulta = V0808-18

Spain: General Directorate of Taxation, *Consulta vinculante V0999-18* (April 18, 2018), https://petete.minhafp.gob.es/consultas/?num_consulta = V0999-18

Sweden: Tax Authority (*Skatteverket*), *Guidelines on the Taxation of Mining of Bitcoins and Other Virtual Currencies* (*Beskattning vid mining av bitcoin och andra virtuella valutor m.m.*) (April 24, 2015); www4.skatteverket.se/rattsligvagledning/338713.html?q = 131 + 191846-15%2F111

Sweden: Tax Authority (*Skatteverket*), *Taxation of bitcoin and other virtual currency for capital gains purposes* (*Beskattning av bitcoin och andra s.k. virtuella valutor i inkomstslaget kapital*) (April 23, 2014), www4.skatteverket.se/rattsligvagledning/327766.html

Switzerland: Canton Lutzern, *Bitcoin & Co. und Steuern* (November 15, 2017), https://steuern.lu.ch/-/media/Steuern/Dokumente/SteuerBulletin/2017/SteuerPraxis201720BitcoinundCo.pdf?la = de-CH

Switzerland: Kanton Zug, *Kryptowährungen* (November 30, 2017), www.zg.ch/behoerden/finanzdirektion/steuerverwaltung/kryptowaehrungen

WEBSITES AND ONLINE ARTICLES

BBC News, *Mt. Gox bitcoin exchange files for bankruptcy* (February 28, 2014), www.bbc.com/news/technology-25233230

Bitcoin, https://bitcoin.org

BitInfoCharts, https://bitinfocharts.com/comparison/bitcoin-transactionfees.html#1y

Bitfinex, www.bitfinex.com

Bitstamp, www.bitstamp.net

Blockchain, https://blockchain.info/pools

Brown, R., *A Simple Model for Smart Contracts* (February 10, 2015), https://gendal.me/2015/02/10/a-simple-model-for-smart-contracts/

Caron, P.L., *Pepperdine Hosts Symposium on the Most Maligned Supreme Court Decisions,* Tax Prof. L. Blog (April 1, 2011), http://taxprof.typepad.com/taxprofblog/2011/04/supreme-mistakes.html

Chaum, D., *Blind signatures for untraceable payments* (1983), www.hit.bme.hu/~buttyan/courses/BMEVIHIM219/2009/Chaum.BlindSigForPayment.1982.PDF.

Coinbase, www.coinbase.com

CoinMarketCap, https://coinmarketcap.com/

Cointelegraph, *Difference Between Bitcoin and Bitcoin Cash,* https://cointelegraph.com/bitcoin-cash-for-beginners/btc-bch-differences#neutral-opinion

Evans, D.S., *Bitcoin Payments: Igniting Or Not?* (February 17, 2014) www.globaleconomicsgroup.com/financial-regulation/bitcoin-payments-igniting-or-not/

Floyd, D., *$6.3 Billion: 2018 ICO Funding has Passed 2017's Total* (April 19, 2018), www.coindesk.com/6-3-billion-2018-ico-funding-already-outpaced-2017/

Gehrke, N., *Japan Income Tax on Virtual Currencies* (January 29, 2018), https://medium.com/tokyo-fintech/japan-income-tax-on-virtual-currencies-8e8c170195a2

Gemini, https://gemini.com/

Greenspan, G. *Beware of the Impossible Smart Contracts*, Blockchain news (April 12, 2016), www.multichain.com/blog/2016/04/beware-impossible-smart-contract/

Grigg, I., *How DigiCash Blew Everything* (February 10, 1999), http://cryptome.org/jya/digicrash.htm

Gronholt-Pedersen, J., *Maersk, IBM to launch blockchain-based platform for global trade* (January 16, 2018), www.reuters.com/article/us-maersk-blockchain-ibm/maersk-ibm-to-launch-blockchain-based-platform-for-global-trade-idUSKBN1F51DE

Gulf News, *Dubai has world's first government entity to conduct transactions through Blockchain network* (October 7, 2017), http://gulfnews.com/business/property/dubai-has-world-s-first-government-entity-to-conduct-transactions-through-blockchain-network-1.2101819

History of Bitcoin, http://historyofbitcoin.org/

ICO Alert, https://www.icoalert.com/

ICO Stats, https://icostats.com/

Kassem, M., *Smart Dubai close to rolling out 20 blockchain-based services* (January 14, 2018), www.thenational.ae/business/smart-dubai-close-to-rolling-out-20-blockchain-based-services-1.695280

Kawamura M., et al., *Japan exempts virtual currencies from consumption tax* (March 31, 2017), www.dlapiper.com/en/netherlands/insights/publications/2017/03/global-tax-news-mar-2017/japan-exempts-virtual-currencies/

Kraken, www.kraken.com

Lanz, J.A. *South Korea Will Announce Crypto Tax Policies in July* (April 2, 2018), https://cryptocurrencynews.com/daily-news/crypto-news/south-korea-crypto-tax-policies/

Mick, J., *Inside the Mega-Hack of Bitcoin: the Full Story* (June 19, 2011), www.dailytech.com/Inside + the + MegaHack + of + Bitcoin + the + Full + Story/article21942.htm.

Nagata, K., *Cryptoprofits are taxable — have you filed?* (February 18, 2018), www.japantimes.co.jp/news/2018/02/18/business/financial-markets/cryptoprofits-taxable-filed/#.W2GJgNUzbcs

Nasdaq, *Nasdaq's Blockchain Technology to Transform the Republic of Estonia's e-Residency Shareholder Participation* (February 12, 2016), http://ir.nasdaq.com/releasedetail.cfm?releaseid = 954654

Prisco, G., *Swiss Tax Authorities Confirm that Bitcoin is VAT-free in Switzerland* (June 12, 2015), https://bitcoinmagazine.com/articles/swiss-tax-authorities-confirm-bitcoin-vat-free-switzerland-1434140401/.

Roberts, J., *Companies Can Put Shareholders on a Blockchain Starting Today* (August 1, 2017), http://fortune.com/2017/08/01/blockchain-shareholders-law/

Roberts, J., *The Diamond Industry Is Obsessed With the Blockchain* (September 12, 2018) http://fortune.com/2017/09/12/diamond-blockchain-everledger/

Sales Tax Handbook, *North Dakota: Sales Tax Handbook - Are Software and Digital Products subject to sales tax?* www.salestaxhandbook.com/north-dakota/sales-tax-taxability/software-and-digital-products

Sales Tax Institute, *Arizona Issues Ruling on Marketplace Nexus* (October 28, 2016), www.salestaxinstitute.com/resources/arizona-issues-ruling-marketplace-nexus

Sales Tax Institute, *Remote Seller Nexus Chart* (accessed: June 1, 2018), www.sales taxinstitute.com/resources/remote-seller-nexus-chart

Sales Tax Institute, *State Sales Tax Rates*, http://salestaxinstitute.com/rates.html.

Sheppard Mullin Richter & Hampton LLP, *Taxation on virtual currency income in China* (December 9, 2008), www.lexology.com/library/detail.aspx?g = 87cd4685-3e8f-4571-83ec-669873ff7942.

Siegel, D., *Understanding the DAO attack* (June 25, 2016), www.coindesk.com/understanding-dao-hack-journalists/

Strategic Coin, *Utility, Equity, and Debt Tokens: an Overview for Institutional Investors*, http://strategiccoin.com/utility-equity-debt-tokens-overview-institutional-inves tors/

Streamlined Sales Tax Governing Board, http://streamlinedsalestax.org

Szabo, N., *Smart Contracts: Building Blocks for Digital Markets* (1996), www.fon.hum .uva.nl/rob/Courses/InformationInSpeech/CDROM/Literature/LOTwinterscho ol2006/szabo.best.vwh.net/smart_contracts_2.html

Tax Foundation, *Unpacking the State and Local Tax Toolkit: Sources of State and Local Tax Collections* (June 20, 2017), https://taxfoundation.org/toolkit-sources-state -local-tax-collections/

TokenMarket, *What is Token?* https://tokenmarket.net/what-is/what-is-token/

US Census Bureau, *E-Stats 2015: Measuring the Electronic* Economy (May 24, 2017), www.census.gov/content/dam/Census/library/publications/2017/econ/e15-es tats.pdf

Vischer Blog, *Taxation of cryptocurrencies* (December 18, 2017), http://blog.vischer.com/en/taxation-of-cryptocurrencies

Wei Dai, *B-Money* (1998), http://weidai.com/bmoney.txt

White, M., *Digitizing Global Trade with Maersk and IBM* (January 16, 2018), www.ibm.com/blogs/blockchain/2018/01/digitizing-global-trade-maersk-ibm/

Wildeboer Dellelce, *Cryptocurrencies and Tax: Five Things Every Canadian Needs to Know* (December 12, 2017), www.wildlaw.ca/resource-centre/legal-updates/20 17/cryptocurrencies-and-tax-five-things-every-canadian-needs-to-know/

Wong, J., *Sweden's blockchain-powered land registry is inching towards reality* (April 3, 2017) https://qz.com/947064/sweden-is-turning-a-blockchain-powered-land-re gistry-into-a-reality/

World Bank, *GDP (current US$)*, https://data.worldbank.org/indicator/NY.GDP.MKTP.CD?year_high_desc = true

Wüst, K. & A. Gervais, *Do you need a Blockchain?* (2017), https://eprint.iacr.org/201 7/375.pdf

Zhao, W., *China's ICO Ban: A Full Translation of Regulator Remarks* (September 5, 2017), www.coindesk.com/chinas-ico-ban-a-full-translation-of-regulator-remarks/

Zuckerman, M.J., *UK Financial Regulator To Release Crypto Review This Year With BoE And Treasury* (April 9, 2018), https://cointelegraph.com/news/uk-financial-regulator-to-release-crypto-review-this-year-with-boe-and-treasury

Zuckerman, M.J., *South Korean Regulators To Release Crypto Tax Framework By June* (April 1, 2018), https://cointelegraph.com/news/south-korean-regulators-to-release-crypto-tax-framework-by-june

Table of Cases

European Union

Germany

Netherlands

United Kingdom

United States

Index

1. Alberto Xavier, *The Taxation of Foreign Investment in Brazil,* 1980 (ISBN 90-200-0582-0).
2. Hugh J. Ault & Albert J. Rädler, *The German Corporation Tax Law with 1980 Amendments,* 1981 (ISBN 90-200-0642-8).
3. Paul R. McDaniel & Hugh J. Ault, *Introduction to United States International Taxation,* 1981 (ISBN 90-6544-004-6).
4. Albert J. Rädler, *German Transfer Pricing/Prix de Transfer en Allemagne,* 1984 (ISBN 90-6544-143-3).
5. Paul R. McDaniel & Stanley S. Surrey, *International Aspects of Tax Expenditures: A Comparative Study,* 1985 (ISBN 90-654-4163-8).
6. Kees van Raad, *Nondiscrimination in International Tax Law,* 1986 (ISBN 90-6544-266-9).
7. Sijbren Cnossen (ed.), *Tax Coordination in the European Community,* 1987 (ISBN 90-6544-272-3).
8. Ben Terra, *Sales Taxation. The Case of Value Added Tax in the European Community,* 1989 (ISBN 90-6544-381-9).
9. Rutsel S.J. Martha, *The Jurisdiction to Tax in International Law: Theory and Practice of Legislative Fiscal Jurisdiction,* 1989 (ISBN 90-654-4416-5).
10. Paul R. McDaniel & Hugh J. Ault, *Introduction to United States International Taxation* (3rd revised edition), 1989 (ISBN 90-6544-423-8).
11. Manuel Pires, *International Juridicial Double Taxation of Income,* 1989 (ISBN 90-6544-426-2).
12. A.H.M. Daniels, *Issues in International Partnership Taxation,* 1991 (ISBN 90-654-4577-3).
13. Arvid A. Skaar, *Permanent Establishment: Erosion of a Tax Treaty Principle,* 1992 (ISBN 90-6544-594-3).
14. Cyrille David & Geerten M.M. Michielse (eds), *Tax Treatment of Financial Instruments,* 1996 (ISBN 90-654-4666-4).
15. Herbert H. Alpert & Kees van Raad (eds), *Essays on International Taxation,* 1993 (ISBN 90-654-4781-4).
16. Wolfgang Gassner, Michael Lang & Eduard Lechner (eds), *Tax Treaties and EC Law,* 1997 (ISBN 90-411-0680-4).
17. Glória Teixeira, *Taxing Corporate Profits in the EU,* 1997 (ISBN 90-411-0703-7).
18. Michael Lang et al. (eds), *Multilateral Tax Treaties,* 1998 (ISBN 90-411-0704-5).
19. Stef van Weeghel, *The Improper Use of Tax Treaties,* 1998 (ISBN 90-411-0737-1).
20. Klaus Vogel (ed.), *Interpretation of Tax Law and Treaties and Transfer Pricing in Japan and Germany,* 1998 (ISBN 90-411-9655-2).
21. Bertil Wiman (ed.), *International Studies in Taxation: Law and Economics; Liber Amicorum Leif Mutén,* 1999 (ISBN 90-411-9692-7).
22. Alfonso J. Martín Jiménez, *Towards Corporate Tax Harmonization in the European Community,* 1999 (ISBN 90-411-9690-0).

23. Ramon J. Jeffery, *The Impact of State Sovereignty on Global Trade and International Taxation*, 1999 (ISBN 90-411-9703-6).
24. A.J. Easson, *Taxation of Foreign Direct Investment*, 1999 (ISBN 90-411-9741-9).
25. Marjaana Helminen, *The Dividend Concept in International Tax Law: Dividend Payments Between Corporate Entities*, 1999 (ISBN 90-411-9765-6).
26. Paul Kirchhof, Moris Lehner, Kees van Raad, Arndt Raupach & Michael-Rodi (eds), *International and Comparative Taxation: Essays in Honour of Klaus Vogel*, 2002 (ISBN 90-411-9841-5).
27. Krister Andersson, Peter Melz & Christer Silfverberg (eds), *Liber Amicorum Sven-Olof Lodin*, 2001 (ISBN 90-411-9850-4).
28. Juan Martín Jovanovich, *Customs Valuation and Transfer Pricing: Is It Possible to Harmonize Customs and Tax Rules?*, Second Edition, 2018 (ISBN 978-90-411-6134-5).
29. Stefano Simontacchi, *Taxation of Capital Gains under the OECD Model Convention: With Special Regard to Immovable Property*, 2007 (ISBN 978-90-411-2549-1).
30. Michael Lang, Josef Schuch, & Claus Staringer (eds), *Tax Treaty Law and EC Law*, 2007 (ISBN 978-90-411-2629-0).
31. Duncan Bentley, *Taxpayers' Rights: Theory Origin and Implementation*, 2007 (ISBN 978-90-411-2650-4).
32. Sergio André Rocha, *Interpretation of Double Taxation Conventions: General Theory and Brazilian Perspective*, 2008 (ISBN 978-90-411-2822-5).
33. Robert F. van Brederode, *Systems of General Sales Taxation: Theory, Policy and Practice*, 2009 (ISBN 978-90-411-2832-4).
34. John G. Head & Richard Krever (eds), *Tax Reform in the 21st Century: A Volume in Memory of Richard Musgrave*, 2009 (ISBN 978-90-411-2829-4).
35. Jens Wittendorff, *Transfer Pricing and the Arm's Length Principle in International Tax Law*, 2010 (ISBN 978-90-411-3270-3).
36. Marjaana Helminen, *The International Tax Law Concept of Dividend*, Second Edition, 2017 (ISBN 978-90-411-8394-1).
37. Robert F. van Brederode (ed.), *Immovable Property under VAT: A Comparative Global Analysis*, 2011 (ISBN 978-90-411-3126-3).
38. Dennis Weber & Stef van Weeghel, *The 2010 OECD Updates: Model Tax Convention & Transfer Pricing Guidelines - A Critical Review*, 2011 (ISBN 978-90-411-3812-5).
39. Yariv Brauner & Martin James McMahon, Jr. (eds), *The Proper Tax Base: Structural Fairness from an International and Comparative Perspective—Essays in Honour of Paul McDaniel*, 2012 (ISBN 978-90-411-3286-4).
40. Robert F. van Brederode (ed.), *Science, Technology and Taxation*, 2012 (ISBN 978-90-411-3125-6).
41. Oskar Henkow, *The VAT/GST Treatment of Public Bodies*, 2013 (ISBN 978-90-411-4663-2).
42. Jean Schaffner, *How Fixed Is a Permanent Establishment?*, 2013 (ISBN 978-90-411-4662-5).

43. Miguel Correia, *Taxation of Corporate Groups*, 2013 (ISBN 978-90-411-4841-4).
44. Veronika Daurer, *Tax Treaties and Developing Countries*, 2014 (ISBN 978-90-411-4982-4).
45. Claire Micheau, *State Aid, Subsidy and Tax Incentives under EU and WTO Law*, 2014 (ISBN 978-90-411-4555-0).
46. Robert F. van Brederode & Richard Krever (eds), *Legal Interpretation of Tax Law*, 2014 (ISBN 978-90-411-4945-9).
47. Radhakishan Rawal, *Taxation of Cross-border Services*, 2014 (ISBN 978-90-411-4947-3).
48. João Dácio Rolim, *Proportionality and Fair Taxation*, 2014 (ISBN 978-90-411-5838-3).
49. Paulo Rosenblatt, *General Anti-avoidance Rules for Major Developing Countries*, 2015 (ISBN 978-90-411-5839-0).
50. Gaspar Lopes Dias V.S., *Tax Arbitrage through Cross-Border Financial Engineering*, 2015 (ISBN 978-90-411-5875-8).
51. Geerten M.M. Michielse & Victor Thuronyi (eds), *Tax Design Issues Worldwide*, 2015 (ISBN 978-90-411-5610-5).
52. Oktavia Weidmann, *Taxation of Derivatives*, 2015 (ISBN 978-90-411-5977-9).
53. Chris Evans, Richard Krever & Peter Mellor (eds), *Tax Simplification*, 2015 (ISBN 978-90-411-5976-2).
54. Reuven Avi-Yonah & Joel Slemrod (eds), *Taxation and Migration*, 2015 (ISBN 978-90-411-6136-9).
55. Alexander Bosman, *Other Income under Tax Treaties: An Analysis of Article 21 of the OECD Model Convention*, 2015 (ISBN 978-90-411-6610-4).
56. John Abrahamson, *International Taxation of Manufacturing and Distribution*, 2016 (ISBN 978-90-411-6664-7).
57. Frederik Boulogne, *Shortcomings in the EU Merger Directive*, 2016 (ISBN 978-90-411-6713-2).
58. Angelika Meindl-Ringler, *Beneficial Ownership in International Tax Law*, 2016 (ISBN 978-90-411-6833-7).
59. Andreas Waltrich, *Cross-Border Taxation of Permanent Establishments: An International Comparison*, 2016 (ISBN 978-90-411-6832-0).
60. Sergio André Rocha & Allison Christians (eds), *Tax Sovereignty in the BEPS Era*, 2017 (ISBN 978-90-411-6707-1).
61. Peter Antony Wilson, *BRICS and International Tax Law*, 2018 (ISBN 978-90-411-9435-0).
62. Louise Otis, Brigitte Alepin & Blanca Moreno-Dodson (eds), *Winning the Tax Wars: Tax Competition and Cooperation*, 2018 (ISBN 978-90-411-9460-2).
63. Marta Castelon, *International Taxation of Income from Services under Double Taxation Conventions: Development, Practice and Policy*, 2018 (ISBN 978-90-411-9594-4).
64. D.M. Broekhuijsen, *A Multilateral Tax Treaty: Designing an Instrument to Modernise International Tax Law*, 2018 (ISBN 978-90-411-9872-3).

65. John Abrahamson, *International Taxation of Energy Production and Distribution*, 2018 (ISBN 978-90-411-9101-4).
66. Leopoldo Parada, *Double Non-taxation and the Use of Hybrid Entities: An Alternative Approach in the New Era of BEPS*, 2018 (ISBN 978-90-411-9991-1).
67. Richard Snoeij, *International Tax Aspects of Sovereign Wealth Investors: A Source State Perspective*, 2018 (ISBN 978-90-411-9431-2).
68. Aleksandra Bal, *Taxation, Virtual Currency and Blockchain*, 2019 (ISBN 978-94-035-0103-1).

www.ingramcontent.com/pod-product-compliance
Ingram Content Group UK Ltd.
Pitfield, Milton Keynes, MK11 3LW, UK
UKHW020243290926
15470UKWH00002B/700

9 789403 501031